FROG

KERORO GUNSOU

VOL # 6 BY MINE YOSHIZAKI

ENCOUNTER XLVI TARGET: THE HINATA HOME!!

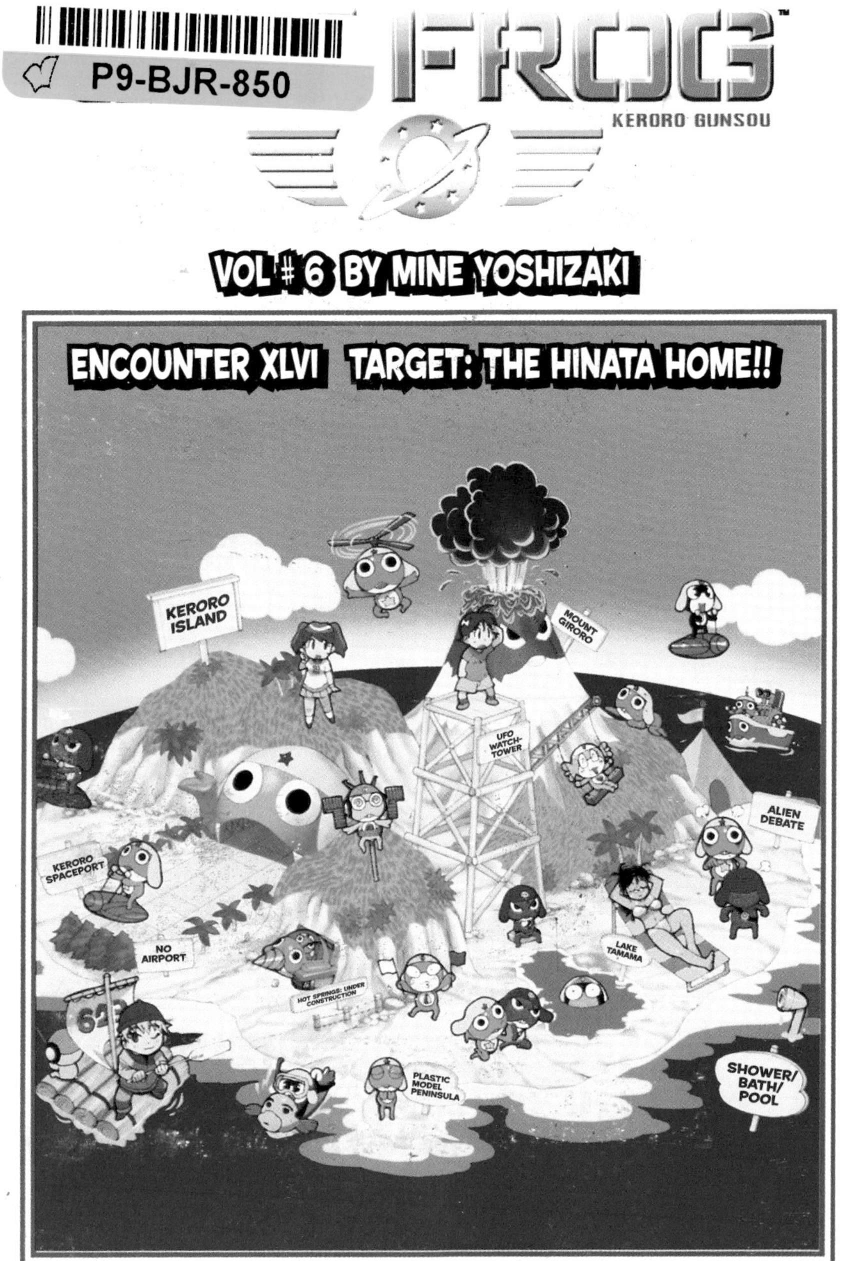
KERORO ISLAND
MOUNT GIRORO
UFO WATCH-TOWER
ALIEN DEBATE
KERORO SPACEPORT
LAKE TAMAMA
NO AIRPORT
HOT SPRINGS: UNDER CONSTRUCTION
62
PLASTIC MODEL PENINSULA
SHOWER/ BATH/ POOL

TOKYOPOP®

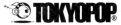

HAMBURG // LONDON // LOS ANGELES // TOKYO

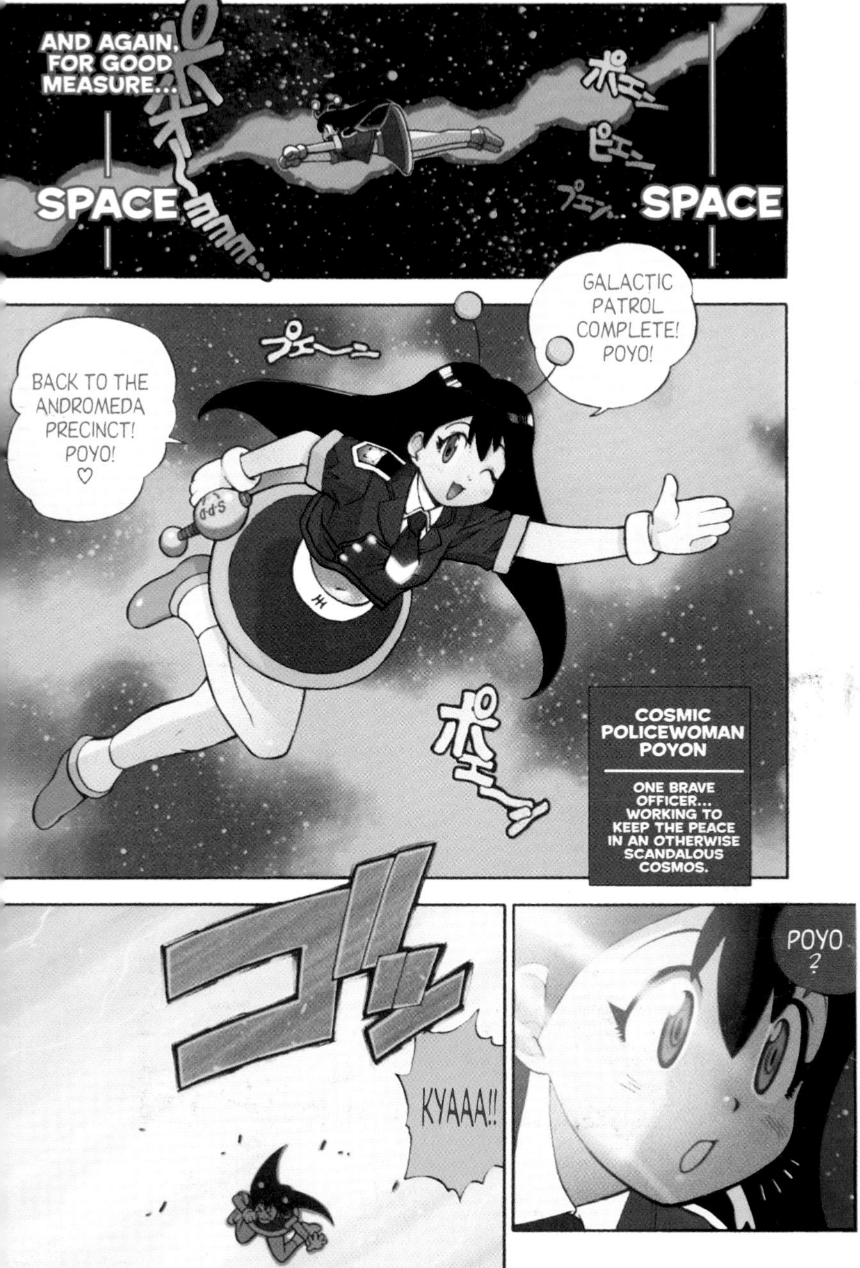
AND AGAIN, FOR GOOD MEASURE...
SPACE
SPACE
GALACTIC PATROL COMPLETE! POYO!
BACK TO THE ANDROMEDA PRECINCT! POYO! ♡
COSMIC POLICEWOMAN POYON
ONE BRAVE OFFICER... WORKING TO KEEP THE PEACE IN AN OTHERWISE SCANDALOUS COSMOS.
POYO?
KYAAA!!

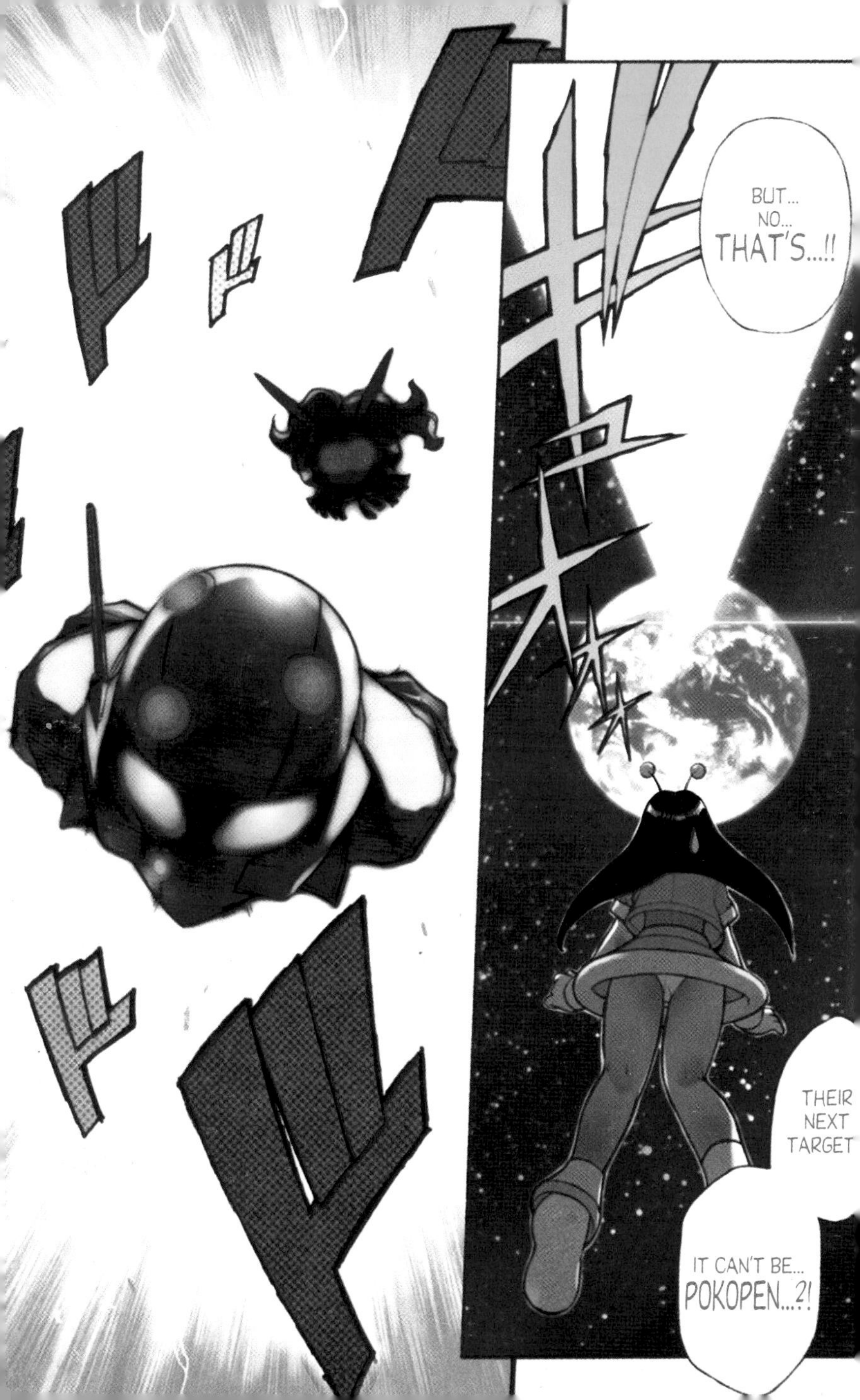
BUT... NO... THAT'S...!!
THEIR NEXT TARGET
IT CAN'T BE... POKOPEN...?!

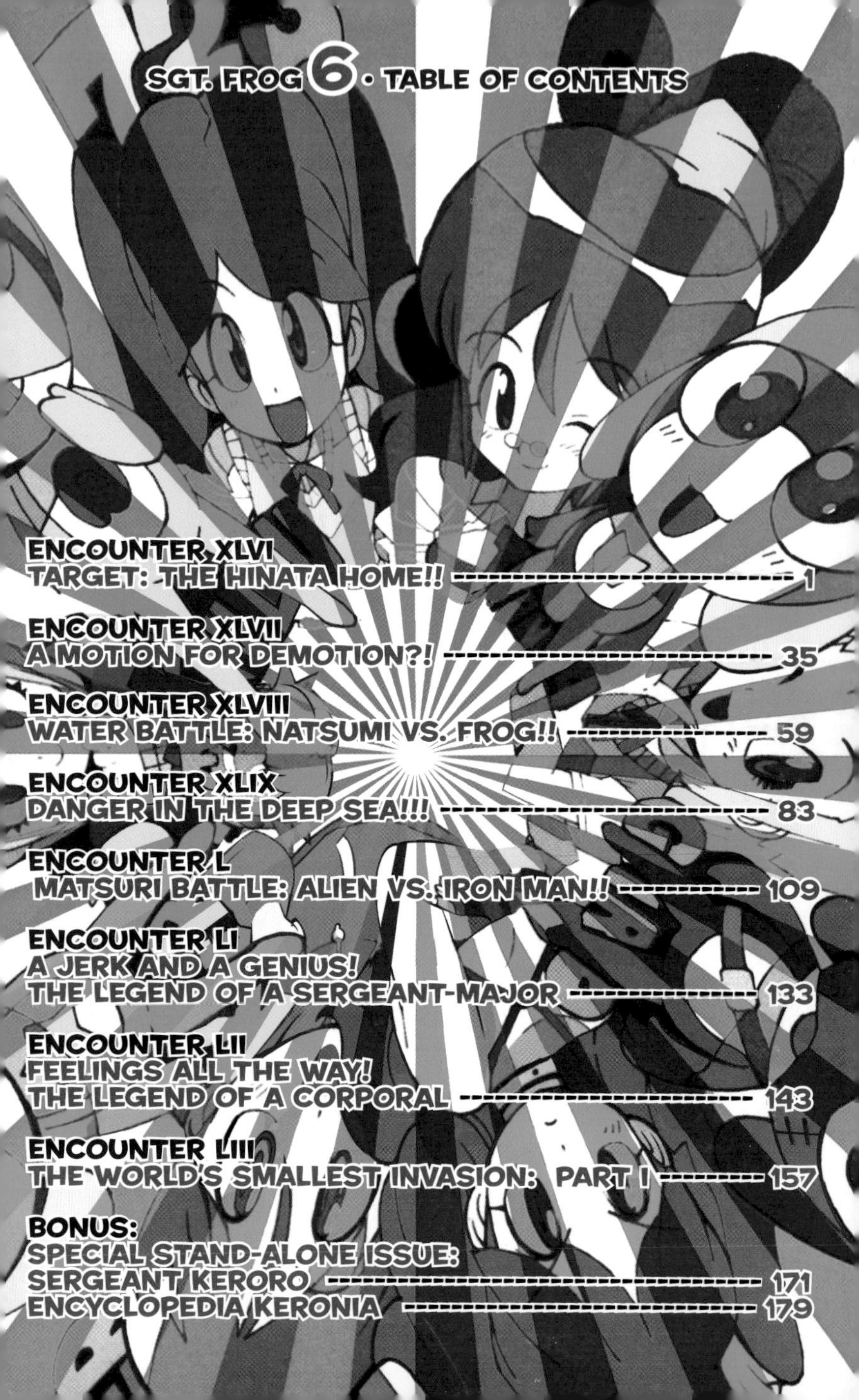

SGT. FROG 6 • TABLE OF CONTENTS

KERORO GUNSOU

VOLUME #6

BY

MINE YOSHIZAKI

HAMBURG // LONDON // LOS ANGELES // TOKYO

SGT. Frog Vol. 6

Created by Mine Yoshizaki

Translation - Yuko Fukami
English Adaptation - Carol Fox
Copy Editor - Troy Lewter
Retouch and Lettering - Jose Macasocol, Jr.
Production Artists - James Dashiell and James Lee
Cover Design - Raymond Makowski

Editor - Paul Morrissey
Digital Imaging Manager - Chris Buford
Pre-Press Manager - Antonio DePietro
Production Managers - Jennifer Miller and Mutsumi Miyazaki
Art Director - Matt Alford
Managing Editor - Jill Freshney
VP of Production - Ron Klamert
Editor-in-Chief - Mike Kiley
President and C.O.O. - John Parker
Publisher and C.E.O. - Stuart Levy

A  Manga

TOKYOPOP Inc.
5900 Wilshire Blvd. Suite 2000
Los Angeles, CA 90036

E-mail: info@TOKYOPOP.com
Come visit us online at www.TOKYOPOP.com

ISBN: 1-59182-708-6

First TOKYOPOP printing: January 2005
10 9 8 7 6 5 4 3 2 1
Printed in the USA

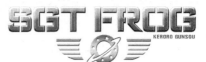

SGT FROG

KERORO GUNSOU

CHARACTER RELATIONSHIPS AND THE STORY SO FAR

(FACT-CHECKING PERFORMED BY SHONEN ACE MAGAZINE)

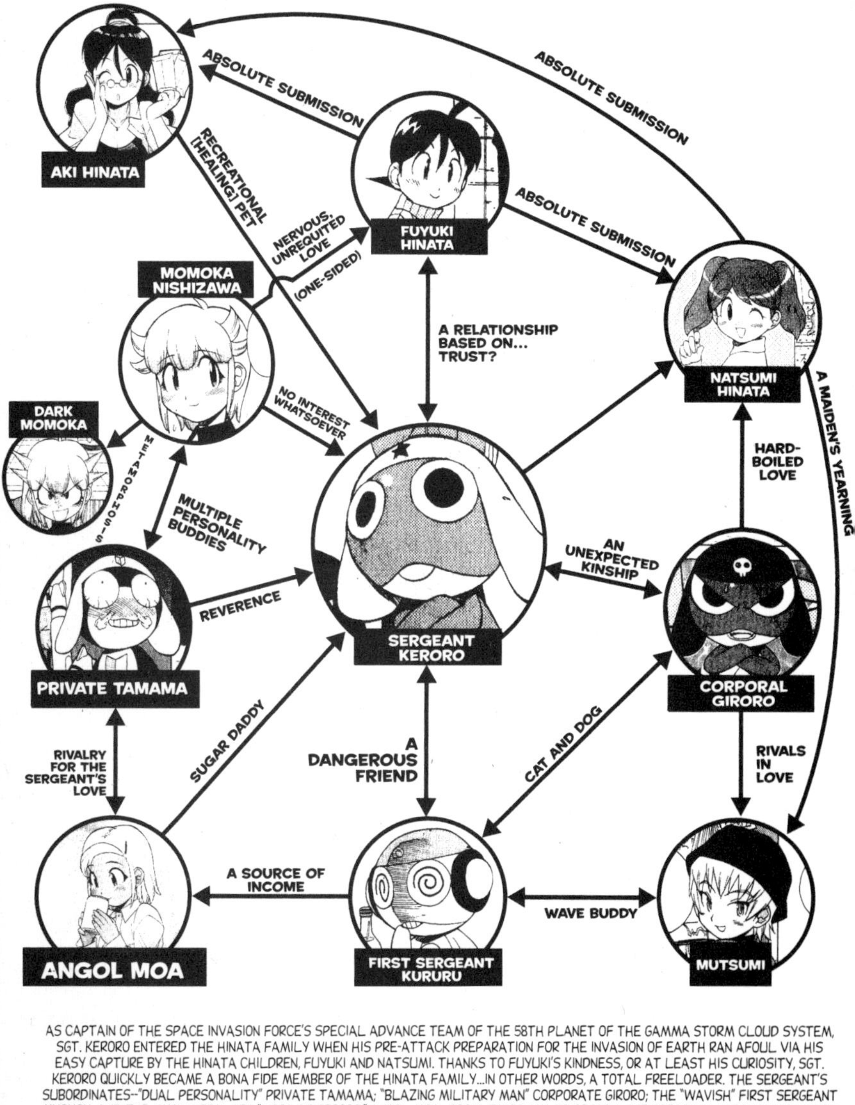
AKI HINATA
FUYUKI HINATA
ABSOLUTE SUBMISSION
ABSOLUTE SUBMISSION
ABSOLUTE SUBMISSION
RECREATIONAL [HEALING] PET
NERVOUS, UNREQUITED LOVE
(ONE-SIDED)
MOMOKA NISHIZAWA
NATSUMI HINATA
A RELATIONSHIP BASED ON... TRUST?
A MAIDEN'S YEARNING
DARK MOMOKA
METAMORPHOSIS
NO INTEREST WHATSOEVER
HARD-BOILED LOVE
MULTIPLE PERSONALITY BUDDIES
AN UNEXPECTED KINSHIP
REVERENCE
SERGEANT KERORO
PRIVATE TAMAMA
CORPORAL GIRORO
SUGAR DADDY
CAT AND DOG
RIVALRY FOR THE SERGEANT'S LOVE
A DANGEROUS FRIEND
RIVALS IN LOVE
A SOURCE OF INCOME
WAVE BUDDY
ANGOL MOA
FIRST SERGEANT KURURU
MUTSUMI

AS CAPTAIN OF THE SPACE INVASION FORCE'S SPECIAL ADVANCE TEAM OF THE 58TH PLANET OF THE GAMMA STORM CLOUD SYSTEM, SGT. KERORO ENTERED THE HINATA FAMILY WHEN HIS PRE-ATTACK PREPARATION FOR THE INVASION OF EARTH RAN AFOUL VIA HIS EASY CAPTURE BY THE HINATA CHILDREN, FUYUKI AND NATSUMI. THANKS TO FUYUKI'S KINDNESS, OR AT LEAST HIS CURIOSITY, SGT. KERORO QUICKLY BECAME A BONA FIDE MEMBER OF THE HINATA FAMILY...IN OTHER WORDS, A TOTAL FREELOADER. THE SERGEANT'S SUBORDINATES--"DUAL PERSONALITY" PRIVATE TAMAMA; "BLAZING MILITARY MAN" CORPORATE GIRORO; THE "WAVISH" FIRST SERGEANT KURURU; AND THE MUCH-HERALDED "LORD OF TERROR," ANGOL MOA--SOON JOINED HIM TO REFORM THE KERORO PLATOON, WHICH DOES AS IT PLEASES IN A TOP-SECRET BASE BENEATH THE HINATA HOME. THUS, HAVE THEIR OBNOXIOUS DAYS CONTINUED...

BUT IN THIS VOLUME, THERE'S GOING TO BE A CHANGE IN PLANS...

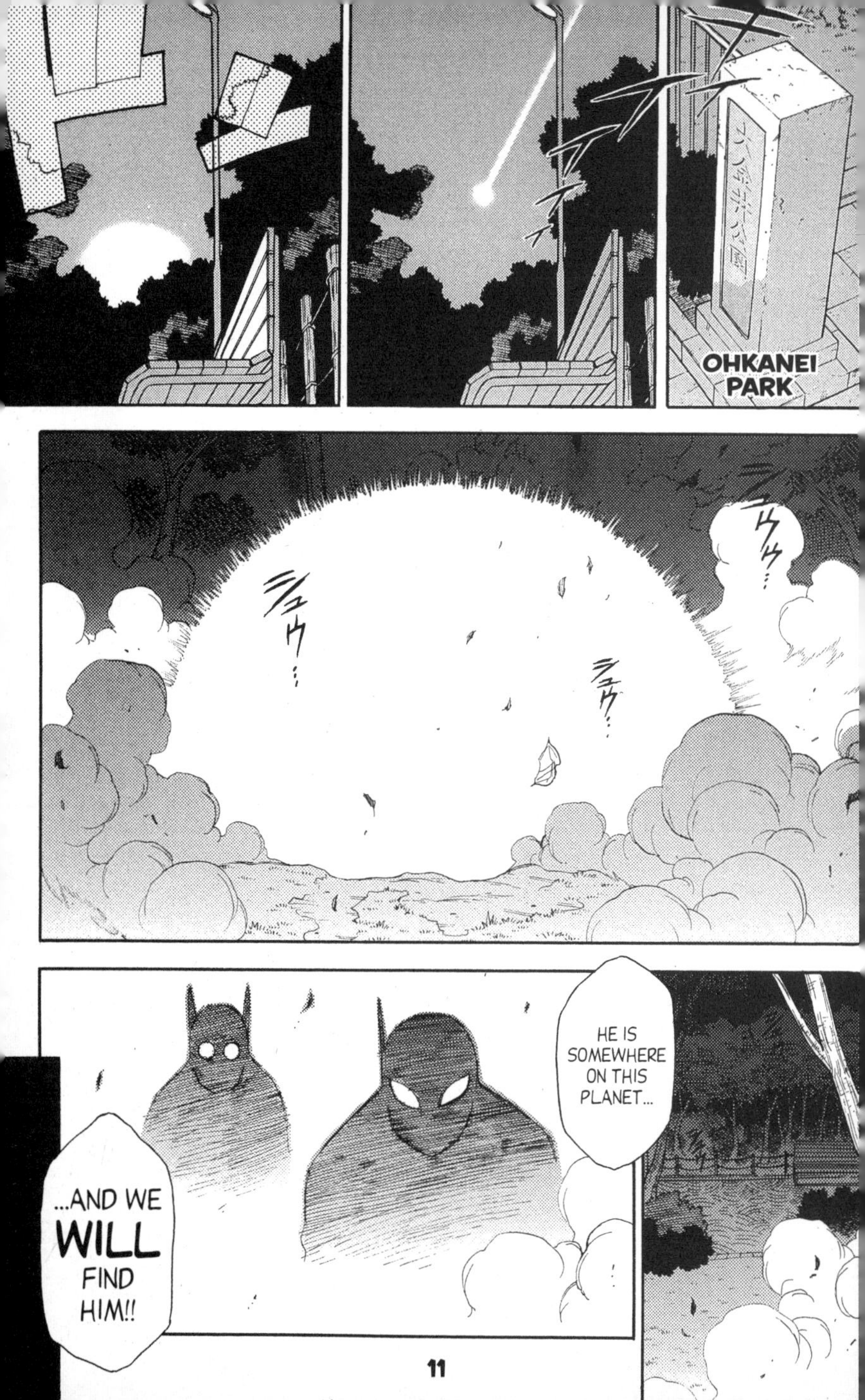
OHKANEI PARK
HE IS SOMEWHERE ON THIS PLANET...
...AND WE WILL FIND HIM!!

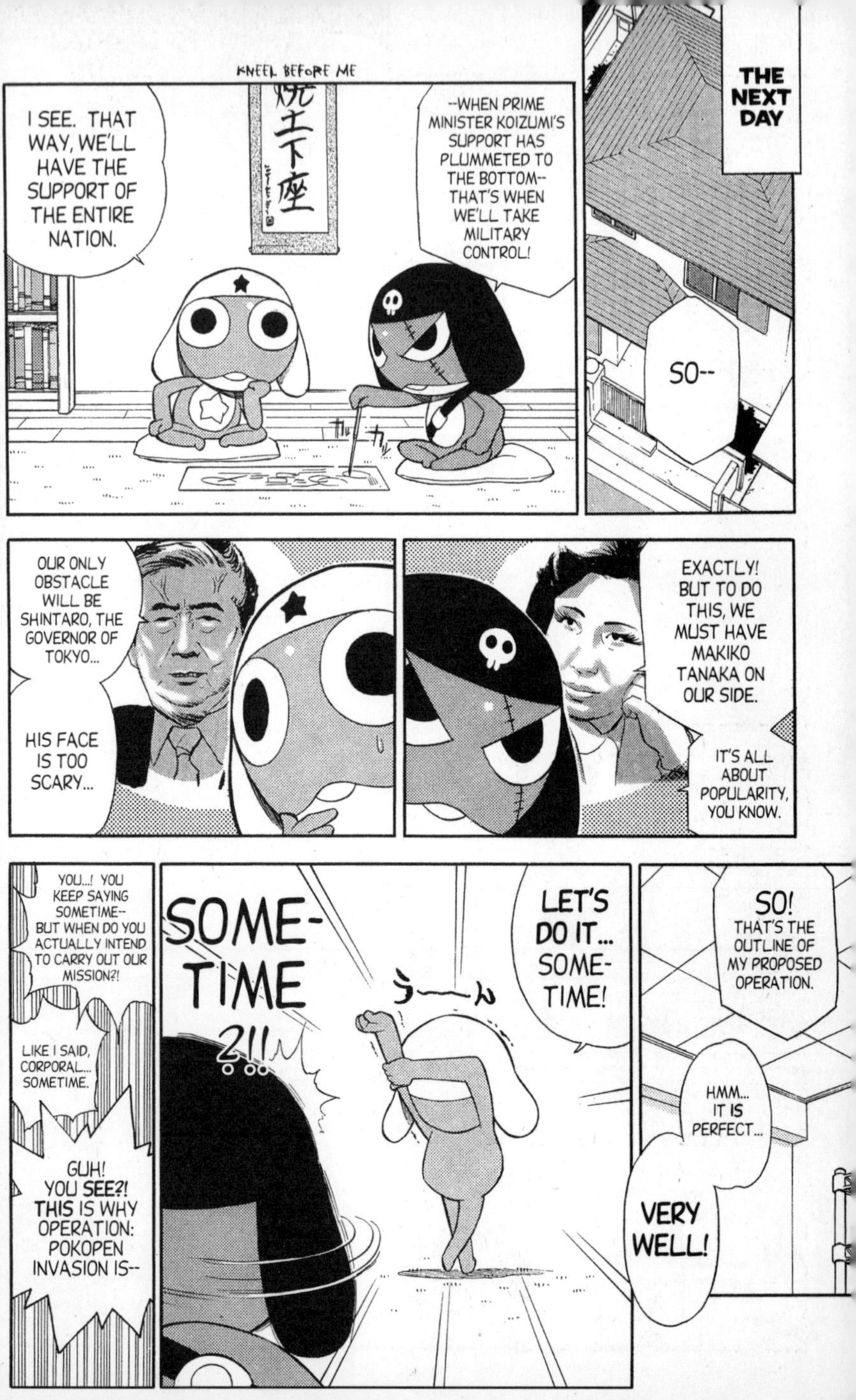
THE NEXT DAY
SO--
KNEEL BEFORE ME
--WHEN PRIME MINISTER KOIZUMI'S SUPPORT HAS PLUMMETED TO THE BOTTOM-- THAT'S WHEN WE'LL TAKE MILITARY CONTROL!
I SEE. THAT WAY, WE'LL HAVE THE SUPPORT OF THE ENTIRE NATION.
EXACTLY! BUT TO DO THIS, WE MUST HAVE MAKIKO TANAKA ON OUR SIDE.
IT'S ALL ABOUT POPULARITY, YOU KNOW.
OUR ONLY OBSTACLE WILL BE SHINTARO, THE GOVERNOR OF TOKYO...
HIS FACE IS TOO SCARY...
SO! THAT'S THE OUTLINE OF MY PROPOSED OPERATION.
HMM... IT IS PERFECT...
VERY WELL!
LET'S DO IT... SOMETIME!
う〜ん
SOME-TIME ?!!
YOU...! YOU KEEP SAYING SOMETIME-- BUT WHEN DO YOU ACTUALLY INTEND TO CARRY OUT OUR MISSION?!
LIKE I SAID, CORPORAL... SOMETIME.
GUH! YOU SEE?! THIS IS WHY OPERATION: POKOPEN INVASION IS--

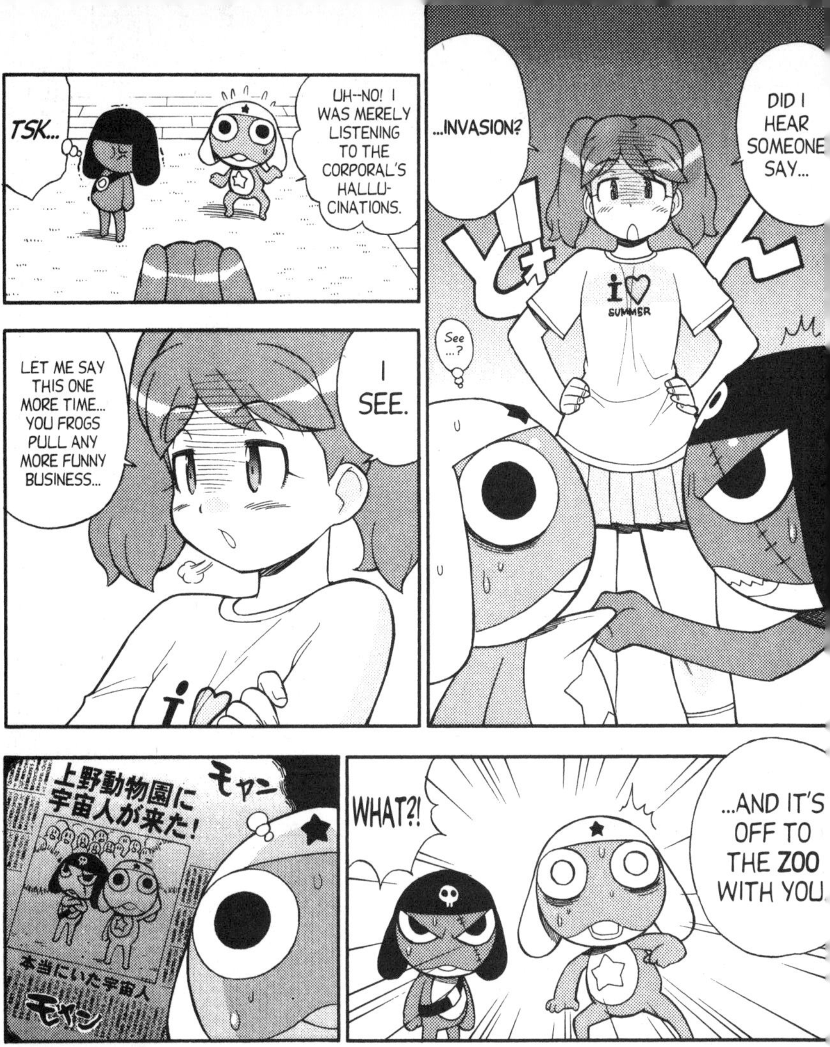
DID I HEAR SOMEONE SAY...
...INVASION?
See ...?
UH--NO! I WAS MERELY LISTENING TO THE CORPORAL'S HALLUCINATIONS.
TSK...
I SEE.
LET ME SAY THIS ONE MORE TIME... YOU FROGS PULL ANY MORE FUNNY BUSINESS...
...AND IT'S OFF TO THE ZOO WITH YOU.
WHAT?!
モヤン
上野動物園に宇宙人が来た!
本当にいた宇宙人
モヤン

Newspaper: Exclusive! Aliens at Ueno Zoo! Their Existence Finally Proven...

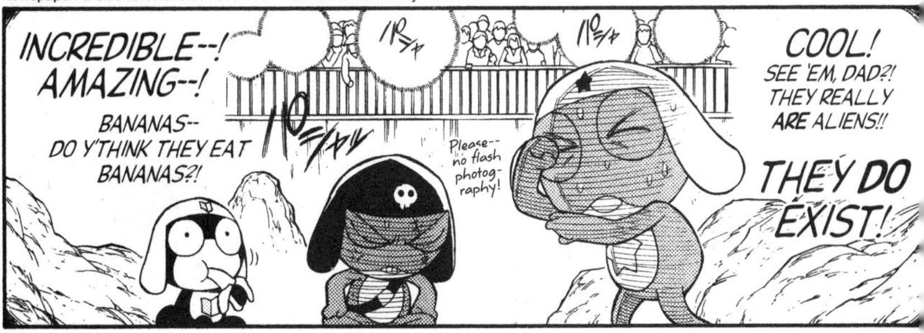
COOL! SEE 'EM, DAD?! THEY REALLY ARE ALIENS!!
THEY DO EXIST!
パシャ
Please-- no flash photography!
パシャ
BANANAS-- DO Y'THINK THEY EAT BANANAS?!
INCREDIBLE--! AMAZING--!

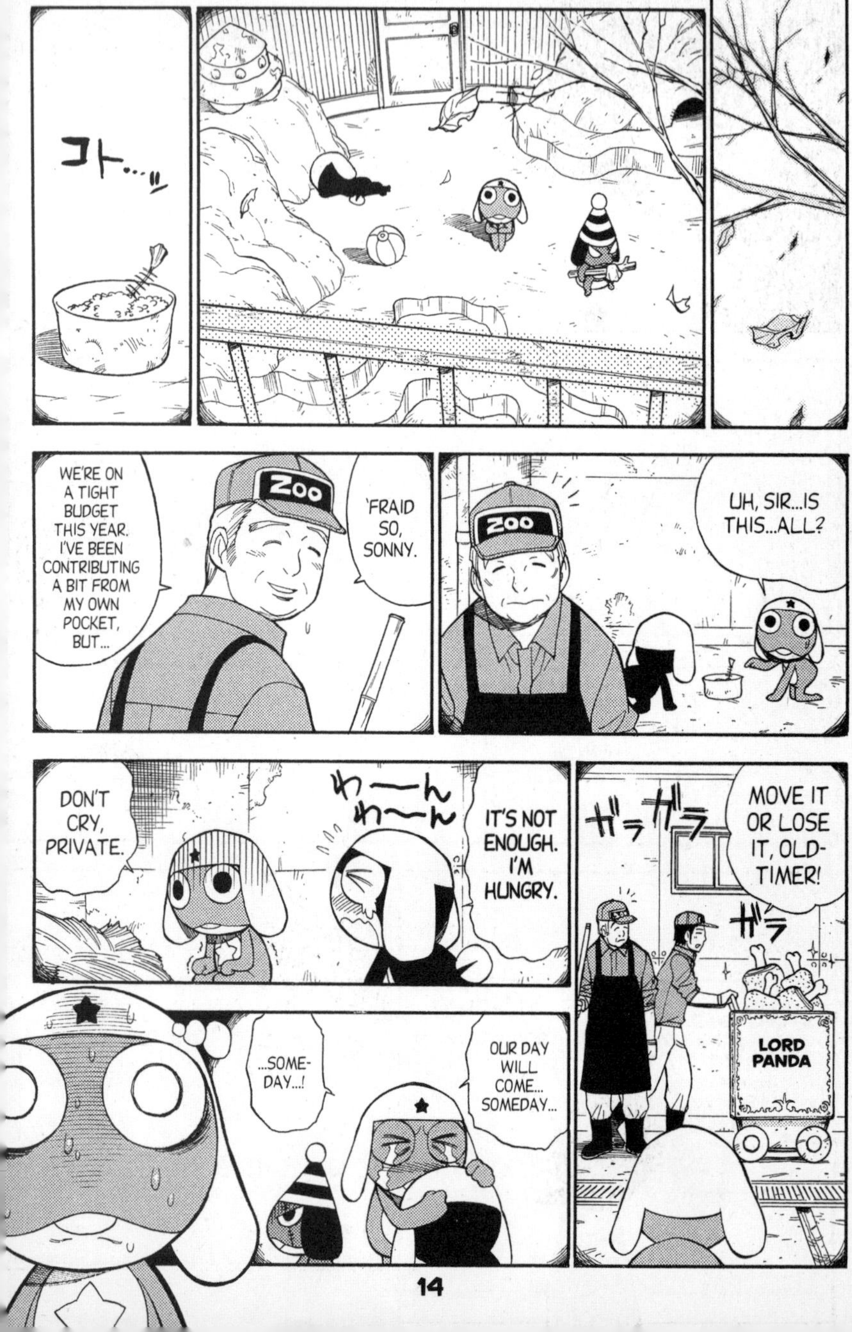
コト…ッ
UH, SIR...IS THIS...ALL?
'FRAID SO, SONNY.
WE'RE ON A TIGHT BUDGET THIS YEAR. I'VE BEEN CONTRIBUTING A BIT FROM MY OWN POCKET, BUT...
MOVE IT OR LOSE IT, OLD-TIMER!
ガラガラ
ガラ
LORD PANDA
IT'S NOT ENOUGH. I'M HUNGRY.
わ〜ん わ〜ん
DON'T CRY, PRIVATE.
OUR DAY WILL COME... SOMEDAY...
...SOME-DAY...!

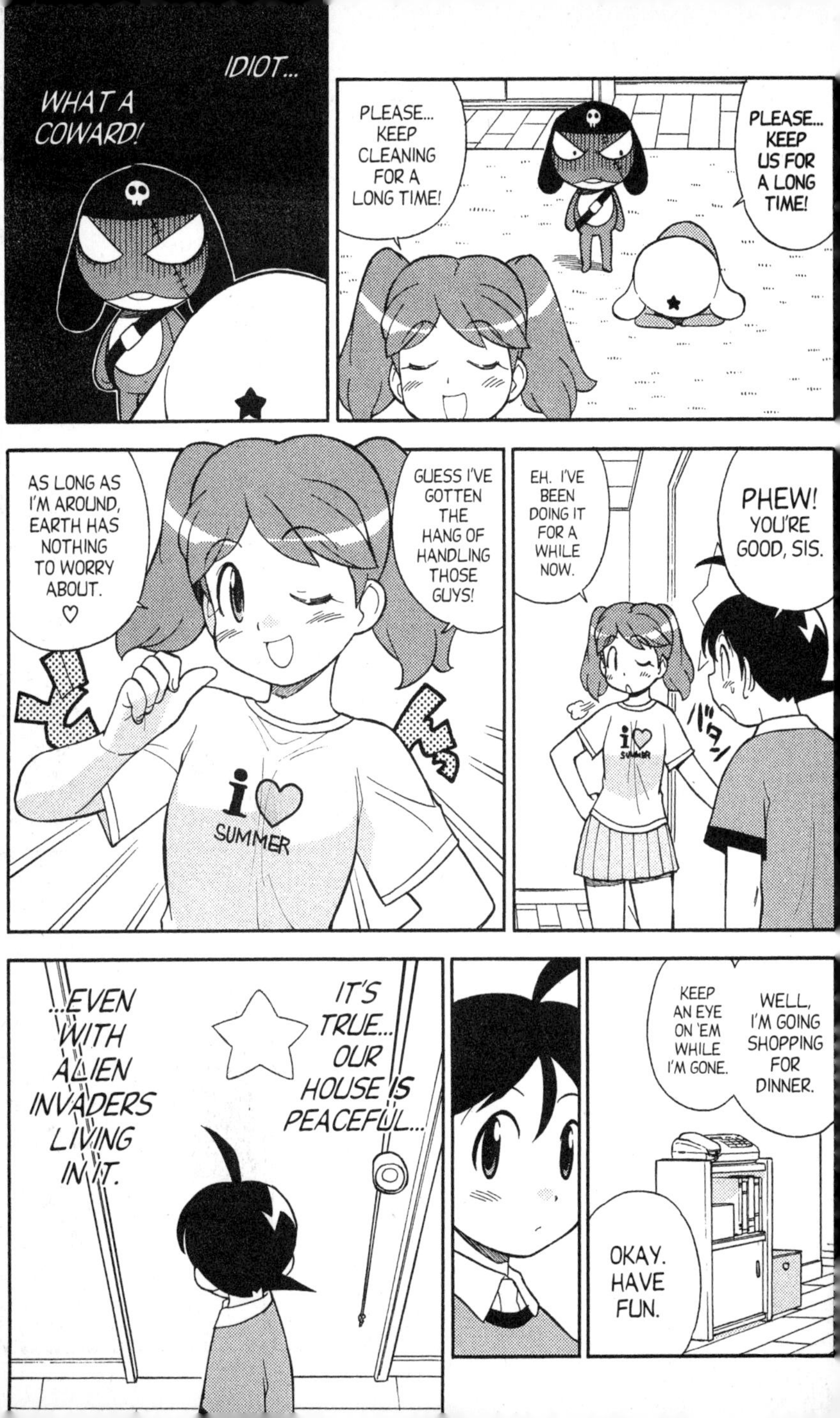
PLEASE... KEEP US FOR A LONG TIME!
PLEASE... KEEP CLEANING FOR A LONG TIME!
IDIOT...
WHAT A COWARD!
PHEW! YOU'RE GOOD, SIS.
EH. I'VE BEEN DOING IT FOR A WHILE NOW.
GUESS I'VE GOTTEN THE HANG OF HANDLING THOSE GUYS!
AS LONG AS I'M AROUND, EARTH HAS NOTHING TO WORRY ABOUT. ♡
I ♥ SUMMER
WELL, I'M GOING SHOPPING FOR DINNER.
KEEP AN EYE ON 'EM WHILE I'M GONE.
OKAY. HAVE FUN.
IT'S TRUE... OUR HOUSE IS PEACEFUL...
...EVEN WITH ALIEN INVADERS LIVING IN IT.

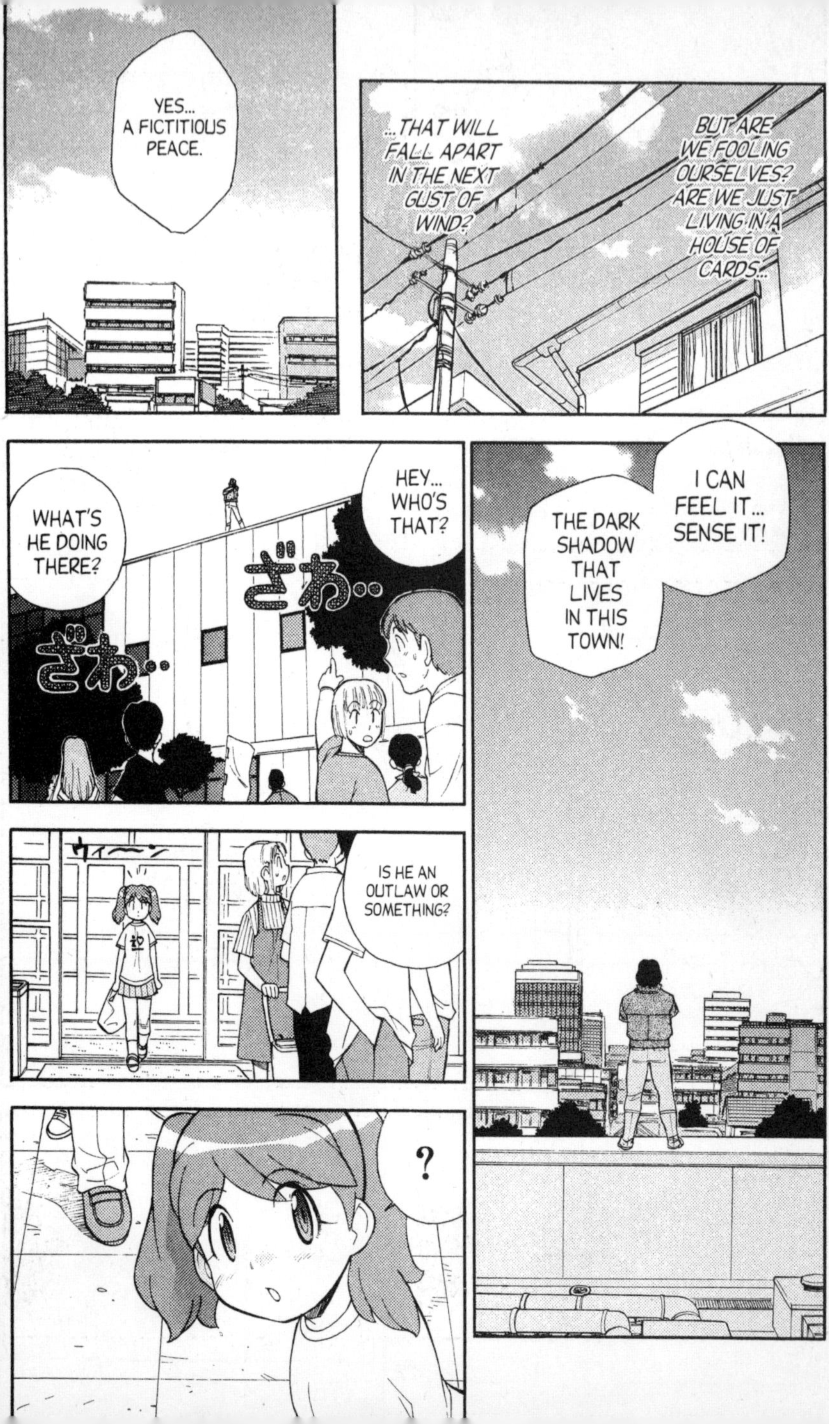

BUT ARE WE FOOLING OURSELVES? ARE WE JUST LIVING IN A HOUSE OF CARDS...
...THAT WILL FALL APART IN THE NEXT GUST OF WIND?
YES... A FICTITIOUS PEACE.
I CAN FEEL IT... SENSE IT!
THE DARK SHADOW THAT LIVES IN THIS TOWN!
HEY... WHO'S THAT?
ざわ‥
WHAT'S HE DOING THERE?
ざわ‥
IS HE AN OUTLAW OR SOMETHING?
ウィ〜ン
?

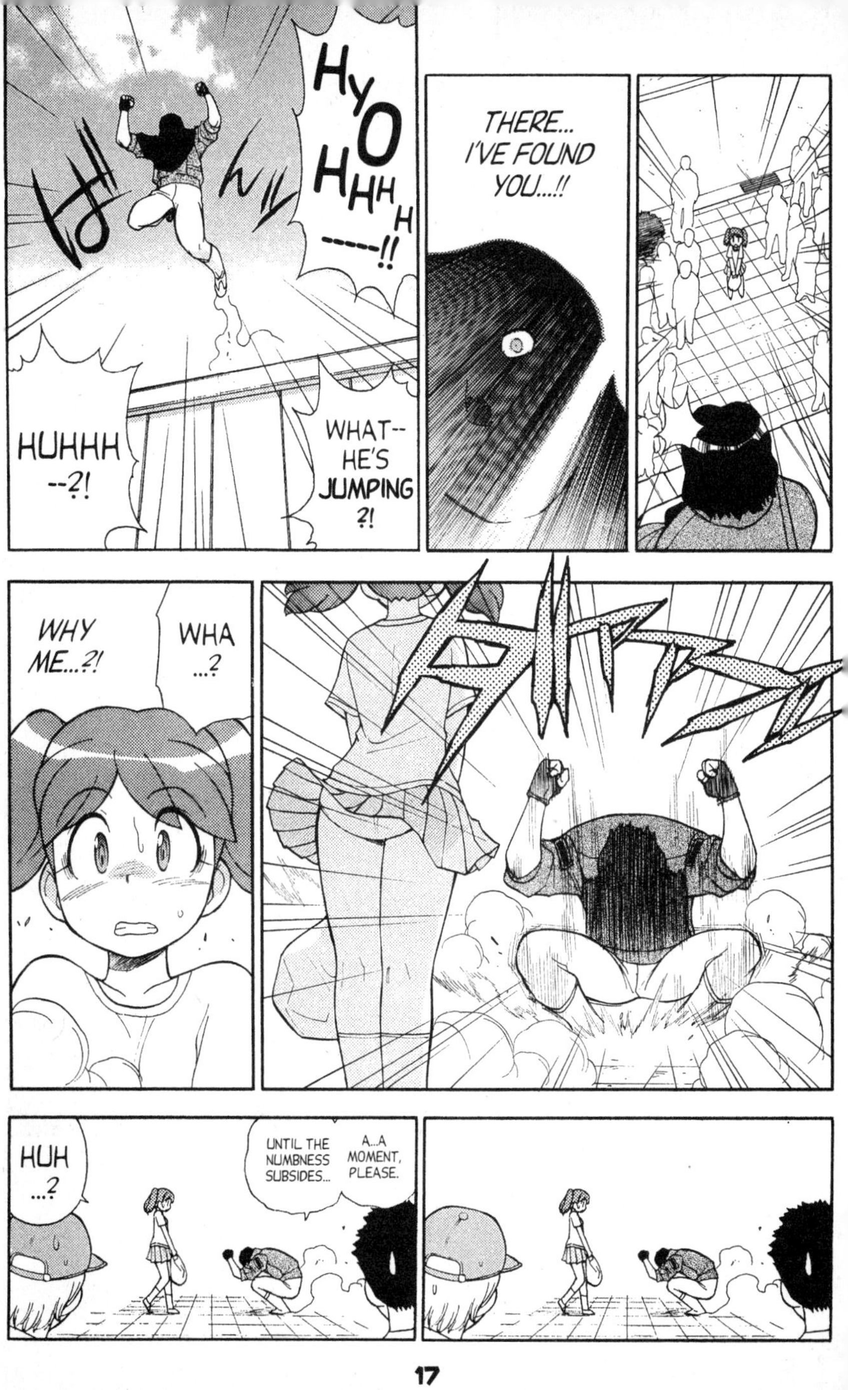
THERE... I'VE FOUND YOU...!!
HYOHHHHH-----!!
WHAT-- HE'S JUMPING?!
HUHHH--?!
WHA...?
WHY ME...?!
A...A MOMENT, PLEASE.
UNTIL THE NUMBNESS SUBSIDES...
HUH...?

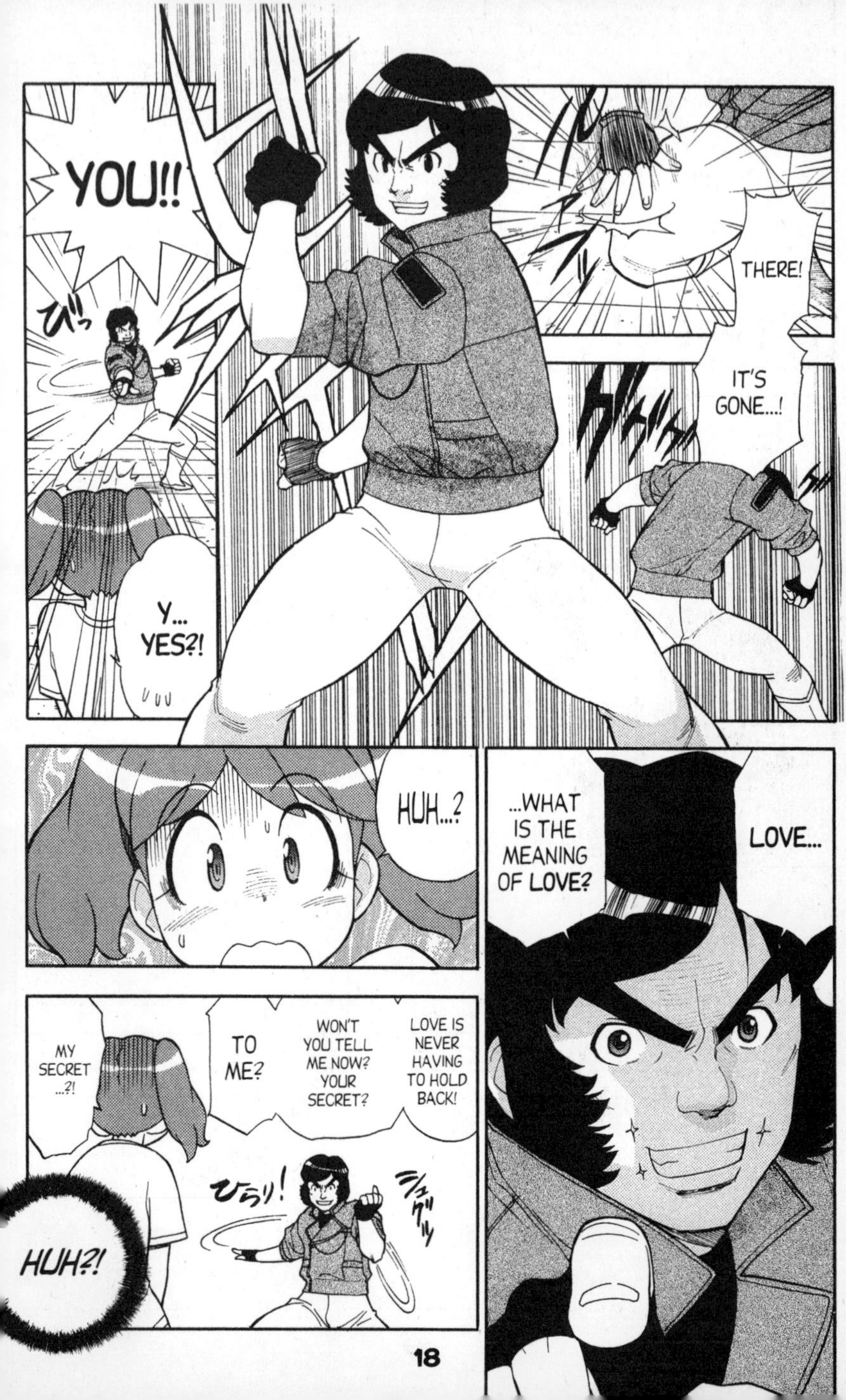
THERE!
IT'S GONE...!
YOU!!
Y... YES?!
LOVE...
...WHAT IS THE MEANING OF LOVE?
HUH...?
LOVE IS NEVER HAVING TO HOLD BACK!
WON'T YOU TELL ME NOW? YOUR SECRET?
TO ME?
MY SECRET ...?!
HUH?!

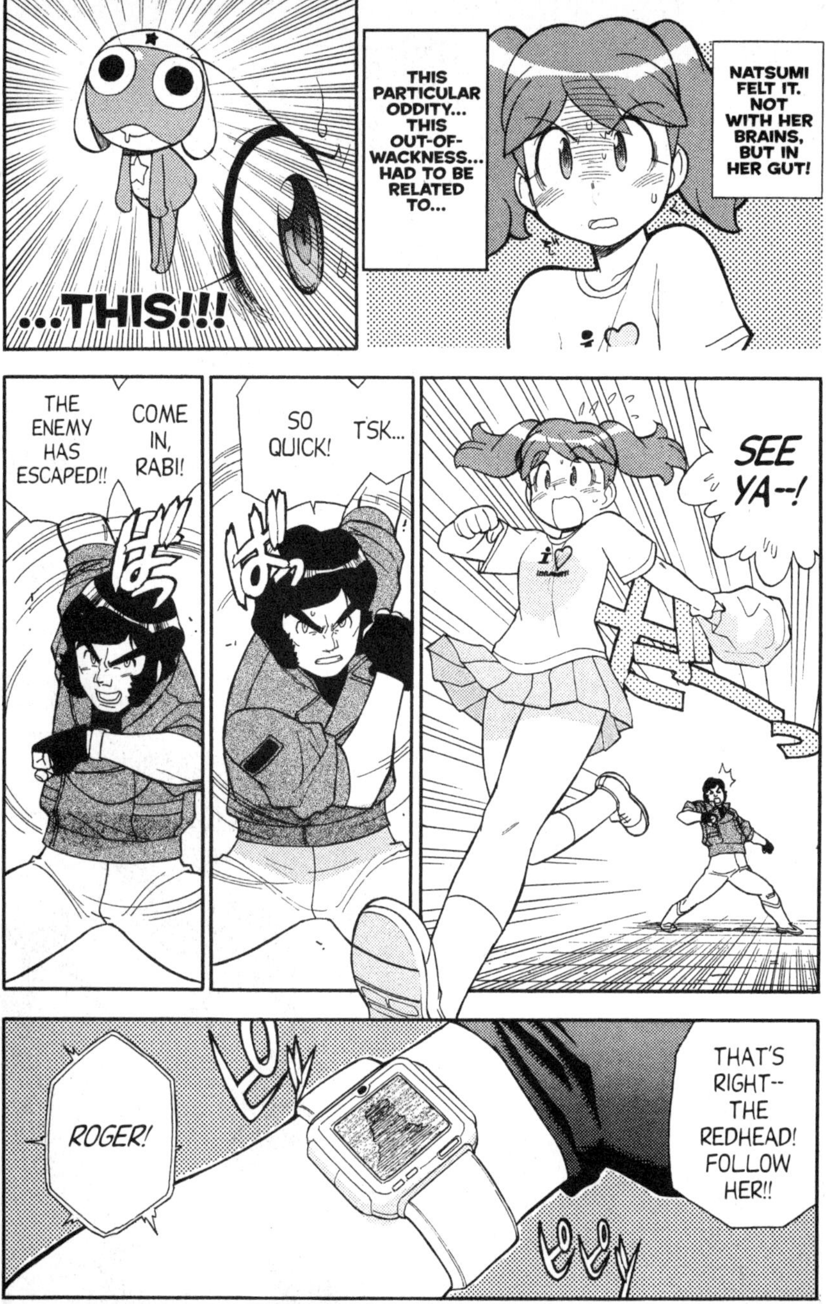
NATSUMI FELT IT. NOT WITH HER BRAINS, BUT IN HER GUT!
THIS PARTICULAR ODDITY... THIS OUT-OF-WACKNESS... HAD TO BE RELATED TO...
...THIS!!!
SEE YA--!
TSK...
SO QUICK!
COME IN, RABI!
THE ENEMY HAS ESCAPED!!
THAT'S RIGHT-- THE REDHEAD! FOLLOW HER!!
ROGER!

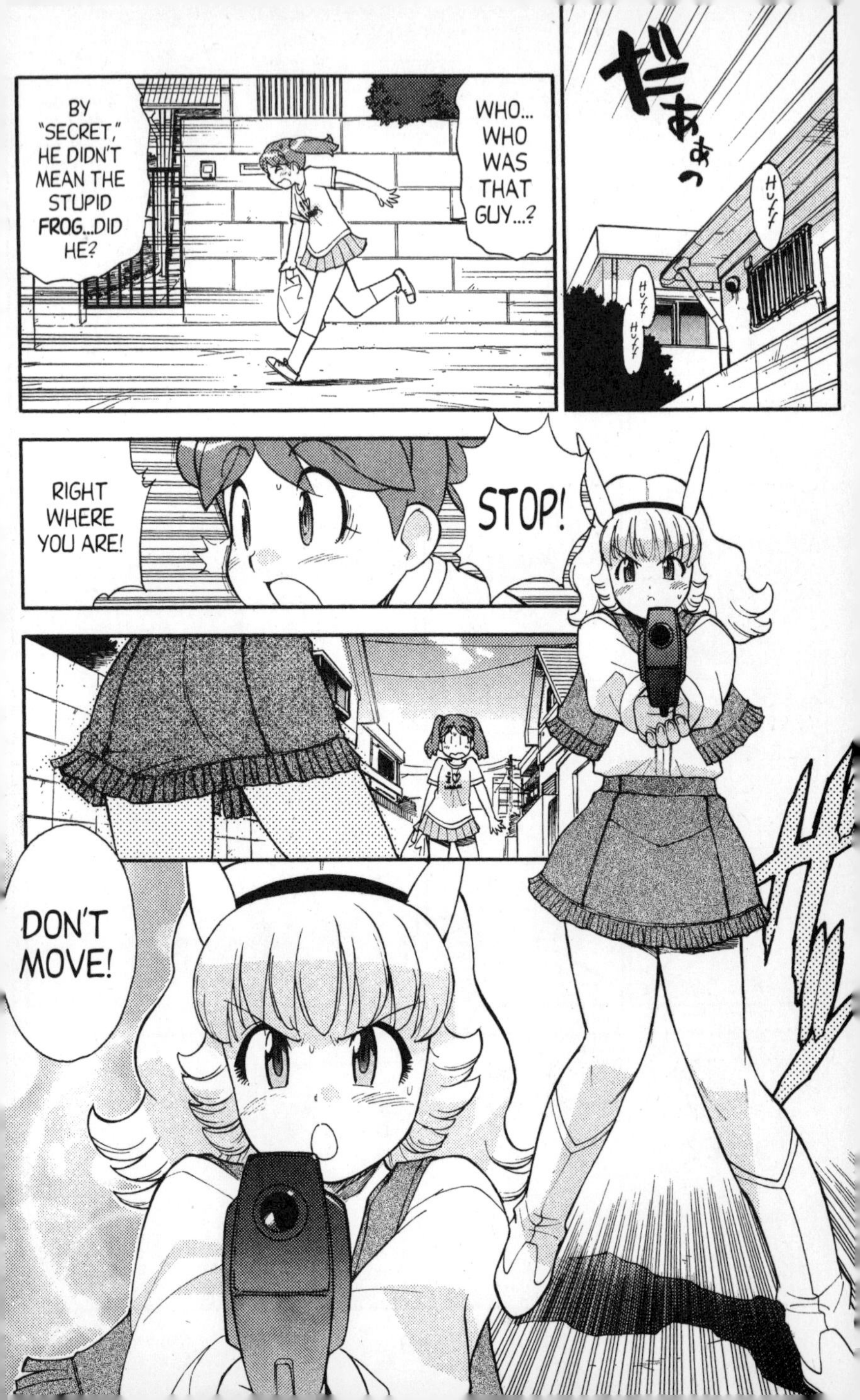
だあっ
Huff
Huff
Huff
WHO... WHO WAS THAT GUY...?
BY "SECRET," HE DIDN'T MEAN THE STUPID FROG...DID HE?
STOP!
RIGHT WHERE YOU ARE!
DON'T MOVE!

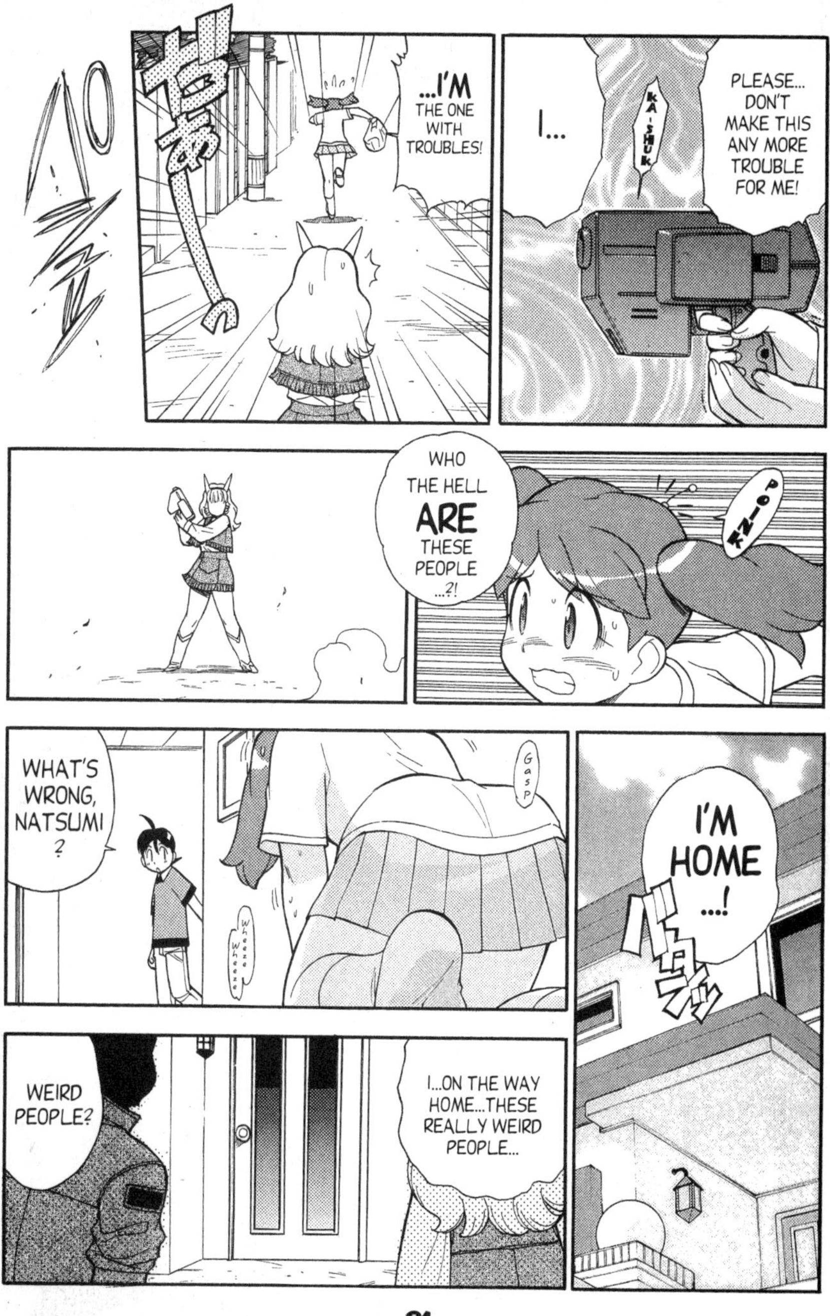
PLEASE... DON'T MAKE THIS ANY MORE TROUBLE FOR ME!
KA-SHUK
I...
...I'M THE ONE WITH TROUBLES!
POINK
WHO THE HELL ARE THESE PEOPLE...?!
I'M HOME...!
Gasp
Wheeze Wheeze
WHAT'S WRONG, NATSUMI?
I...ON THE WAY HOME...THESE REALLY WEIRD PEOPLE...
WEIRD PEOPLE?

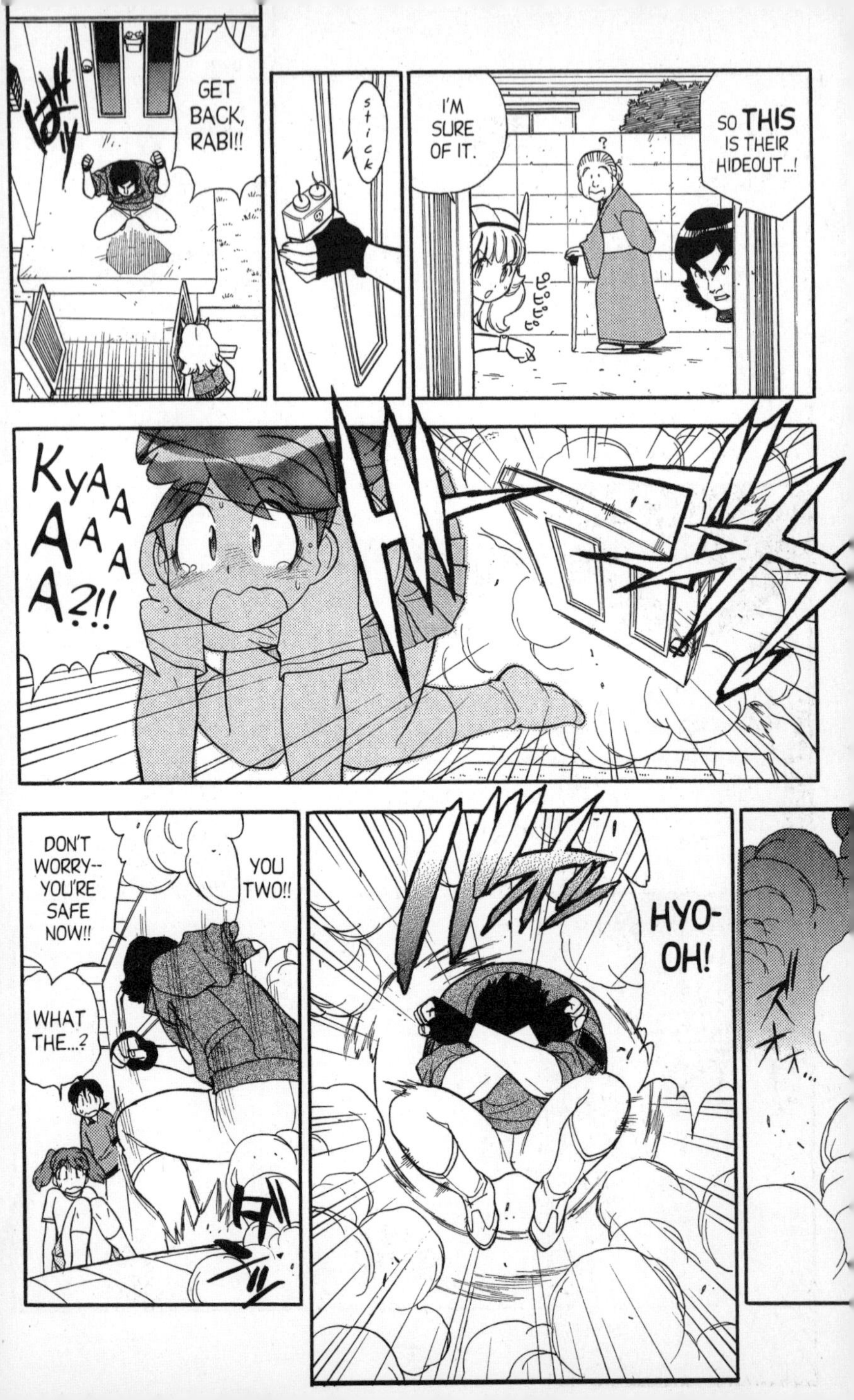
SO THIS IS THEIR HIDEOUT...!
?
I'M SURE OF IT.
stick
GET BACK, RABI!!
KyAAAAAAA?!!
HYO-OH!
YOU TWO!!
DON'T WORRY-- YOU'RE SAFE NOW!!
WHAT THE...?

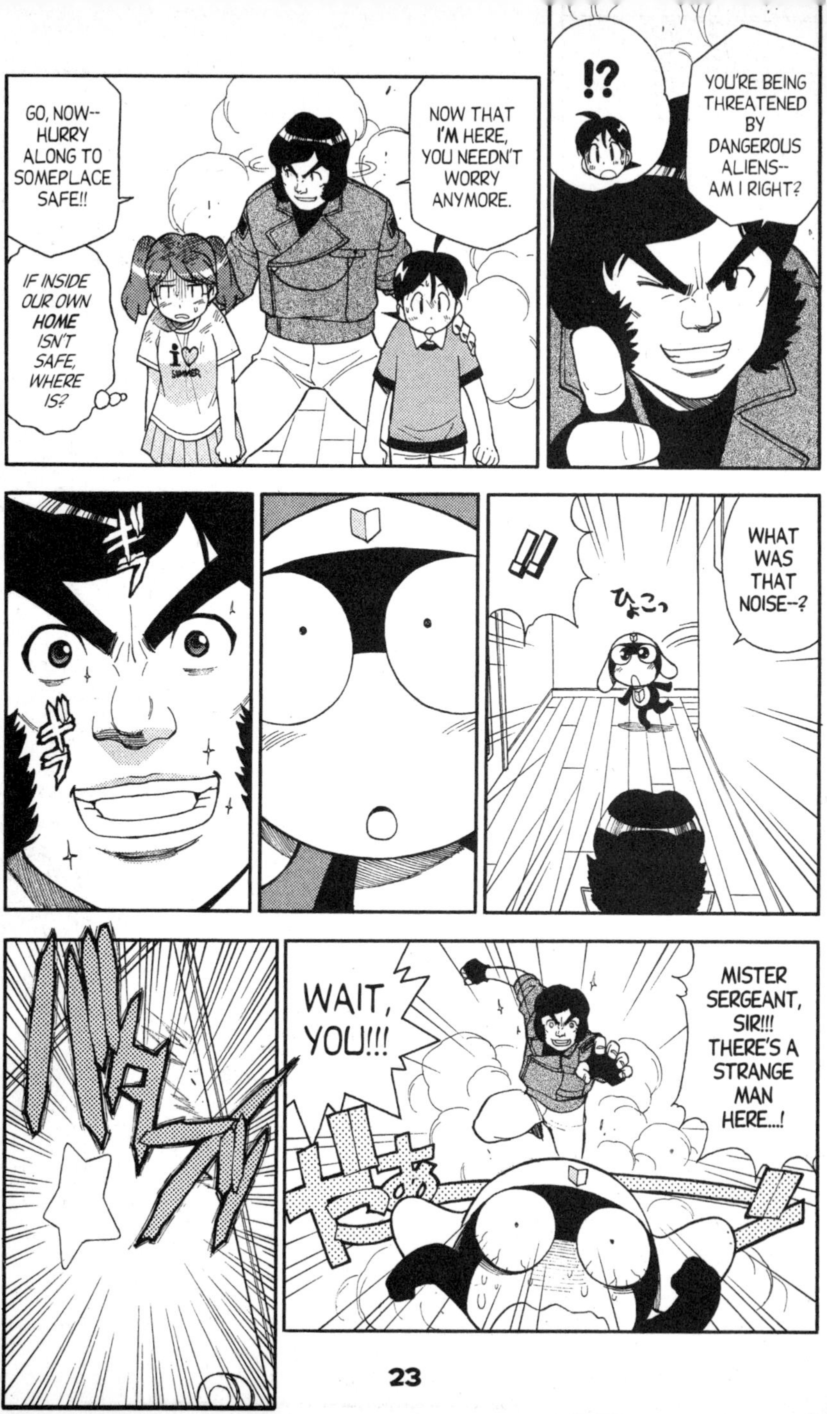
!?
YOU'RE BEING THREATENED BY DANGEROUS ALIENS-- AM I RIGHT?
NOW THAT I'M HERE, YOU NEEDN'T WORRY ANYMORE.
GO, NOW-- HURRY ALONG TO SOMEPLACE SAFE!!
IF INSIDE OUR OWN HOME ISN'T SAFE, WHERE IS?
WHAT WAS THAT NOISE--?
ひょこっ
ギラ
ギラ
MISTER SERGEANT, SIR!!! THERE'S A STRANGE MAN HERE...!
WAIT, YOU!!!

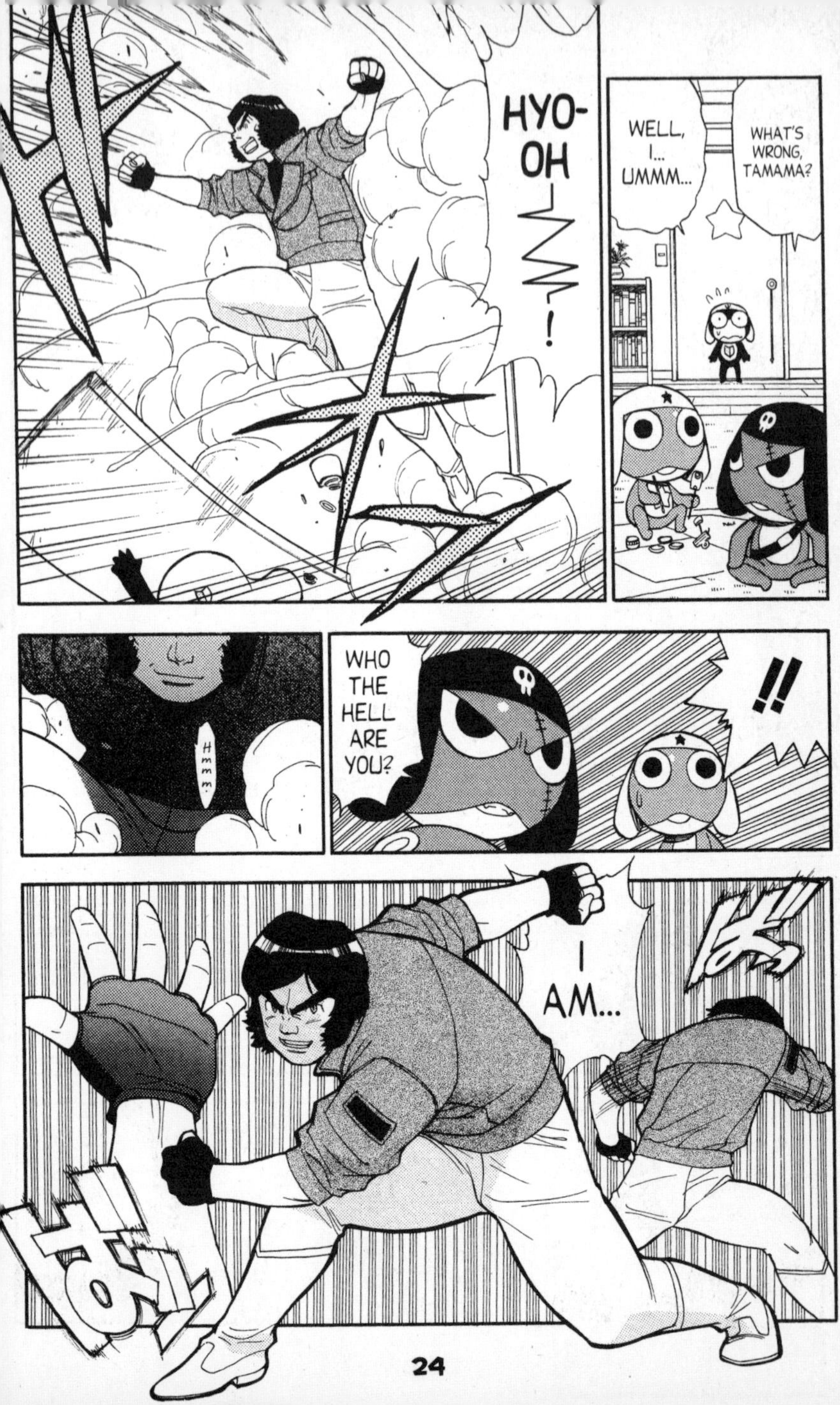

WHAT'S WRONG, TAMAMA?
WELL, I... UMMM...
HYO-OH
!
WHO THE HELL ARE YOU?
!!
Hmmm.
I AM...

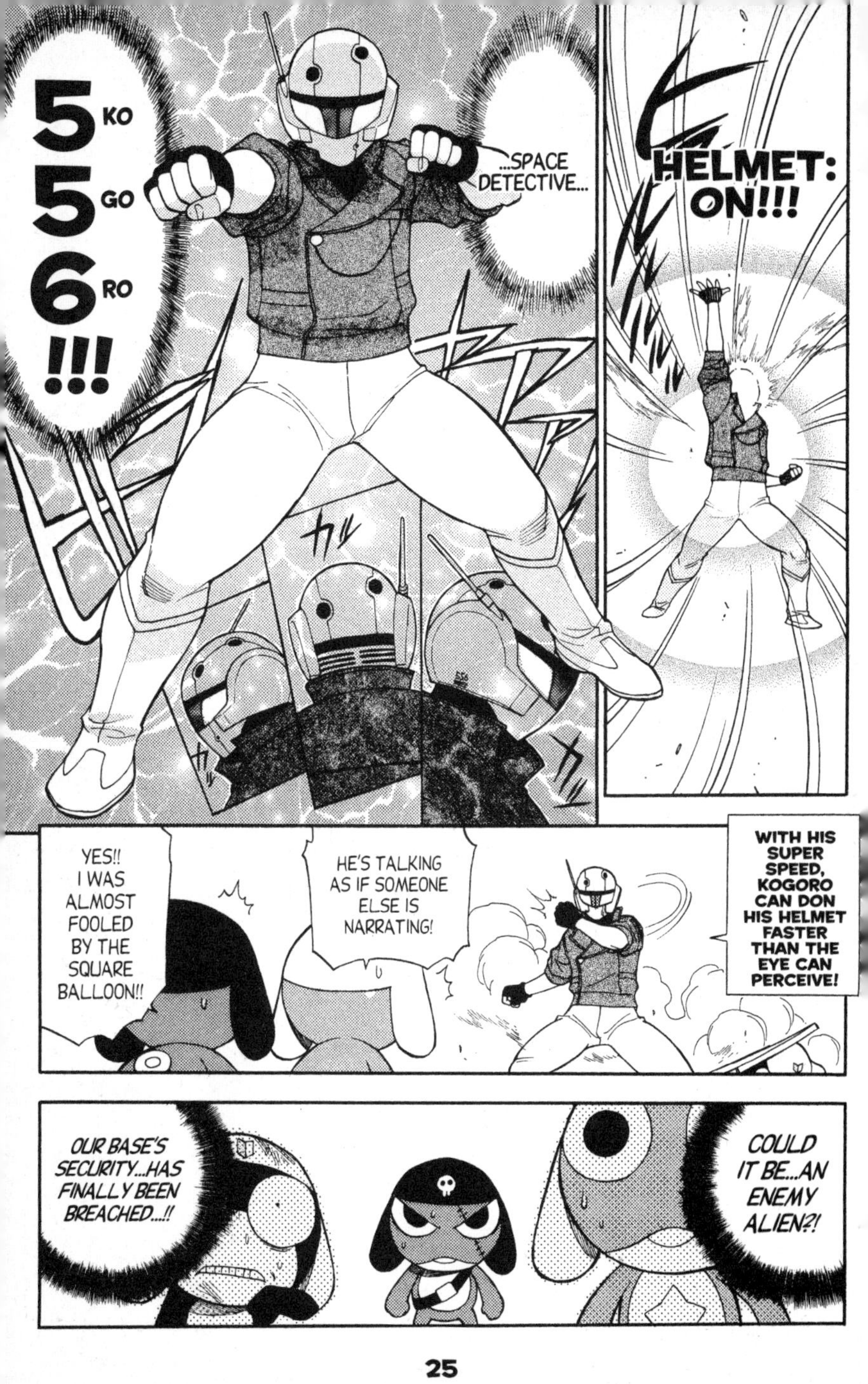
HELMET: ON!!!
...SPACE DETECTIVE...
5KO 5GO 6RO!!!
WITH HIS SUPER SPEED, KOGORO CAN DON HIS HELMET FASTER THAN THE EYE CAN PERCEIVE!
HE'S TALKING AS IF SOMEONE ELSE IS NARRATING!
YES!! I WAS ALMOST FOOLED BY THE SQUARE BALLOON!!
COULD IT BE...AN ENEMY ALIEN?!
OUR BASE'S SECURITY...HAS FINALLY BEEN BREACHED...!!

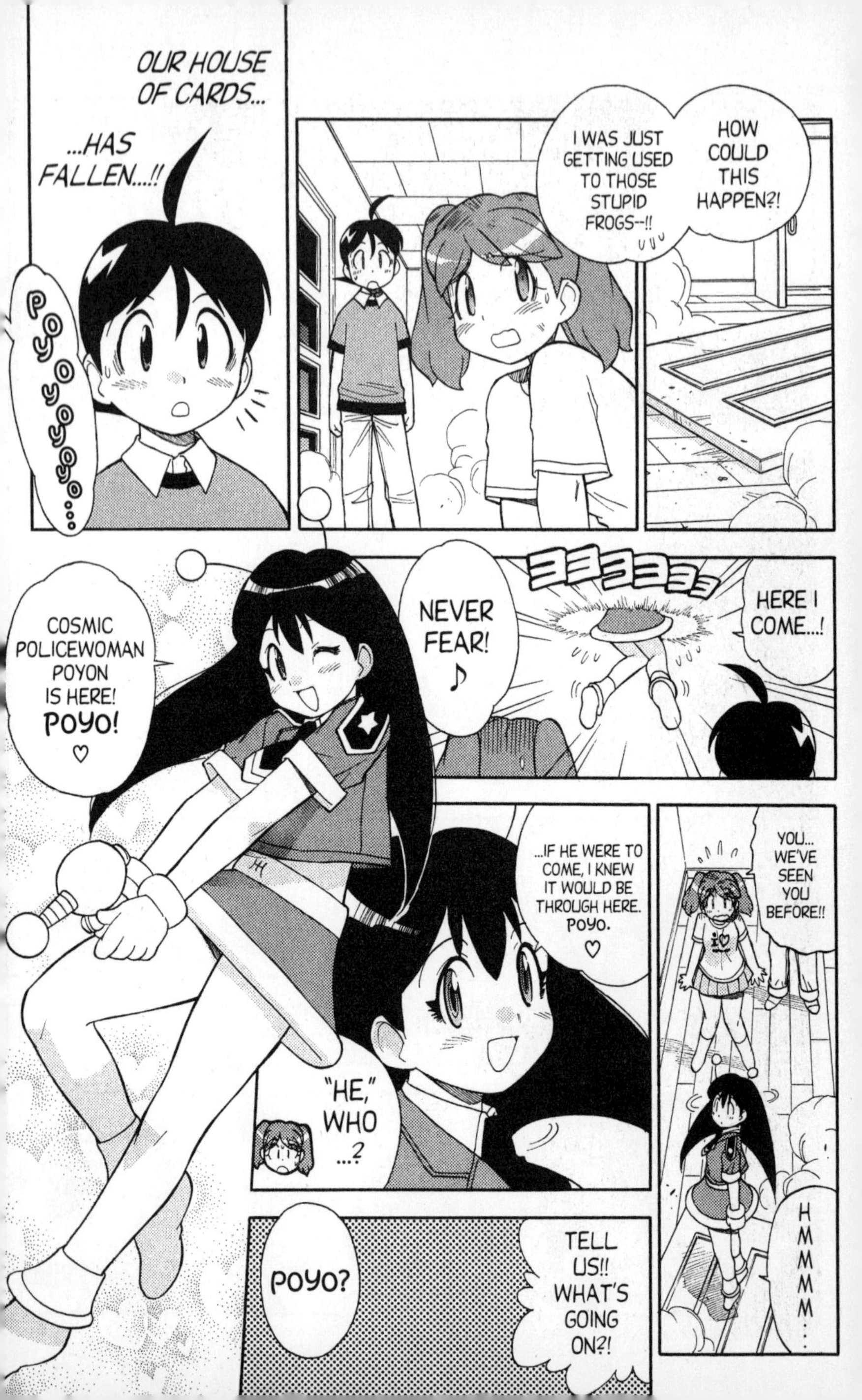

HOW COULD THIS HAPPEN?!
I WAS JUST GETTING USED TO THOSE STUPID FROGS--!!
OUR HOUSE OF CARDS...
...HAS FALLEN...!!
POYOYOYOYOYO...
HERE I COME...!
NEVER FEAR! ♪
COSMIC POLICEWOMAN POYON IS HERE! POYO! ♡
YOU... WE'VE SEEN YOU BEFORE!!
HMMMM...
...IF HE WERE TO COME, I KNEW IT WOULD BE THROUGH HERE. POYO. ♡
"HE," WHO ...?
TELL US!! WHAT'S GOING ON?!
POYO?

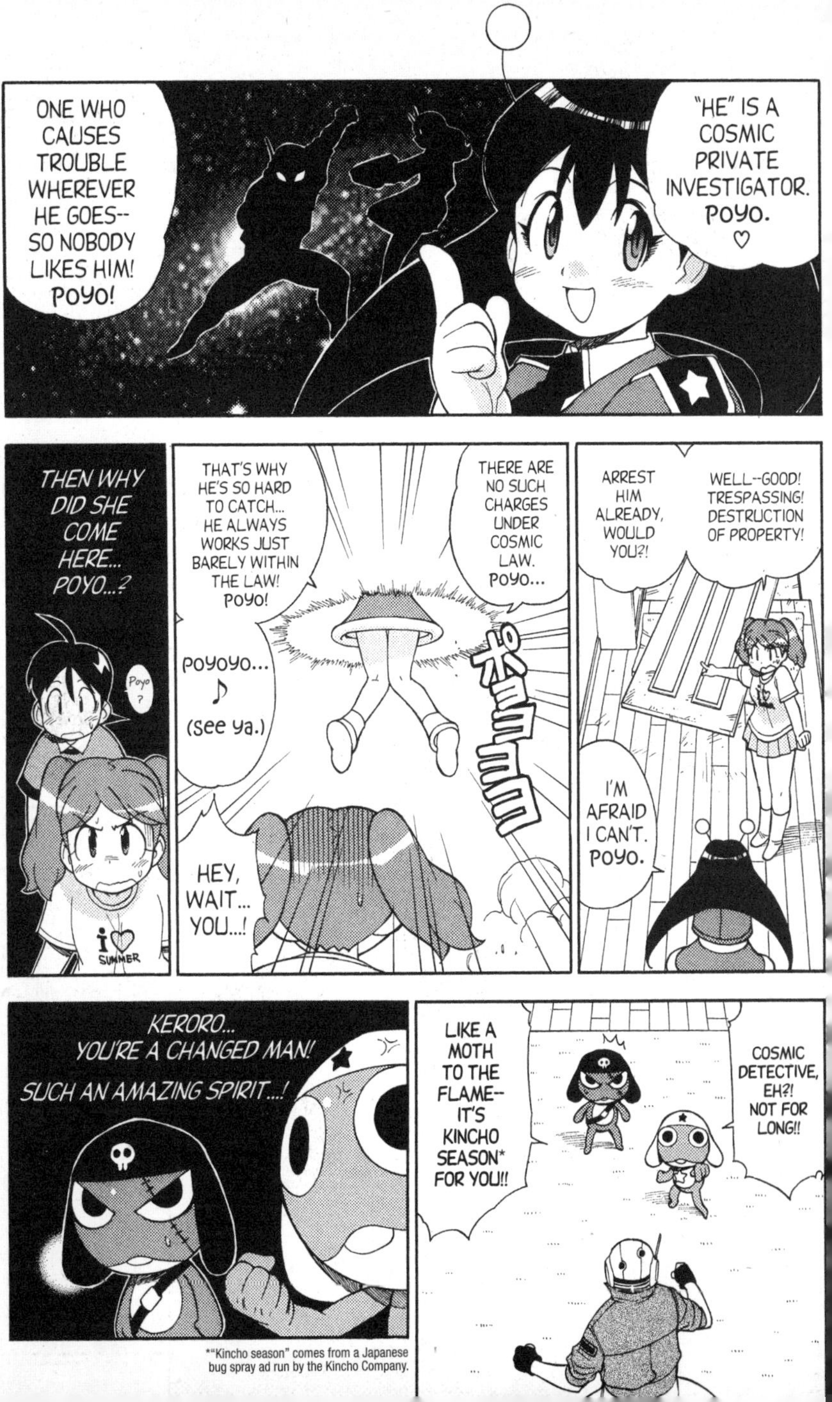
"HE" IS A COSMIC PRIVATE INVESTIGATOR. POYO. ♡
ONE WHO CAUSES TROUBLE WHEREVER HE GOES-- SO NOBODY LIKES HIM! POYO!
WELL--GOOD! TRESPASSING! DESTRUCTION OF PROPERTY!
ARREST HIM ALREADY, WOULD YOU?!
I'M AFRAID I CAN'T. POYO.
THERE ARE NO SUCH CHARGES UNDER COSMIC LAW. POYO...
THAT'S WHY HE'S SO HARD TO CATCH... HE ALWAYS WORKS JUST BARELY WITHIN THE LAW! POYO!
POYOYO... ♪ (see ya.)
HEY, WAIT... YOU...!
THEN WHY DID SHE COME HERE... POYO...?
Poyo ?
I ♥ SUMMER
COSMIC DETECTIVE, EH?! NOT FOR LONG!!
LIKE A MOTH TO THE FLAME-- IT'S KINCHO SEASON* FOR YOU!!
KERORO... YOU'RE A CHANGED MAN!
SUCH AN AMAZING SPIRIT...!

*"Kincho season" comes from a Japanese bug spray ad run by the Kincho Company.

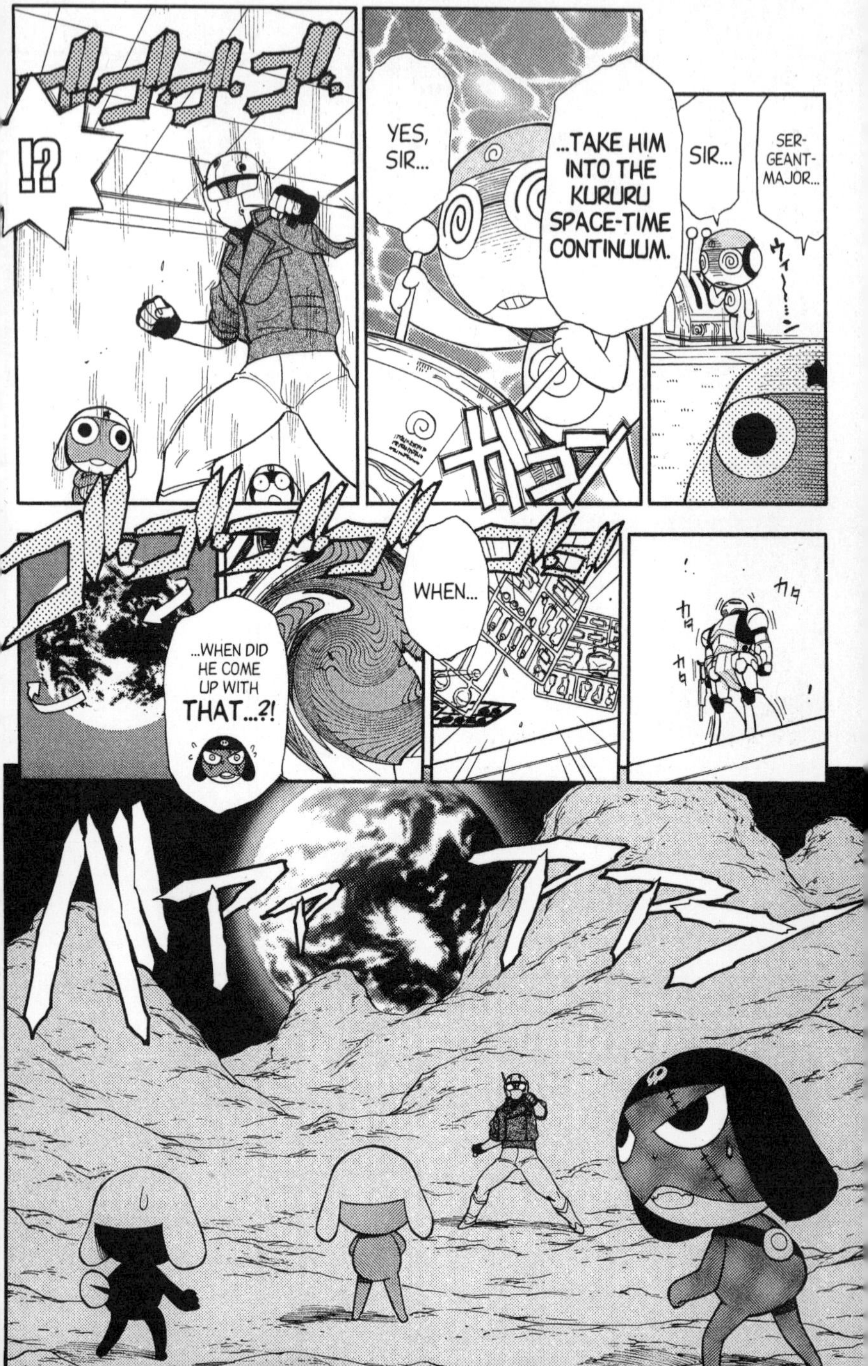

SER-GEANT-MAJOR...
SIR...
...TAKE HIM INTO THE KURURU SPACE-TIME CONTINUUM.
YES, SIR...
!?
WHEN...
...WHEN DID HE COME UP WITH THAT...?!

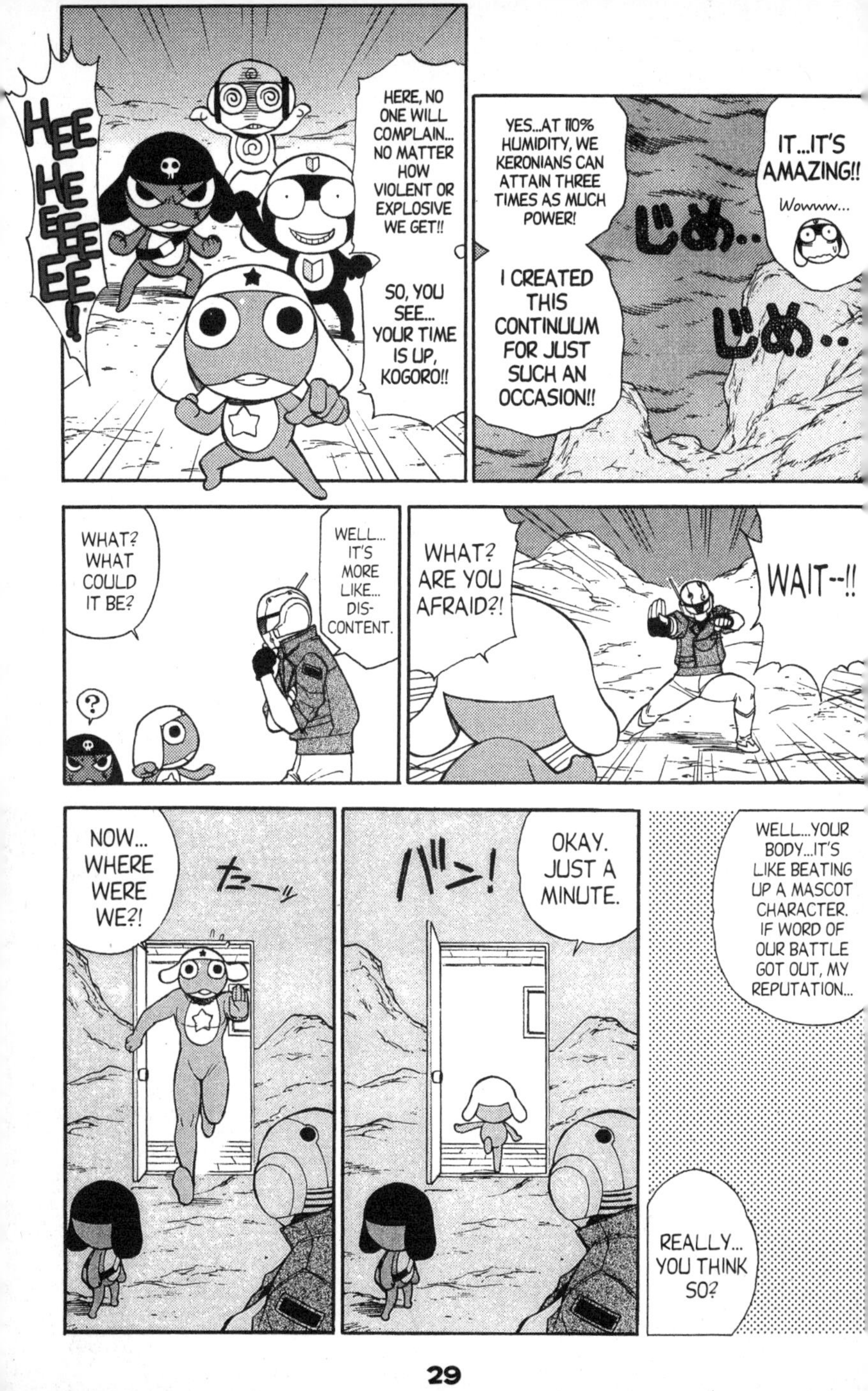
IT...IT'S AMAZING!!
Wowww...
じめ..
じめ..
YES...AT 110% HUMIDITY, WE KERONIANS CAN ATTAIN THREE TIMES AS MUCH POWER!
I CREATED THIS CONTINUUM FOR JUST SUCH AN OCCASION!!
HERE, NO ONE WILL COMPLAIN... NO MATTER HOW VIOLENT OR EXPLOSIVE WE GET!!
SO, YOU SEE... YOUR TIME IS UP, KOGORO!!
HEE HE EEEEE!!
WAIT--!!
WHAT? ARE YOU AFRAID?!
WELL... IT'S MORE LIKE... DIS-CONTENT.
WHAT? WHAT COULD IT BE?
?
WELL...YOUR BODY...IT'S LIKE BEATING UP A MASCOT CHARACTER. IF WORD OF OUR BATTLE GOT OUT, MY REPUTATION...
REALLY... YOU THINK SO?
OKAY. JUST A MINUTE.
バン!
NOW... WHERE WERE WE?!
たーッ

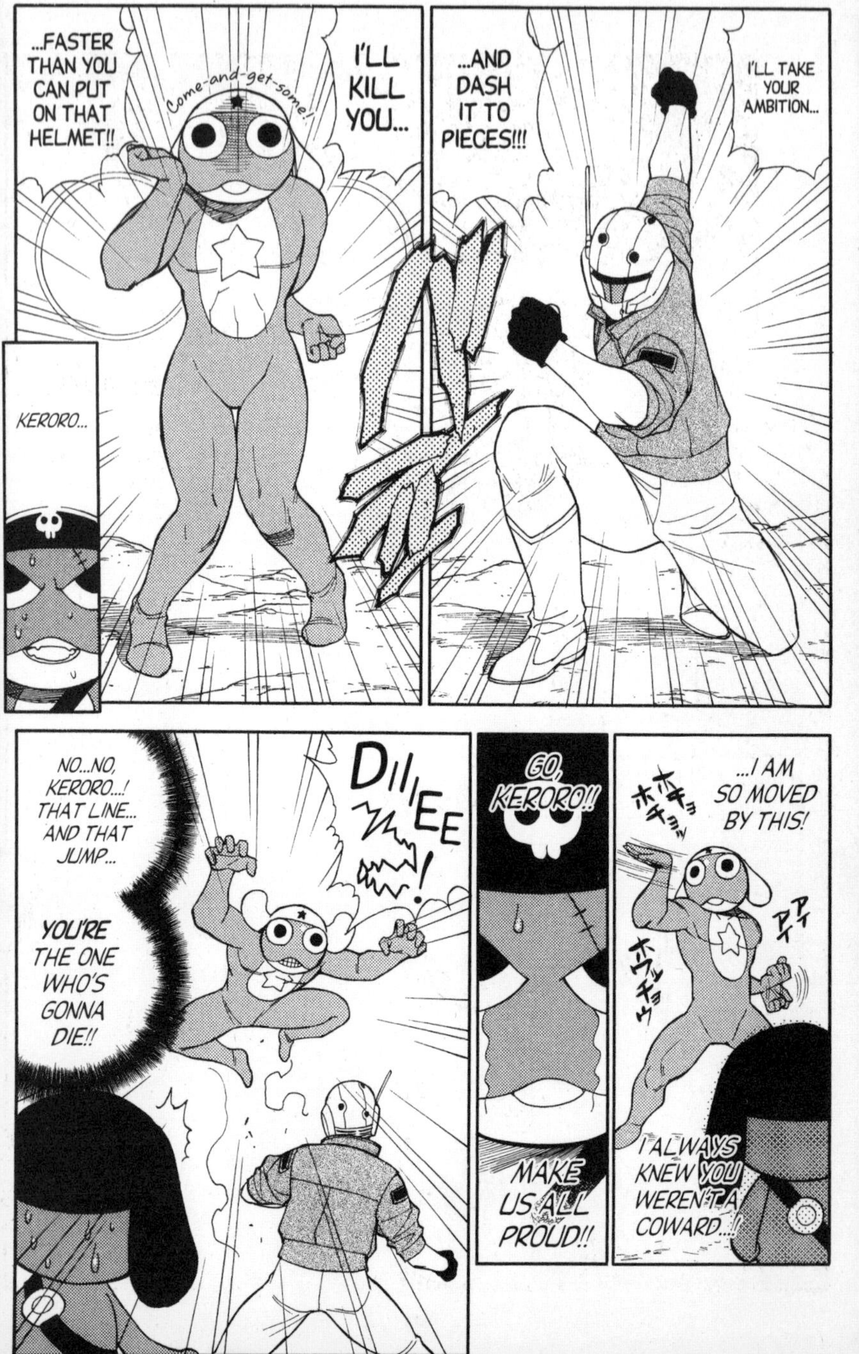

I'LL TAKE YOUR AMBITION...
...AND DASH IT TO PIECES!!!
I'LL KILL YOU...
...FASTER THAN YOU CAN PUT ON THAT HELMET!!
Come-and-get-some!
KERORO...
...I AM SO MOVED BY THIS!
I ALWAYS KNEW YOU WEREN'T A COWARD...!!
GO, KERORO!!
MAKE US ALL PROUD!!
DIIIEEE!
NO...NO, KERORO...! THAT LINE... AND THAT JUMP...
YOU'RE THE ONE WHO'S GONNA DIE!!

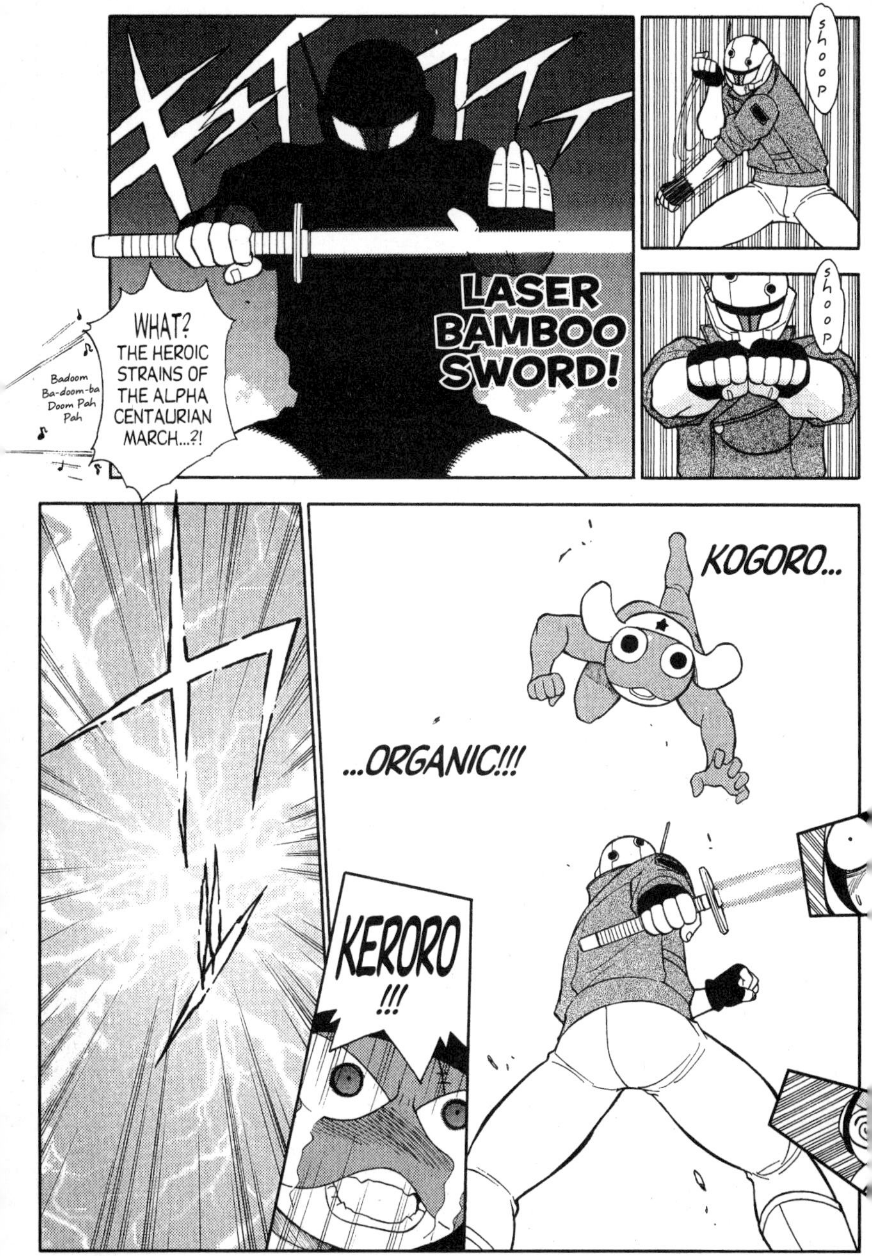
shoop
shoop
LASER BAMBOO SWORD!
WHAT? THE HEROIC STRAINS OF THE ALPHA CENTAURIAN MARCH...?!
Badoom Ba-doom-ba Doom Pah Pah
KOGORO...
...ORGANIC!!!
KERORO !!!

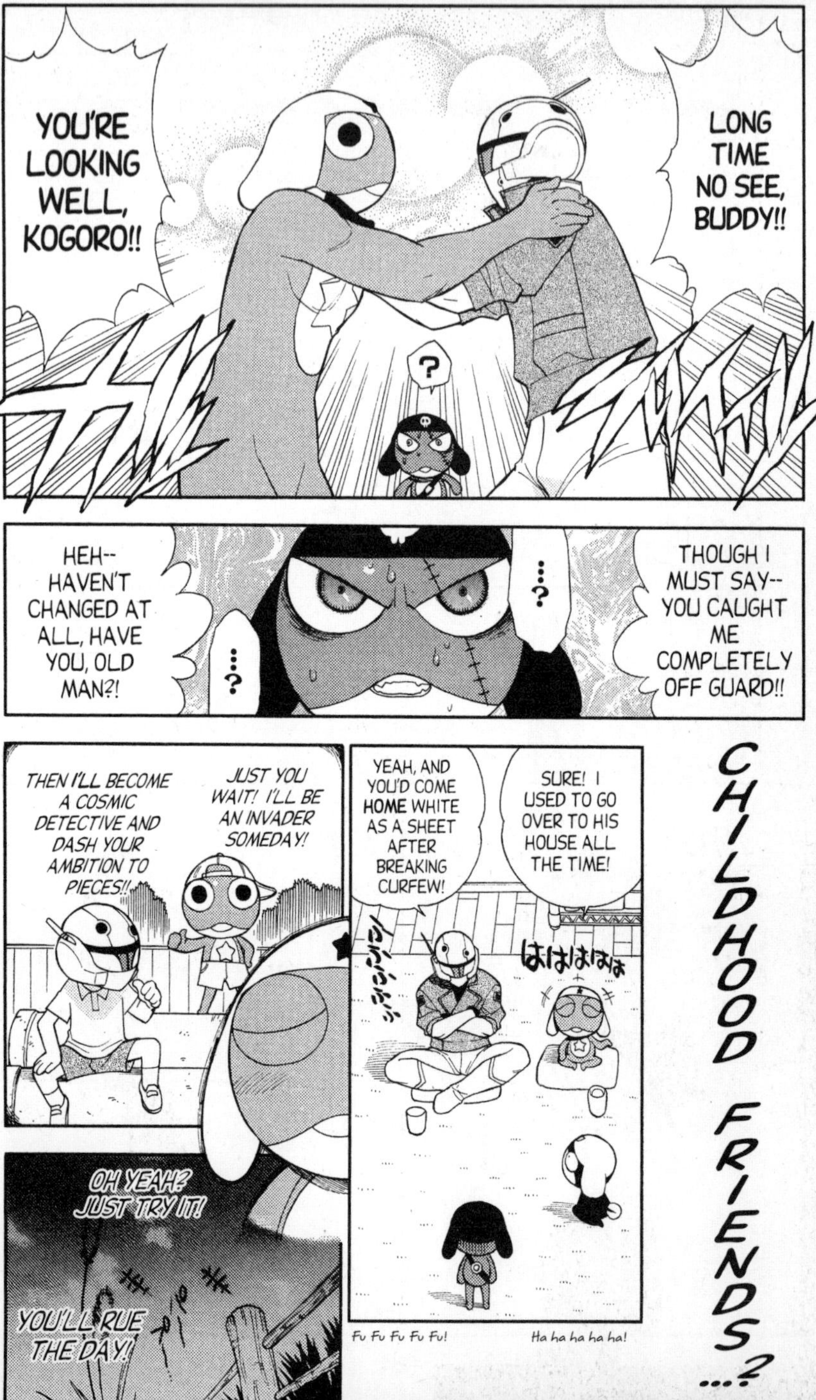

LONG TIME NO SEE, BUDDY!!
YOU'RE LOOKING WELL, KOGORO!!
?
THOUGH I MUST SAY-- YOU CAUGHT ME COMPLETELY OFF GUARD!!
...?
...?
HEH-- HAVEN'T CHANGED AT ALL, HAVE YOU, OLD MAN?!
CHILDHOOD FRIENDS...?
SURE! I USED TO GO OVER TO HIS HOUSE ALL THE TIME!
YEAH, AND YOU'D COME HOME WHITE AS A SHEET AFTER BREAKING CURFEW!
はははははは
ふふふふふ
Ha ha ha ha ha!
Fu Fu Fu Fu Fu!
JUST YOU WAIT! I'LL BE AN INVADER SOMEDAY!
THEN I'LL BECOME A COSMIC DETECTIVE AND DASH YOUR AMBITION TO PIECES!!
OH YEAH? JUST TRY IT!
YOU'LL RUE THE DAY!

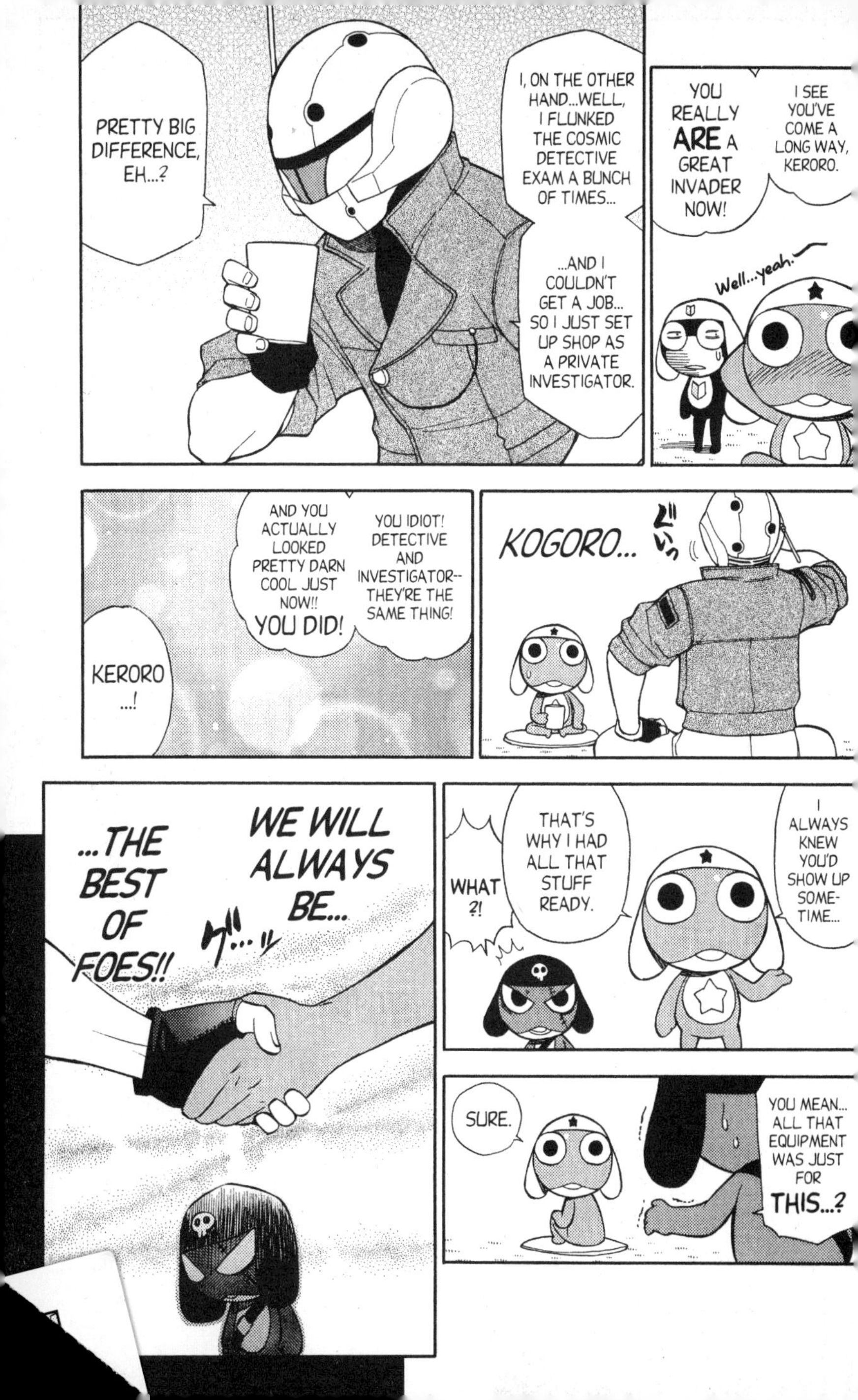
I SEE YOU'VE COME A LONG WAY, KERORO.
YOU REALLY ARE A GREAT INVADER NOW!
Well...yeah.
I, ON THE OTHER HAND...WELL, I FLUNKED THE COSMIC DETECTIVE EXAM A BUNCH OF TIMES...
...AND I COULDN'T GET A JOB... SO I JUST SET UP SHOP AS A PRIVATE INVESTIGATOR.
PRETTY BIG DIFFERENCE, EH...?
KOGORO...
YOU IDIOT! DETECTIVE AND INVESTIGATOR-- THEY'RE THE SAME THING!
AND YOU ACTUALLY LOOKED PRETTY DARN COOL JUST NOW!! YOU DID!
KERORO ...!
I ALWAYS KNEW YOU'D SHOW UP SOME-TIME...
THAT'S WHY I HAD ALL THAT STUFF READY.
WHAT?!
YOU MEAN... ALL THAT EQUIPMENT WAS JUST FOR THIS...?
SURE.
WE WILL ALWAYS BE...
...THE BEST OF FOES!!

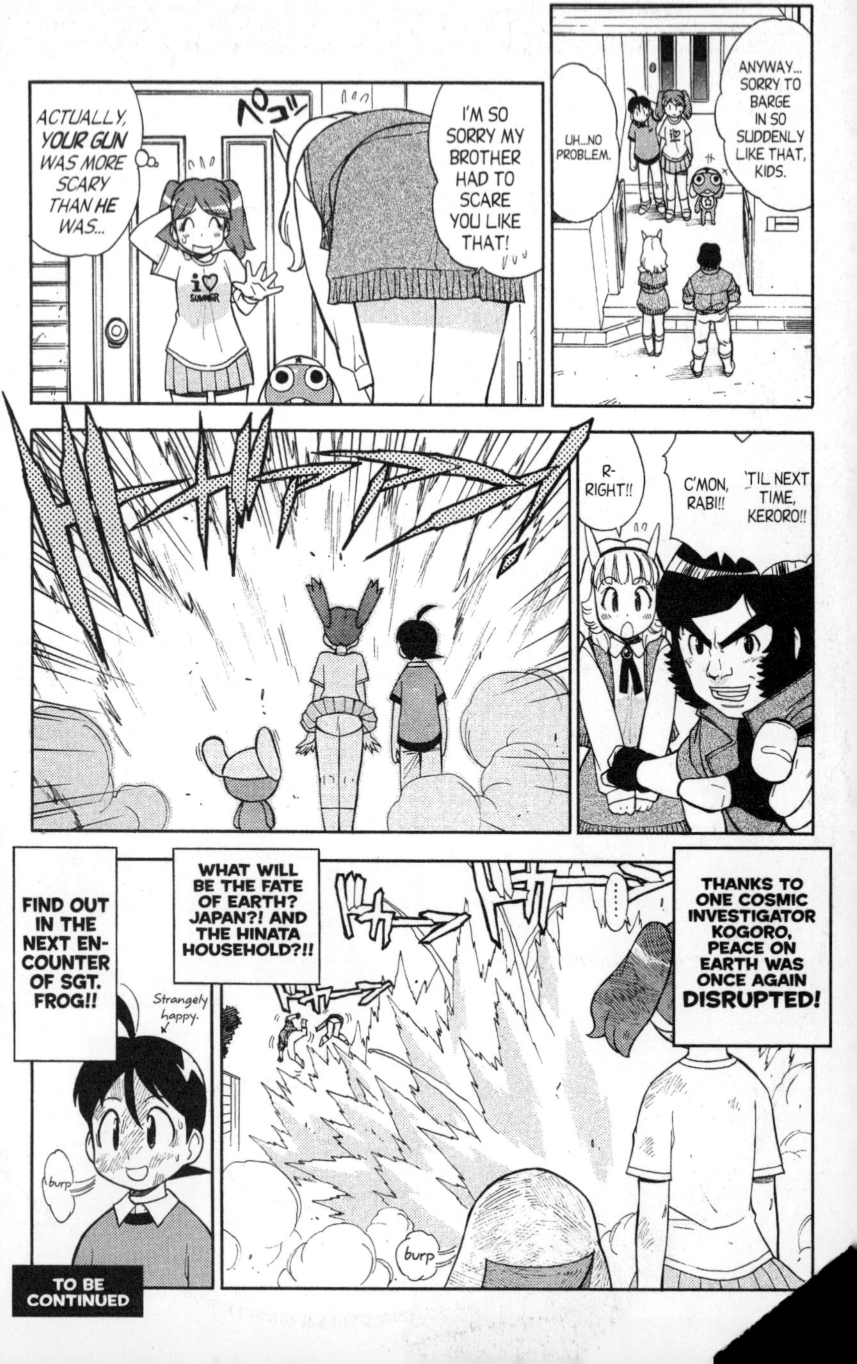
ANYWAY... SORRY TO BARGE IN SO SUDDENLY LIKE THAT, KIDS.
UH...NO PROBLEM.
I'M SO SORRY MY BROTHER HAD TO SCARE YOU LIKE THAT!
ACTUALLY, YOUR GUN WAS MORE SCARY THAN HE WAS...
'TIL NEXT TIME, KERORO!!
C'MON, RABI!!
R- RIGHT!!
THANKS TO ONE COSMIC INVESTIGATOR KOGORO, PEACE ON EARTH WAS ONCE AGAIN DISRUPTED!
......
burp
WHAT WILL BE THE FATE OF EARTH? JAPAN?! AND THE HINATA HOUSEHOLD?!!
FIND OUT IN THE NEXT EN-COUNTER OF SGT. FROG!!
Strangely happy.
burp
TO BE CONTINUED

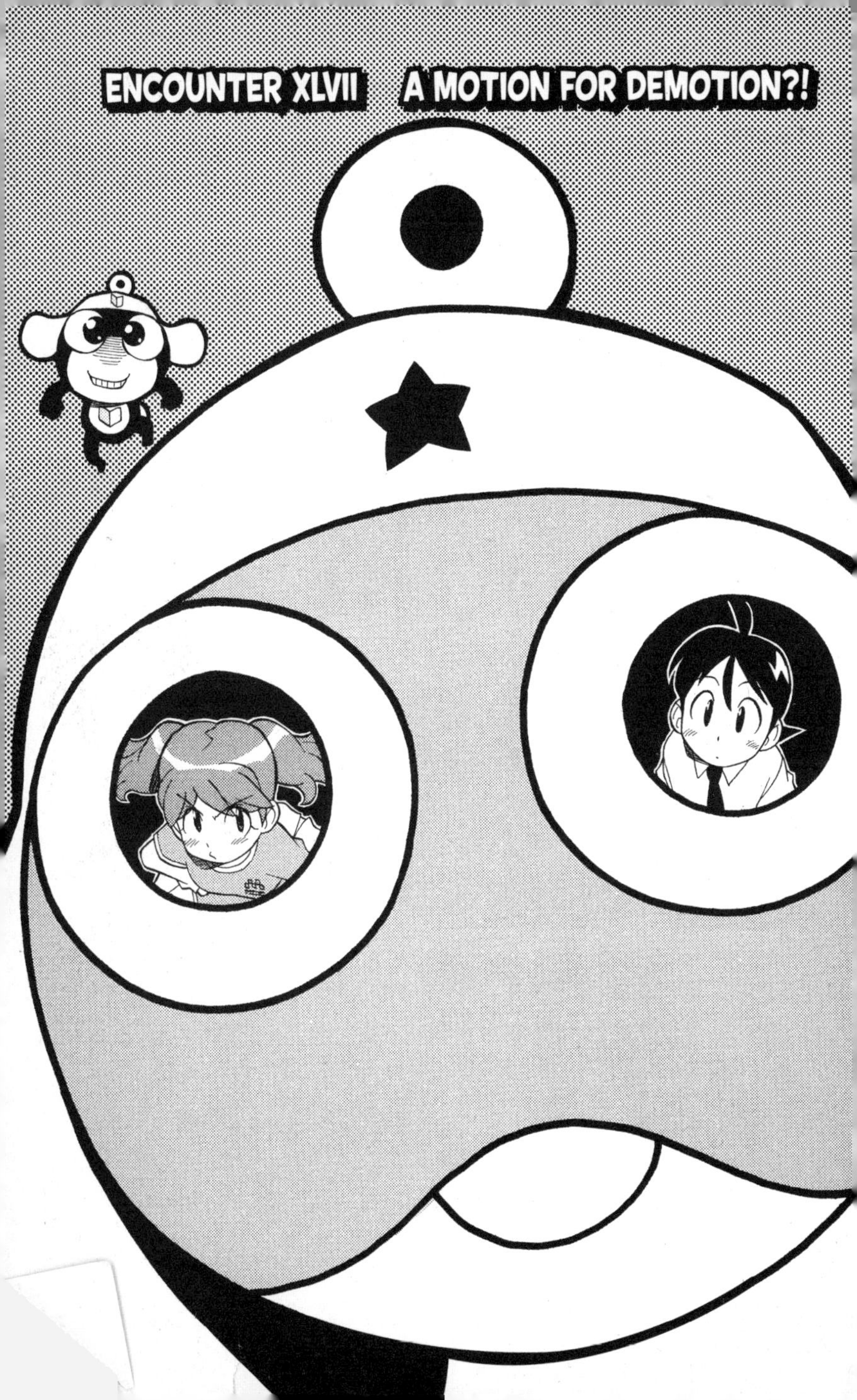
ENCOUNTER XLVII A MOTION FOR DEMOTION?!

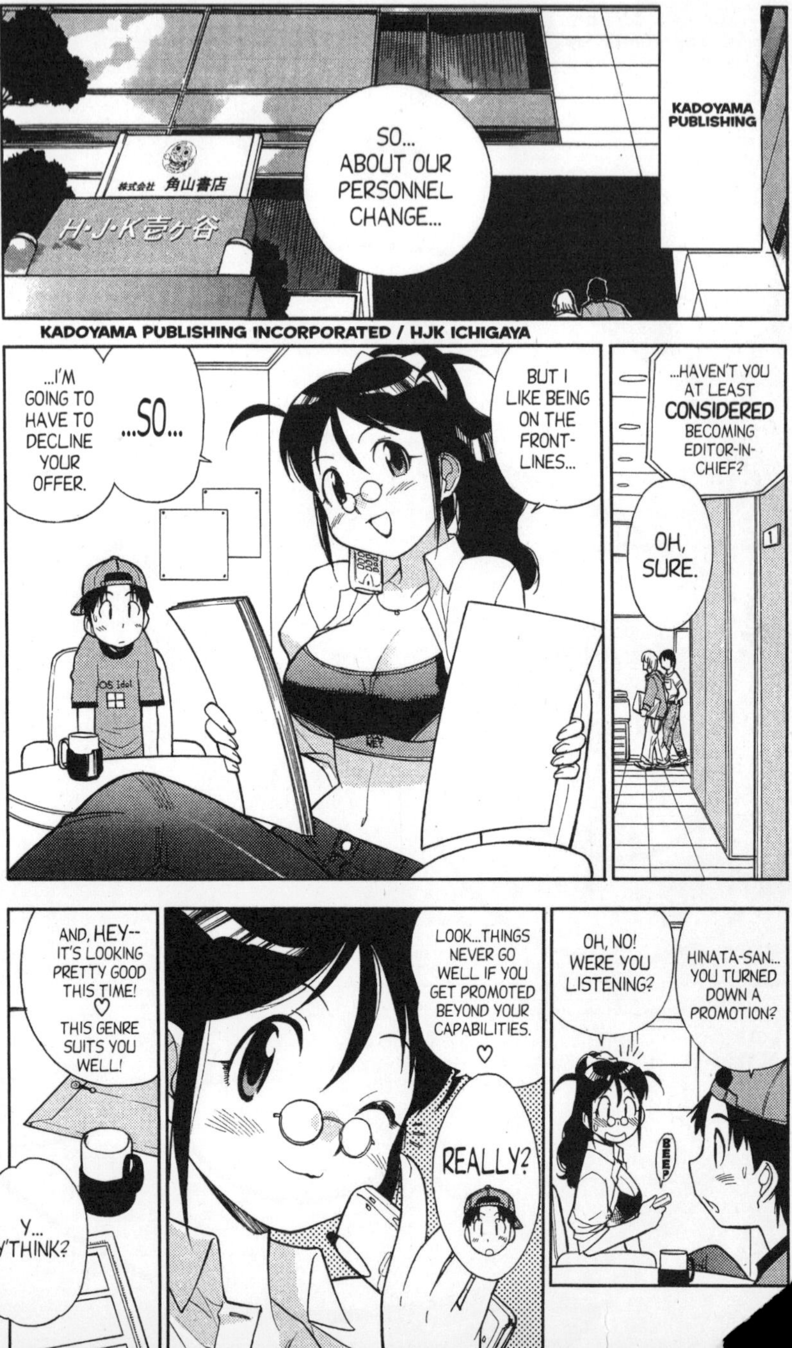
KADOYAMA PUBLISHING
SO... ABOUT OUR PERSONNEL CHANGE...
株式会社 角山書店
H・J・K壱ヶ谷
KADOYAMA PUBLISHING INCORPORATED / HJK ICHIGAYA
...HAVEN'T YOU AT LEAST CONSIDERED BECOMING EDITOR-IN-CHIEF?
OH, SURE.
BUT I LIKE BEING ON THE FRONT-LINES...
...SO...
...I'M GOING TO HAVE TO DECLINE YOUR OFFER.
HINATA-SAN... YOU TURNED DOWN A PROMOTION?
OH, NO! WERE YOU LISTENING?
LOOK...THINGS NEVER GO WELL IF YOU GET PROMOTED BEYOND YOUR CAPABILITIES. ♡
REALLY?
AND, HEY-- IT'S LOOKING PRETTY GOOD THIS TIME! ♡ THIS GENRE SUITS YOU WELL!
Y... Y'THINK?

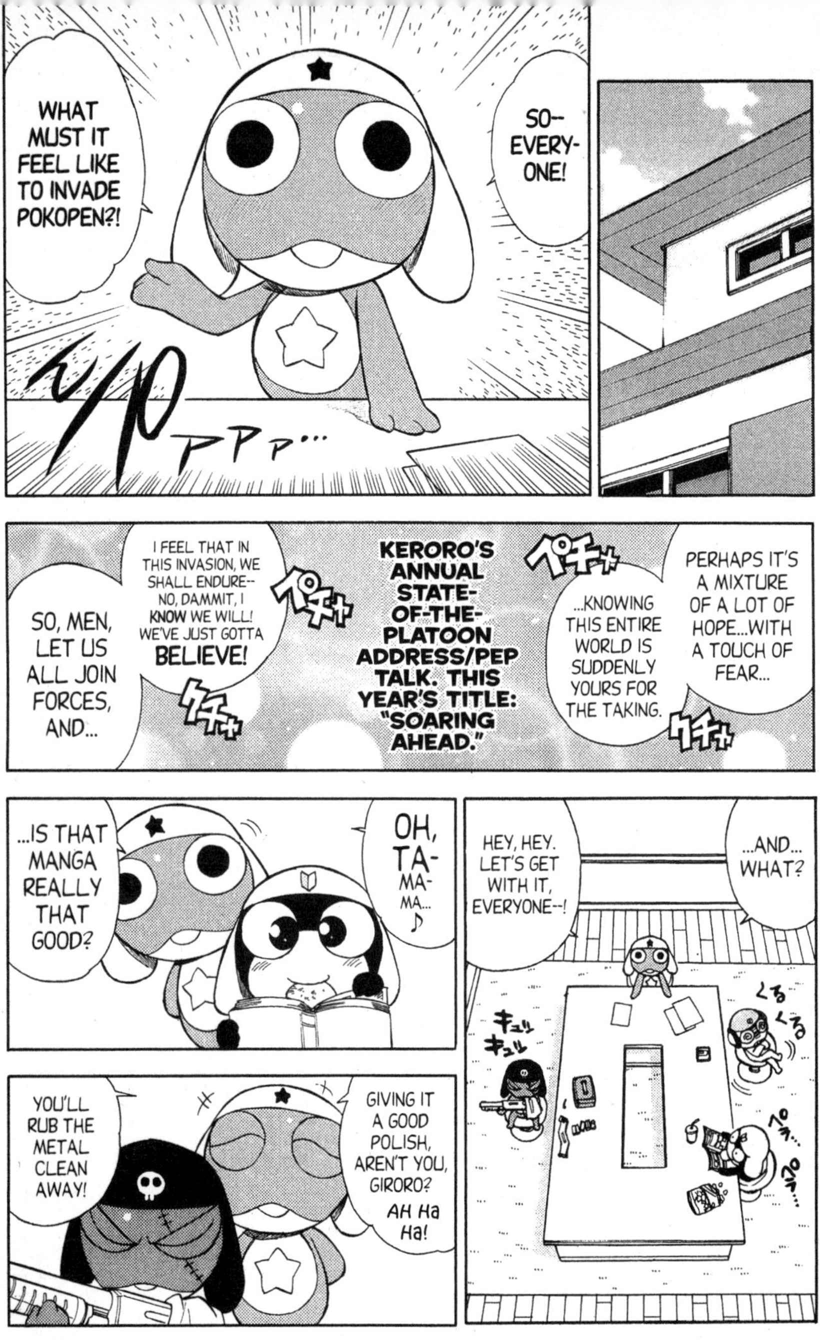
SO-- EVERY-ONE!
WHAT MUST IT FEEL LIKE TO INVADE POKOPEN?!
PERHAPS IT'S A MIXTURE OF A LOT OF HOPE...WITH A TOUCH OF FEAR...
...KNOWING THIS ENTIRE WORLD IS SUDDENLY YOURS FOR THE TAKING.
KERORO'S ANNUAL STATE-OF-THE-PLATOON ADDRESS/PEP TALK. THIS YEAR'S TITLE: "SOARING AHEAD."
I FEEL THAT IN THIS INVASION, WE SHALL ENDURE-- NO, DAMMIT, I KNOW WE WILL! WE'VE JUST GOTTA BELIEVE!
SO, MEN, LET US ALL JOIN FORCES, AND...
...AND... WHAT?
HEY, HEY. LET'S GET WITH IT, EVERYONE--!
OH, TA-MA-MA... ♪
...IS THAT MANGA REALLY THAT GOOD?
GIVING IT A GOOD POLISH, AREN'T YOU, GIRORO? AH HA HA!
YOU'LL RUB THE METAL CLEAN AWAY!

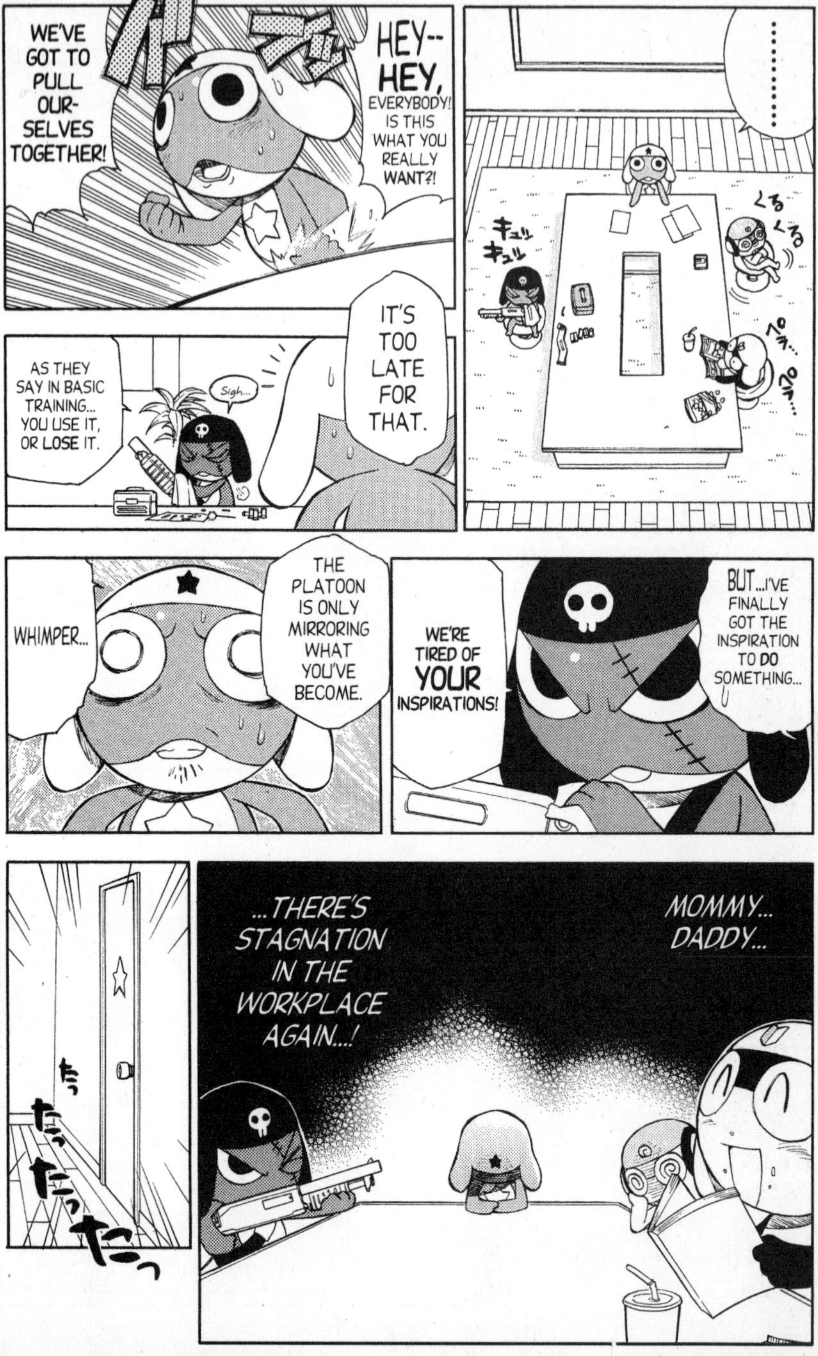
……
くるくる
キュッ キュッ
ペラ… ペラ…
HEY-- HEY, EVERYBODY! IS THIS WHAT YOU REALLY WANT?!
WE'VE GOT TO PULL OUR-SELVES TOGETHER!
IT'S TOO LATE FOR THAT.
Sigh...
AS THEY SAY IN BASIC TRAINING... YOU USE IT, OR LOSE IT.
BUT...I'VE FINALLY GOT THE INSPIRATION TO DO SOMETHING...
WE'RE TIRED OF YOUR INSPIRATIONS!
THE PLATOON IS ONLY MIRRORING WHAT YOU'VE BECOME.
WHIMPER...
MOMMY... DADDY...
...THERE'S STAGNATION IN THE WORKPLACE AGAIN...!

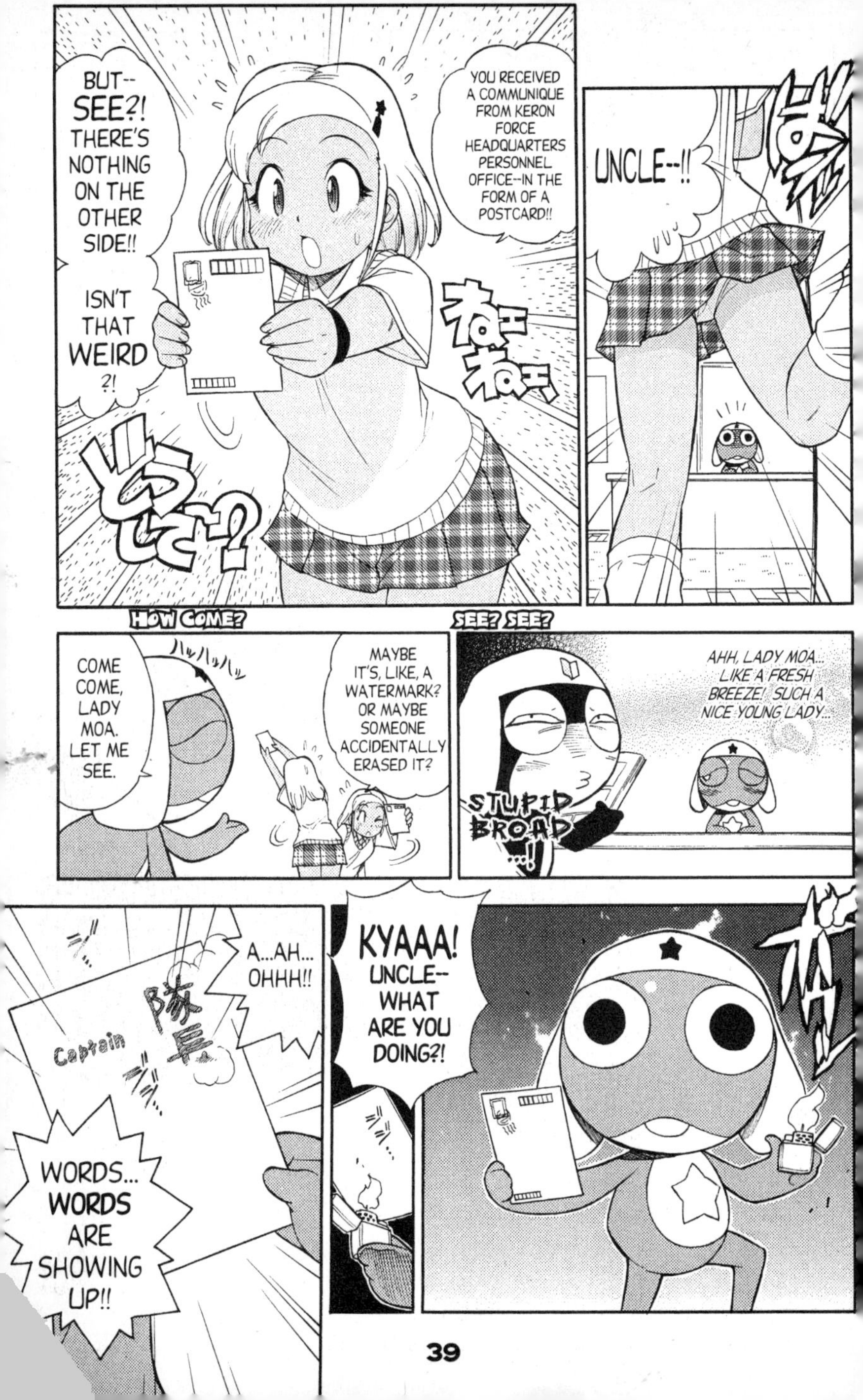
UNCLE--!!
SEE? SEE?
YOU RECEIVED A COMMUNIQUE FROM KERON FORCE HEADQUARTERS PERSONNEL OFFICE--IN THE FORM OF A POSTCARD!!
BUT-- SEE?! THERE'S NOTHING ON THE OTHER SIDE!!
ISN'T THAT WEIRD ?!
HOW COME?
AHH, LADY MOA... LIKE A FRESH BREEZE! SUCH A NICE YOUNG LADY...
STUPID BROAD ...!
MAYBE IT'S, LIKE, A WATERMARK? OR MAYBE SOMEONE ACCIDENTALLY ERASED IT?
COME COME, LADY MOA. LET ME SEE.
KYAAA! UNCLE-- WHAT ARE YOU DOING?!
A...AH... OHHH!!
Captain
WORDS... WORDS ARE SHOWING UP!!

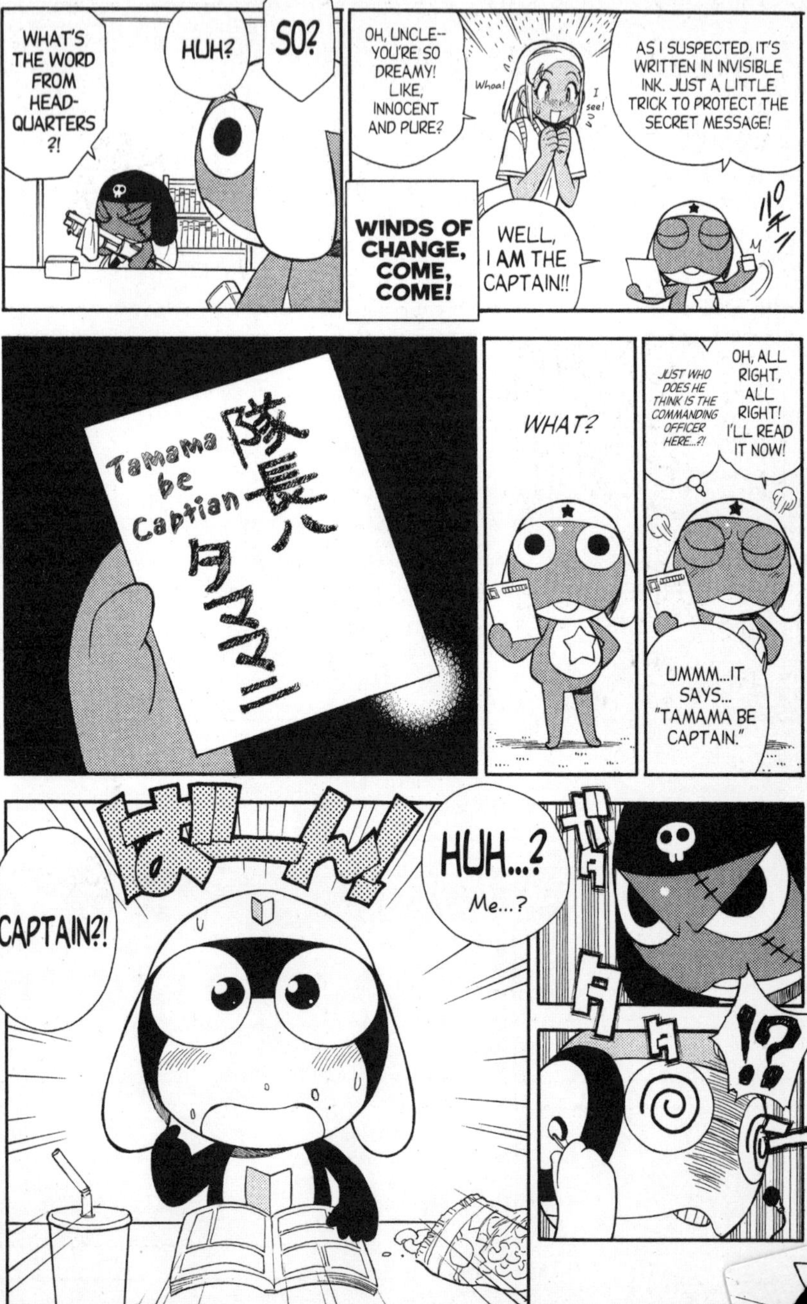
AS I SUSPECTED, IT'S WRITTEN IN INVISIBLE INK. JUST A LITTLE TRICK TO PROTECT THE SECRET MESSAGE!
I see!
Whoa!
OH, UNCLE-- YOU'RE SO DREAMY! LIKE, INNOCENT AND PURE?
WELL, I AM THE CAPTAIN!!
WINDS OF CHANGE, COME, COME!
SO?
HUH?
WHAT'S THE WORD FROM HEAD-QUARTERS ?!
OH, ALL RIGHT, ALL RIGHT! I'LL READ IT NOW!
JUST WHO DOES HE THINK IS THE COMMANDING OFFICER HERE...?!
UMMM...IT SAYS... "TAMAMA BE CAPTAIN."
WHAT?
隊長ハタママニ
Tamama be Captian
!?
HUH...?
Me...?
ばーん!!
CAPTAIN?!

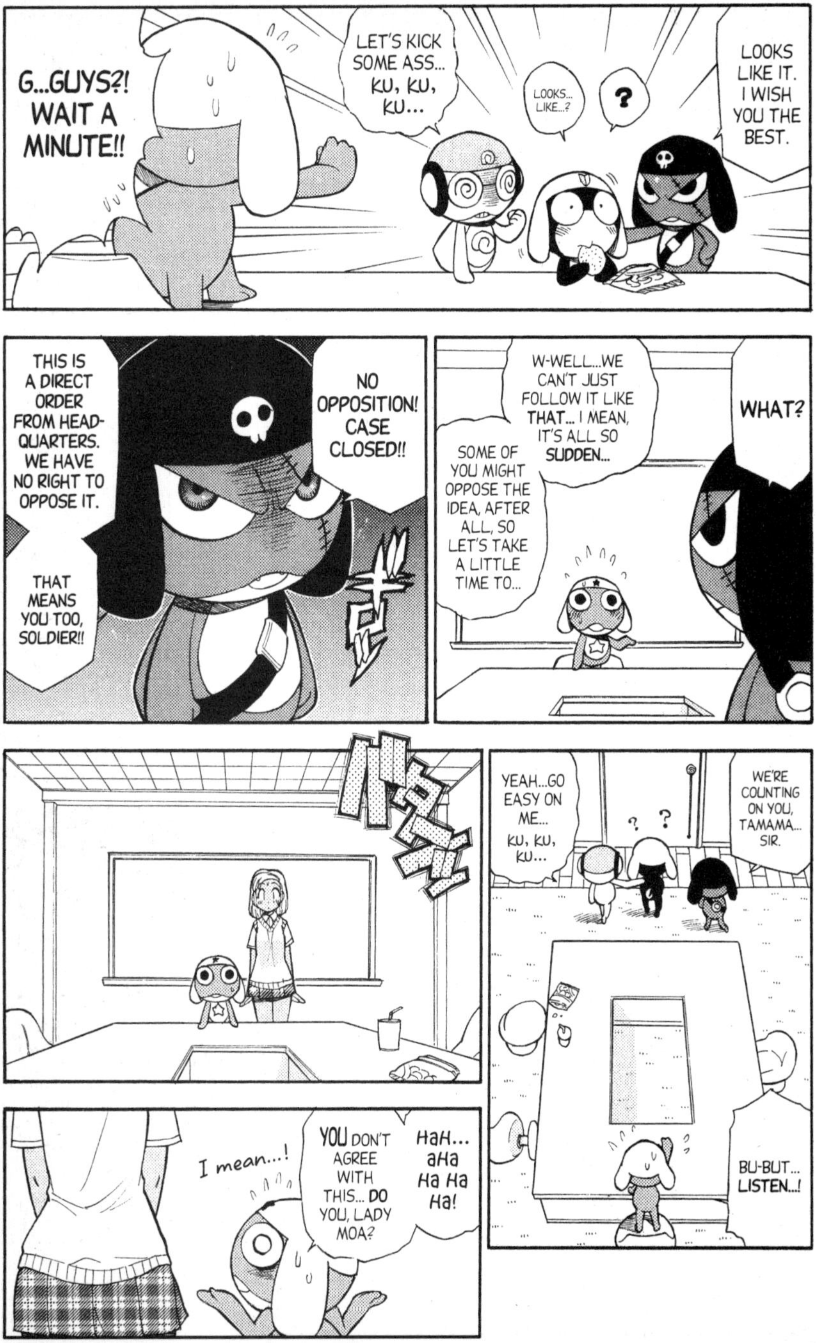
LOOKS LIKE IT. I WISH YOU THE BEST.
?
LOOKS... LIKE...?
LET'S KICK SOME ASS... KU, KU, KU...
G...GUYS?! WAIT A MINUTE!!
WHAT?
W-WELL...WE CAN'T JUST FOLLOW IT LIKE THAT... I MEAN, IT'S ALL SO SUDDEN...
SOME OF YOU MIGHT OPPOSE THE IDEA, AFTER ALL, SO LET'S TAKE A LITTLE TIME TO...
NO OPPOSITION! CASE CLOSED!!
THIS IS A DIRECT ORDER FROM HEADQUARTERS. WE HAVE NO RIGHT TO OPPOSE IT.
THAT MEANS YOU TOO, SOLDIER!!
WE'RE COUNTING ON YOU, TAMAMA... SIR.
YEAH...GO EASY ON ME... KU, KU, KU...
? ?
BU-BUT... LISTEN...!
HaH... aHa Ha Ha Ha!
YOU DON'T AGREE WITH THIS... DO YOU, LADY MOA?
I mean...!

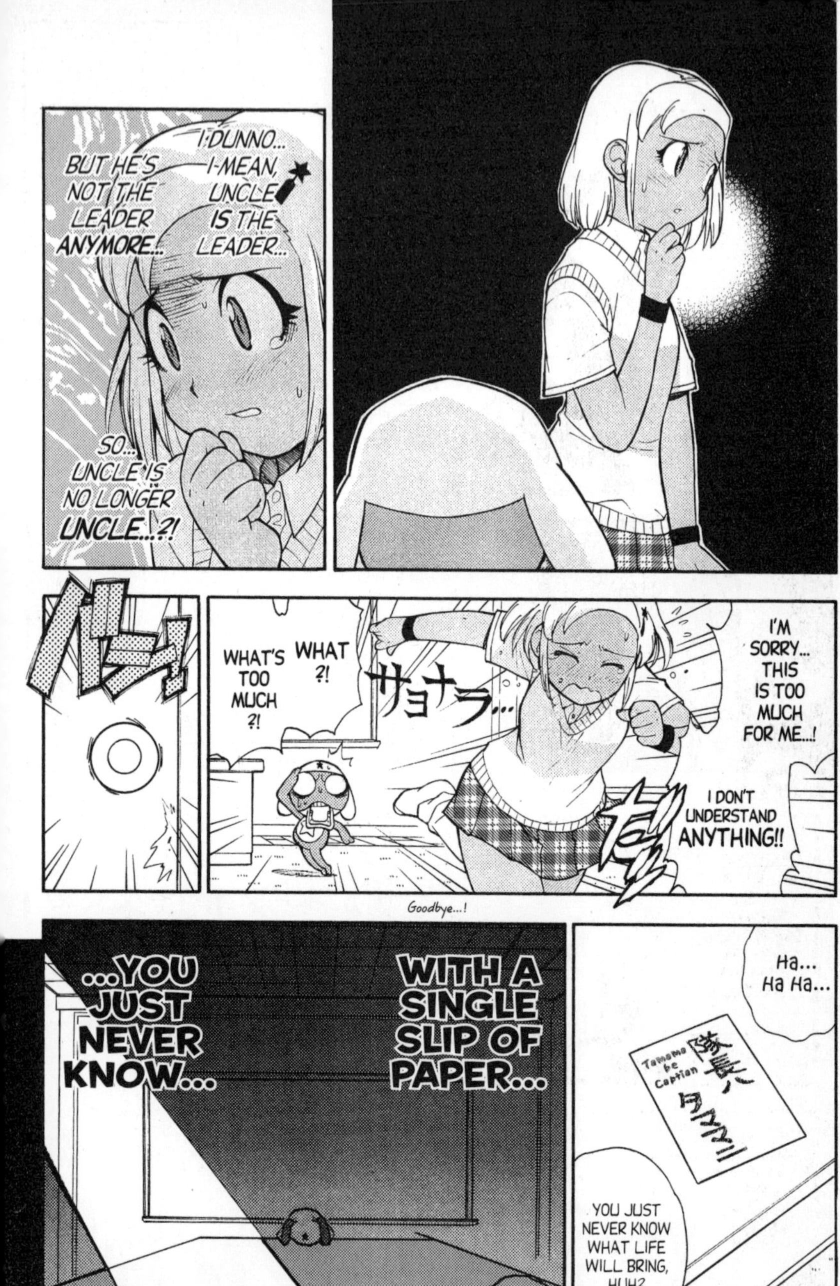
I DUNNO... I MEAN, UNCLE IS THE LEADER...
BUT HE'S NOT THE LEADER ANYMORE...
SO... UNCLE IS NO LONGER UNCLE...?!
I'M SORRY... THIS IS TOO MUCH FOR ME...!
サヨナラ...
WHAT ?!
WHAT'S TOO MUCH ?!
I DON'T UNDERSTAND ANYTHING!!
Goodbye...!
Ha... Ha Ha...
隊長ハタママ
Tamama be Captian
YOU JUST NEVER KNOW WHAT LIFE WILL BRING, HUH?
WITH A SINGLE SLIP OF PAPER...
...YOU JUST NEVER KNOW...

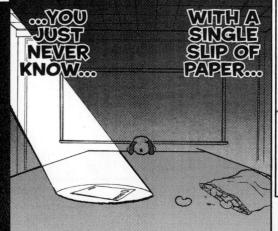

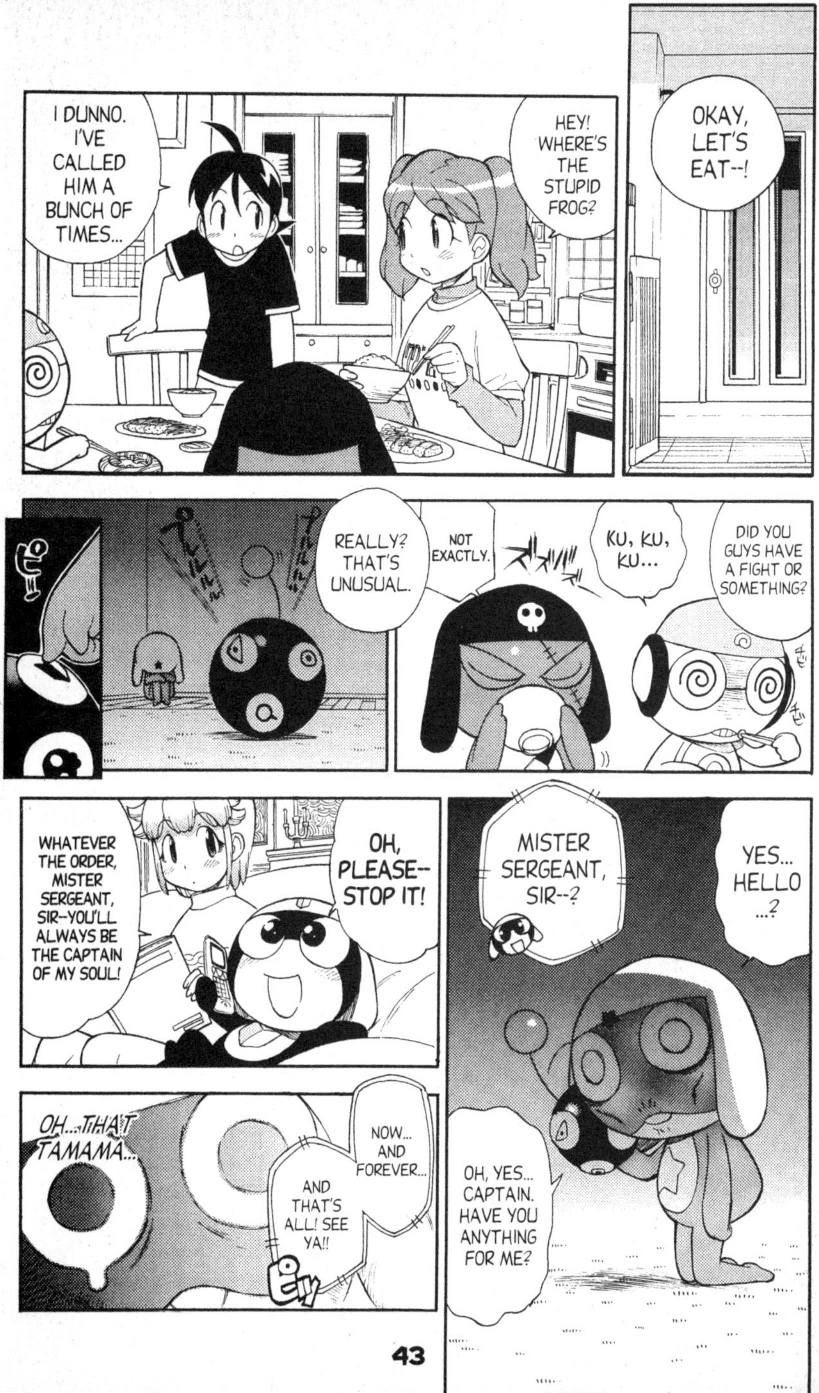
OKAY, LET'S EAT--!
HEY! WHERE'S THE STUPID FROG?
I DUNNO. I'VE CALLED HIM A BUNCH OF TIMES...
DID YOU GUYS HAVE A FIGHT OR SOMETHING?
KU, KU, KU...
NOT EXACTLY.
REALLY? THAT'S UNUSUAL.
YES... HELLO ...?
MISTER SERGEANT, SIR--?
OH, YES... CAPTAIN. HAVE YOU ANYTHING FOR ME?
OH, PLEASE-- STOP IT!
WHATEVER THE ORDER, MISTER SERGEANT, SIR--YOU'LL ALWAYS BE THE CAPTAIN OF MY SOUL!
NOW... AND FOREVER...
AND THAT'S ALL! SEE YA!!
OH...THAT TAMAMA...

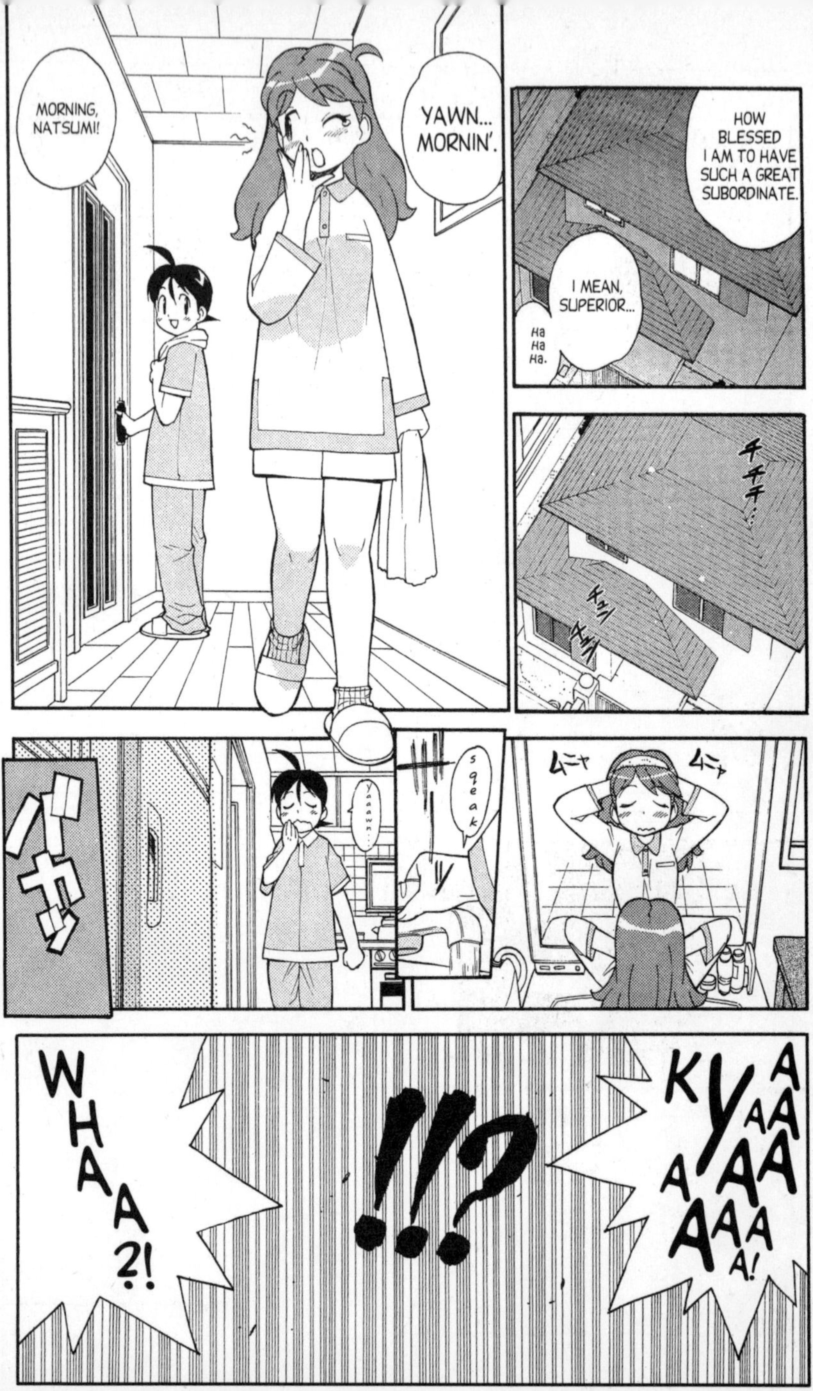

HOW BLESSED I AM TO HAVE SUCH A GREAT SUBORDINATE.
I MEAN, SUPERIOR...
Ha Ha Ha.
チチチ...
チュン チュン
YAWN... MORNIN'.
MORNING, NATSUMI!
ムニャ ムニャ
sqeak
yaaawn...
パカッ
KYAAAAAAAAAAA!
!!?
WHAAA?!

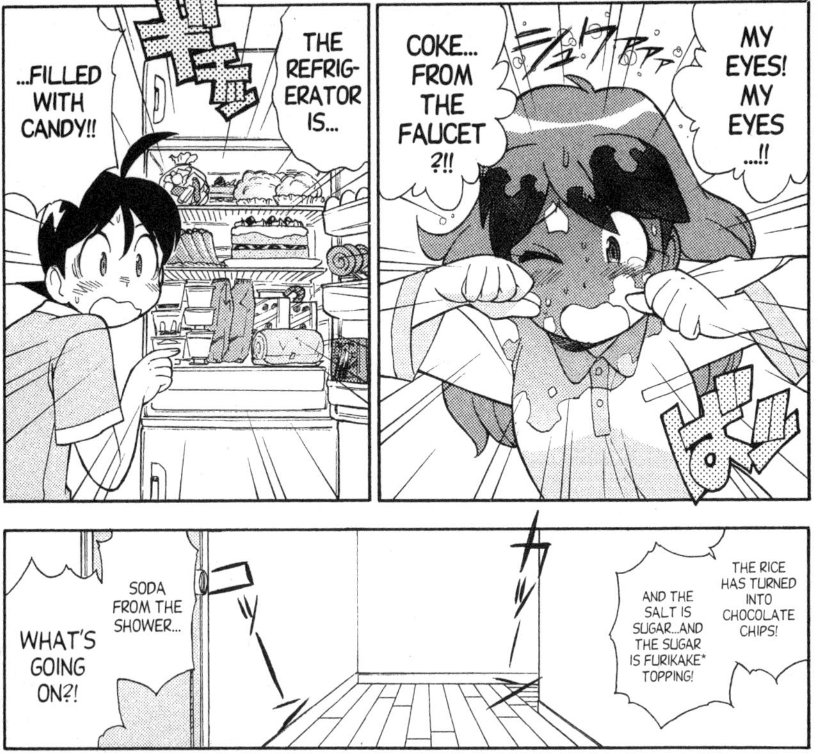
MY EYES! MY EYES ...!!
COKE... FROM THE FAUCET ?!!
THE REFRIG-ERATOR IS...
...FILLED WITH CANDY!!
THE RICE HAS TURNED INTO CHOCOLATE CHIPS!
AND THE SALT IS SUGAR...AND THE SUGAR IS FURIKAKE* TOPPING!
SODA FROM THE SHOWER...
WHAT'S GOING ON?!

*In Japan, furikake is a seasoning people put on rice when there's nothing else to eat with it.

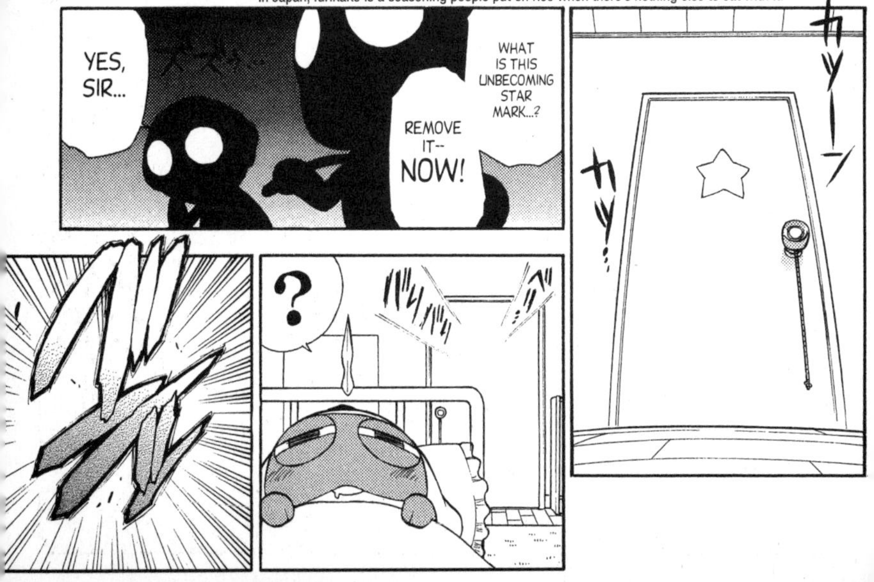
WHAT IS THIS UNBECOMING STAR MARK...?
REMOVE IT-- NOW!
YES, SIR...
?

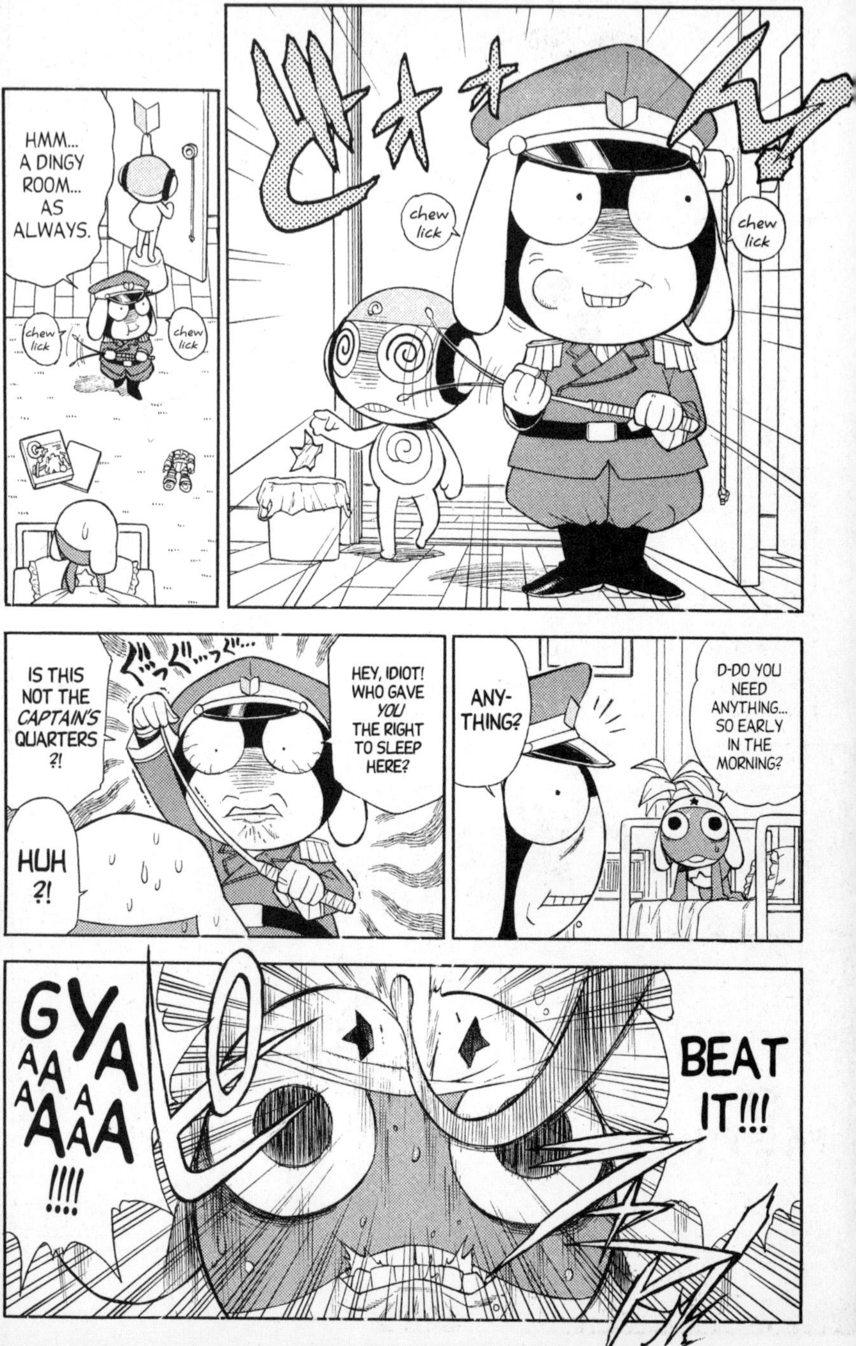
chew lick
chew lick
HMM... A DINGY ROOM... AS ALWAYS.
chew lick
chew lick
D-DO YOU NEED ANYTHING... SO EARLY IN THE MORNING?
ANY-THING?
HEY, IDIOT! WHO GAVE *YOU* THE RIGHT TO SLEEP HERE?
IS THIS NOT THE *CAPTAIN'S* QUARTERS?!
HUH?!
BEAT IT!!!
GYAAAAAAAAA!!!!

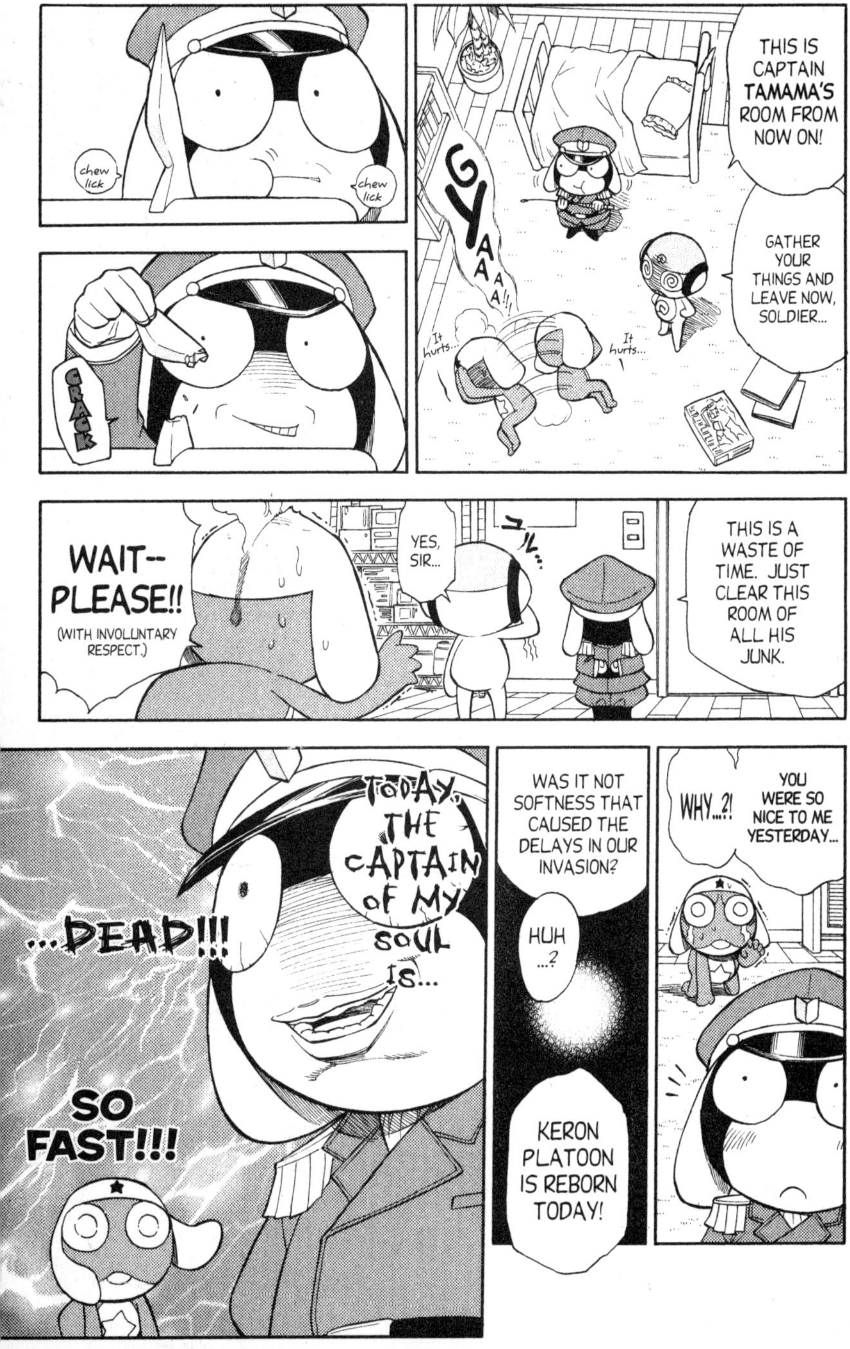
THIS IS CAPTAIN TAMAMA'S ROOM FROM NOW ON!
GATHER YOUR THINGS AND LEAVE NOW, SOLDIER...
GYAAAA!!
It hurts...
It hurts...
chew lick
chew lick
CRACK
THIS IS A WASTE OF TIME. JUST CLEAR THIS ROOM OF ALL HIS JUNK.
YES, SIR...
WAIT-- PLEASE!!
(WITH INVOLUNTARY RESPECT.)
YOU WERE SO NICE TO ME YESTERDAY...
WHY...?!
WAS IT NOT SOFTNESS THAT CAUSED THE DELAYS IN OUR INVASION?
HUH...?
KERON PLATOON IS REBORN TODAY!
TODAY, THE CAPTAIN OF MY SOUL IS...
...DEAD!!!
SO FAST!!!

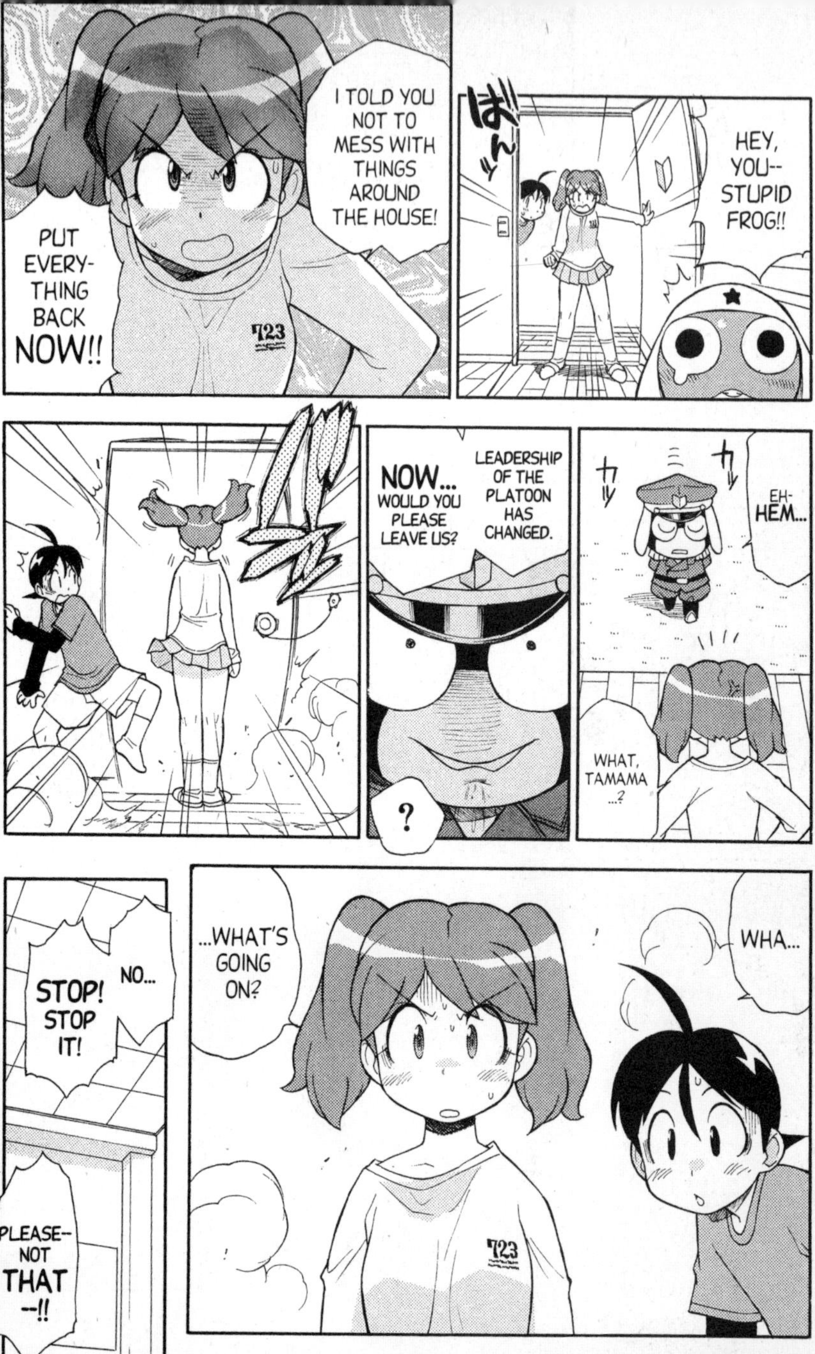
ばんッ
HEY, YOU-- STUPID FROG!!
I TOLD YOU NOT TO MESS WITH THINGS AROUND THE HOUSE!
PUT EVERY-THING BACK NOW!!
カッ カッ
EH-HEM...
WHAT, TAMAMA...?
LEADERSHIP OF THE PLATOON HAS CHANGED.
NOW... WOULD YOU PLEASE LEAVE US?
?
WHA...
...WHAT'S GOING ON?
NO...
STOP! STOP IT!
PLEASE--NOT THAT--!!

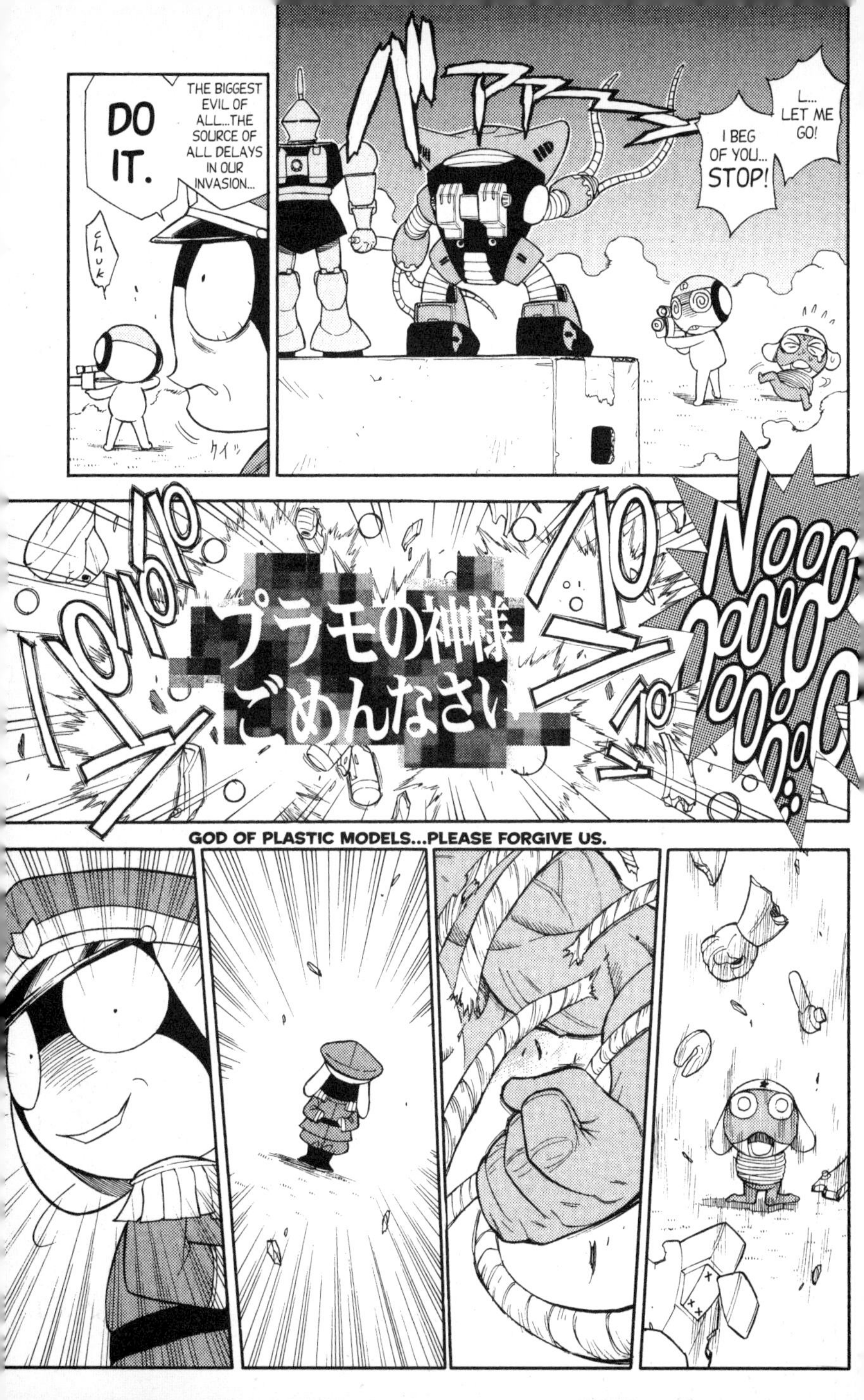
L... LET ME GO!
I BEG OF YOU... STOP!
THE BIGGEST EVIL OF ALL...THE SOURCE OF ALL DELAYS IN OUR INVASION...
DO IT.
chuk
クイッ
プラモの神様ごめんなさい
Nooooooo...
GOD OF PLASTIC MODELS...PLEASE FORGIVE US.

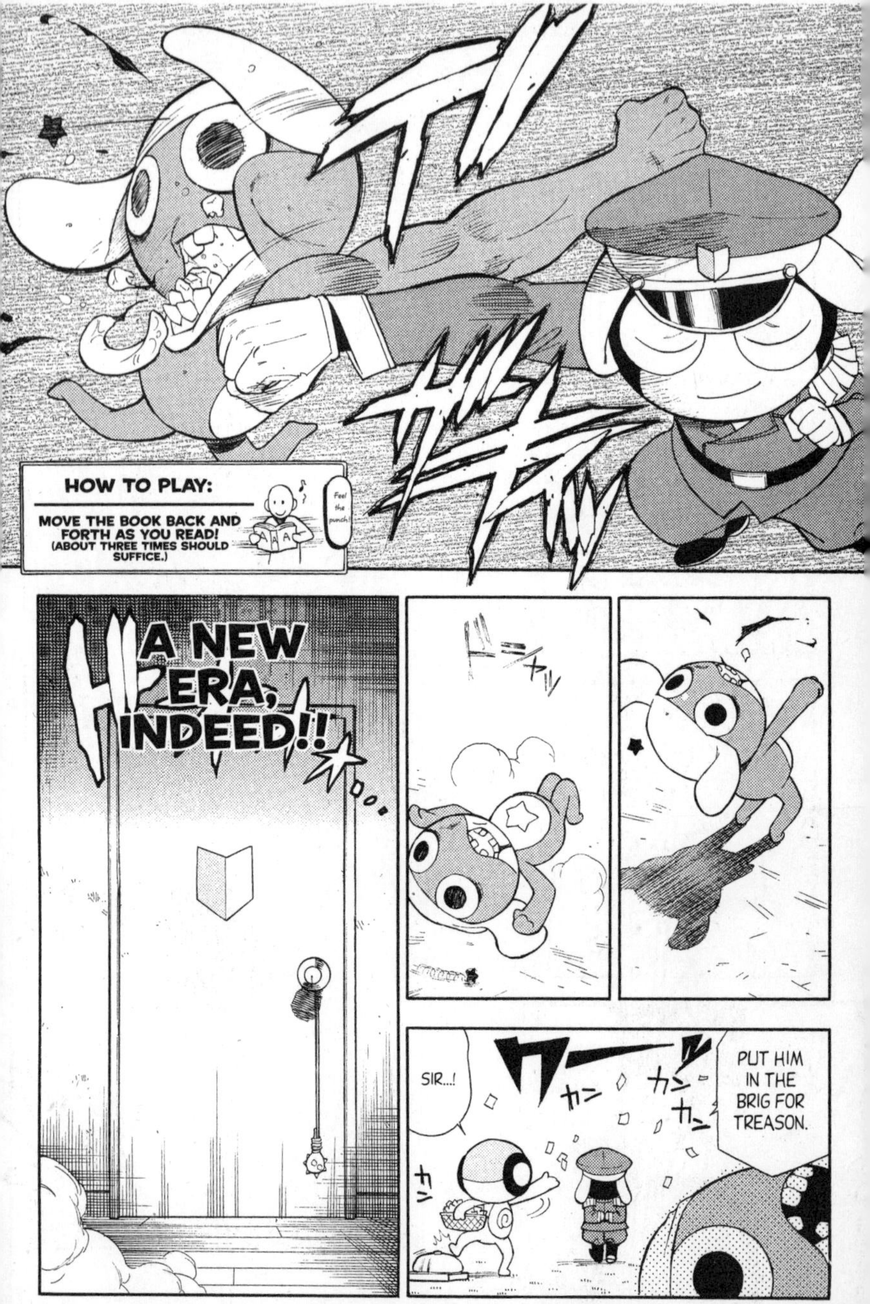
HOW TO PLAY:
MOVE THE BOOK BACK AND FORTH AS YOU READ! (ABOUT THREE TIMES SHOULD SUFFICE.)
Feel the punch!
PUT HIM IN THE BRIG FOR TREASON.
SIR...!
A NEW ERA, INDEED!!

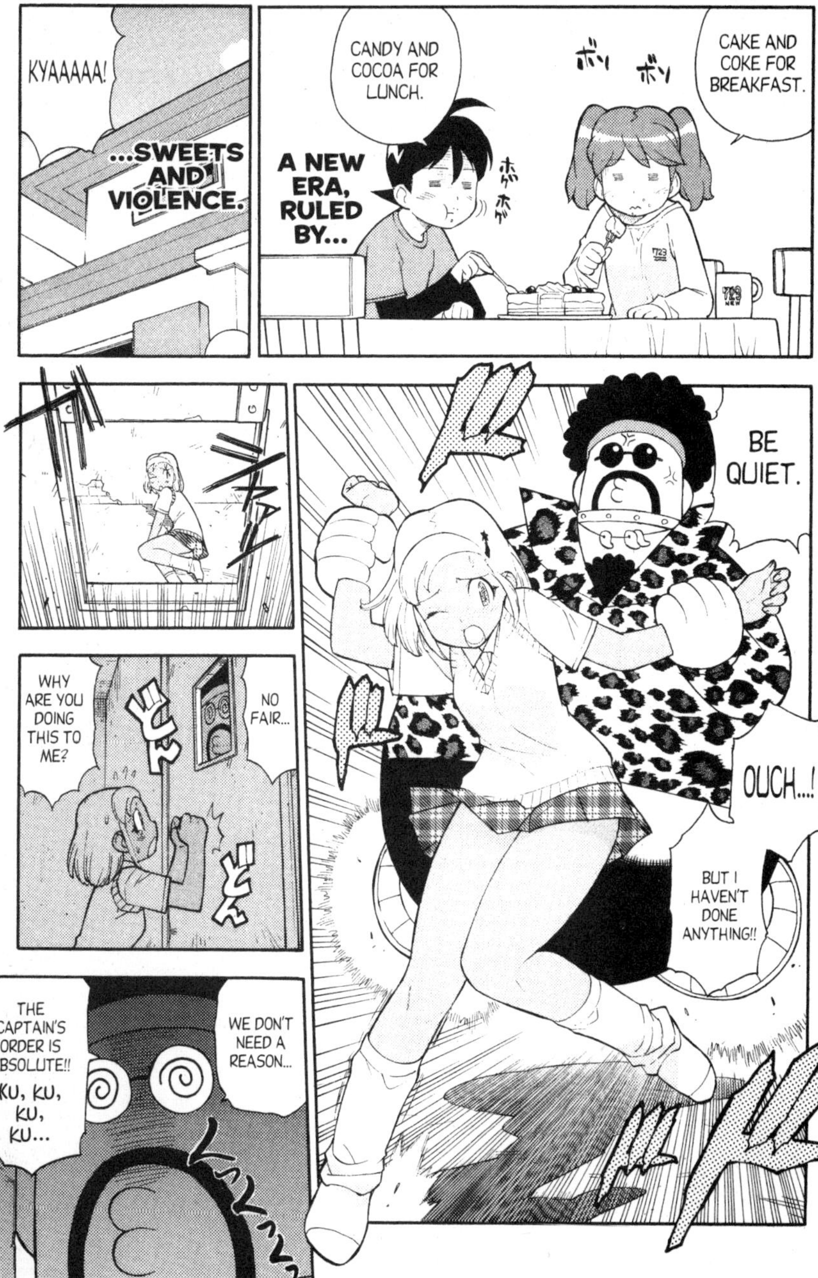
CAKE AND COKE FOR BREAKFAST.
CANDY AND COCOA FOR LUNCH.
A NEW ERA, RULED BY...
KYAAAAA!
...SWEETS AND VIOLENCE.
BE QUIET.
OUCH...!
BUT I HAVEN'T DONE ANYTHING!!
NO FAIR...
WHY ARE YOU DOING THIS TO ME?
どん
どん
WE DON'T NEED A REASON...
THE CAPTAIN'S ORDER IS ABSOLUTE!!
KU, KU, KU, KU...

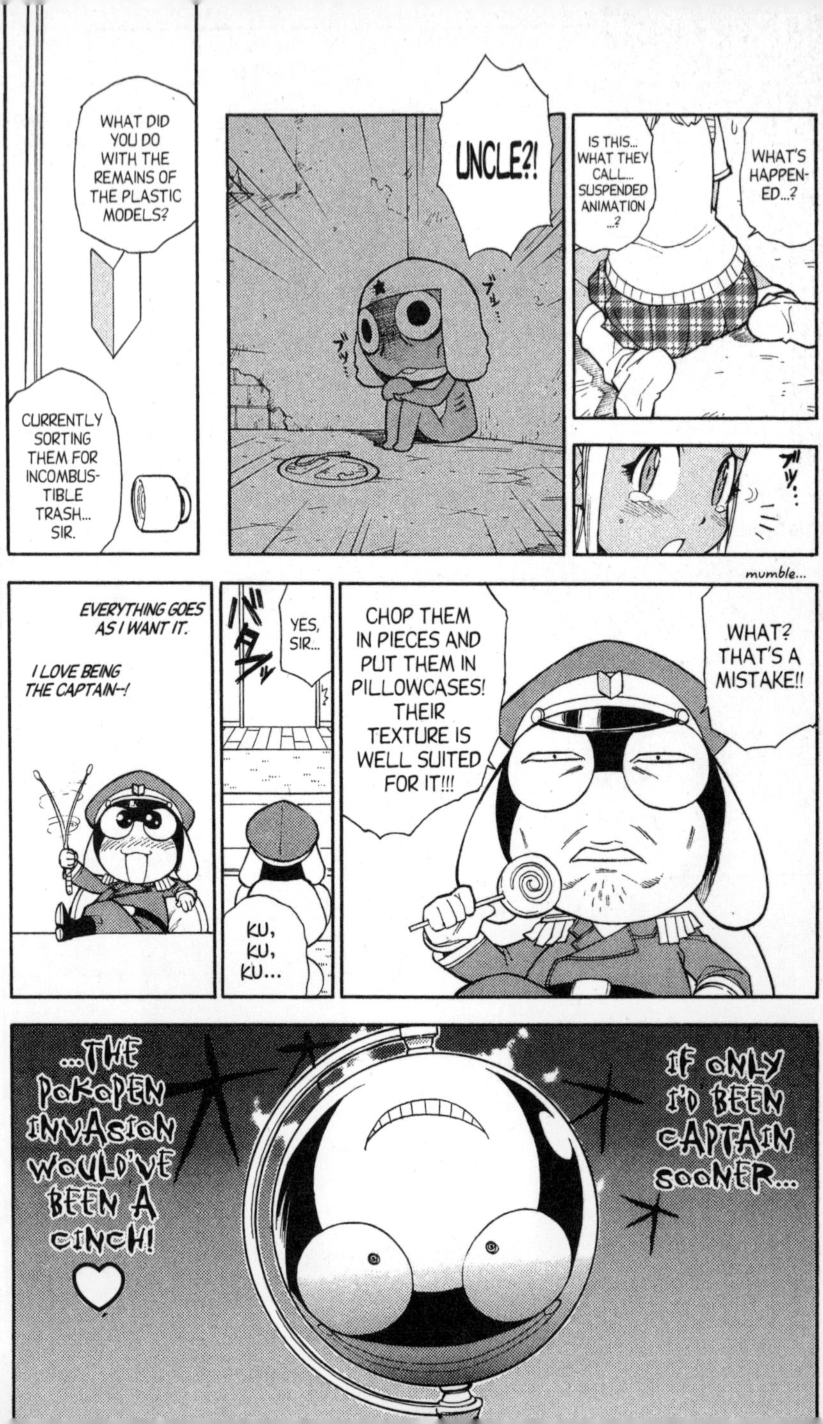
WHAT'S HAPPENED...?
IS THIS... WHAT THEY CALL... SUSPENDED ANIMATION...?
mumble...
UNCLE?!
WHAT DID YOU DO WITH THE REMAINS OF THE PLASTIC MODELS?
CURRENTLY SORTING THEM FOR INCOMBUSTIBLE TRASH... SIR.
WHAT? THAT'S A MISTAKE!!
CHOP THEM IN PIECES AND PUT THEM IN PILLOWCASES! THEIR TEXTURE IS WELL SUITED FOR IT!!!
YES, SIR...
KU, KU, KU...
EVERYTHING GOES AS I WANT IT.
I LOVE BEING THE CAPTAIN--!
IF ONLY I'D BEEN CAPTAIN SOONER...
...THE POKOPEN INVASION WOULD'VE BEEN A CINCH! ♥

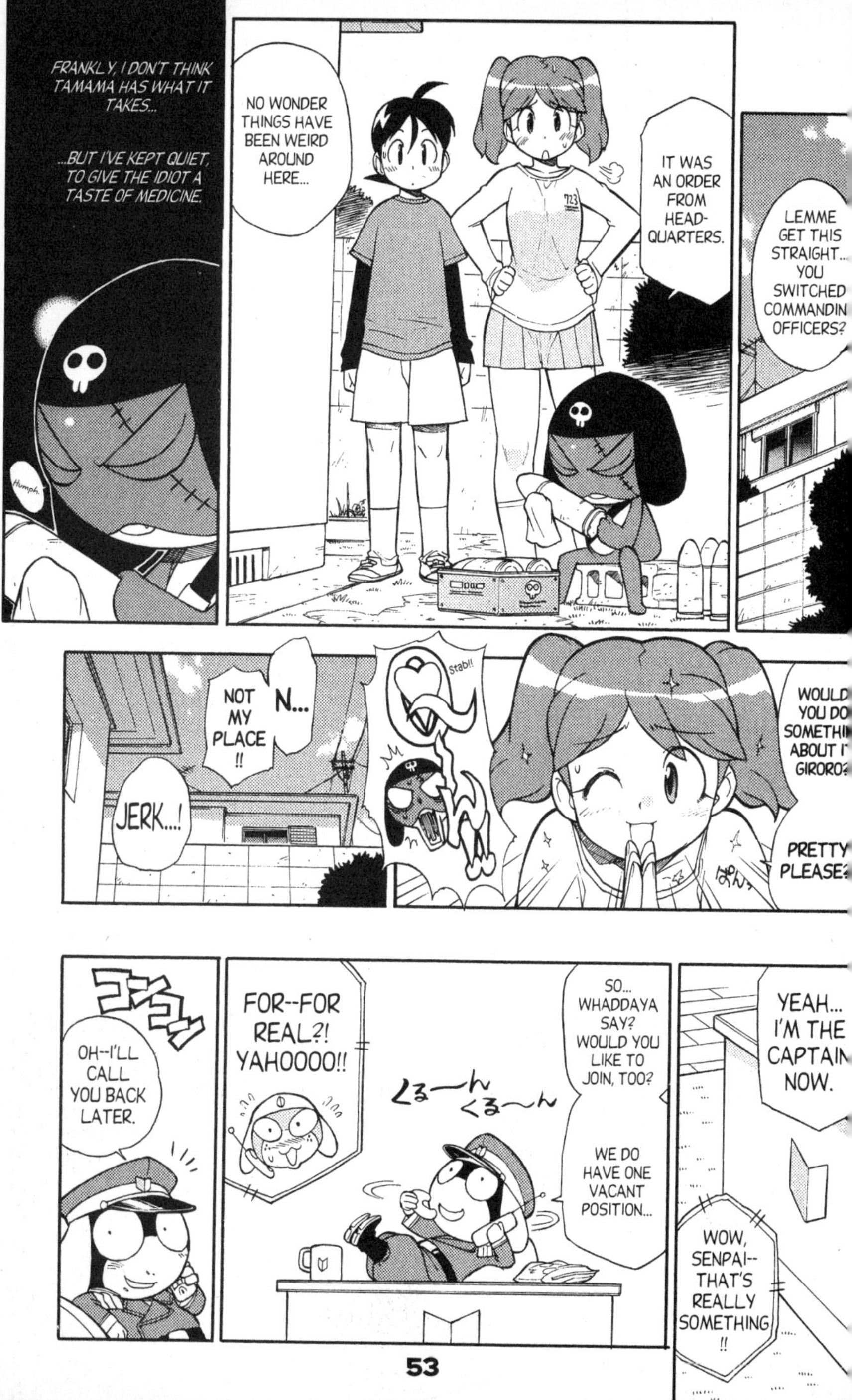
LEMME GET THIS STRAIGHT... YOU SWITCHED COMMANDIN OFFICERS?
IT WAS AN ORDER FROM HEAD-QUARTERS.
NO WONDER THINGS HAVE BEEN WEIRD AROUND HERE...
FRANKLY, I DON'T THINK TAMAMA HAS WHAT IT TAKES...
...BUT I'VE KEPT QUIET, TO GIVE THE IDIOT A TASTE OF MEDICINE.
Humph.
WOULD YOU DO SOMETHIN ABOUT I GIRORO?
PRETTY PLEASE?
Stab!!
N...
NOT MY PLACE !!
JERK...!
YEAH... I'M THE CAPTAIN NOW.
WOW, SENPAI-- THAT'S REALLY SOMETHING !!
SO... WHADDAYA SAY? WOULD YOU LIKE TO JOIN, TOO?
くる～ん くる～ん
WE DO HAVE ONE VACANT POSITION...
FOR--FOR REAL?! YAHOOOO!!
OH--I'LL CALL YOU BACK LATER.

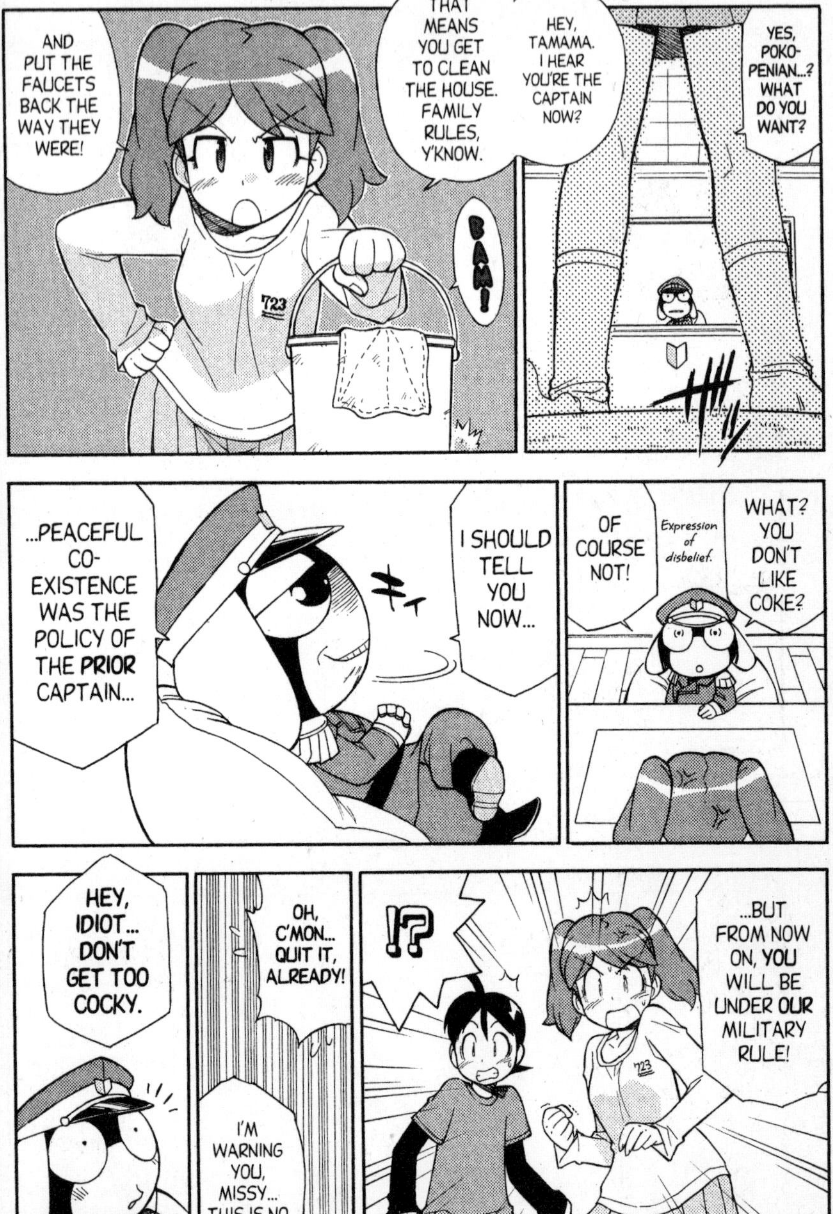
YES, POKO-PENIAN...? WHAT DO YOU WANT?
HEY, TAMAMA. I HEAR YOU'RE THE CAPTAIN NOW?
THAT MEANS YOU GET TO CLEAN THE HOUSE. FAMILY RULES, Y'KNOW.
BAM!
AND PUT THE FAUCETS BACK THE WAY THEY WERE!
WHAT? YOU DON'T LIKE COKE?
Expression of disbelief.
OF COURSE NOT!
I SHOULD TELL YOU NOW...
キィ
...PEACEFUL CO-EXISTENCE WAS THE POLICY OF THE PRIOR CAPTAIN...
...BUT FROM NOW ON, YOU WILL BE UNDER OUR MILITARY RULE!
!?
OH, C'MON... QUIT IT, ALREADY!
I'M WARNING YOU, MISSY... THIS IS NO JOKE...!
HEY, IDIOT... DON'T GET TOO COCKY.

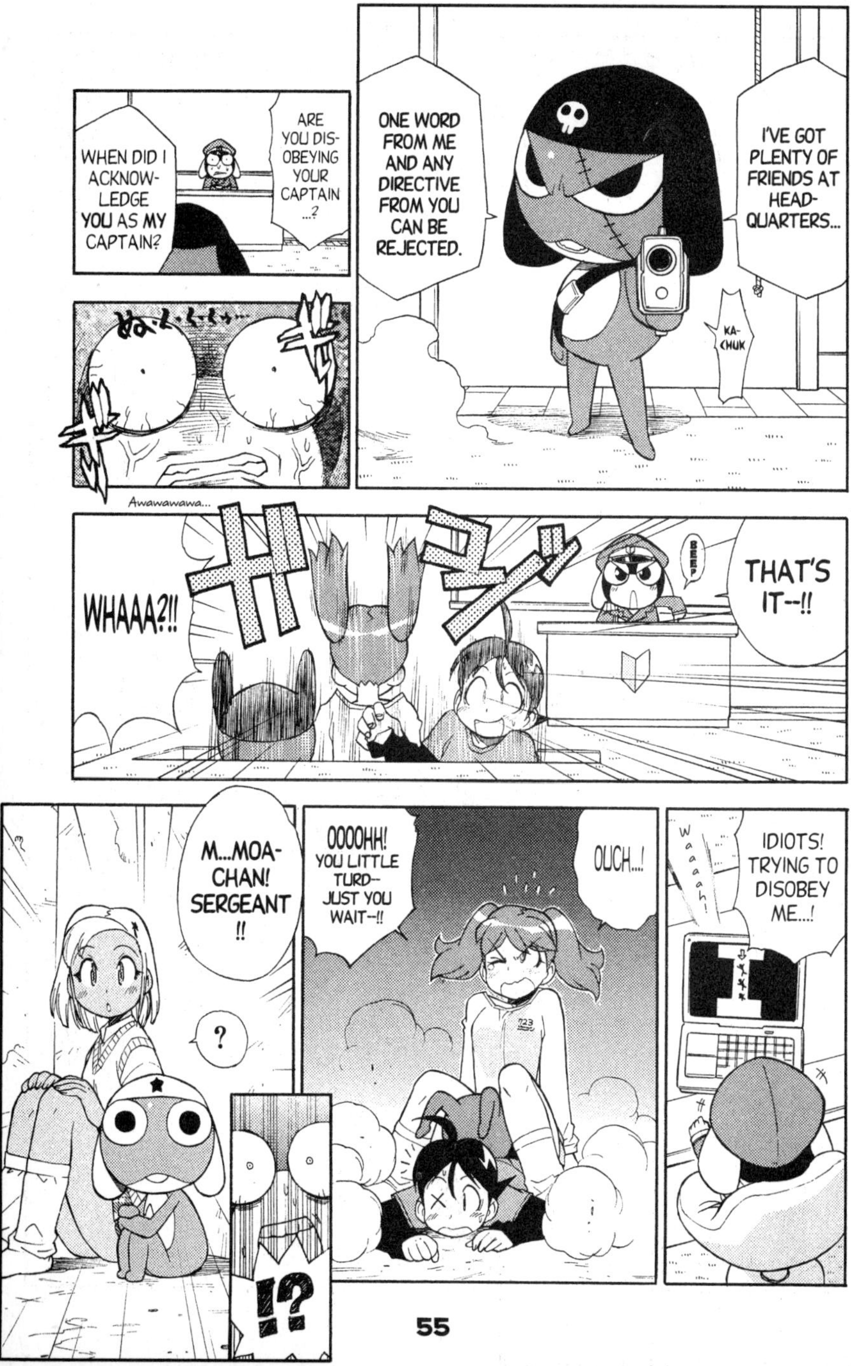
I'VE GOT PLENTY OF FRIENDS AT HEAD-QUARTERS...
ONE WORD FROM ME AND ANY DIRECTIVE FROM YOU CAN BE REJECTED.
KA-CHUK
ARE YOU DIS-OBEYING YOUR CAPTAIN...?
WHEN DID I ACKNOW-LEDGE YOU AS MY CAPTAIN?
Awawawawa...
THAT'S IT--!!
BEEP
WHAAA?!!
IDIOTS! TRYING TO DISOBEY ME...!
Waaaah!
OUCH...!
OOOOHH! YOU LITTLE TURD-- JUST YOU WAIT--!!
M...MOA-CHAN! SERGEANT!!
?
!?

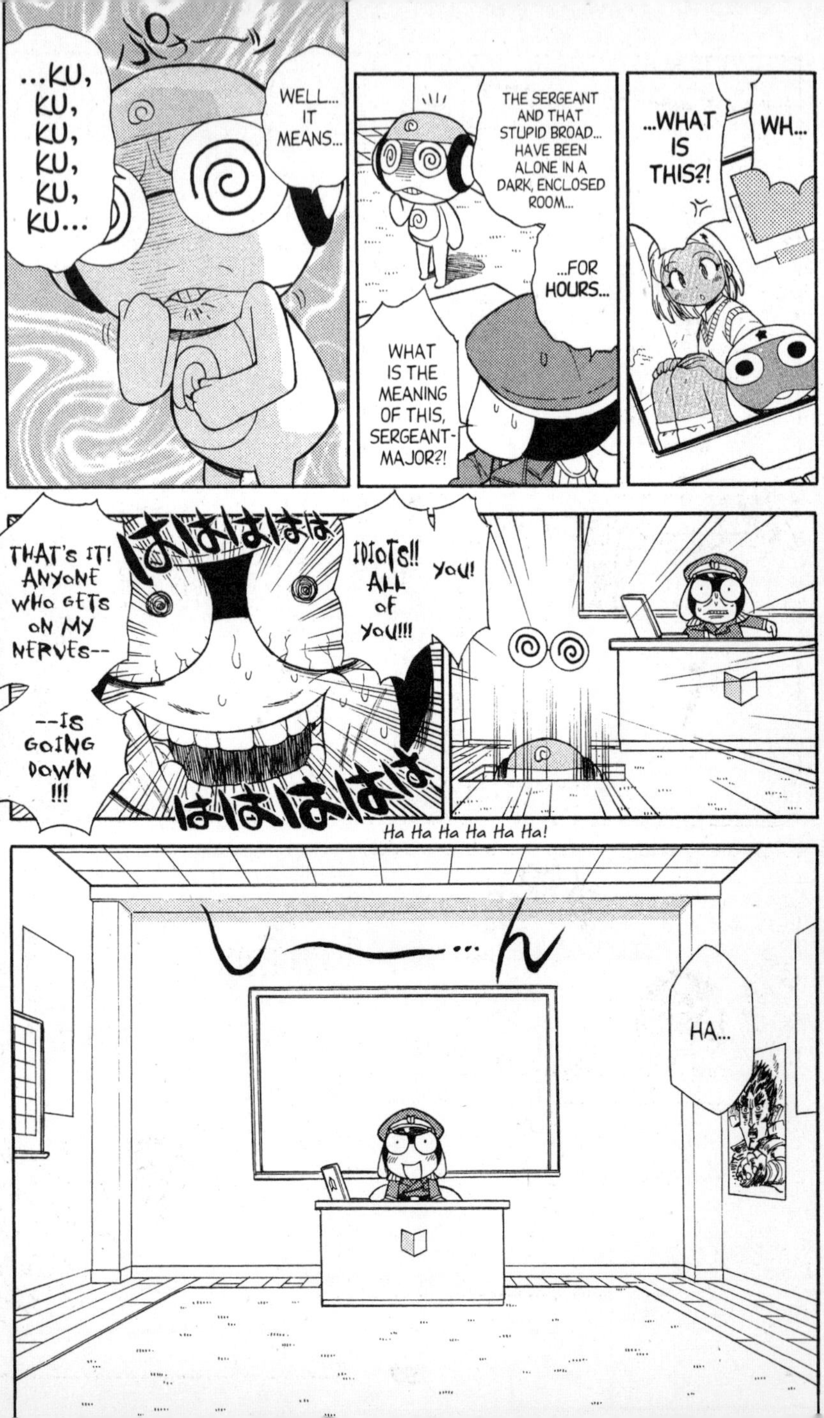
WH...
...WHAT IS THIS?!
THE SERGEANT AND THAT STUPID BROAD... HAVE BEEN ALONE IN A DARK, ENCLOSED ROOM...
...FOR HOURS...
WHAT IS THE MEANING OF THIS, SERGEANT-MAJOR?!
WELL... IT MEANS...
...KU, KU, KU, KU, KU, KU...
YOU!
IDIOTS!! ALL OF YOU!!!
はははははは
THAT'S IT! ANYONE WHO GETS ON MY NERVES--
--IS GOING DOWN!!!
ははははは
Ha Ha Ha Ha Ha Ha!
HA...
し——…ん

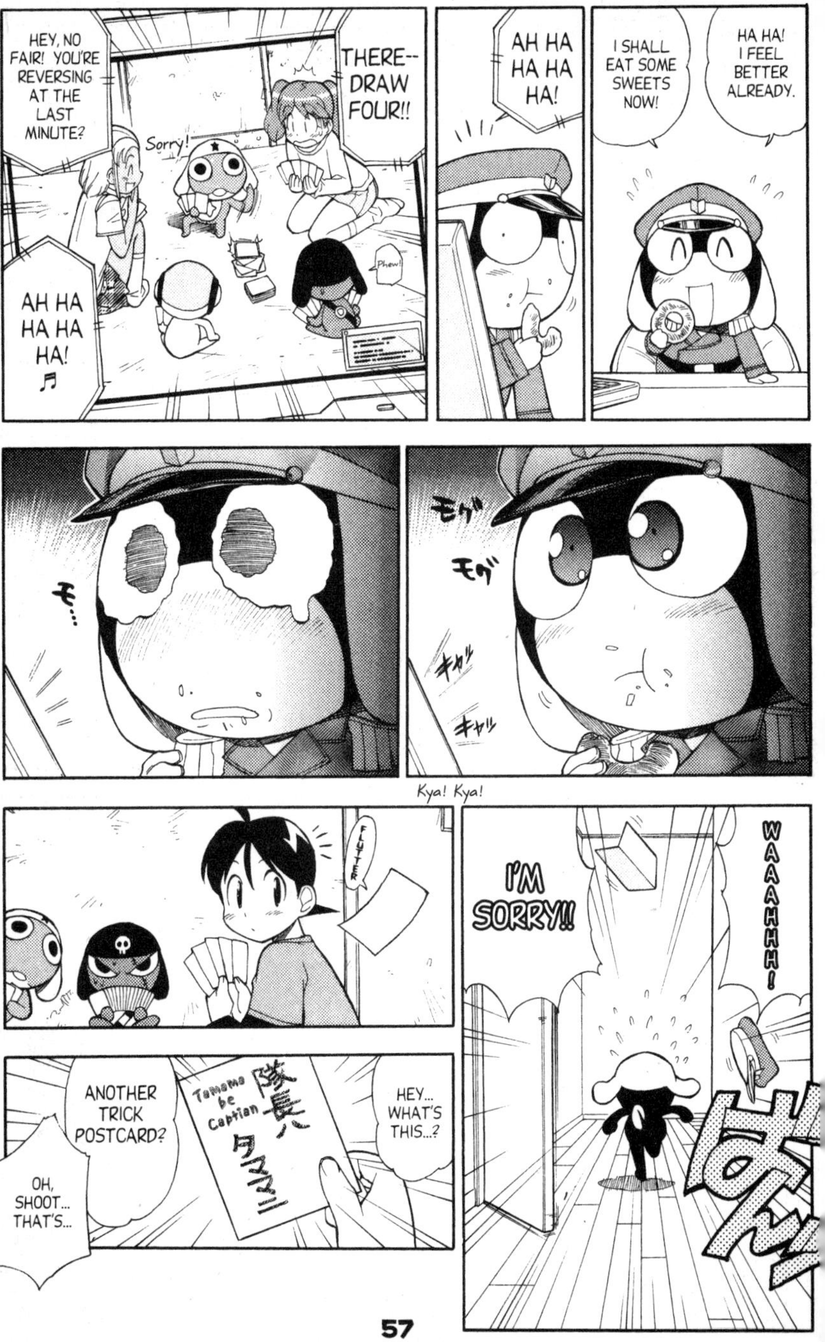
HA HA! I FEEL BETTER ALREADY.
I SHALL EAT SOME SWEETS NOW!
AH HA HA HA HA!
THERE-- DRAW FOUR!!
HEY, NO FAIR! YOU'RE REVERSING AT THE LAST MINUTE?
Sorry!
Phew!
AH HA HA HA HA! ♪
モグ
モグ
キャッ
キャッ
モ…
Kya! Kya!
WAAAAHHHH!
I'M SORRY!!
FLUTTER
HEY... WHAT'S THIS...?
隊長ハタママ二
Tamama be Captian
ANOTHER TRICK POSTCARD?
OH, SHOOT... THAT'S...

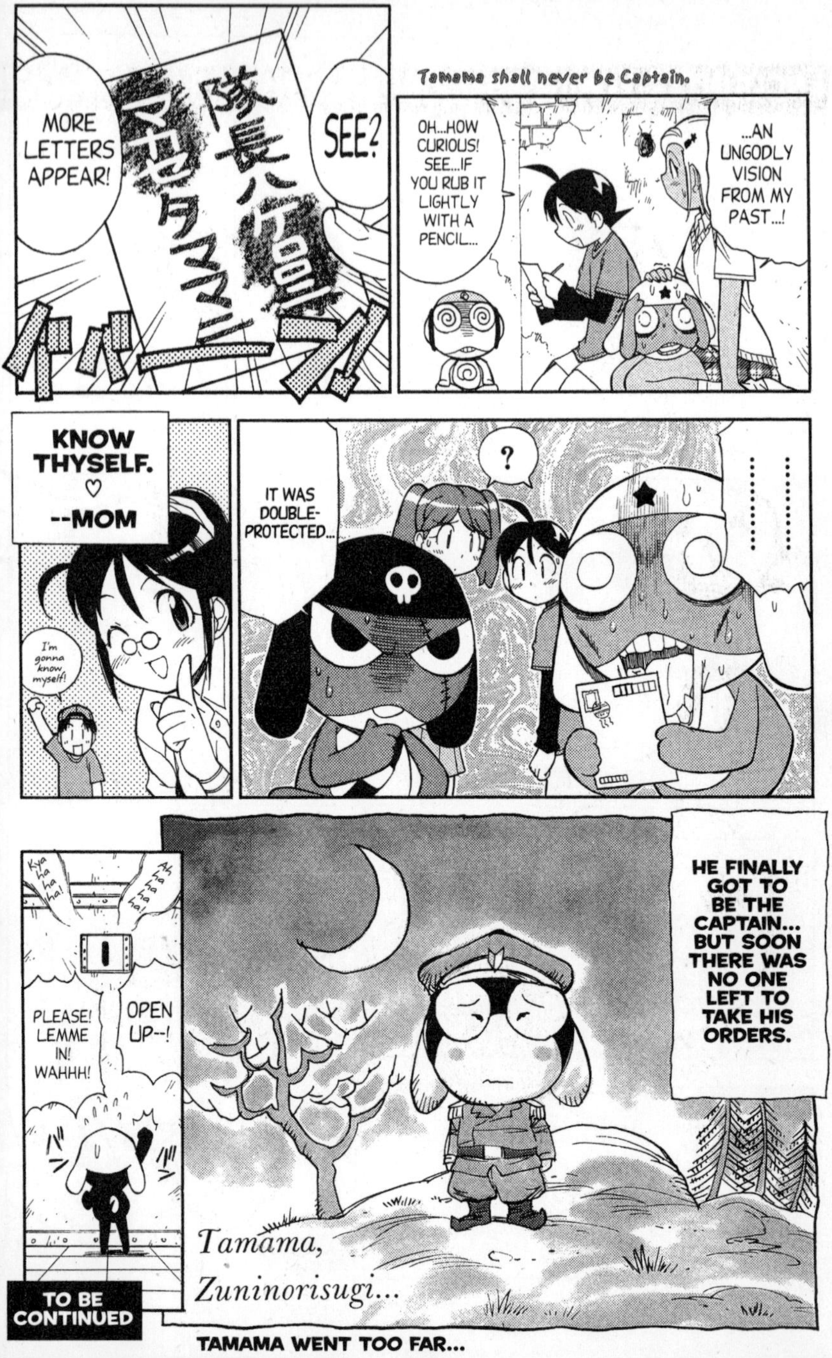
Tamama shall never be Captain.
...AN UNGODLY VISION FROM MY PAST...!
OH...HOW CURIOUS! SEE...IF YOU RUB IT LIGHTLY WITH A PENCIL...
SEE?
MORE LETTERS APPEAR!
......
?
IT WAS DOUBLE-PROTECTED...
KNOW THYSELF. ♡ --MOM
I'm gonna know myself!
HE FINALLY GOT TO BE THE CAPTAIN... BUT SOON THERE WAS NO ONE LEFT TO TAKE HIS ORDERS.
Tamama, Zuninorisugi...
Ah ha ha ha ha!
Kya ha ha ha!
OPEN UP--!
PLEASE! LEMME IN! WAHHH!
TO BE CONTINUED
TAMAMA WENT TOO FAR...

OUNTER XLVIII WATER BATTLE: NATSUMI VS. FROG!!

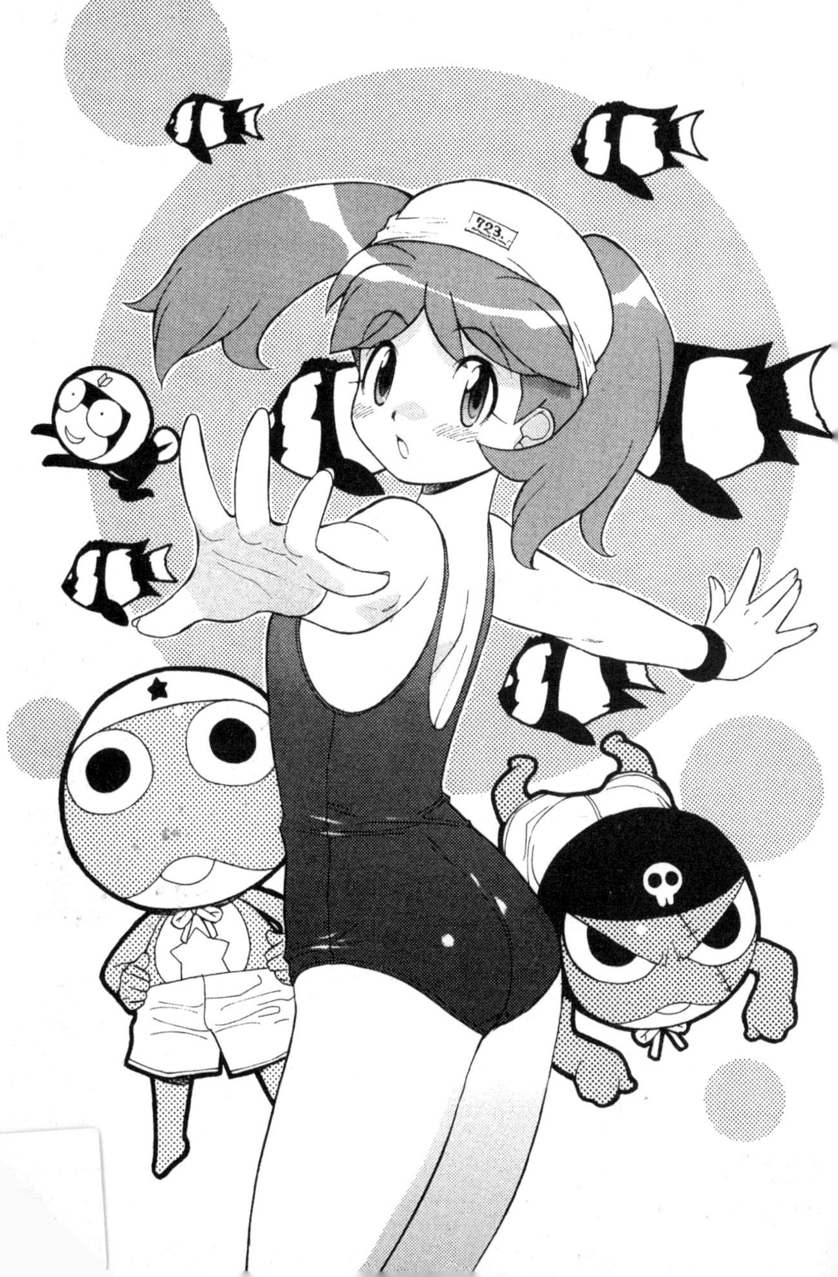
723.

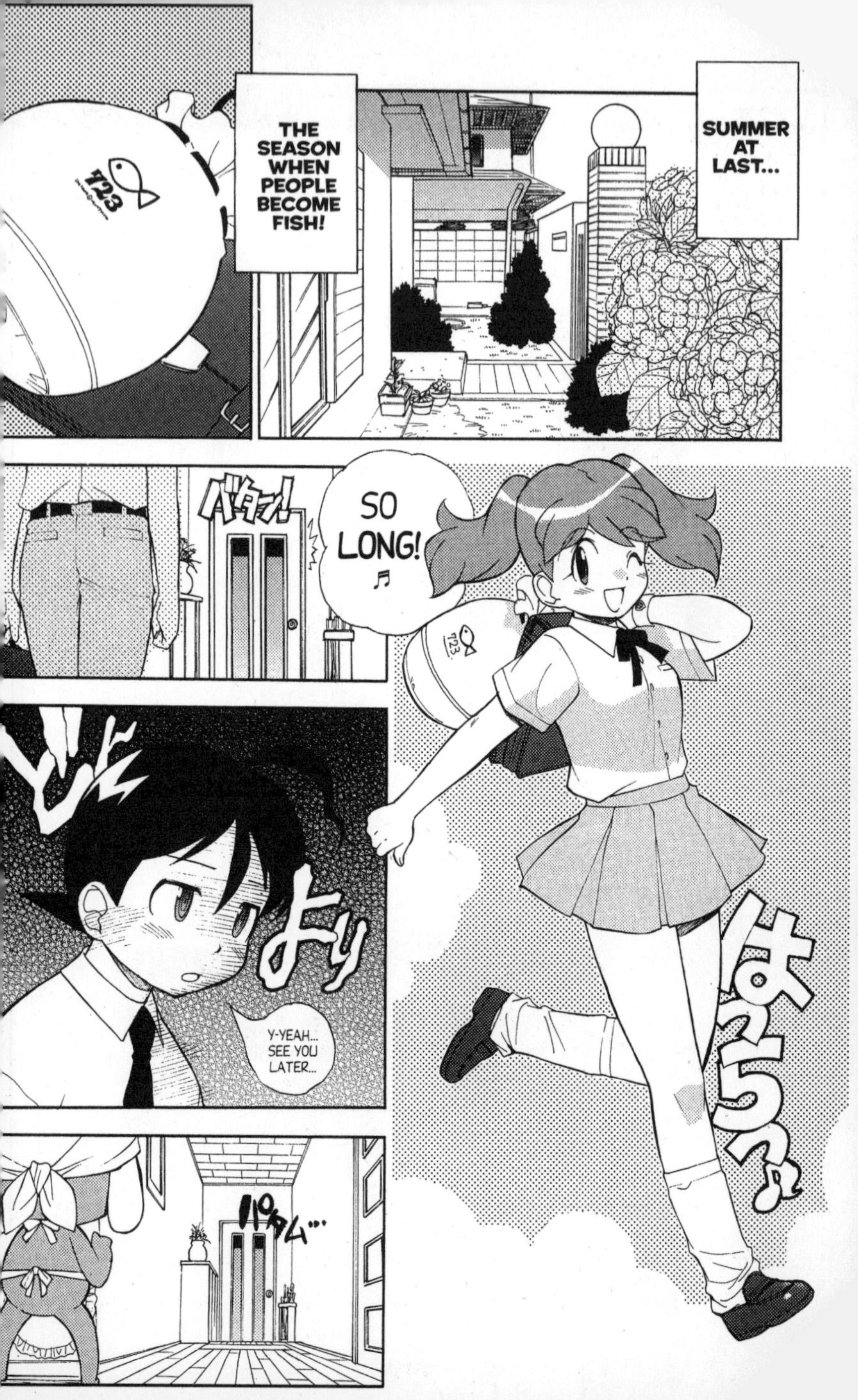
SUMMER AT LAST...
THE SEASON WHEN PEOPLE BECOME FISH!
SO LONG! ♪
バタン!
より
Y-YEAH... SEE YOU LATER...
パタム…

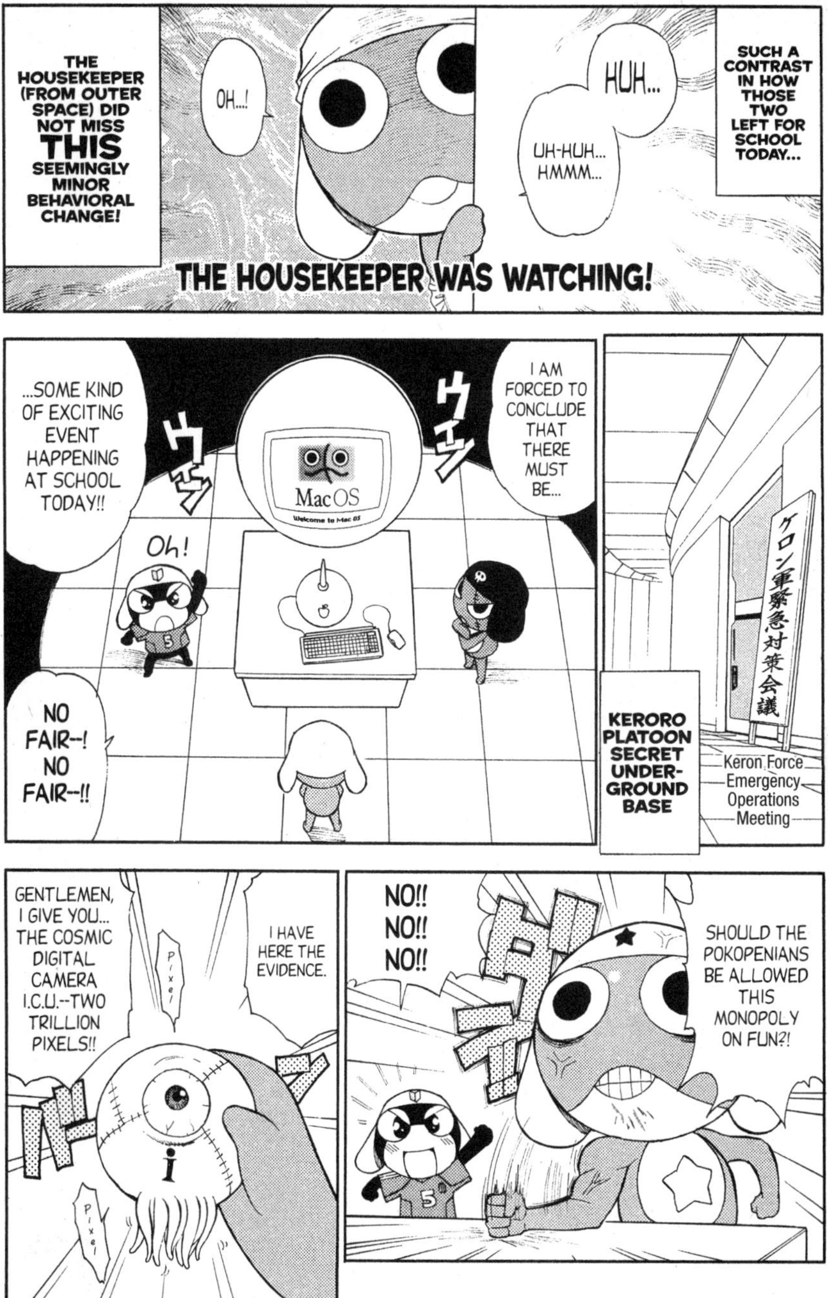
SUCH A CONTRAST IN HOW THOSE TWO LEFT FOR SCHOOL TODAY...
HUH...
UH-HUH... HMMM...
OH...!
THE HOUSEKEEPER (FROM OUTER SPACE) DID NOT MISS **THIS** SEEMINGLY MINOR BEHAVIORAL CHANGE!
THE HOUSEKEEPER WAS WATCHING!
ケロン軍緊急対策会議
KERORO PLATOON SECRET UNDERGROUND BASE
Keron Force Emergency Operations Meeting
I AM FORCED TO CONCLUDE THAT THERE MUST BE...
...SOME KIND OF EXCITING EVENT HAPPENING AT SCHOOL TODAY!!
Mac OS
Welcome to Mac OS
Oh!
NO FAIR--! NO FAIR--!!
SHOULD THE POKOPENIANS BE ALLOWED THIS MONOPOLY ON FUN?!
NO!! NO!! NO!!
I HAVE HERE THE EVIDENCE.
GENTLEMEN, I GIVE YOU... THE COSMIC DIGITAL CAMERA I.C.U.--TWO TRILLION PIXELS!!
Pixel
Pixel

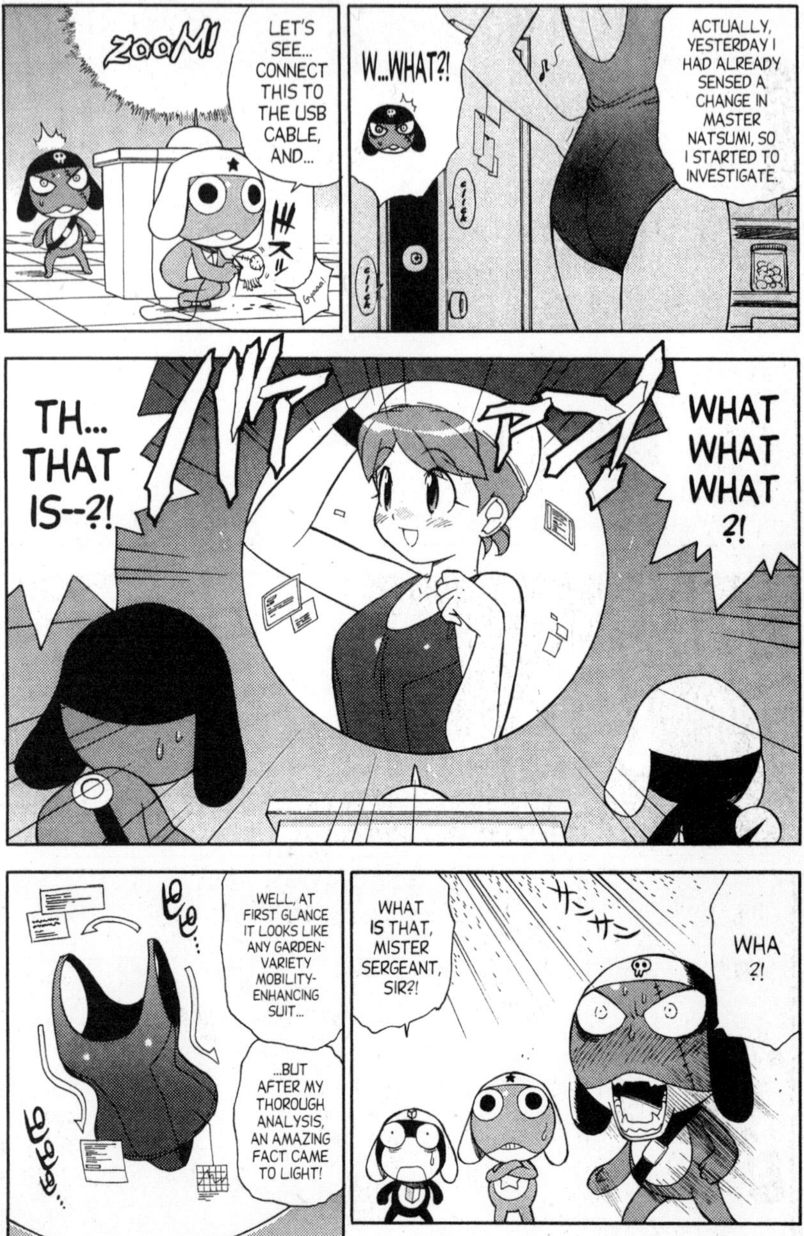
ACTUALLY, YESTERDAY I HAD ALREADY SENSED A CHANGE IN MASTER NATSUMI, SO I STARTED TO INVESTIGATE.
W...WHAT?!
LET'S SEE... CONNECT THIS TO THE USB CABLE, AND...
ZOOM!
Gyaaa!
WHAT WHAT WHAT ?!
TH... THAT IS--?!
WHA ?!
WHAT IS THAT, MISTER SERGEANT, SIR?!
WELL, AT FIRST GLANCE IT LOOKS LIKE ANY GARDEN-VARIETY MOBILITY-ENHANCING SUIT...
...BUT AFTER MY THOROUGH ANALYSIS, AN AMAZING FACT CAME TO LIGHT!

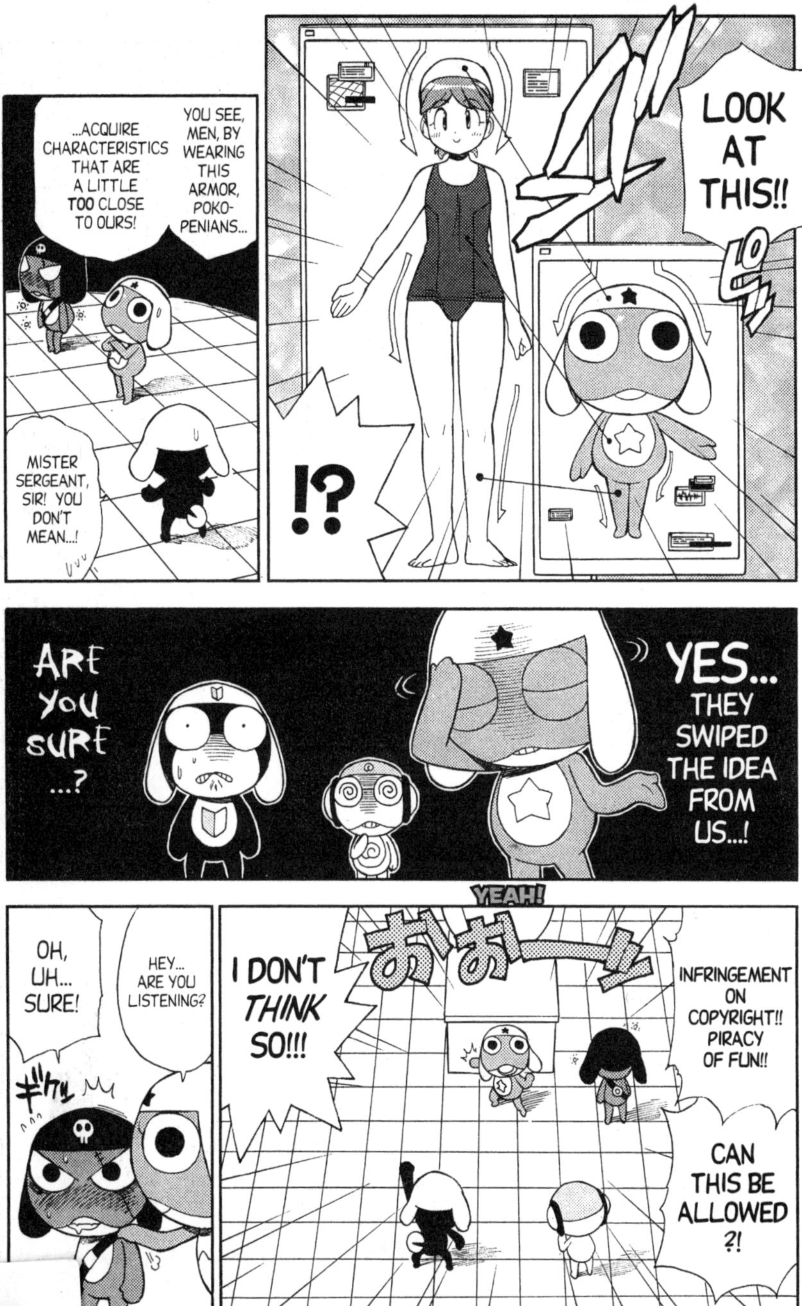
LOOK AT THIS!!
!?
YOU SEE, MEN, BY WEARING THIS ARMOR, POKO-PENIANS...
...ACQUIRE CHARACTERISTICS THAT ARE A LITTLE TOO CLOSE TO OURS!
MISTER SERGEANT, SIR! YOU DON'T MEAN...!
YES... THEY SWIPED THE IDEA FROM US...!
ARE YOU SURE ...?
INFRINGEMENT ON COPYRIGHT!! PIRACY OF FUN!!
YEAH!
おおーっ
CAN THIS BE ALLOWED ?!
I DON'T THINK SO!!!
HEY... ARE YOU LISTENING?
OH, UH... SURE!

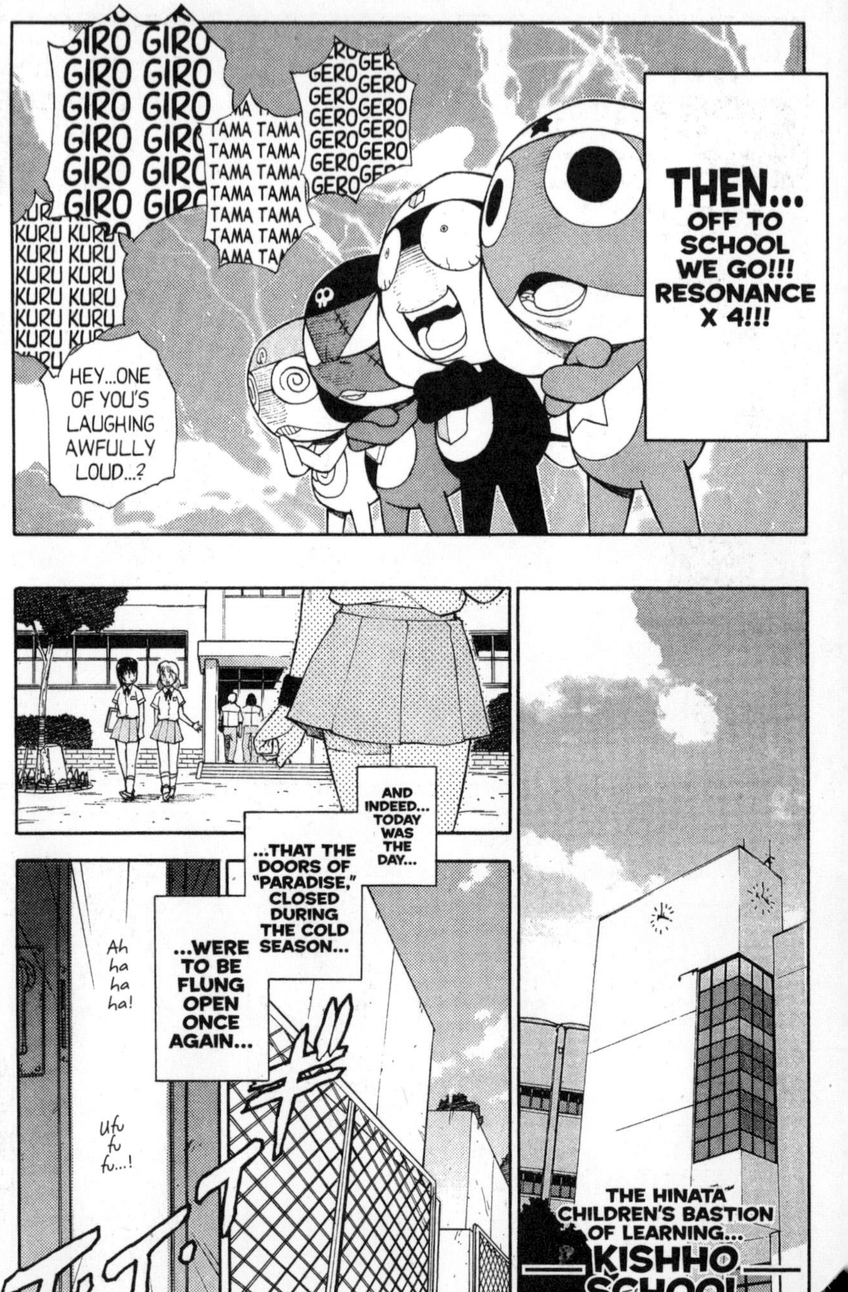
THEN... OFF TO SCHOOL WE GO!!! RESONANCE X 4!!!
GERO GERO GERO GERO GERO GERO GERO GERO GERO GERO
TAMA TAMA TAMA TAMA TAMA TAMA TAMA TAMA TAMA TAMA TAMA TAMA
GIRO GIRO GIRO GIRO GIRO GIRO GIRO GIRO GIRO GIRO GIRO GIRO
KURU KURU KURU KURU KURU KURU KURU KURU KURU KURU KURU KURU
HEY...ONE OF YOU'S LAUGHING AWFULLY LOUD...?
THE HINATA CHILDREN'S BASTION OF LEARNING...
KISHHO SCHOOL
AND INDEED... TODAY WAS THE DAY...
...THAT THE DOORS OF "PARADISE," CLOSED DURING THE COLD SEASON...
...WERE TO BE FLUNG OPEN ONCE AGAIN...
Ah ha ha ha!
Ufu fu fu...!

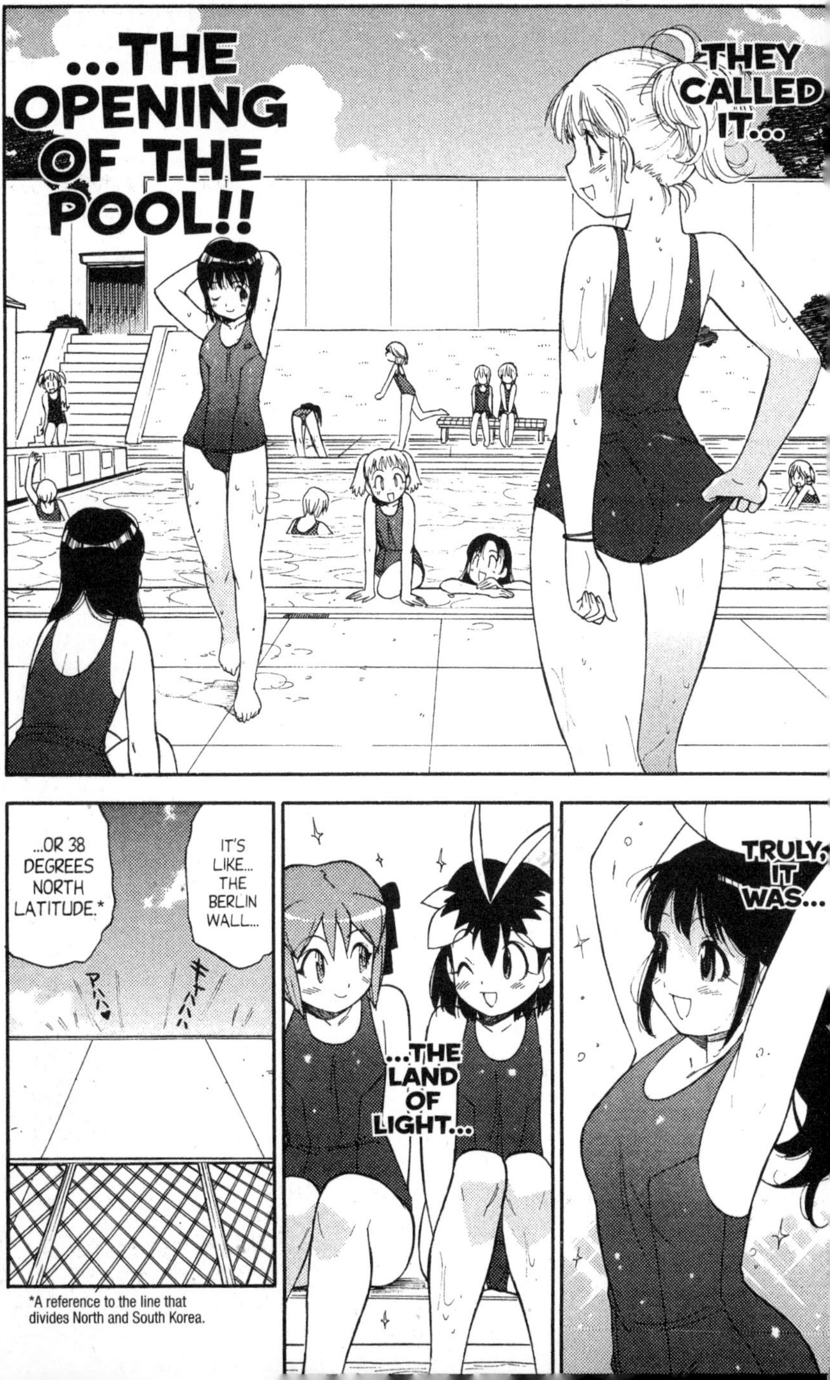
THEY CALLED IT...
...THE OPENING OF THE POOL!!
TRULY, IT WAS...
...THE LAND OF LIGHT...
IT'S LIKE... THE BERLIN WALL...
...OR 38 DEGREES NORTH LATITUDE.*

*A reference to the line that divides North and South Korea.

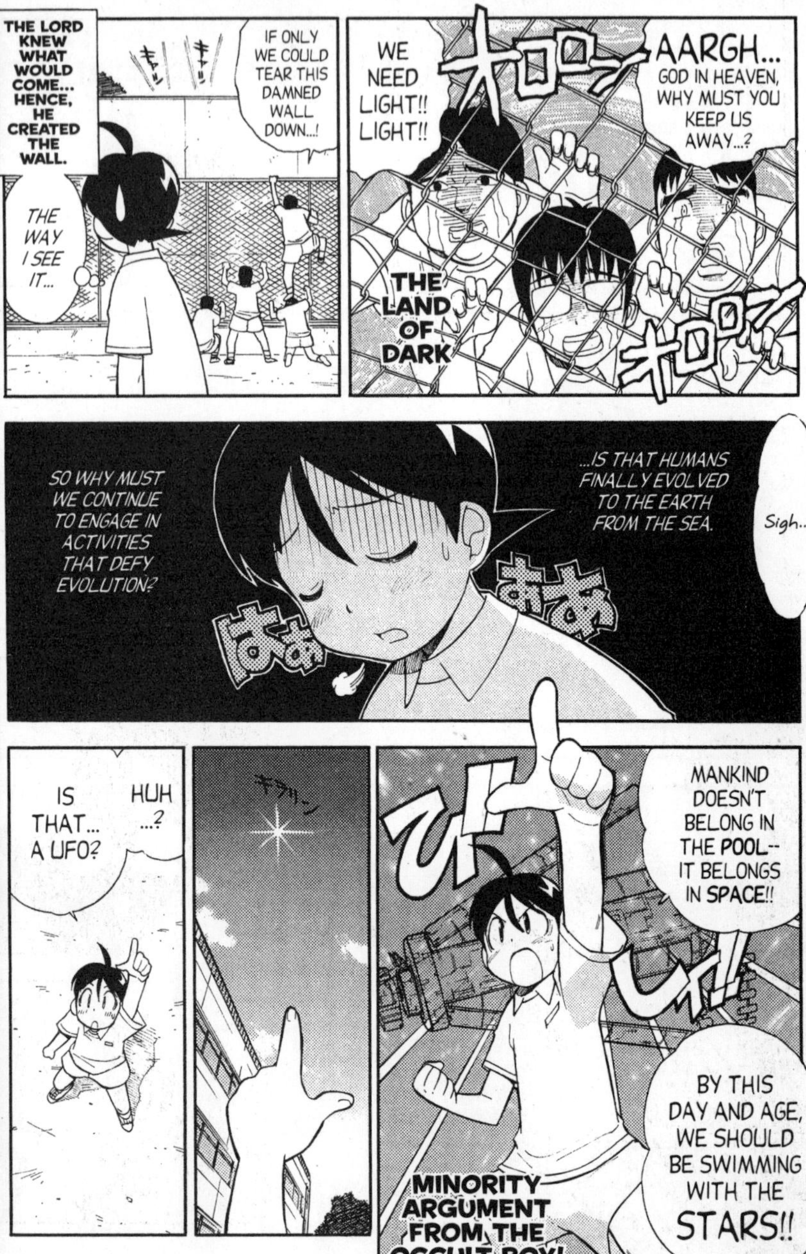
AARGH... GOD IN HEAVEN, WHY MUST YOU KEEP US AWAY...?
WE NEED LIGHT!! LIGHT!!
THE LAND OF DARK
IF ONLY WE COULD TEAR THIS DAMNED WALL DOWN...!
THE LORD KNEW WHAT WOULD COME... HENCE, HE CREATED THE WALL.
THE WAY I SEE IT...
Sigh...
...IS THAT HUMANS FINALLY EVOLVED TO THE EARTH FROM THE SEA.
SO WHY MUST WE CONTINUE TO ENGAGE IN ACTIVITIES THAT DEFY EVOLUTION?
MANKIND DOESN'T BELONG IN THE POOL-- IT BELONGS IN SPACE!!
BY THIS DAY AND AGE, WE SHOULD BE SWIMMING WITH THE STARS!!
MINORITY ARGUMENT FROM THE OCCULT BOY!
HUH...?
IS THAT... A UFO?

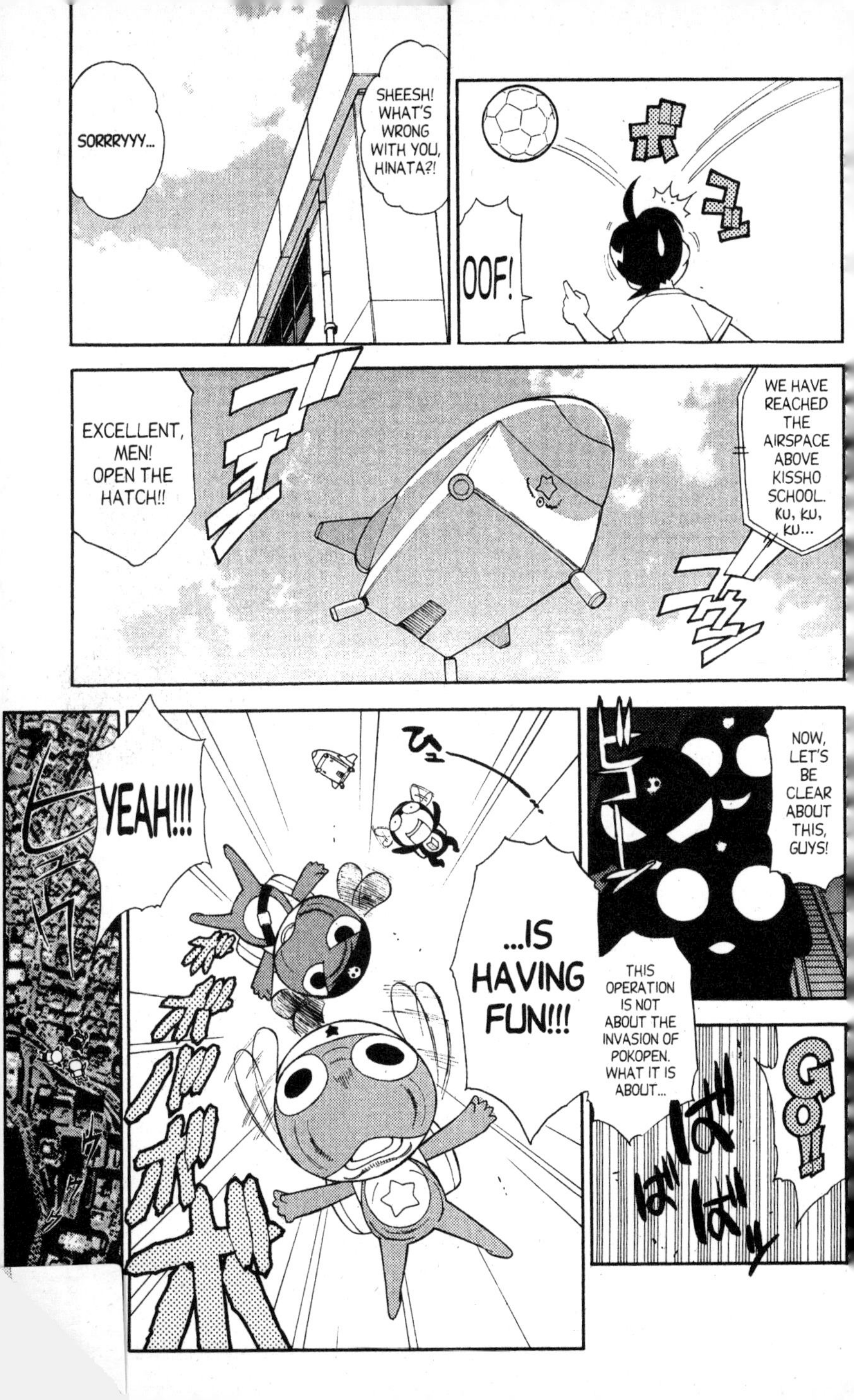

OOF!
SHEESH! WHAT'S WRONG WITH YOU, HINATA?!
SORRRYYY...
WE HAVE REACHED THE AIRSPACE ABOVE KISSHO SCHOOL. KU, KU, KU...
EXCELLENT, MEN! OPEN THE HATCH!!
NOW, LET'S BE CLEAR ABOUT THIS, GUYS!
GO!
THIS OPERATION IS NOT ABOUT THE INVASION OF POKOPEN. WHAT IT IS ABOUT...
...IS HAVING FUN!!!
YEAH!!!

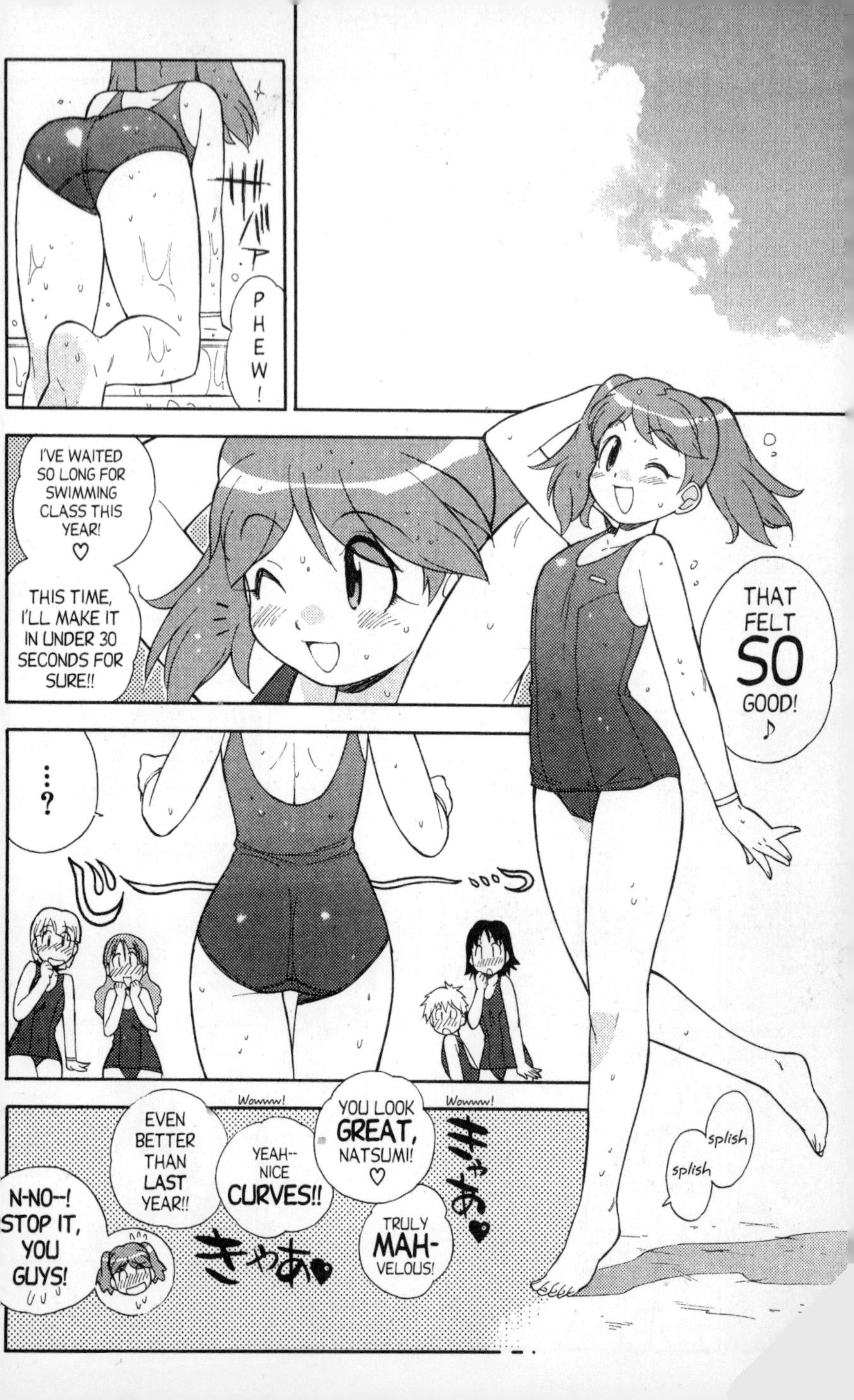
THAT FELT SO GOOD! ♪
splish
splish
ザバァ
PHEW!
I'VE WAITED SO LONG FOR SWIMMING CLASS THIS YEAR! ♡
THIS TIME, I'LL MAKE IT IN UNDER 30 SECONDS FOR SURE!!
...?
Wowww!
きゃあ♥
YOU LOOK GREAT, NATSUMI! ♡
Wowww!
TRULY MAH-VELOUS!
YEAH-- NICE CURVES!!
EVEN BETTER THAN LAST YEAR!!
きゃあ♥
N-NO--! STOP IT, YOU GUYS!

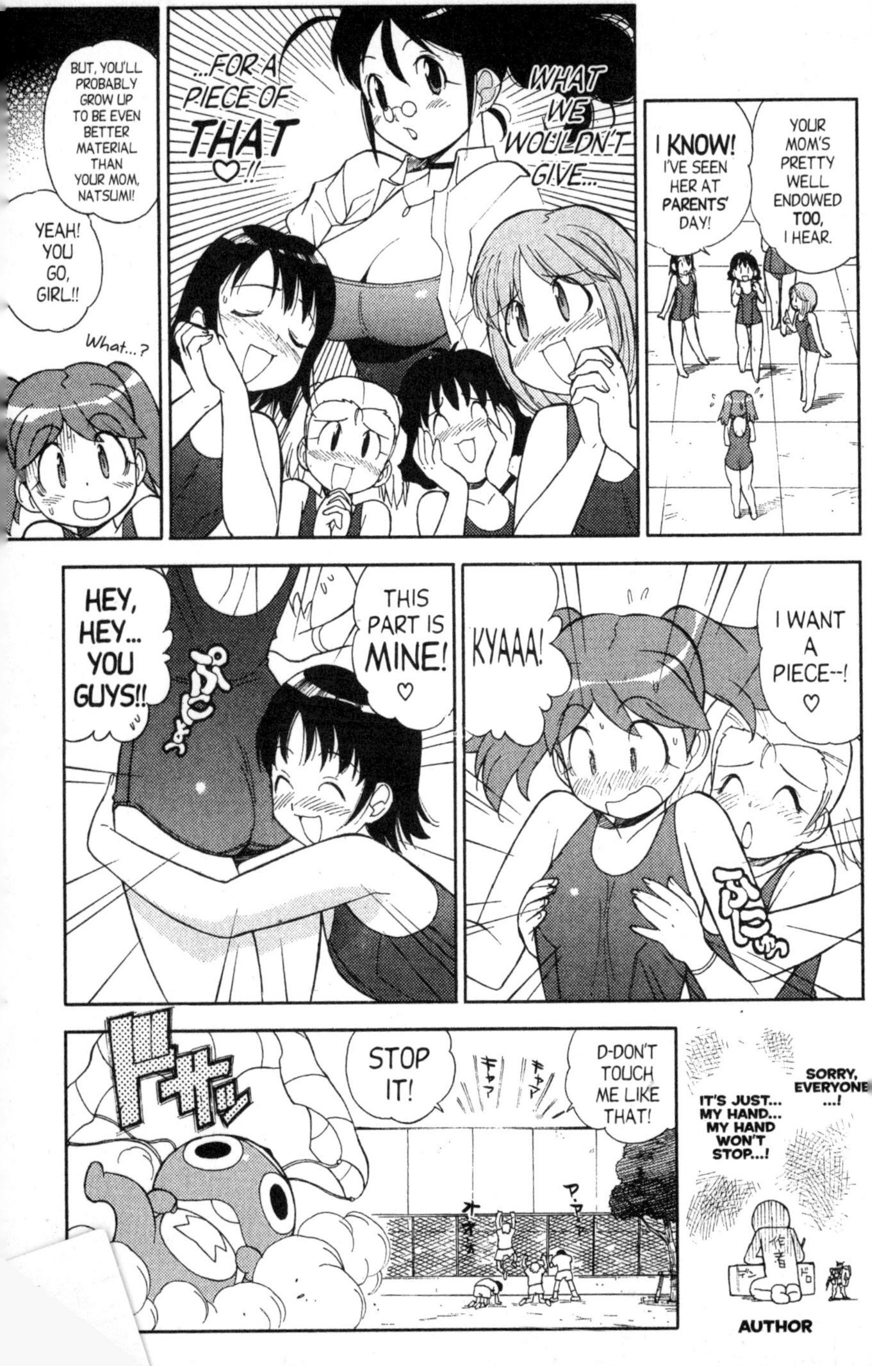
YOUR MOM'S PRETTY WELL ENDOWED TOO, I HEAR.
I KNOW! I'VE SEEN HER AT PARENTS' DAY!
WHAT WE WOULDN'T GIVE...
...FOR A PIECE OF THAT ♡!!
BUT, YOU'LL PROBABLY GROW UP TO BE EVEN BETTER MATERIAL THAN YOUR MOM, NATSUMI!
YEAH! YOU GO, GIRL!!
What...?
I WANT A PIECE--! ♡
KYAAA!
THIS PART IS MINE! ♡
HEY, HEY... YOU GUYS!!
SORRY, EVERYONE...!
IT'S JUST... MY HAND... MY HAND WON'T STOP...!
AUTHOR
D-DON'T TOUCH ME LIKE THAT!
STOP IT!

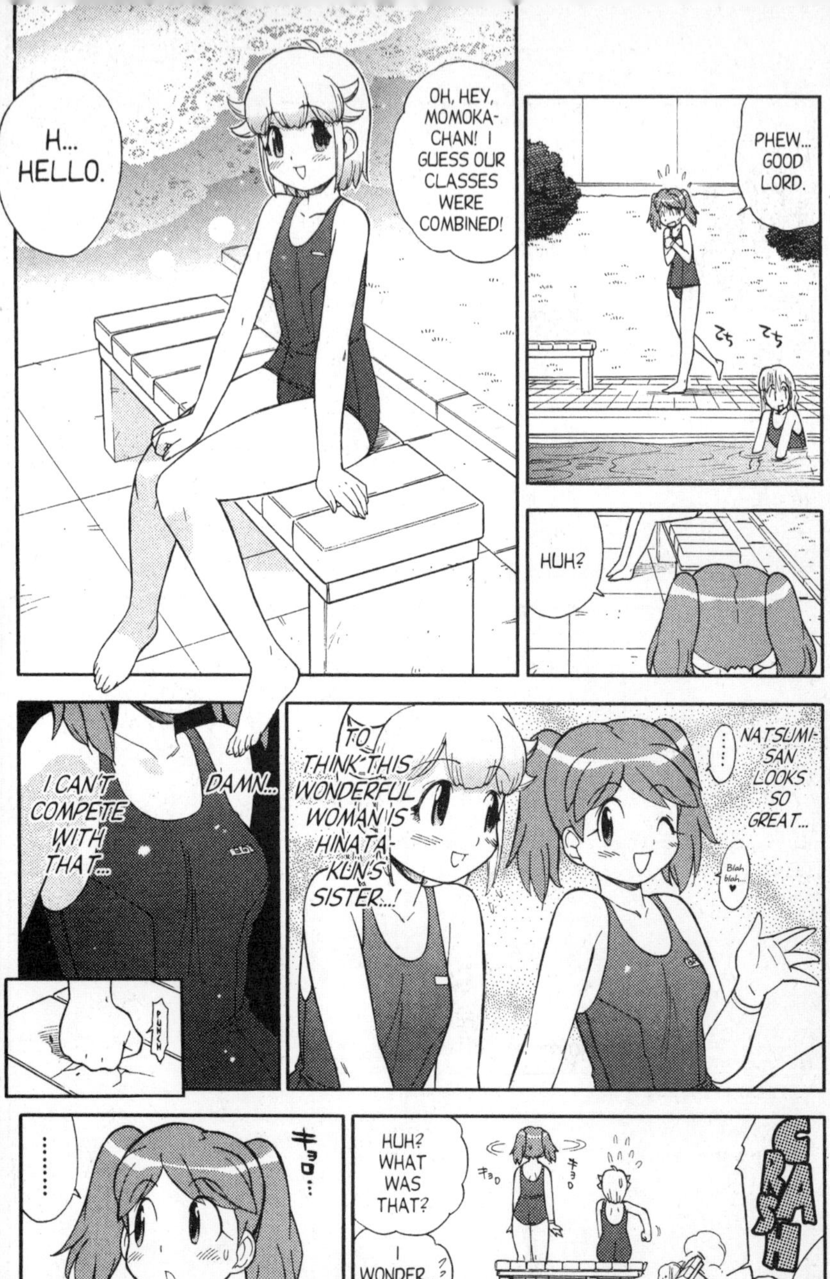
PHEW... GOOD LORD.
てち てち
HUH?
OH, HEY, MOMOKA-CHAN! I GUESS OUR CLASSES WERE COMBINED!
H... HELLO.
......
NATSUMI-SAN LOOKS SO GREAT...
Blah blah... ♥
TO THINK THIS WONDERFUL WOMAN IS HINATA-KUN'S SISTER...!
DAMN...
I CAN'T COMPETE WITH THAT...
PUNCH
CRASH
HUH? WHAT WAS THAT?
キョロ
キョロ
I WONDER... HA HA HA!
キョロ...
....

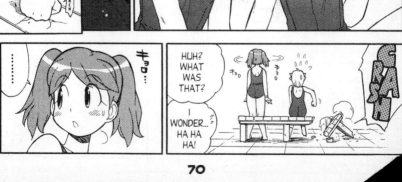

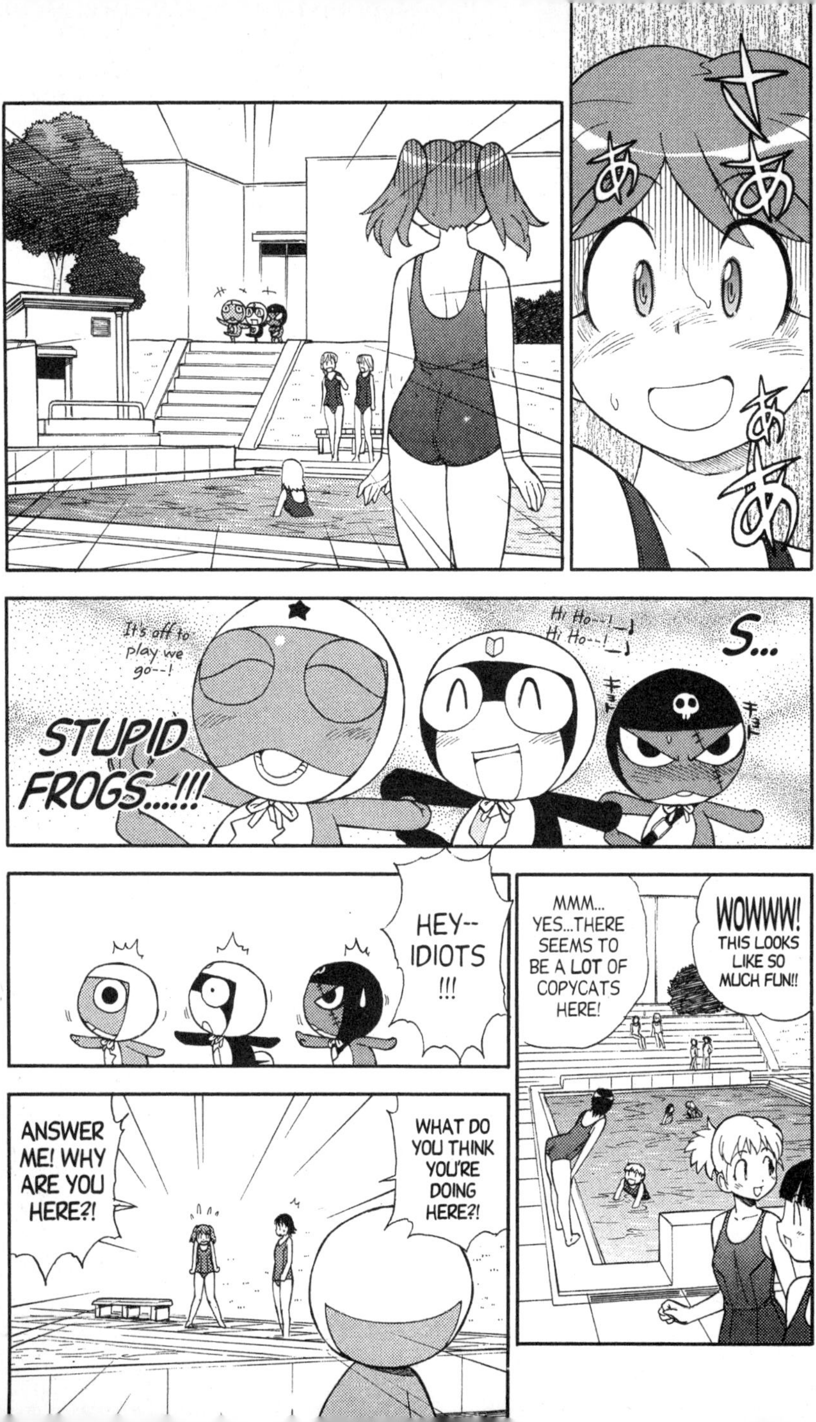

あ あ
ああ
S...
Hi Ho--! Hi Ho--!
It's off to play we go--!
STUPID FROGS...!!!
WOWWW! THIS LOOKS LIKE SO MUCH FUN!!
MMM... YES...THERE SEEMS TO BE A LOT OF COPYCATS HERE!
HEY-- IDIOTS !!!
WHAT DO YOU THINK YOU'RE DOING HERE?!
ANSWER ME! WHY ARE YOU HERE?!

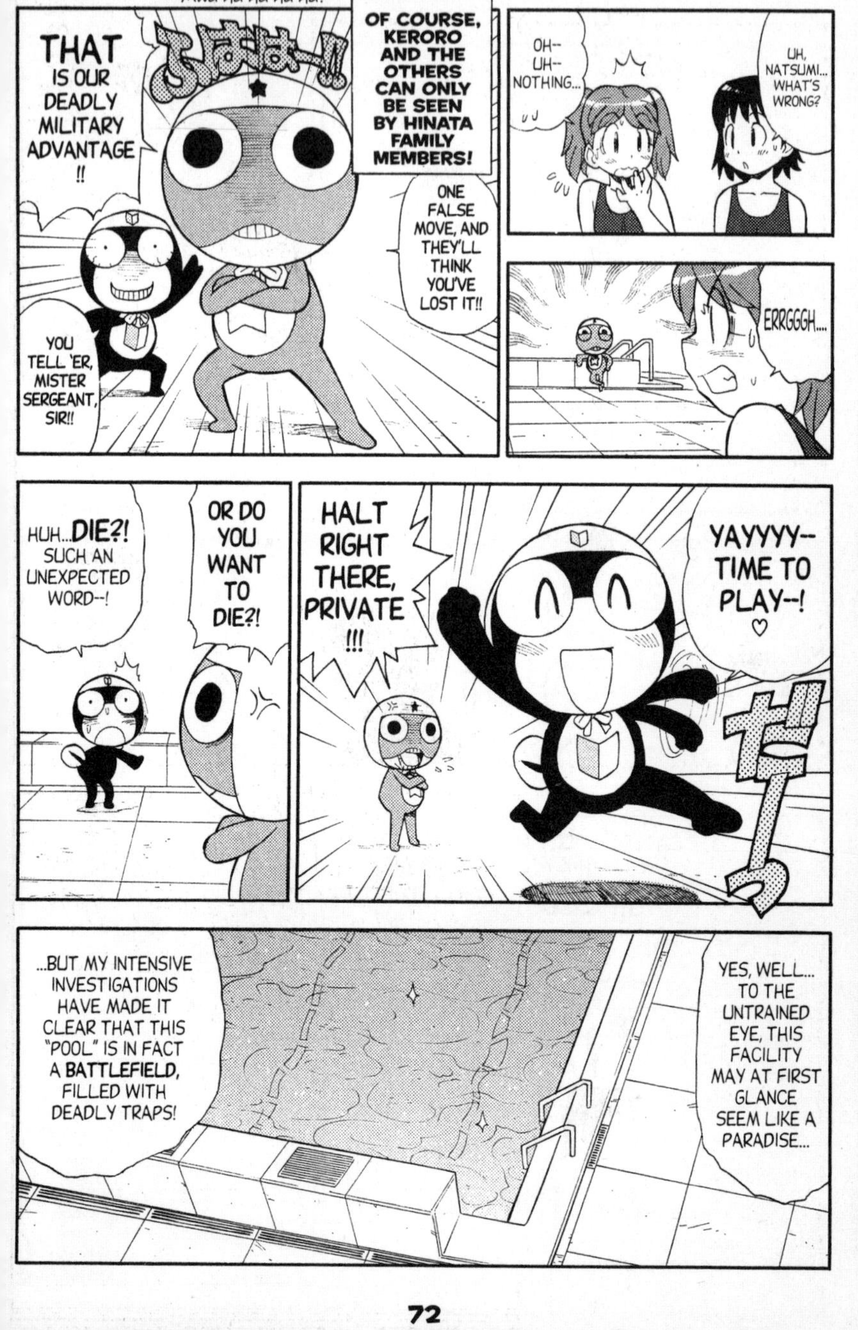

UH, NATSUMI... WHAT'S WRONG?
OH-- UH-- NOTHING...
ERRGGGH....
OF COURSE, KERORO AND THE OTHERS CAN ONLY BE SEEN BY HINATA FAMILY MEMBERS!
Mwa ha ha ha ha!
THAT IS OUR DEADLY MILITARY ADVANTAGE!!
ONE FALSE MOVE, AND THEY'LL THINK YOU'VE LOST IT!!
YOU TELL 'ER, MISTER SERGEANT, SIR!!
YAYYYY-- TIME TO PLAY--! ♡
HALT RIGHT THERE, PRIVATE!!!
OR DO YOU WANT TO DIE?!
HUH...DIE?! SUCH AN UNEXPECTED WORD--!
YES, WELL... TO THE UNTRAINED EYE, THIS FACILITY MAY AT FIRST GLANCE SEEM LIKE A PARADISE...
...BUT MY INTENSIVE INVESTIGATIONS HAVE MADE IT CLEAR THAT THIS "POOL" IS IN FACT A BATTLEFIELD, FILLED WITH DEADLY TRAPS!

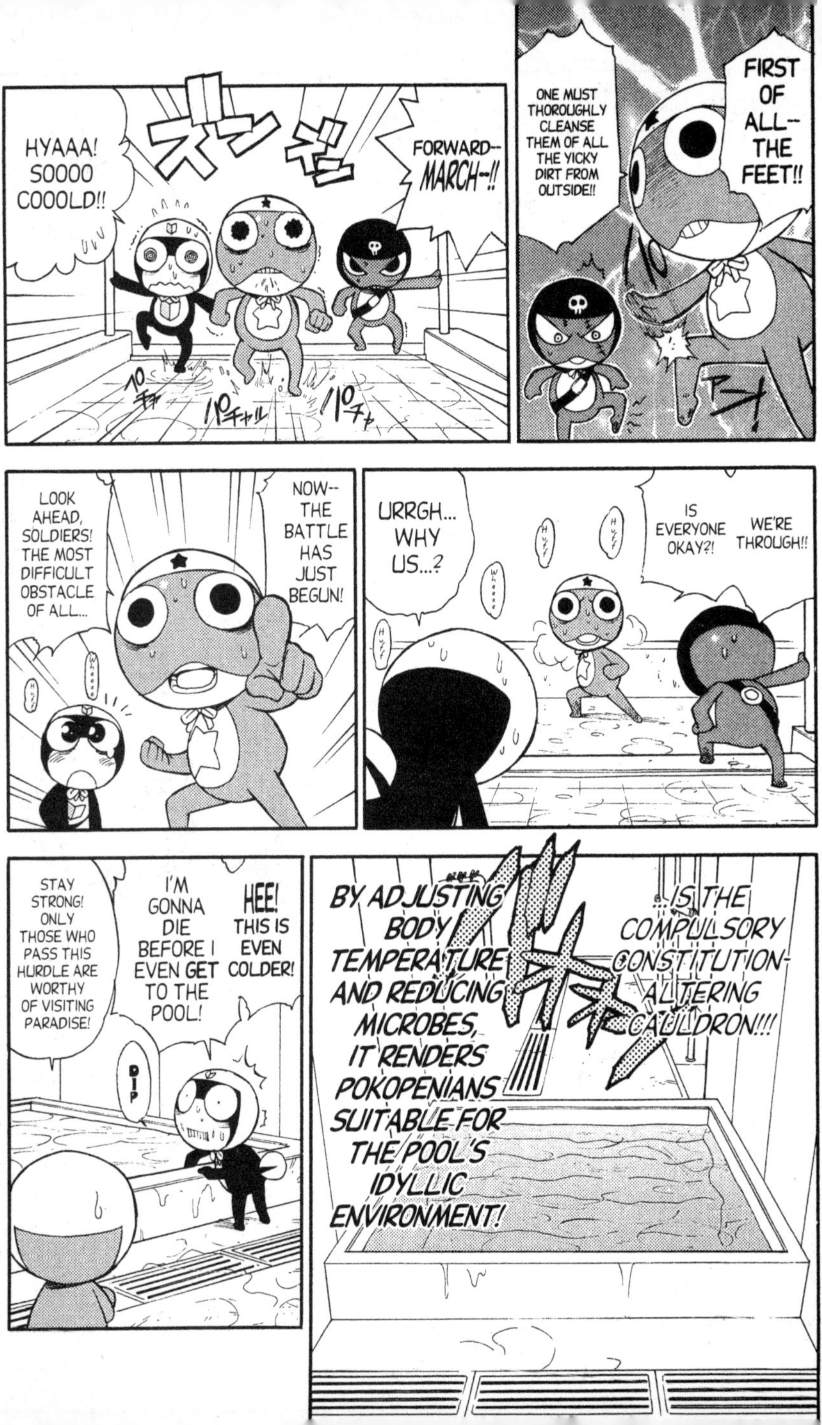
FIRST OF ALL-- THE FEET!!
ONE MUST THOROUGHLY CLEANSE THEM OF ALL THE YICKY DIRT FROM OUTSIDE!!
FORWARD-- MARCH--!!
HYAAA! SOOOO COOOLD!!
WE'RE THROUGH!!
IS EVERYONE OKAY?!
URRGH... WHY US...?
NOW-- THE BATTLE HAS JUST BEGUN!
LOOK AHEAD, SOLDIERS! THE MOST DIFFICULT OBSTACLE OF ALL...
...IS THE COMPULSORY CONSTITUTION-ALTERING CAULDRON!!!
BY ADJUSTING BODY TEMPERATURE AND REDUCING MICROBES, IT RENDERS POKOPENIANS SUITABLE FOR THE POOL'S IDYLLIC ENVIRONMENT!
HEE! THIS IS EVEN COLDER!
I'M GONNA DIE BEFORE I EVEN GET TO THE POOL!
STAY STRONG! ONLY THOSE WHO PASS THIS HURDLE ARE WORTHY OF VISITING PARADISE!
DIP

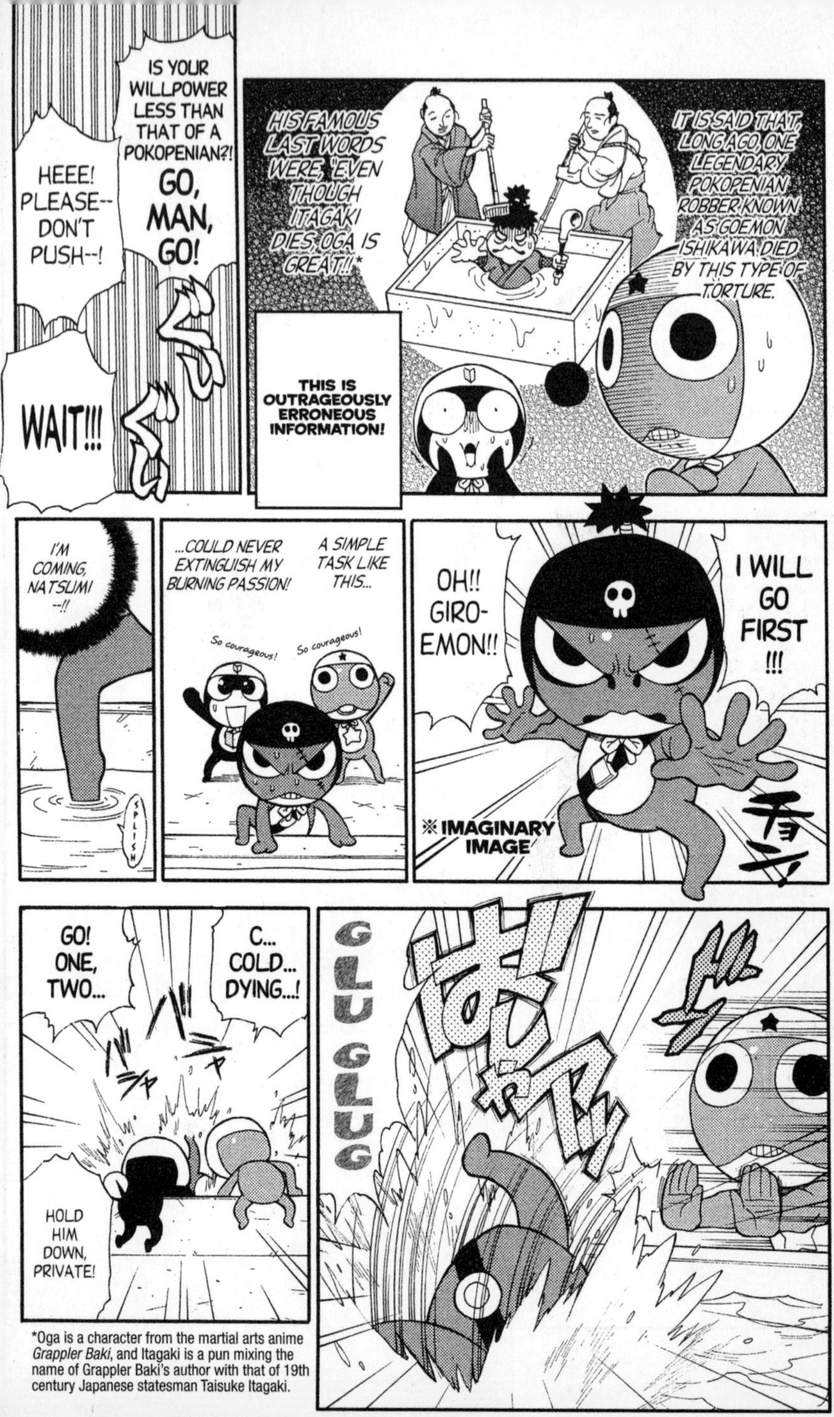
IT IS SAID THAT, LONG AGO, ONE LEGENDARY POKOPENIAN ROBBER KNOWN AS GOEMON ISHIKAWA DIED BY THIS TYPE OF TORTURE.
HIS FAMOUS LAST WORDS WERE, "EVEN THOUGH ITAGAKI DIES, OGA IS GREAT!!"*
THIS IS OUTRAGEOUSLY ERRONEOUS INFORMATION!
IS YOUR WILLPOWER LESS THAN THAT OF A POKOPENIAN?!
GO, MAN, GO!
HEEE! PLEASE-- DON'T PUSH--!
WAIT!!!
I WILL GO FIRST!!!
OH!! GIRO-EMON!!
※IMAGINARY IMAGE
A SIMPLE TASK LIKE THIS...
...COULD NEVER EXTINGUISH MY BURNING PASSION!
So courageous!
So courageous!
I'M COMING, NATSUMI--!!
SPLISH
GLUG GLUG
C... COLD... DYING...!
GO! ONE, TWO...
HOLD HIM DOWN, PRIVATE!

*Oga is a character from the martial arts anime *Grappler Baki*, and Itagaki is a pun mixing the name of Grappler Baki's author with that of 19th century Japanese statesman Taisuke Itagaki.

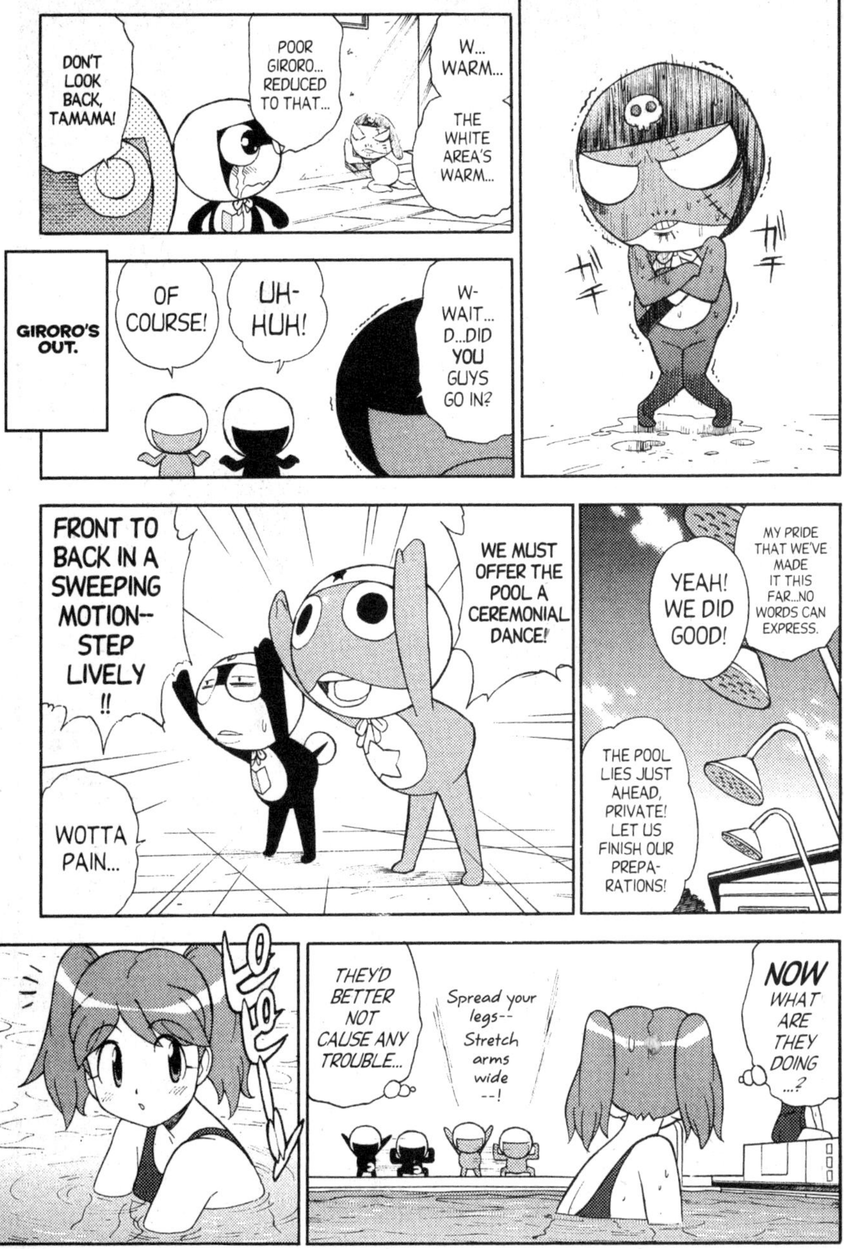
ガチ
ガチ
W... WARM...
THE WHITE AREA'S WARM...
POOR GIRORO... REDUCED TO THAT...
DON'T LOOK BACK, TAMAMA!
W-WAIT... D...DID YOU GUYS GO IN?
UH-HUH!
OF COURSE!
GIRORO'S OUT.
MY PRIDE THAT WE'VE MADE IT THIS FAR...NO WORDS CAN EXPRESS.
YEAH! WE DID GOOD!
THE POOL LIES JUST AHEAD, PRIVATE! LET US FINISH OUR PREPA-RATIONS!
WE MUST OFFER THE POOL A CEREMONIAL DANCE!
FRONT TO BACK IN A SWEEPING MOTION--STEP LIVELY !!
WOTTA PAIN...
NOW WHAT ARE THEY DOING ...?
Spread your legs-- Stretch arms wide --!
THEY'D BETTER NOT CAUSE ANY TROUBLE...

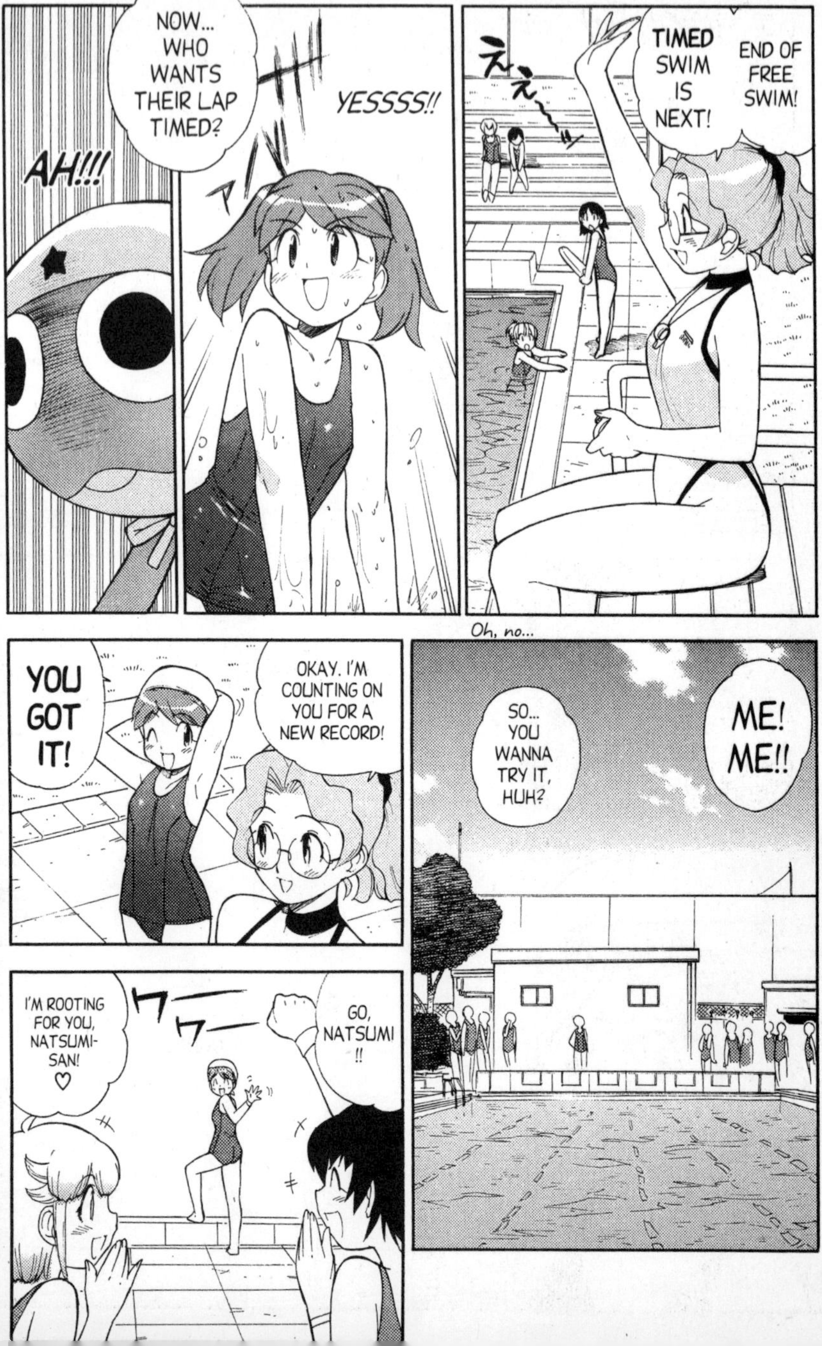
END OF FREE SWIM!
TIMED SWIM IS NEXT!
えぇ~~ッ
NOW... WHO WANTS THEIR LAP TIMED?
YESSSS!!
ア
AH!!!
Oh, no...
ME! ME!!
SO... YOU WANNA TRY IT, HUH?
OKAY. I'M COUNTING ON YOU FOR A NEW RECORD!
YOU GOT IT!
GO, NATSUMI!!
ワーワー
I'M ROOTING FOR YOU, NATSUMI-SAN! ♡

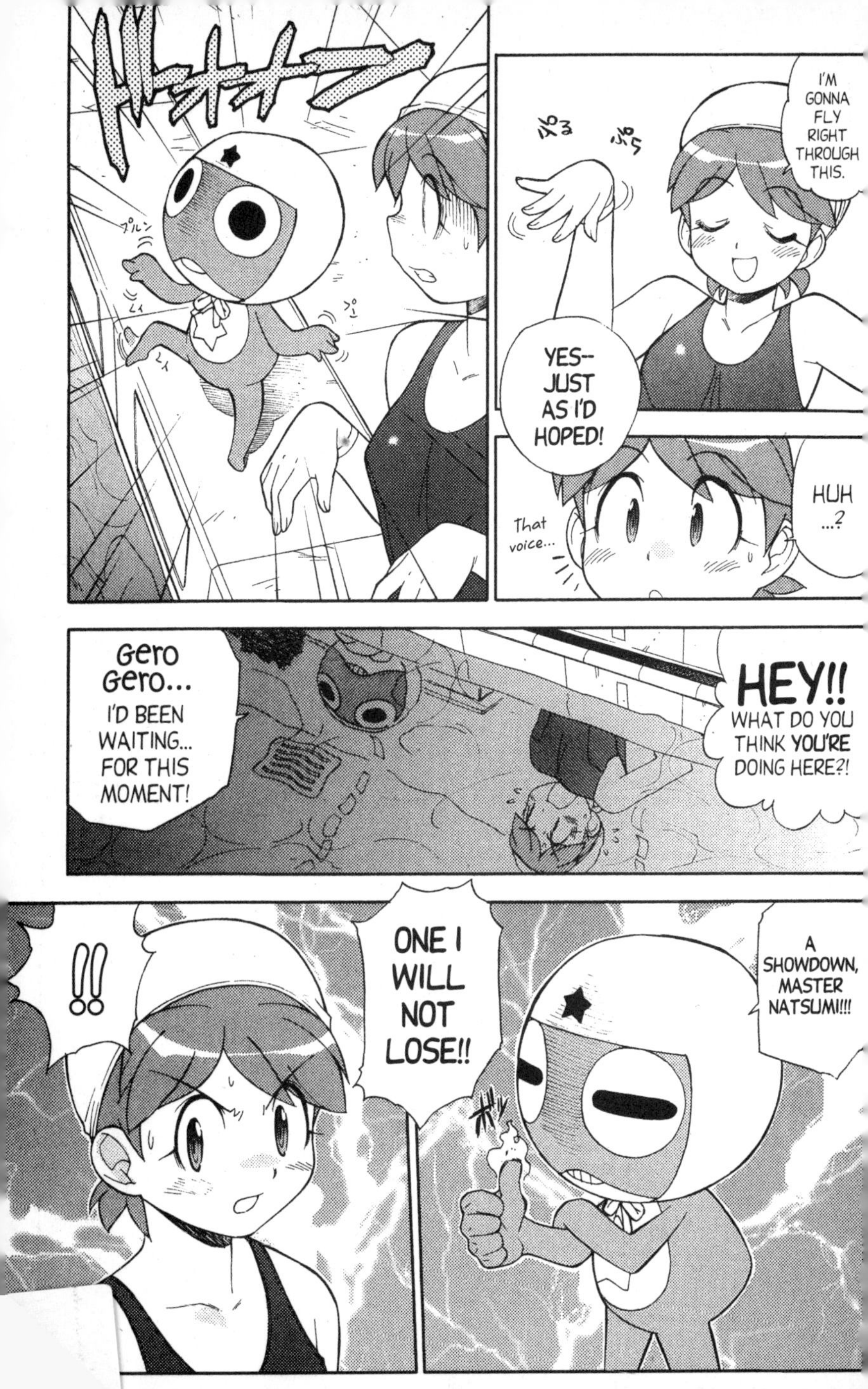
I'M GONNA FLY RIGHT THROUGH THIS.
YES-- JUST AS I'D HOPED!
HUH ...?
That voice...
HEY!! WHAT DO YOU THINK YOU'RE DOING HERE?!
Gero Gero... I'D BEEN WAITING... FOR THIS MOMENT!
A SHOWDOWN, MASTER NATSUMI!!!
ONE I WILL NOT LOSE!!
!!

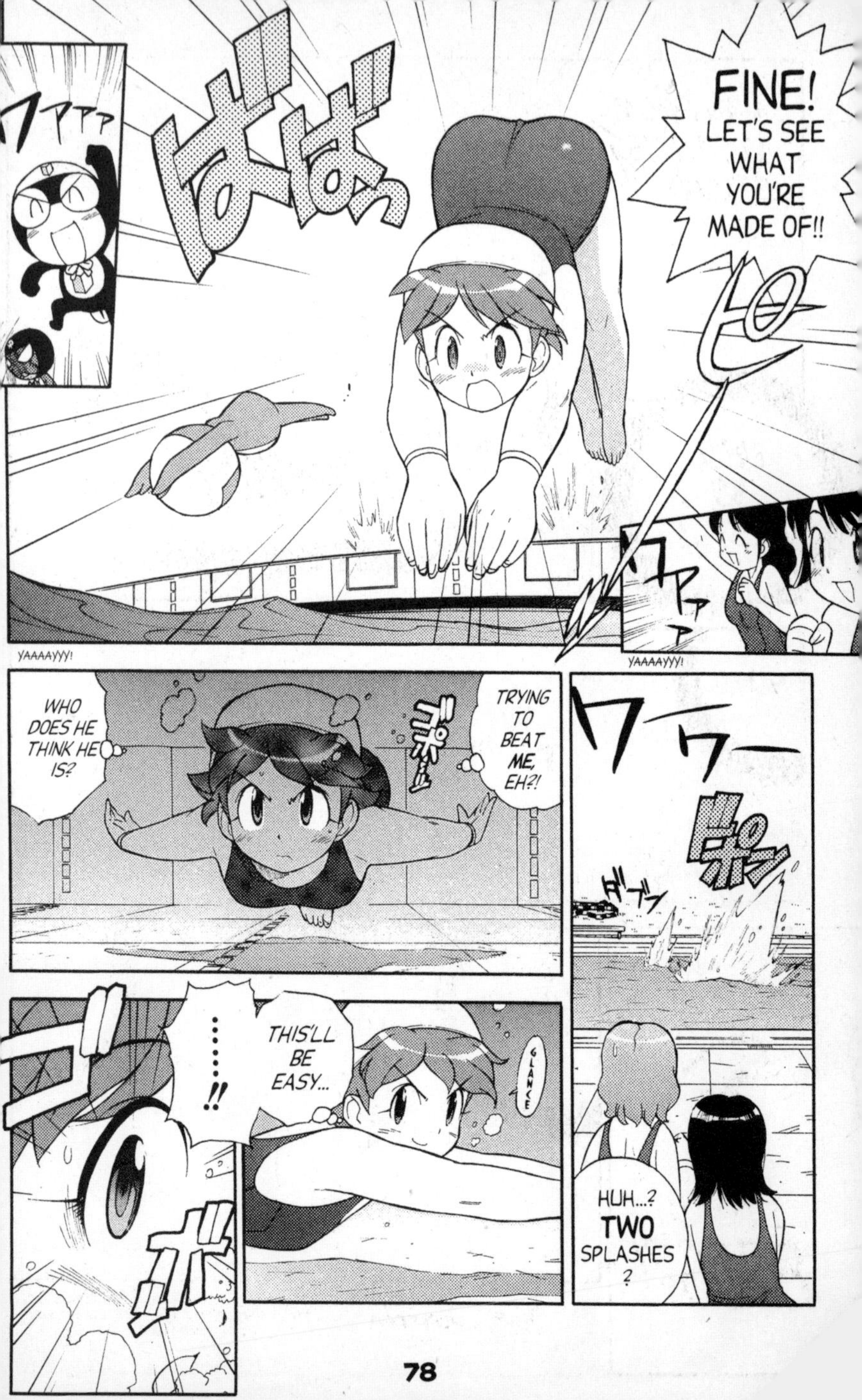
FINE! LET'S SEE WHAT YOU'RE MADE OF!!
YAAAAYYY!
YAAAAYYY!
TRYING TO BEAT ME, EH?!
WHO DOES HE THINK HE IS?
HUH...? TWO SPLASHES?
GLANCE
THIS'LL BE EASY...
......!!

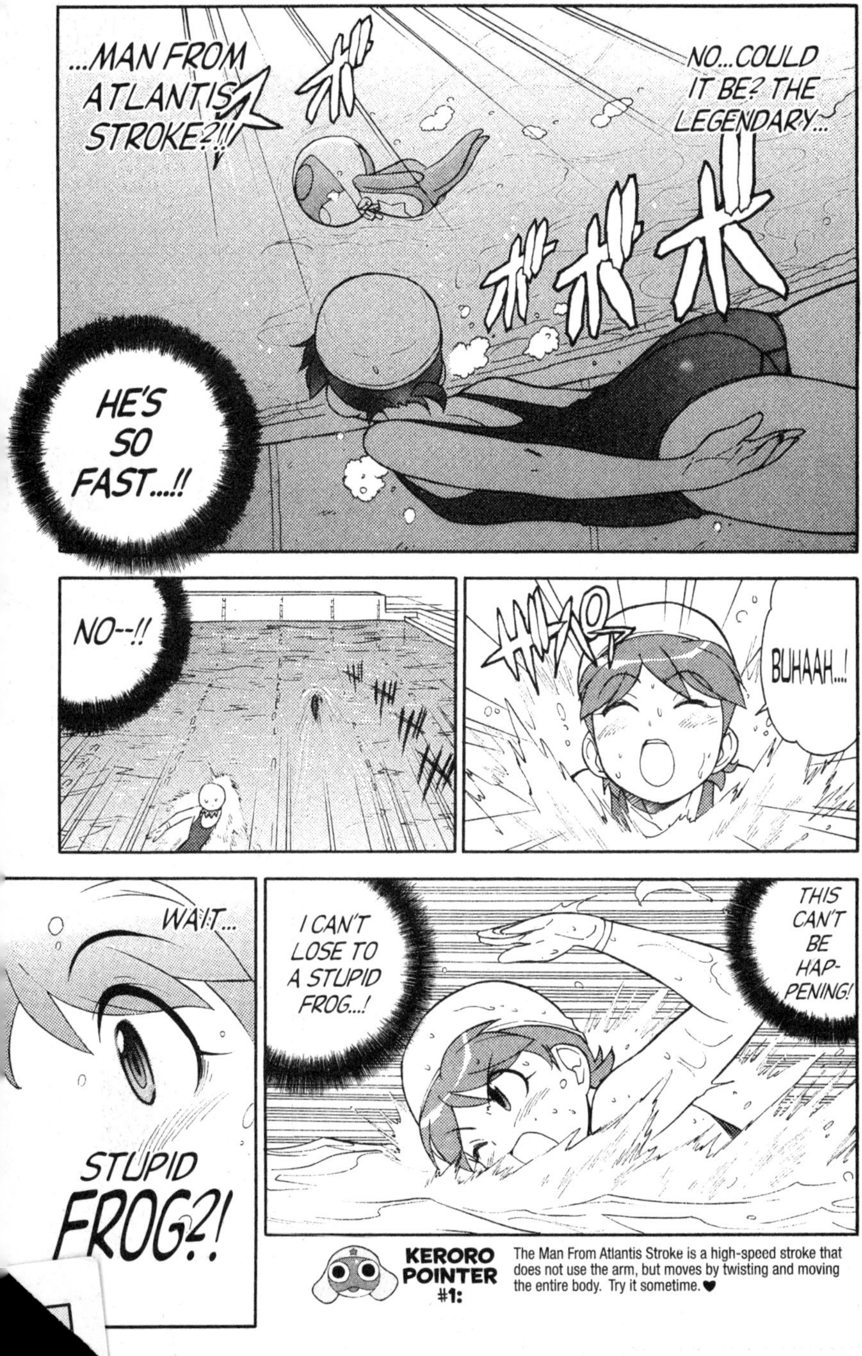
NO...COULD IT BE? THE LEGENDARY...
...MAN FROM ATLANTIS STROKE?!!
HE'S SO FAST...!!
BUHAAH...!
NO--!!
THIS CAN'T BE HAP-PENING!
I CAN'T LOSE TO A STUPID FROG...!
WAIT...
STUPID FROG?!

KERORO POINTER #1: The Man From Atlantis Stroke is a high-speed stroke that does not use the arm, but moves by twisting and moving the entire body. Try it sometime. ♥

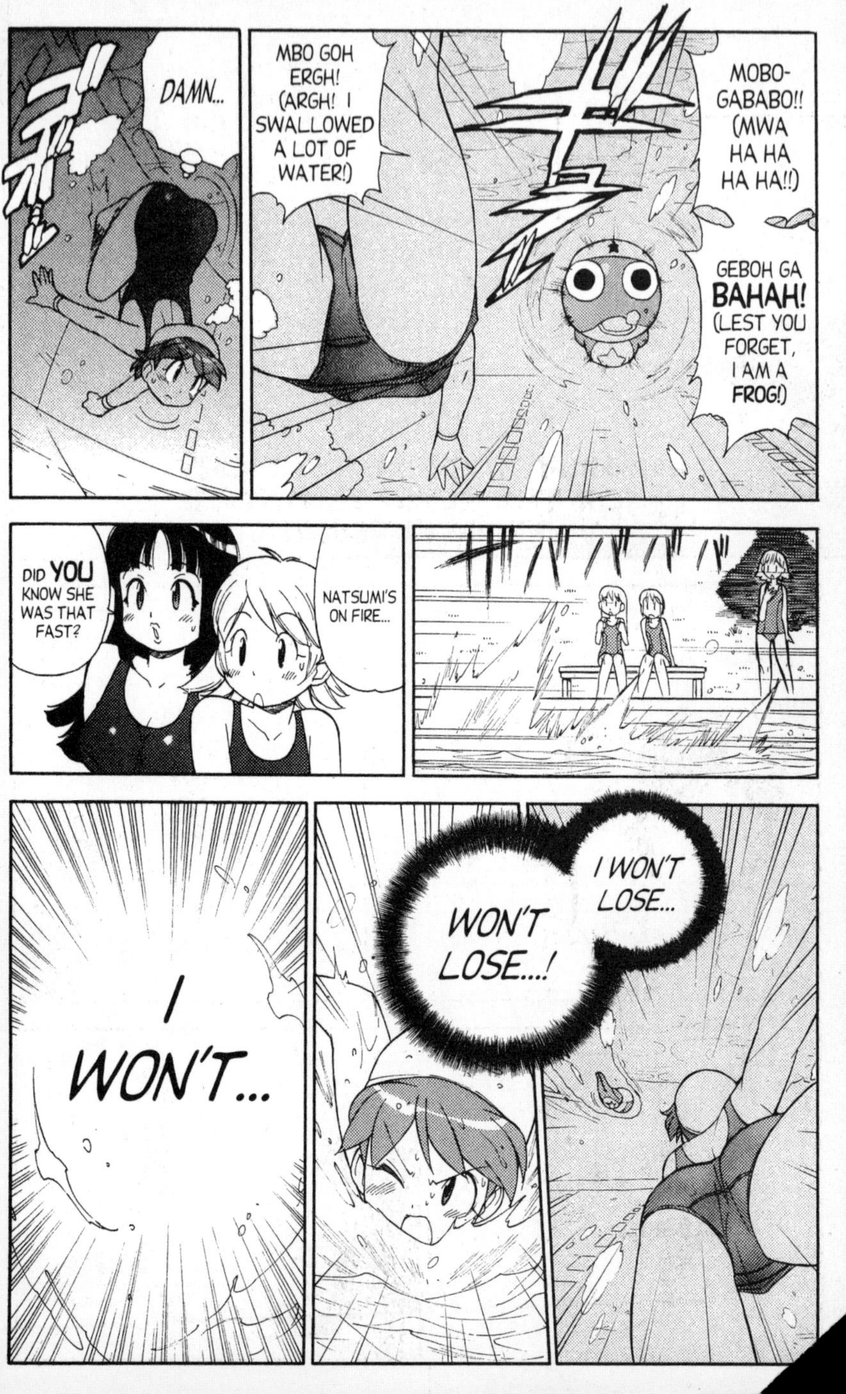
MOBO-GABABO!! (MWA HA HA HA HA!!)
GEBOH GA BAHAH! (LEST YOU FORGET, I AM A FROG!)
MBO GOH ERGH! (ARGH! I SWALLOWED A LOT OF WATER!)
DAMN...
NATSUMI'S ON FIRE...
DID YOU KNOW SHE WAS THAT FAST?
I WON'T LOSE...
WON'T LOSE...!
I WON'T...

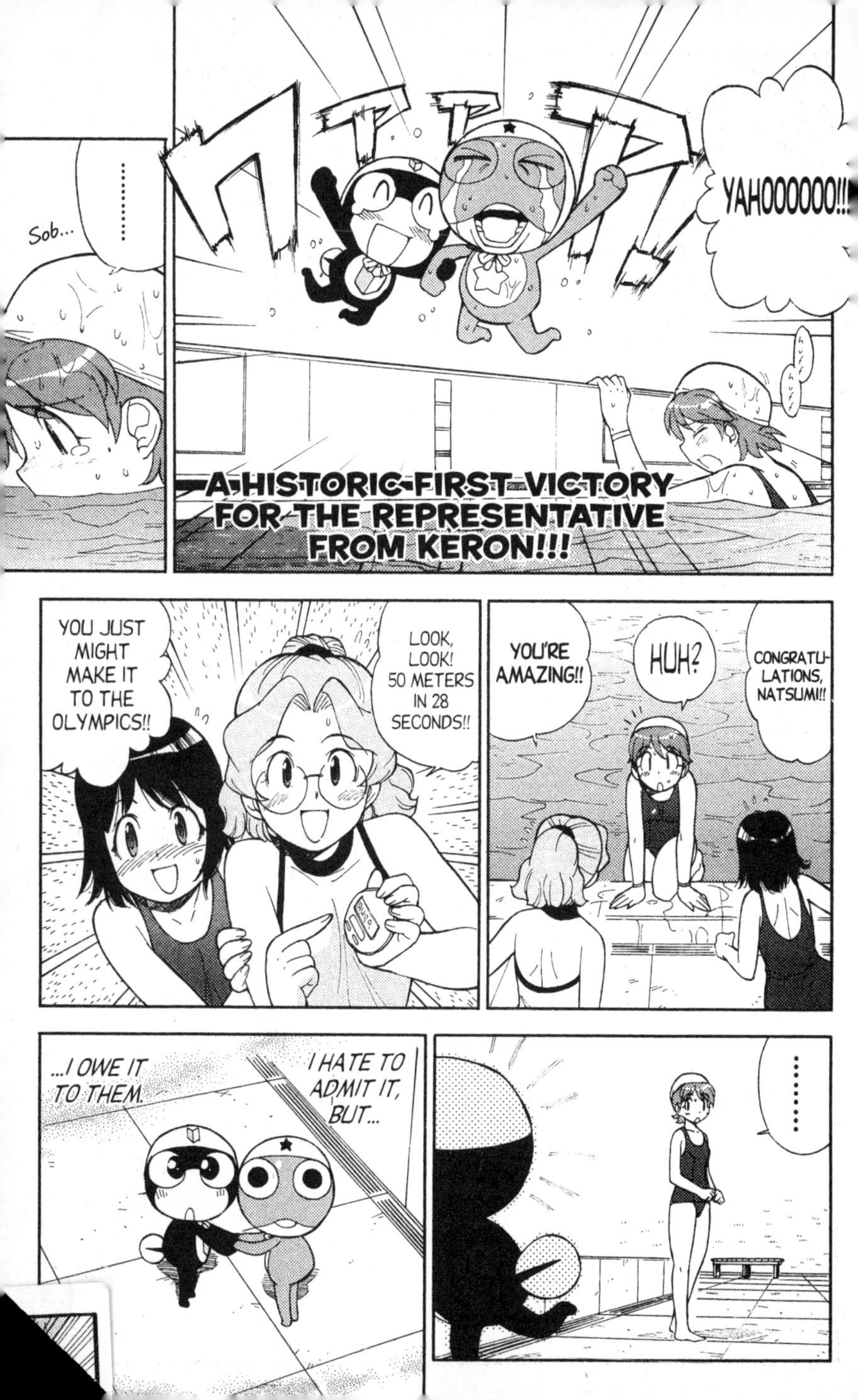
YAHOOOOOO!!!
huff huff
A HISTORIC FIRST VICTORY FOR THE REPRESENTATIVE FROM KERON!!!
....
Sob...
CONGRATULATIONS, NATSUMI!!
HUH?
YOU'RE AMAZING!!
LOOK, LOOK! 50 METERS IN 28 SECONDS!!
YOU JUST MIGHT MAKE IT TO THE OLYMPICS!!
....
I HATE TO ADMIT IT, BUT...
...I OWE IT TO THEM.

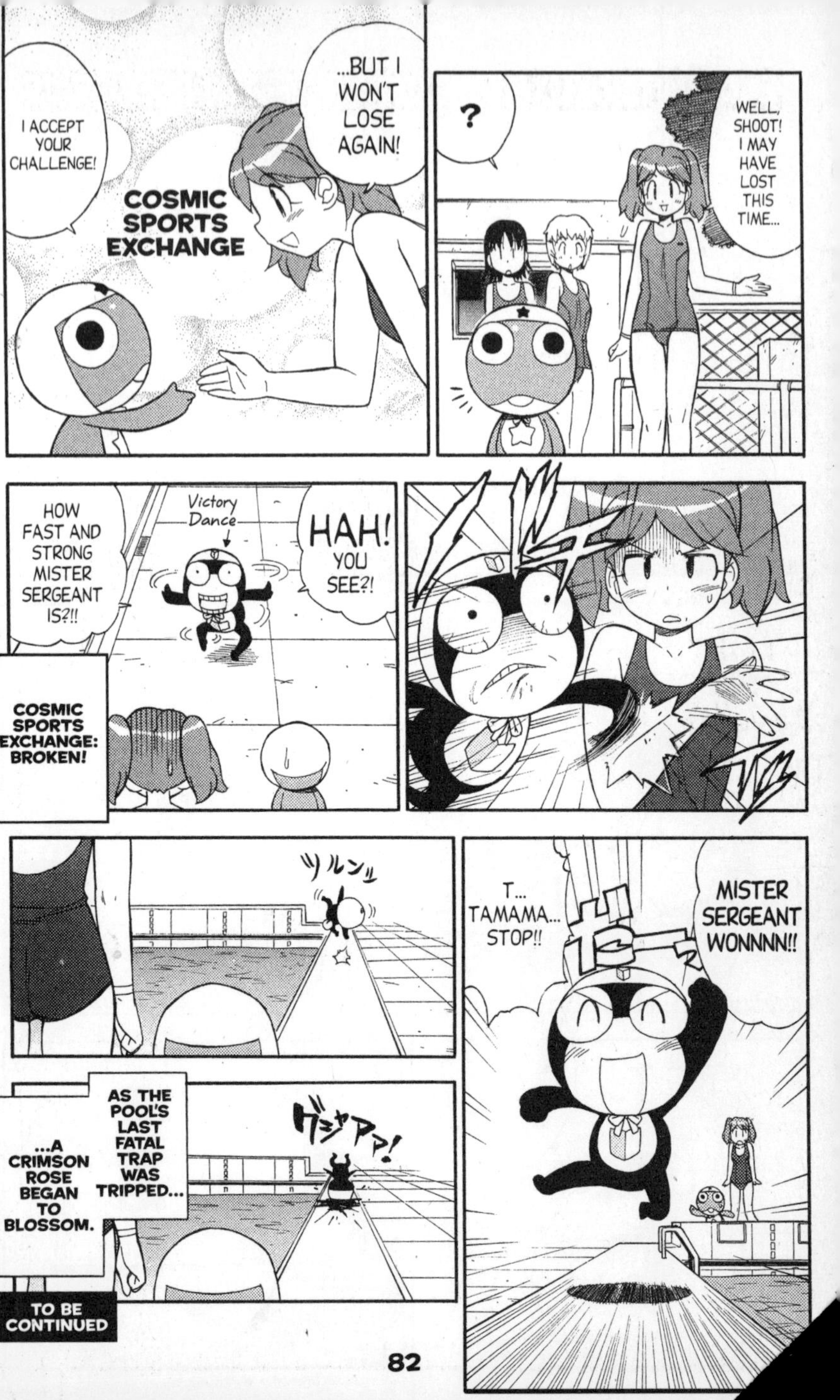
WELL, SHOOT! I MAY HAVE LOST THIS TIME...
?
...BUT I WON'T LOSE AGAIN!
I ACCEPT YOUR CHALLENGE!
COSMIC SPORTS EXCHANGE
HAH! YOU SEE?!
Victory Dance
HOW FAST AND STRONG MISTER SERGEANT IS?!!
COSMIC SPORTS EXCHANGE: BROKEN!
MISTER SERGEANT WONNNN!!
T... TAMAMA... STOP!!
ツルンッ
グシャアァ!
AS THE POOL'S LAST FATAL TRAP WAS TRIPPED...
...A CRIMSON ROSE BEGAN TO BLOSSOM.
TO BE CONTINUED

ENCOUNTER XLIX DANGER IN THE DEEP SEA!!!

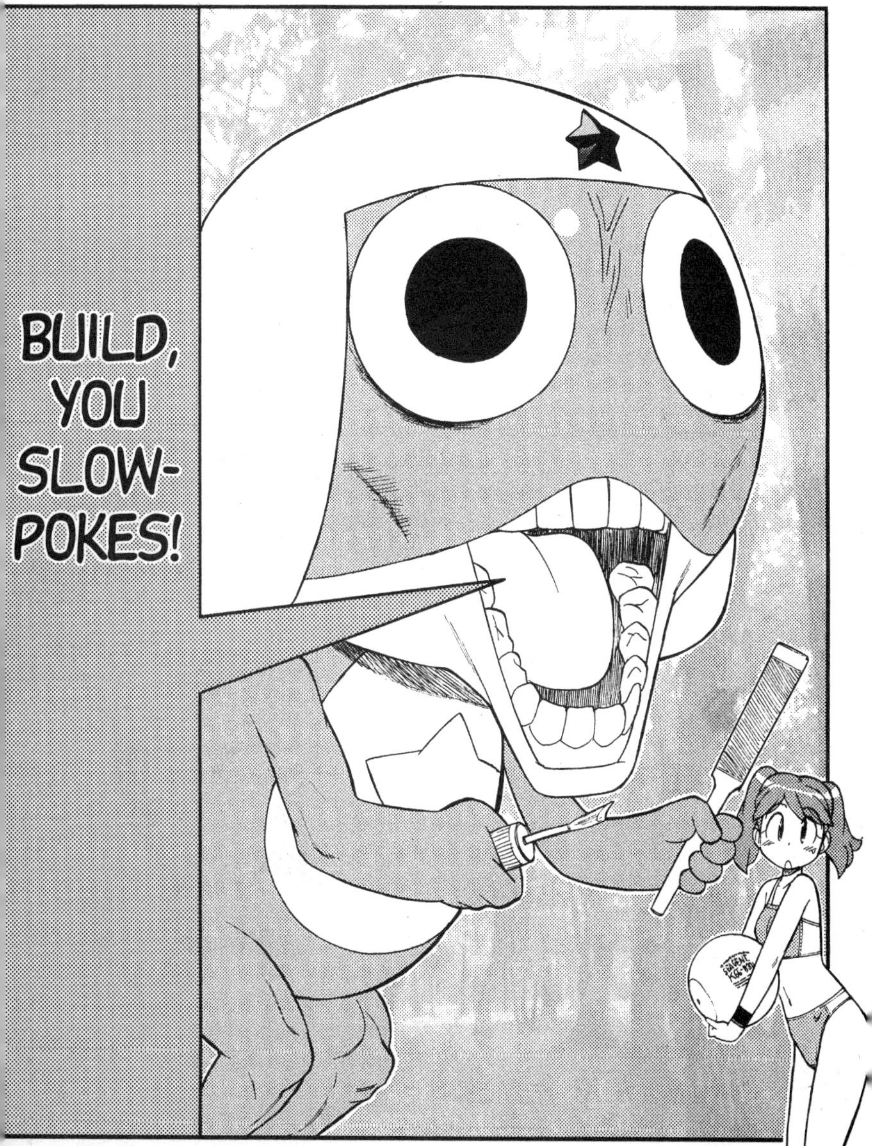
BUILD, YOU SLOW-POKES!

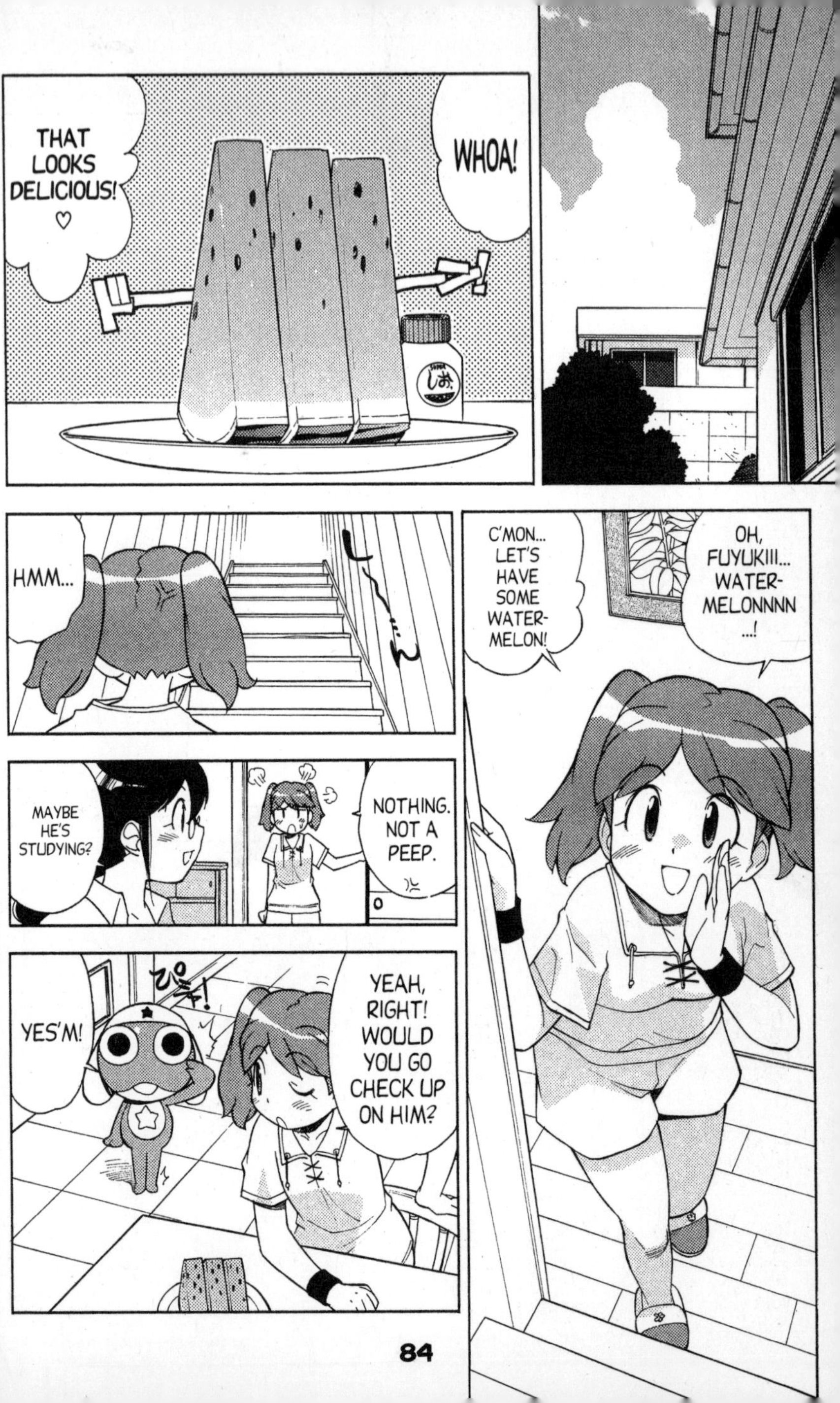
WHOA!
THAT LOOKS DELICIOUS! ♡
OH, FUYUKIII... WATER-MELONNNN ...!
C'MON... LET'S HAVE SOME WATER-MELON!
HMM...
NOTHING. NOT A PEEP.
MAYBE HE'S STUDYING?
YEAH, RIGHT! WOULD YOU GO CHECK UP ON HIM?
YES'M!

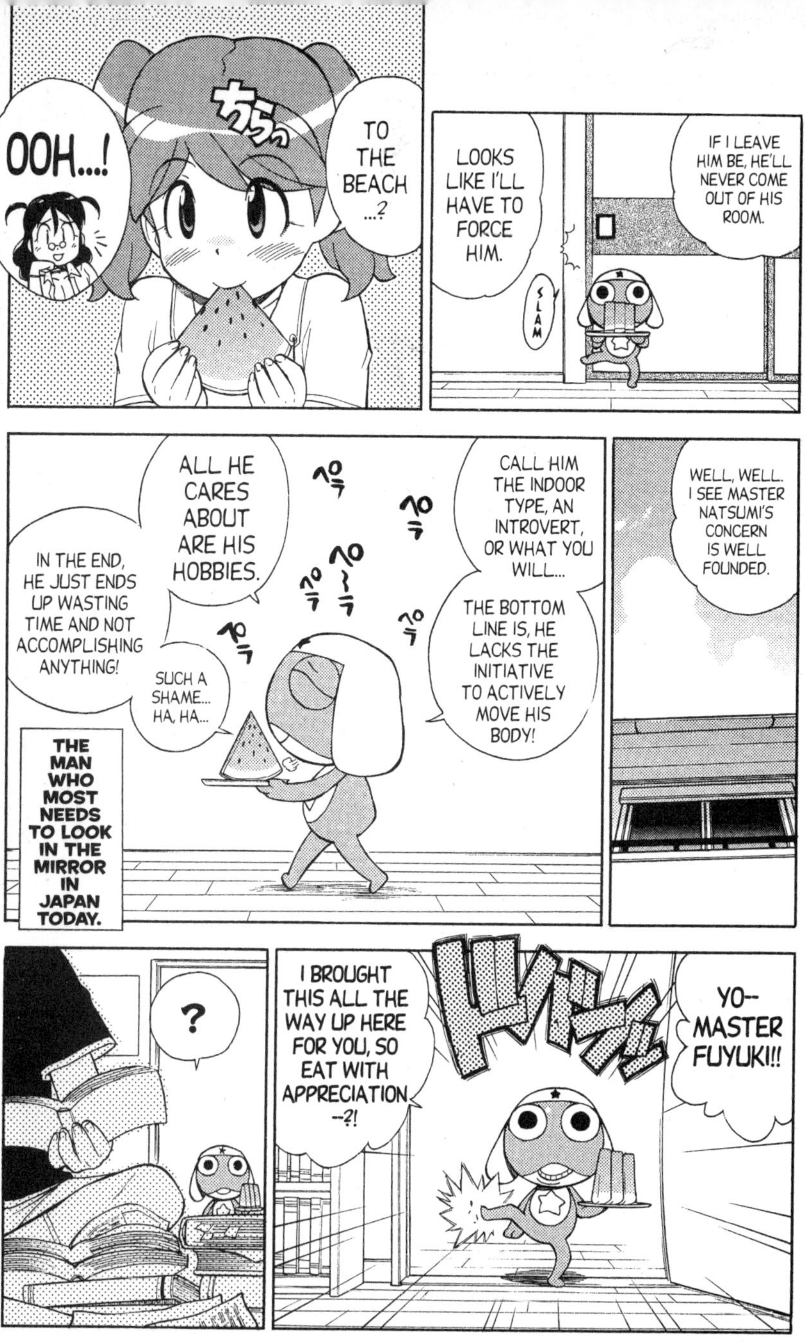
IF I LEAVE HIM BE, HE'LL NEVER COME OUT OF HIS ROOM.
LOOKS LIKE I'LL HAVE TO FORCE HIM.
SLAM
TO THE BEACH ...?
OOH...!
WELL, WELL. I SEE MASTER NATSUMI'S CONCERN IS WELL FOUNDED.
CALL HIM THE INDOOR TYPE, AN INTROVERT, OR WHAT YOU WILL...
THE BOTTOM LINE IS, HE LACKS THE INITIATIVE TO ACTIVELY MOVE HIS BODY!
ALL HE CARES ABOUT ARE HIS HOBBIES.
IN THE END, HE JUST ENDS UP WASTING TIME AND NOT ACCOMPLISHING ANYTHING!
SUCH A SHAME... HA, HA...
THE MAN WHO MOST NEEDS TO LOOK IN THE MIRROR IN JAPAN TODAY.
YO-- MASTER FUYUKI!!
I BROUGHT THIS ALL THE WAY UP HERE FOR YOU, SO EAT WITH APPRECIATION --?!
?

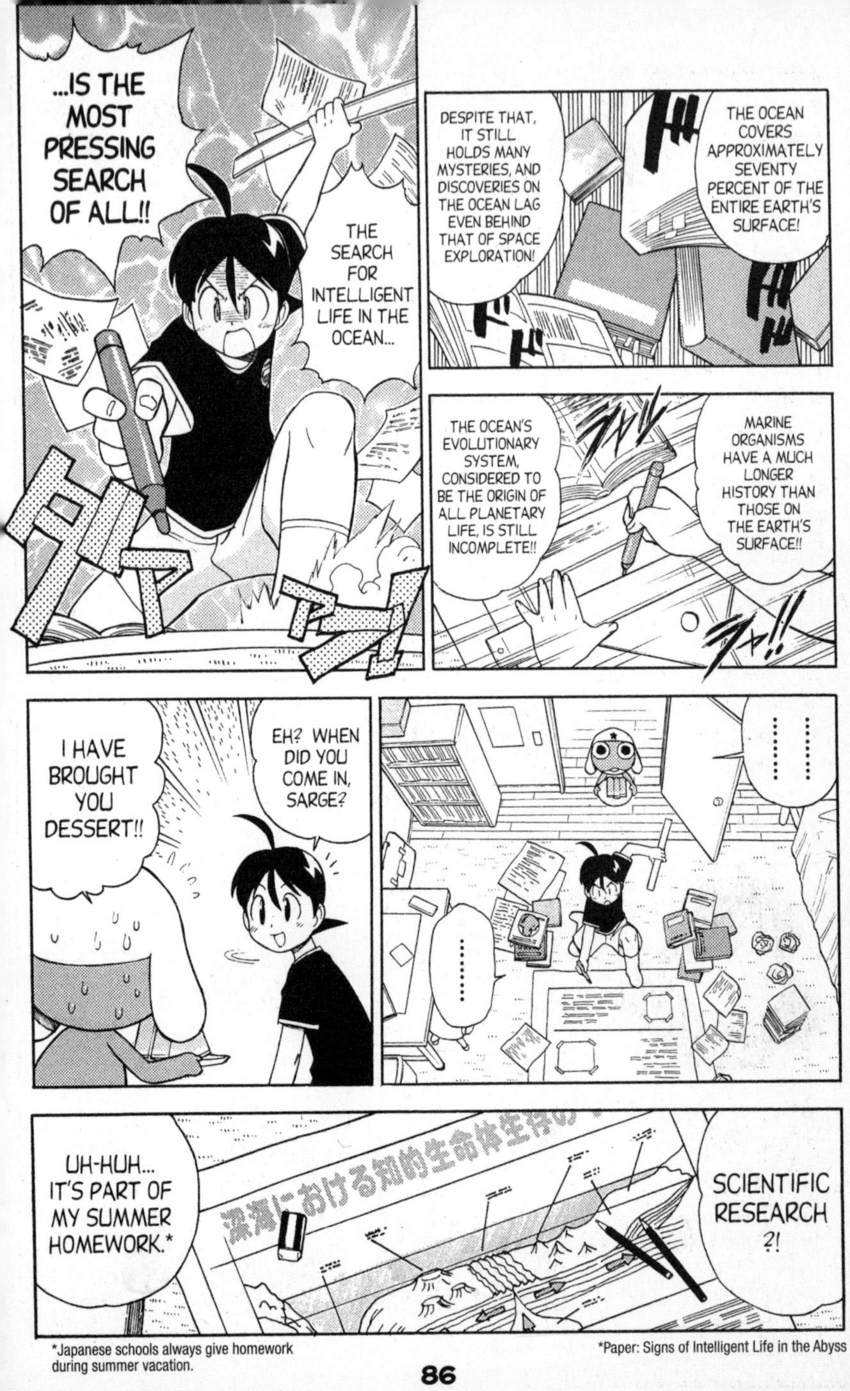
THE OCEAN COVERS APPROXIMATELY SEVENTY PERCENT OF THE ENTIRE EARTH'S SURFACE!
DESPITE THAT, IT STILL HOLDS MANY MYSTERIES, AND DISCOVERIES ON THE OCEAN LAG EVEN BEHIND THAT OF SPACE EXPLORATION!
MARINE ORGANISMS HAVE A MUCH LONGER HISTORY THAN THOSE ON THE EARTH'S SURFACE!!
THE OCEAN'S EVOLUTIONARY SYSTEM, CONSIDERED TO BE THE ORIGIN OF ALL PLANETARY LIFE, IS STILL INCOMPLETE!!
THE SEARCH FOR INTELLIGENT LIFE IN THE OCEAN...
...IS THE MOST PRESSING SEARCH OF ALL!!
......
......
EH? WHEN DID YOU COME IN, SARGE?
I HAVE BROUGHT YOU DESSERT!!
SCIENTIFIC RESEARCH ?!
深海における知的生命体生存
UH-HUH... IT'S PART OF MY SUMMER HOMEWORK.*

*Japanese schools always give homework during summer vacation.

*Paper: Signs of Intelligent Life in the Abyss

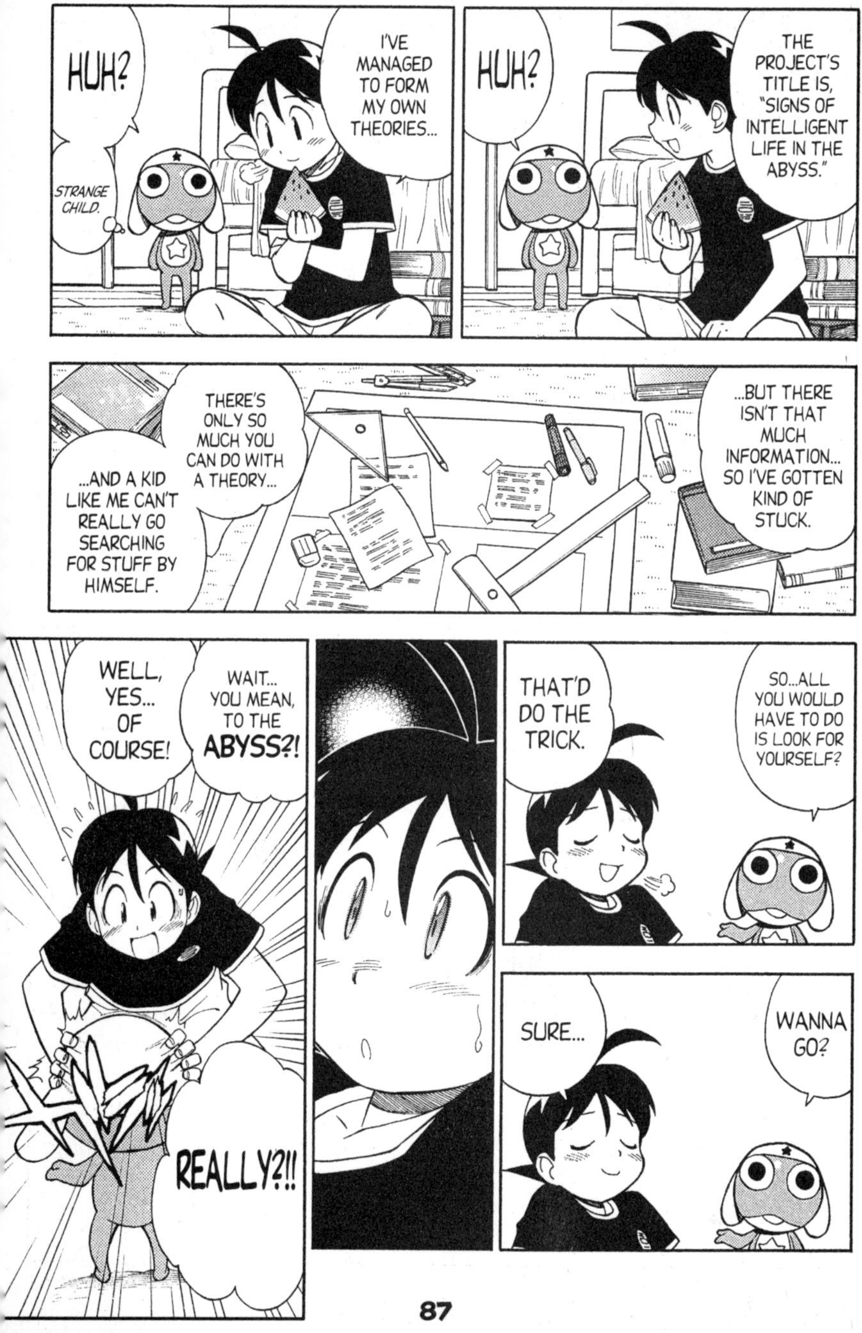
THE PROJECT'S TITLE IS, "SIGNS OF INTELLIGENT LIFE IN THE ABYSS."
HUH?
I'VE MANAGED TO FORM MY OWN THEORIES...
HUH?
STRANGE CHILD.
...BUT THERE ISN'T THAT MUCH INFORMATION... SO I'VE GOTTEN KIND OF STUCK.
THERE'S ONLY SO MUCH YOU CAN DO WITH A THEORY...
...AND A KID LIKE ME CAN'T REALLY GO SEARCHING FOR STUFF BY HIMSELF.
SO...ALL YOU WOULD HAVE TO DO IS LOOK FOR YOURSELF?
THAT'D DO THE TRICK.
WANNA GO?
SURE...
WAIT... YOU MEAN, TO THE ABYSS?!
WELL, YES... OF COURSE!
REALLY?!!

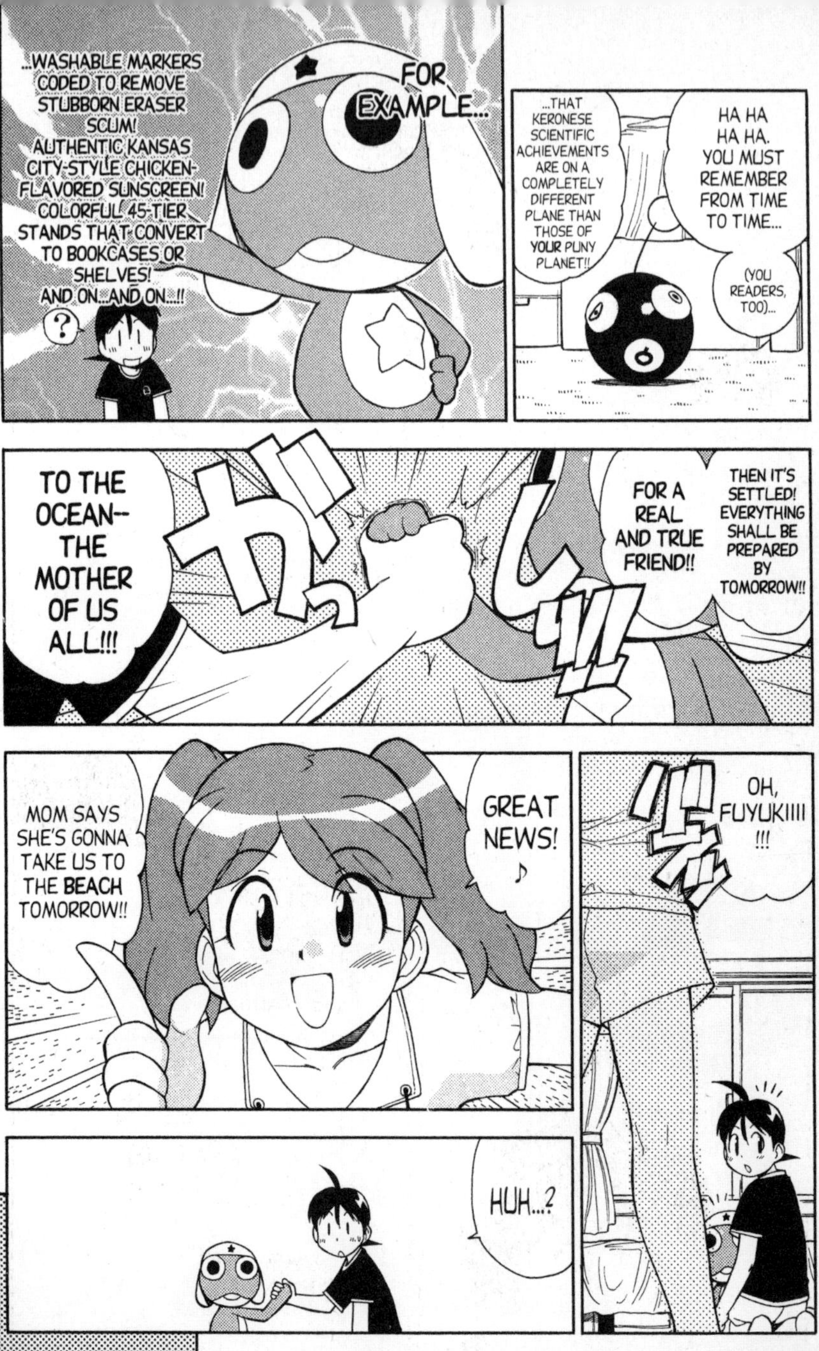
HA HA HA HA. YOU MUST REMEMBER FROM TIME TO TIME...
(YOU READERS, TOO)...
...THAT KERONESE SCIENTIFIC ACHIEVEMENTS ARE ON A COMPLETELY DIFFERENT PLANE THAN THOSE OF **YOUR** PUNY PLANET!!
FOR EXAMPLE...
...WASHABLE MARKERS CODED TO REMOVE STUBBORN ERASER SCUM! AUTHENTIC KANSAS CITY-STYLE CHICKEN-FLAVORED SUNSCREEN! COLORFUL 45-TIER STANDS THAT CONVERT TO BOOKCASES OR SHELVES! AND ON...AND ON...!!
?
THEN IT'S SETTLED! EVERYTHING SHALL BE PREPARED BY TOMORROW!!
FOR A REAL AND TRUE FRIEND!!
がっしぃ!!!
TO THE OCEAN-- THE MOTHER OF US ALL!!!
OH, FUYUKIIII!!!
GREAT NEWS! ♪
MOM SAYS SHE'S GONNA TAKE US TO THE **BEACH** TOMORROW!!
HUH...?

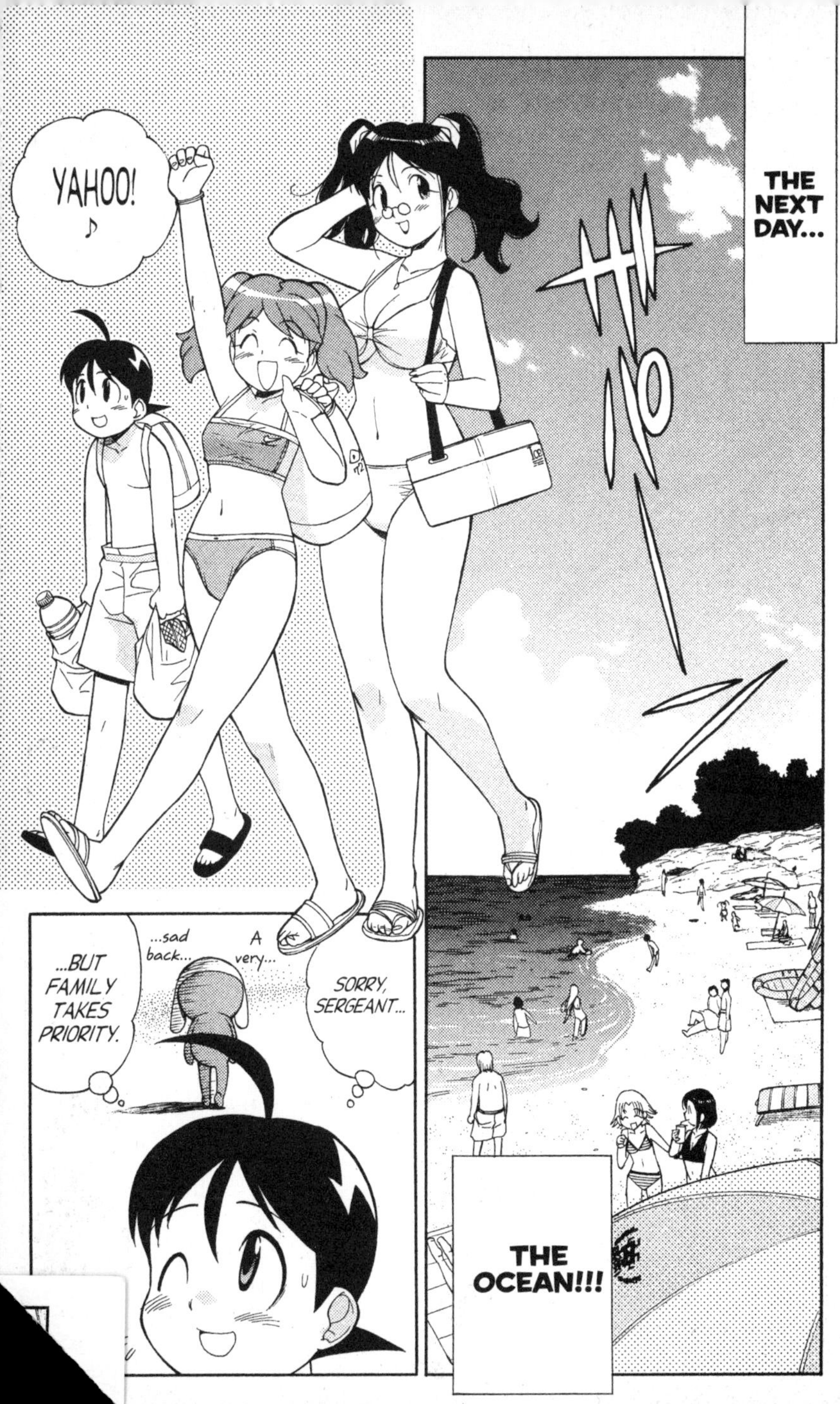
THE NEXT DAY...
THE OCEAN!!!
YAHOO! ♪
SORRY, SERGEANT...
A very...
...sad back...
...BUT FAMILY TAKES PRIORITY.

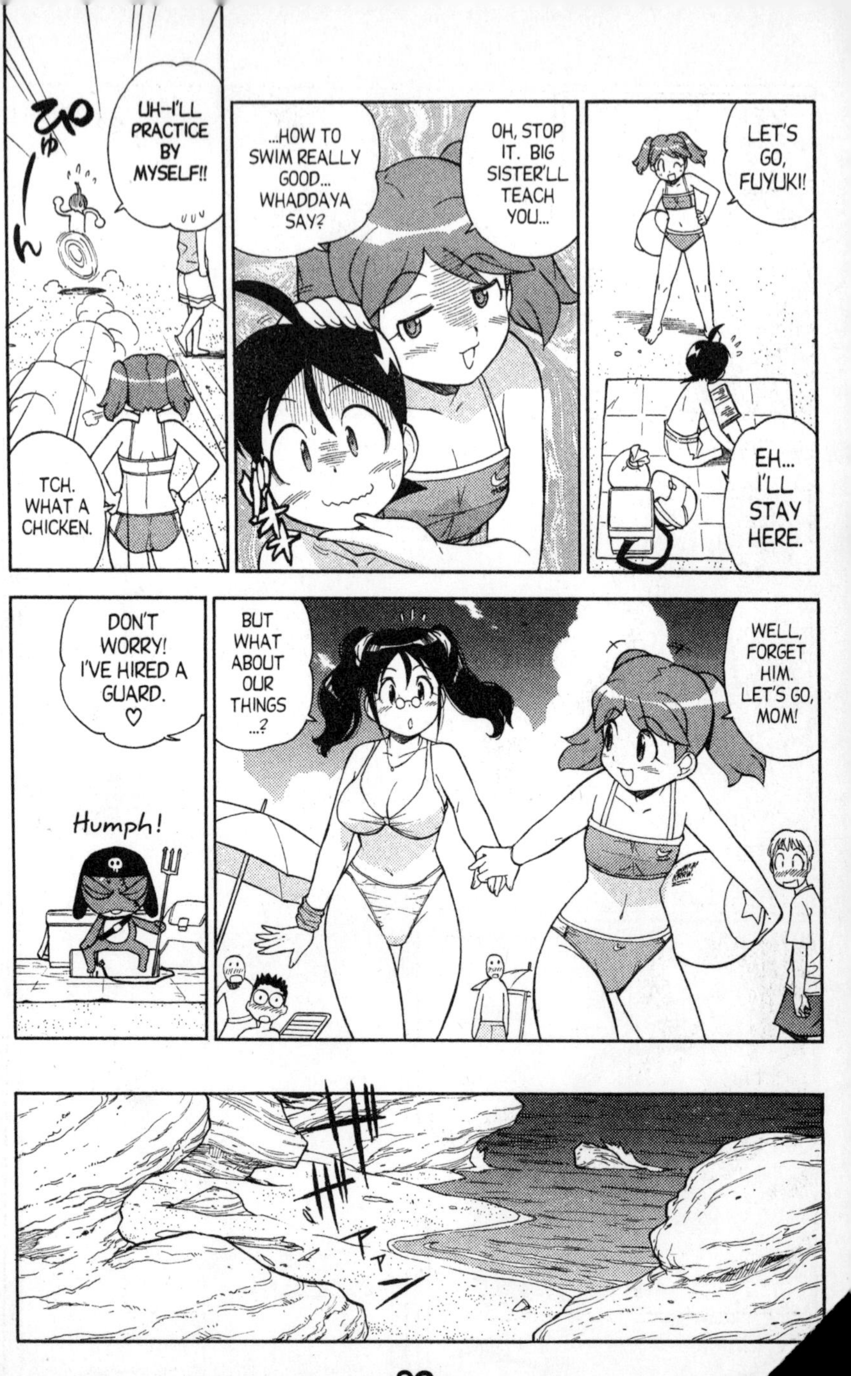
LET'S GO, FUYUKI!
EH... I'LL STAY HERE.
OH, STOP IT. BIG SISTER'LL TEACH YOU...
...HOW TO SWIM REALLY GOOD... WHADDAYA SAY?
UH-I'LL PRACTICE BY MYSELF!!
TCH. WHAT A CHICKEN.
WELL, FORGET HIM. LET'S GO, MOM!
BUT WHAT ABOUT OUR THINGS ...?
DON'T WORRY! I'VE HIRED A GUARD. ♡
Humph!

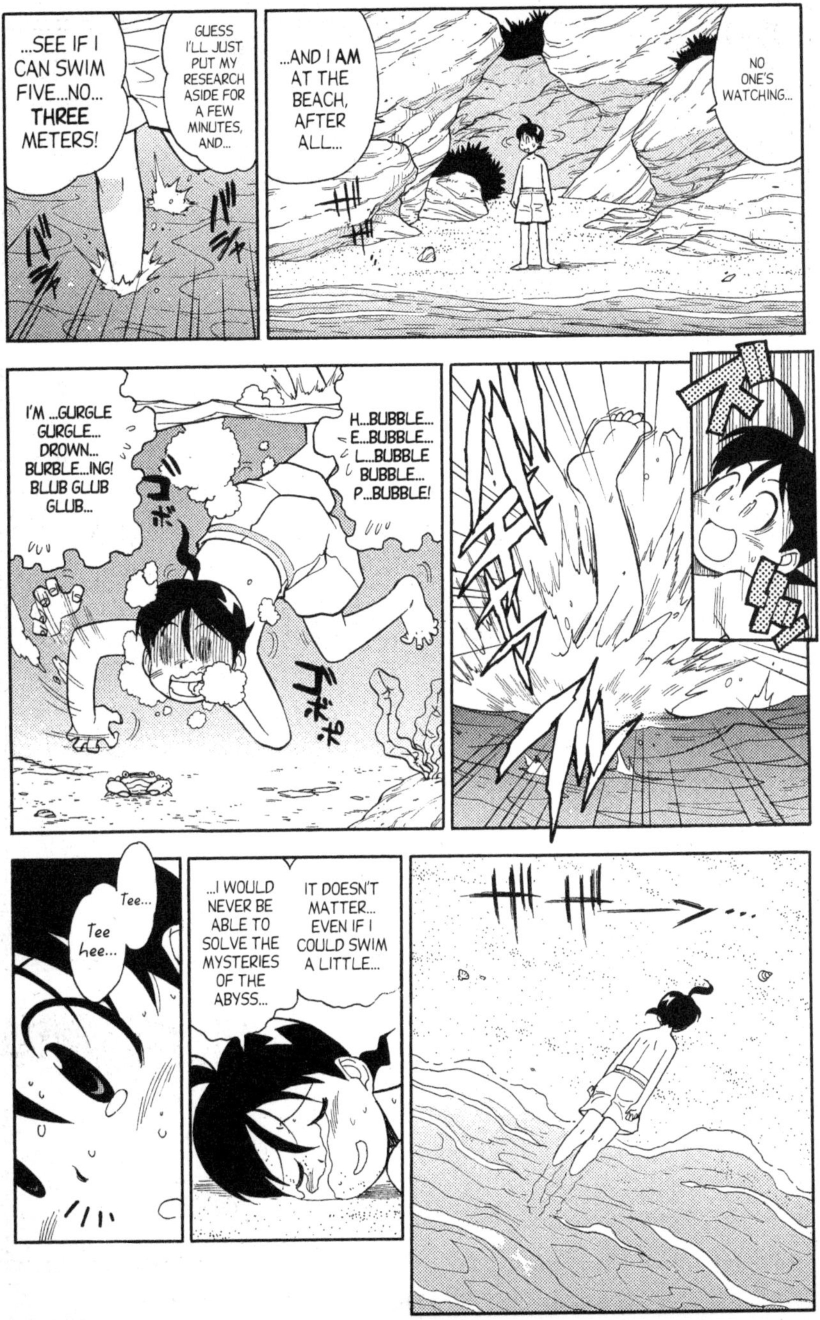
NO ONE'S WATCHING...
...AND I AM AT THE BEACH, AFTER ALL...
GUESS I'LL JUST PUT MY RESEARCH ASIDE FOR A FEW MINUTES, AND...
...SEE IF I CAN SWIM FIVE...NO... THREE METERS!
H...BUBBLE... E...BUBBLE... L...BUBBLE BUBBLE... P...BUBBLE!
I'M ...GURGLE GURGLE... DROWN... BURBLE...ING! BLUB GLUB GLUB...
IT DOESN'T MATTER... EVEN IF I COULD SWIM A LITTLE...
...I WOULD NEVER BE ABLE TO SOLVE THE MYSTERIES OF THE ABYSS...
Tee...
Tee hee...

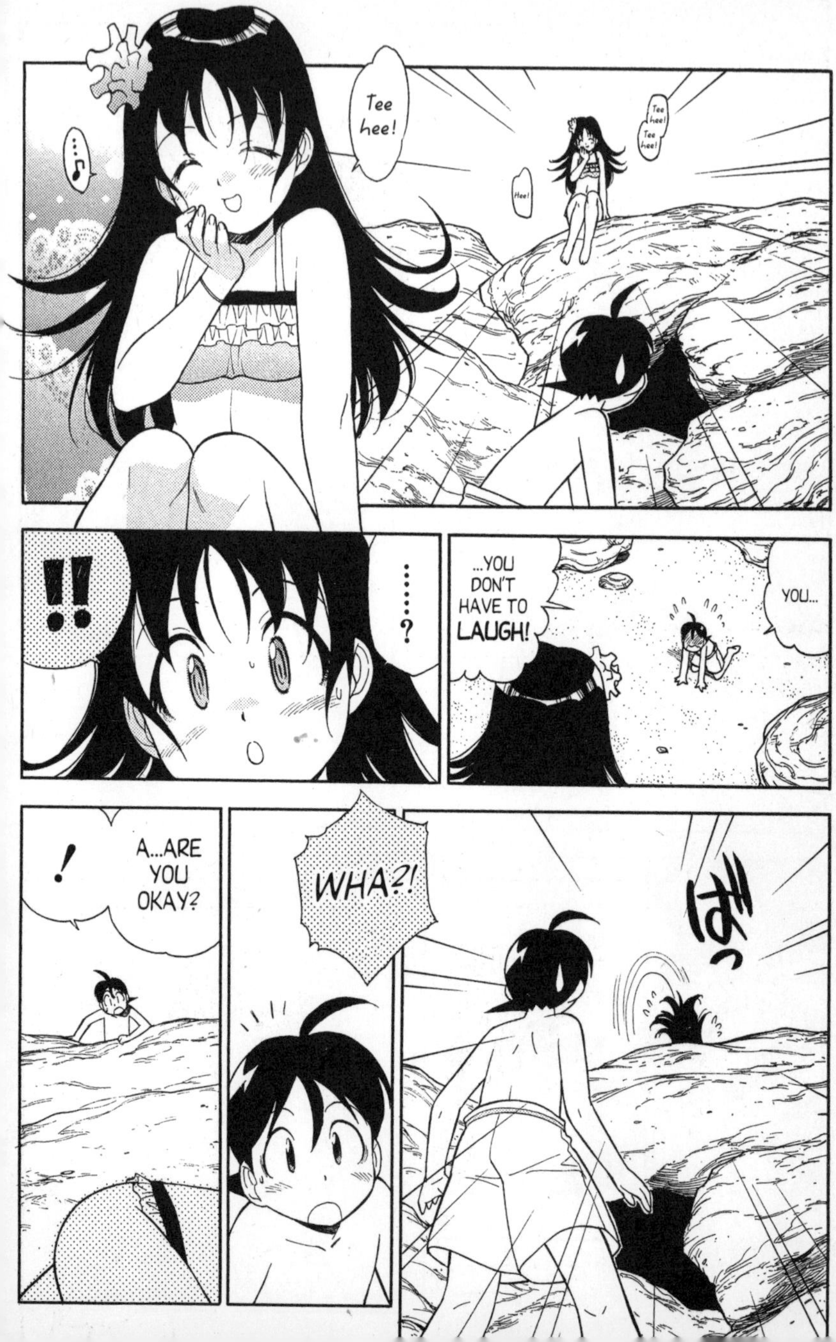

Tee hee!
Tee hee!
Hee!
Tee hee!
...♪
YOU...
...YOU DON'T HAVE TO LAUGH!
......?
!!
ばっ
WHA?!
A...ARE YOU OKAY?
!

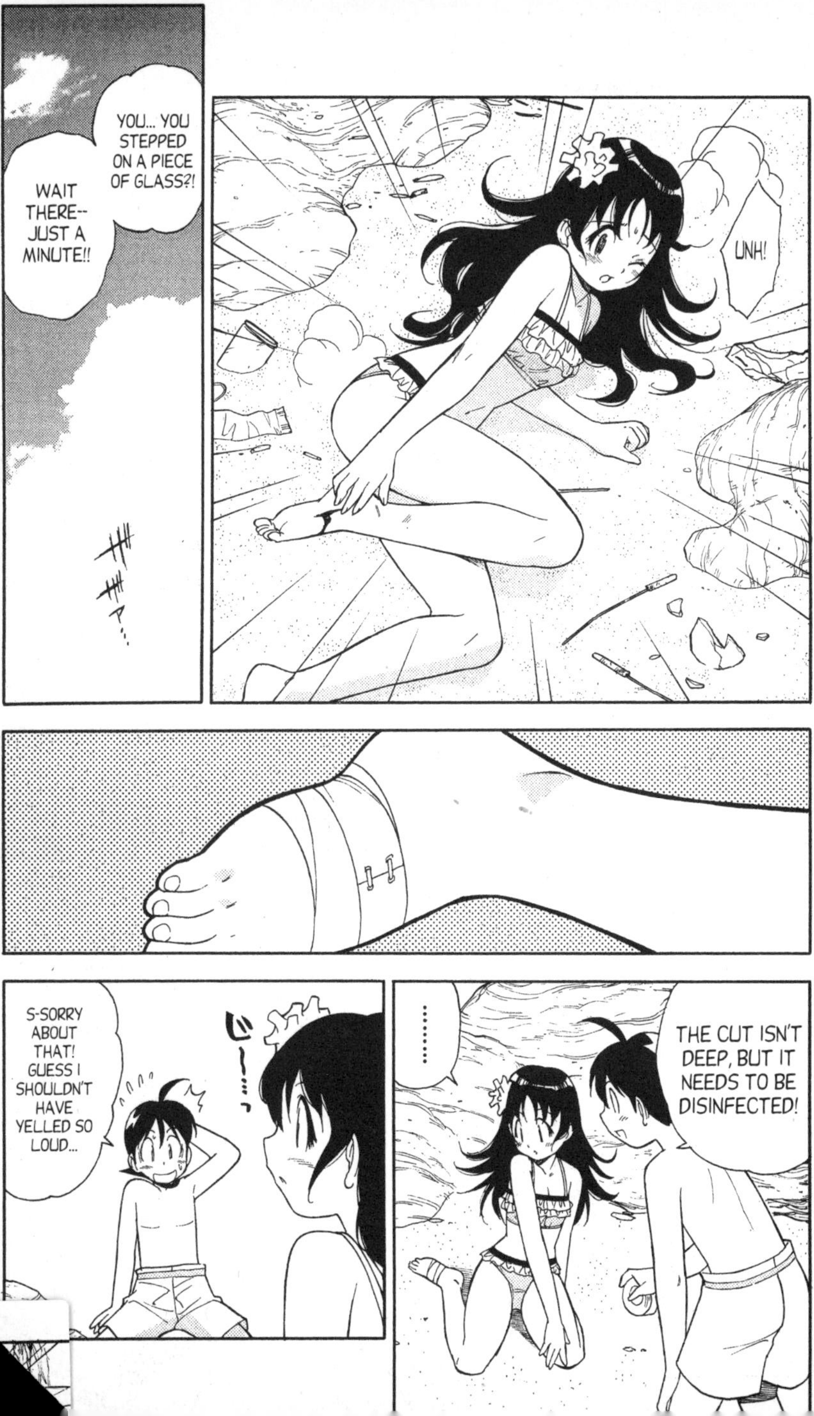
UNH!
YOU... YOU STEPPED ON A PIECE OF GLASS?!
WAIT THERE-- JUST A MINUTE!!
THE CUT ISN'T DEEP, BUT IT NEEDS TO BE DISINFECTED!
....
S-SORRY ABOUT THAT! GUESS I SHOULDN'T HAVE YELLED SO LOUD...

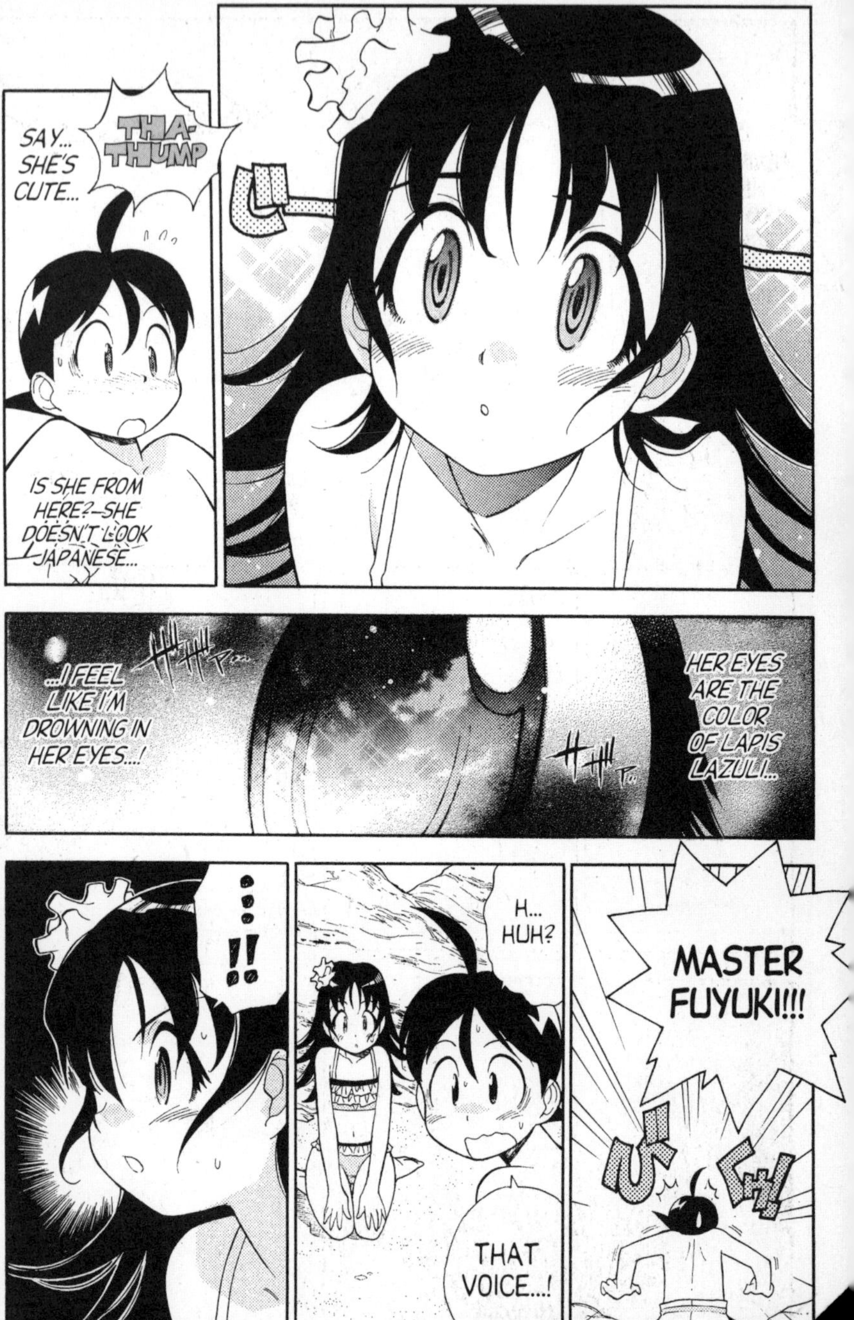
SAY... SHE'S CUTE...
THA-THUMP
IS SHE FROM HERE?—SHE DOESN'T LOOK JAPANESE...
HER EYES ARE THE COLOR OF LAPIS LAZULI...
...I FEEL LIKE I'M DROWNING IN HER EYES...!
MASTER FUYUKI!!!!
H... HUH?
THAT VOICE...!
...!!

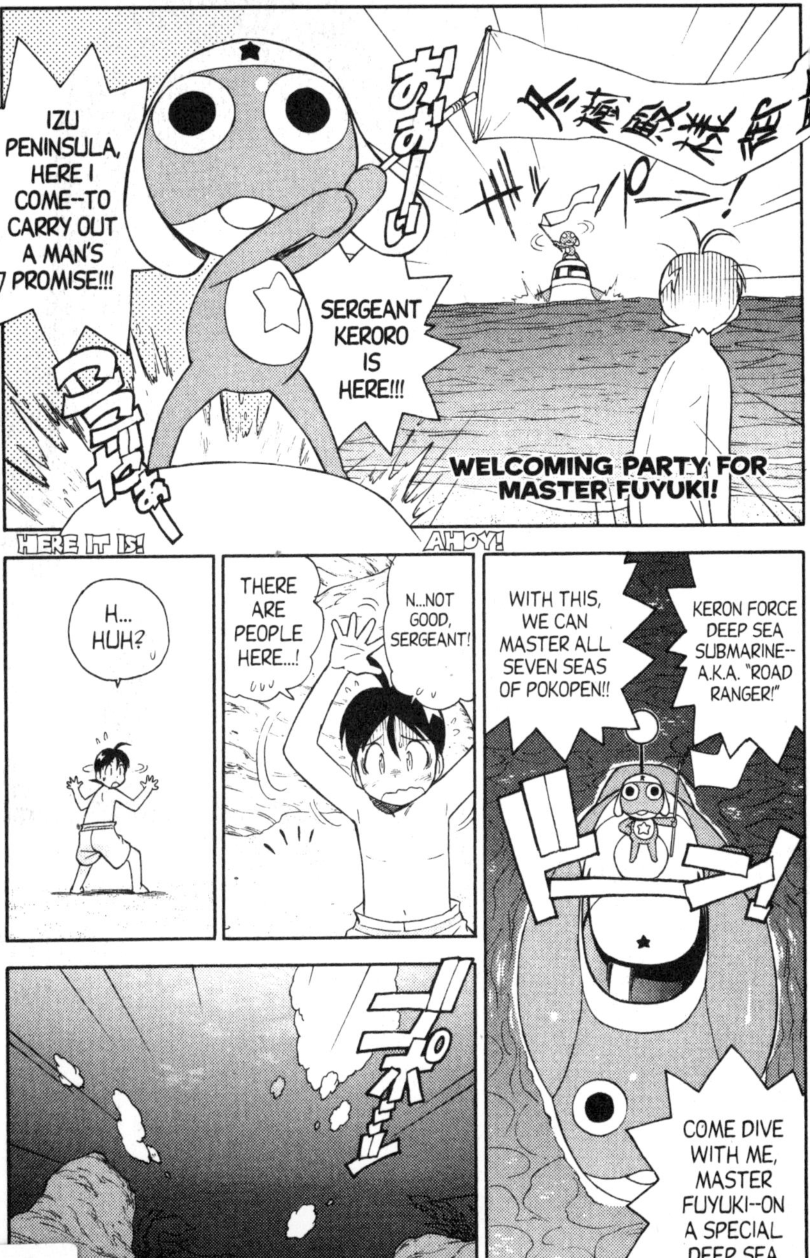
SERGEANT KERORO IS HERE!!!
IZU PENINSULA, HERE I COME--TO CARRY OUT A MAN'S PROMISE!!!
WELCOMING PARTY FOR MASTER FUYUKI!
AHOY!
HERE IT IS!
KERON FORCE DEEP SEA SUBMARINE--A.K.A. "ROAD RANGER!"
WITH THIS, WE CAN MASTER ALL SEVEN SEAS OF POKOPEN!!
COME DIVE WITH ME, MASTER FUYUKI--ON A SPECIAL DEEP SEA TOUR!!
N...NOT GOOD, SERGEANT!
THERE ARE PEOPLE HERE...!
H... HUH?

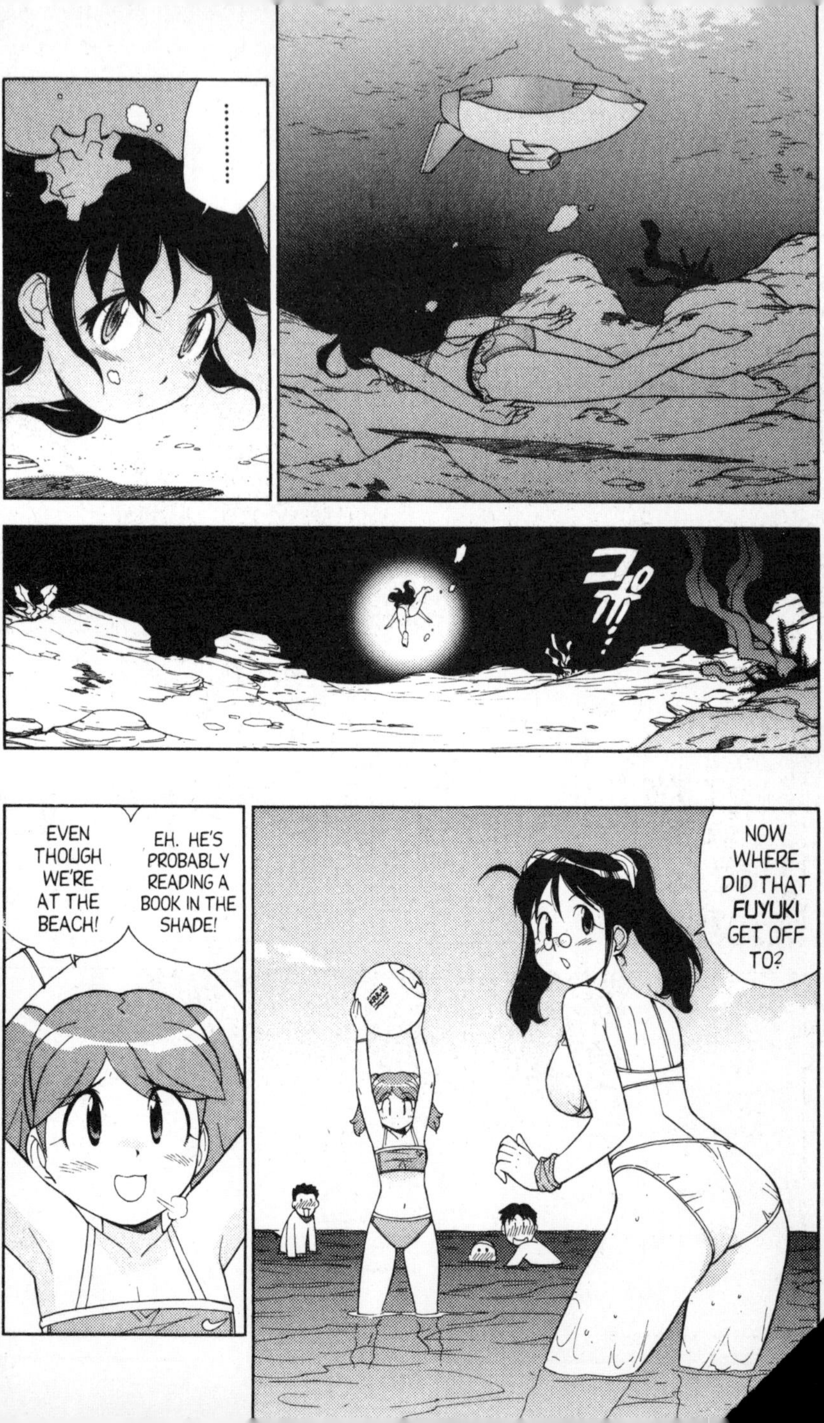
....
コポ
NOW WHERE DID THAT FUYUKI GET OFF TO?
EH. HE'S PROBABLY READING A BOOK IN THE SHADE!
EVEN THOUGH WE'RE AT THE BEACH!

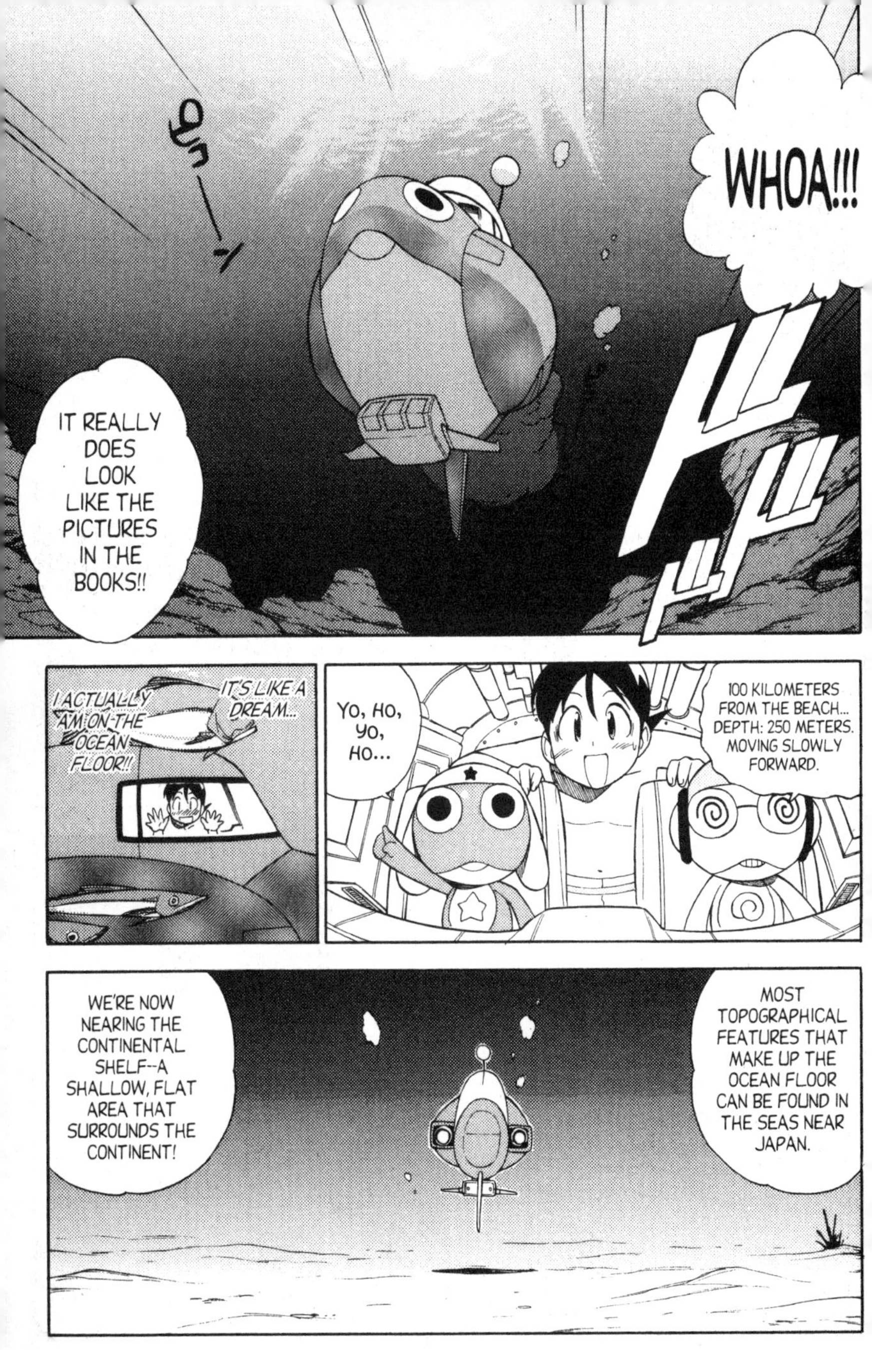
WHOA!!!
IT REALLY DOES LOOK LIKE THE PICTURES IN THE BOOKS!!
100 KILOMETERS FROM THE BEACH... DEPTH: 250 METERS. MOVING SLOWLY FORWARD.
YO, HO, YO, HO...
IT'S LIKE A DREAM...
I ACTUALLY AM ON THE OCEAN FLOOR!!
MOST TOPOGRAPHICAL FEATURES THAT MAKE UP THE OCEAN FLOOR CAN BE FOUND IN THE SEAS NEAR JAPAN.
WE'RE NOW NEARING THE CONTINENTAL SHELF--A SHALLOW, FLAT AREA THAT SURROUNDS THE CONTINENT!

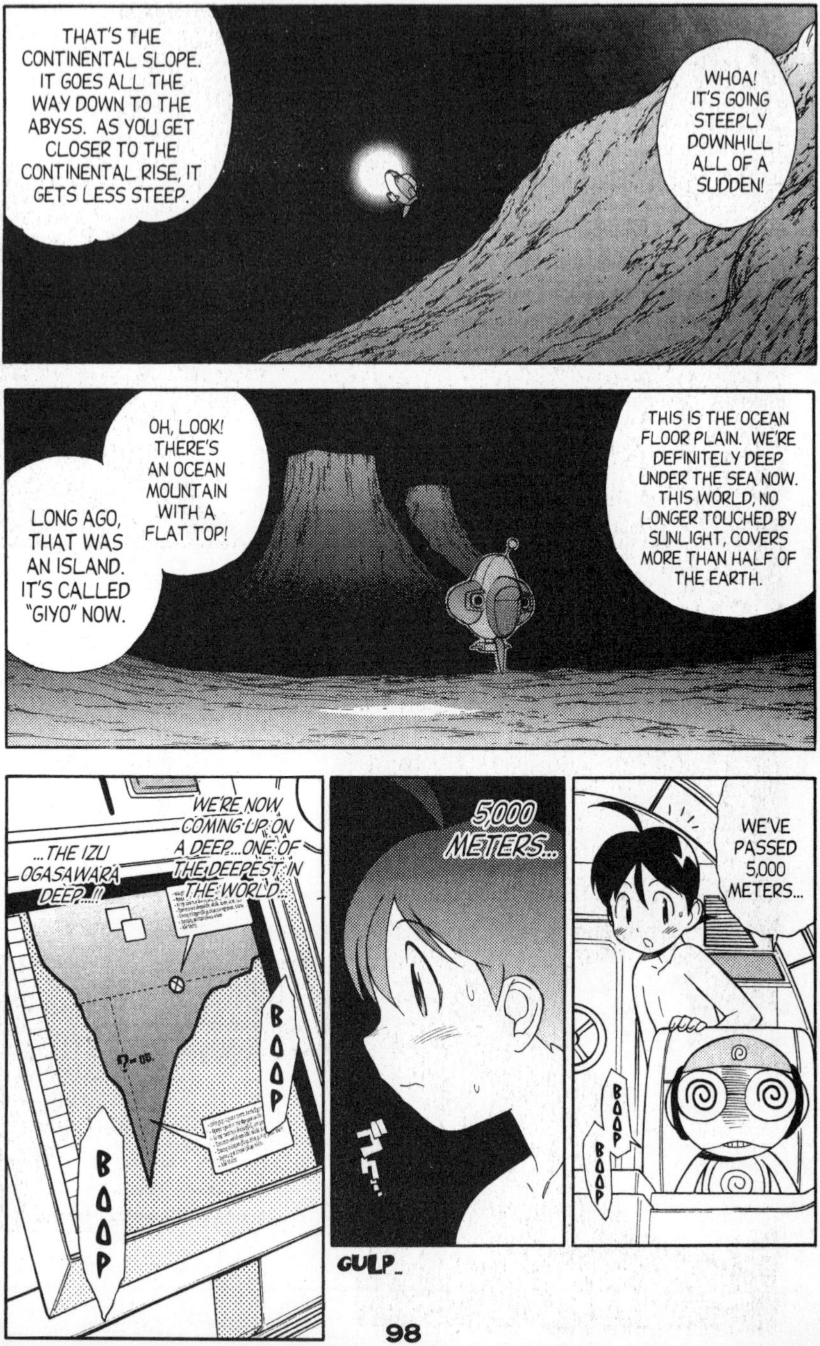

WHOA! IT'S GOING STEEPLY DOWNHILL ALL OF A SUDDEN!
THAT'S THE CONTINENTAL SLOPE. IT GOES ALL THE WAY DOWN TO THE ABYSS. AS YOU GET CLOSER TO THE CONTINENTAL RISE, IT GETS LESS STEEP.
THIS IS THE OCEAN FLOOR PLAIN. WE'RE DEFINITELY DEEP UNDER THE SEA NOW. THIS WORLD, NO LONGER TOUCHED BY SUNLIGHT, COVERS MORE THAN HALF OF THE EARTH.
OH, LOOK! THERE'S AN OCEAN MOUNTAIN WITH A FLAT TOP!
LONG AGO, THAT WAS AN ISLAND. IT'S CALLED "GIYO" NOW.
WE'VE PASSED 5,000 METERS...
BOOP
BOOP
5,000 METERS...
GULP...
WE'RE NOW COMING UP ON A DEEP...ONE OF THE DEEPEST IN THE WORLD...
...THE IZU OGASAWARA DEEP...!!
BOOP
BOOP

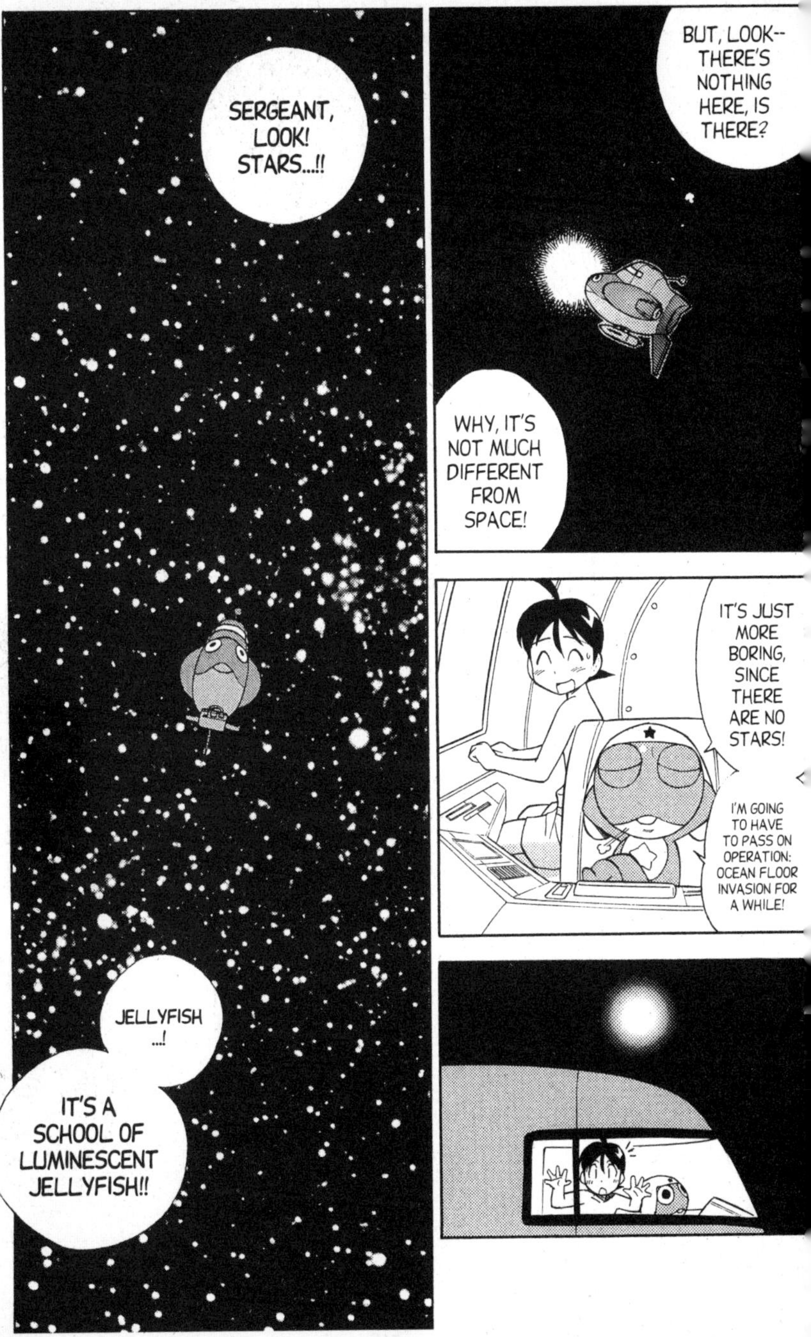
BUT, LOOK-- THERE'S NOTHING HERE, IS THERE?
WHY, IT'S NOT MUCH DIFFERENT FROM SPACE!
IT'S JUST MORE BORING, SINCE THERE ARE NO STARS!
I'M GOING TO HAVE TO PASS ON OPERATION: OCEAN FLOOR INVASION FOR A WHILE!
SERGEANT, LOOK! STARS...!!
JELLYFISH ...!
IT'S A SCHOOL OF LUMINESCENT JELLYFISH!!

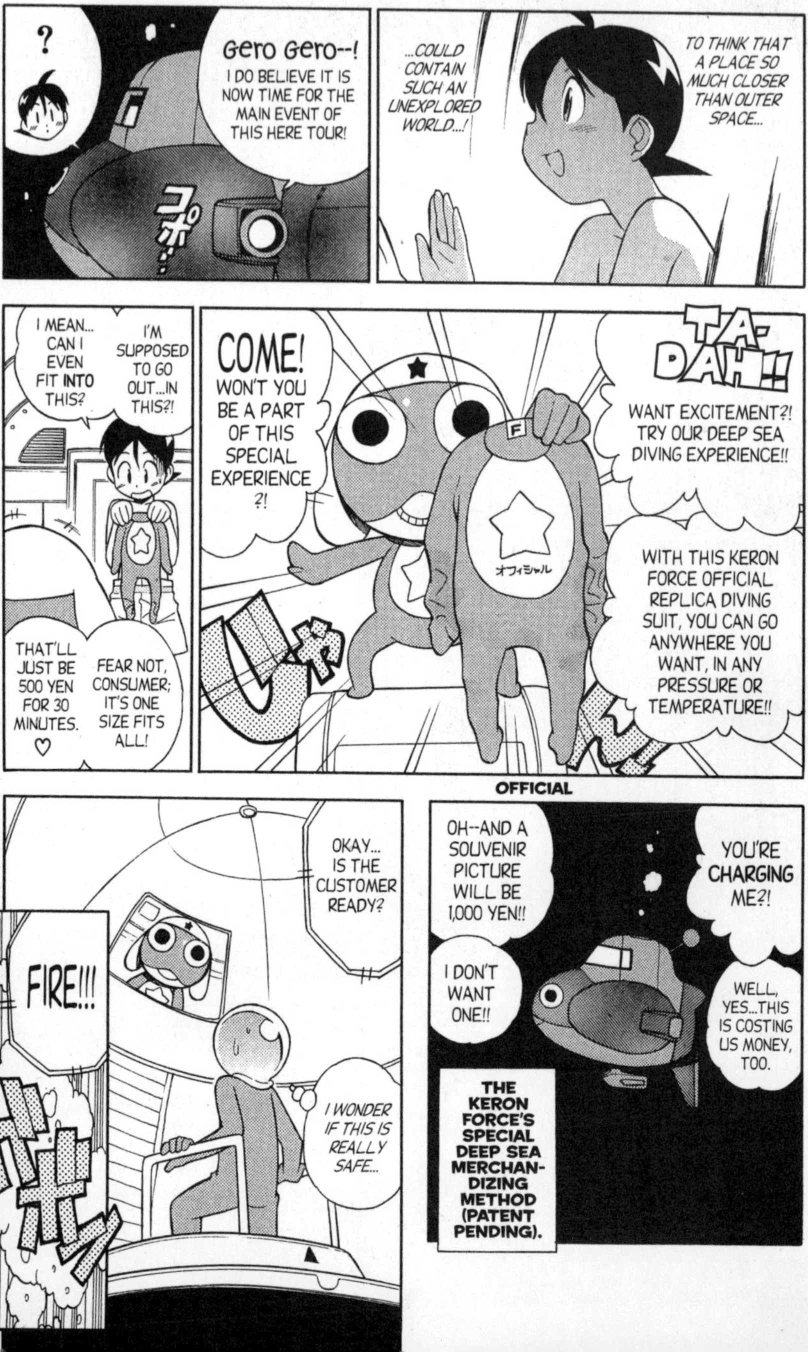
TO THINK THAT A PLACE SO MUCH CLOSER THAN OUTER SPACE...
...COULD CONTAIN SUCH AN UNEXPLORED WORLD...!
Gero Gero--! I DO BELIEVE IT IS NOW TIME FOR THE MAIN EVENT OF THIS HERE TOUR!
?
TA-DAH!!
WANT EXCITEMENT?! TRY OUR DEEP SEA DIVING EXPERIENCE!!
WITH THIS KERON FORCE OFFICIAL REPLICA DIVING SUIT, YOU CAN GO ANYWHERE YOU WANT, IN ANY PRESSURE OR TEMPERATURE!!
COME! WON'T YOU BE A PART OF THIS SPECIAL EXPERIENCE?!
オフィシャル
I'M SUPPOSED TO GO OUT...IN THIS?!
I MEAN... CAN I EVEN FIT INTO THIS?
FEAR NOT, CONSUMER; IT'S ONE SIZE FITS ALL!
THAT'LL JUST BE 500 YEN FOR 30 MINUTES. ♡
OFFICIAL
YOU'RE CHARGING ME?!
OH--AND A SOUVENIR PICTURE WILL BE 1,000 YEN!!
WELL, YES...THIS IS COSTING US MONEY, TOO.
I DON'T WANT ONE!!
THE KERON FORCE'S SPECIAL DEEP SEA MERCHANDIZING METHOD (PATENT PENDING).
OKAY... IS THE CUSTOMER READY?
FIRE!!!
I WONDER IF THIS IS REALLY SAFE...

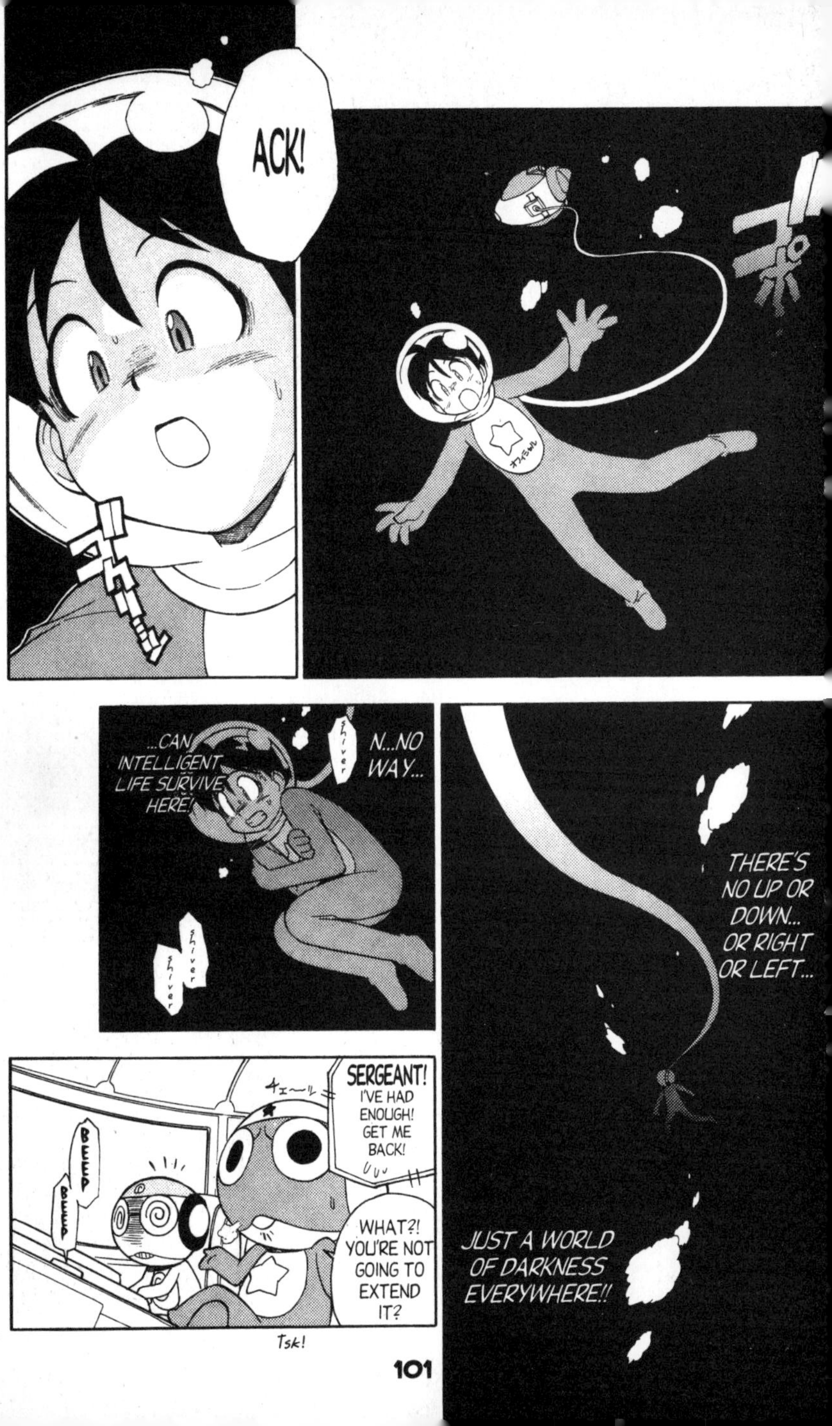
ACK!
THERE'S NO UP OR DOWN... OR RIGHT OR LEFT...
JUST A WORLD OF DARKNESS EVERYWHERE!!
N...NO WAY...
...CAN INTELLIGENT LIFE SURVIVE HERE!?
shiver
shiver shiver
SERGEANT! I'VE HAD ENOUGH! GET ME BACK!
WHAT?! YOU'RE NOT GOING TO EXTEND IT?
BEEP
BEEP
Tsk!

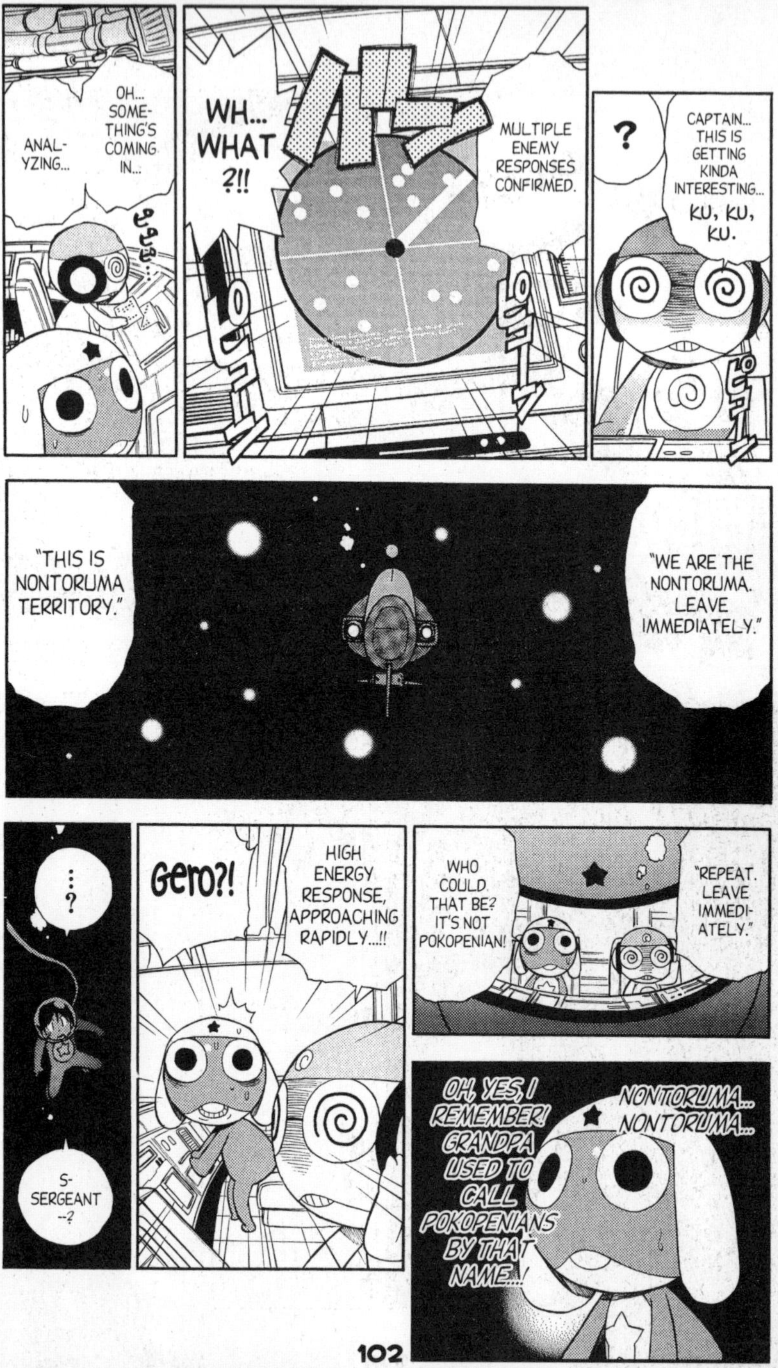
?
CAPTAIN... THIS IS GETTING KINDA INTERESTING... KU, KU, KU.
MULTIPLE ENEMY RESPONSES CONFIRMED.
WH... WHAT ?!!
OH... SOME-THING'S COMING IN...
ANAL-YZING...
"WE ARE THE NONTORUMA. LEAVE IMMEDIATELY."
"THIS IS NONTORUMA TERRITORY."
"REPEAT. LEAVE IMMEDI-ATELY."
WHO COULD THAT BE? IT'S NOT POKOPENIAN!
NONTORUMA... NONTORUMA...
OH, YES, I REMEMBER! GRANDPA USED TO CALL POKOPENIANS BY THAT NAME...!
HIGH ENERGY RESPONSE, APPROACHING RAPIDLY...!!
Gero?!
...?
S-SERGEANT--?

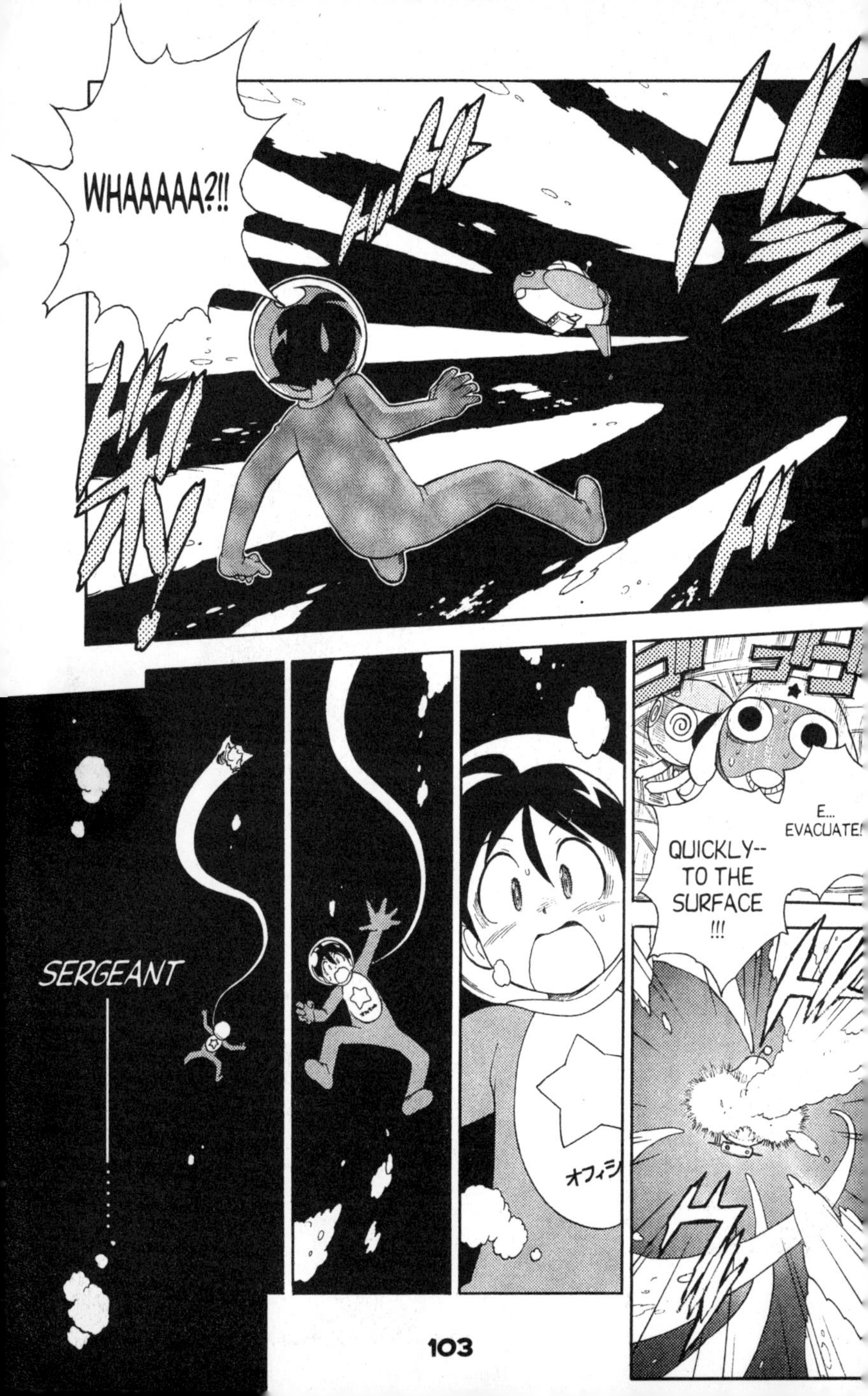
WHAAAAA?!!
E... EVACUATE!
QUICKLY-- TO THE SURFACE !!!
オフィシ
SERGEANT ——......

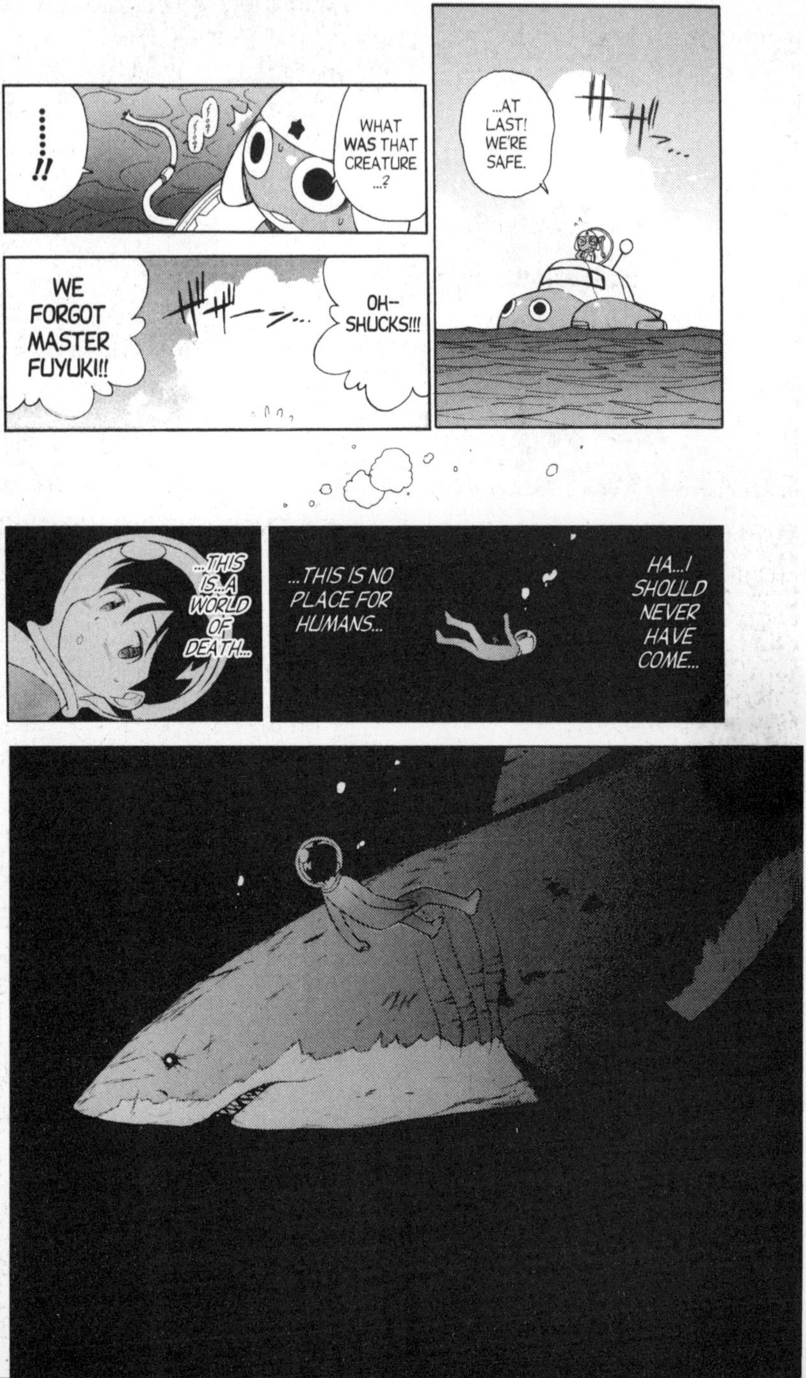
...AT LAST! WE'RE SAFE.
WHAT WAS THAT CREATURE ...?
......!!
OH- SHUCKS!!!
WE FORGOT MASTER FUYUKI!!
HA...I SHOULD NEVER HAVE COME...
...THIS IS NO PLACE FOR HUMANS...
...THIS IS...A WORLD OF DEATH...

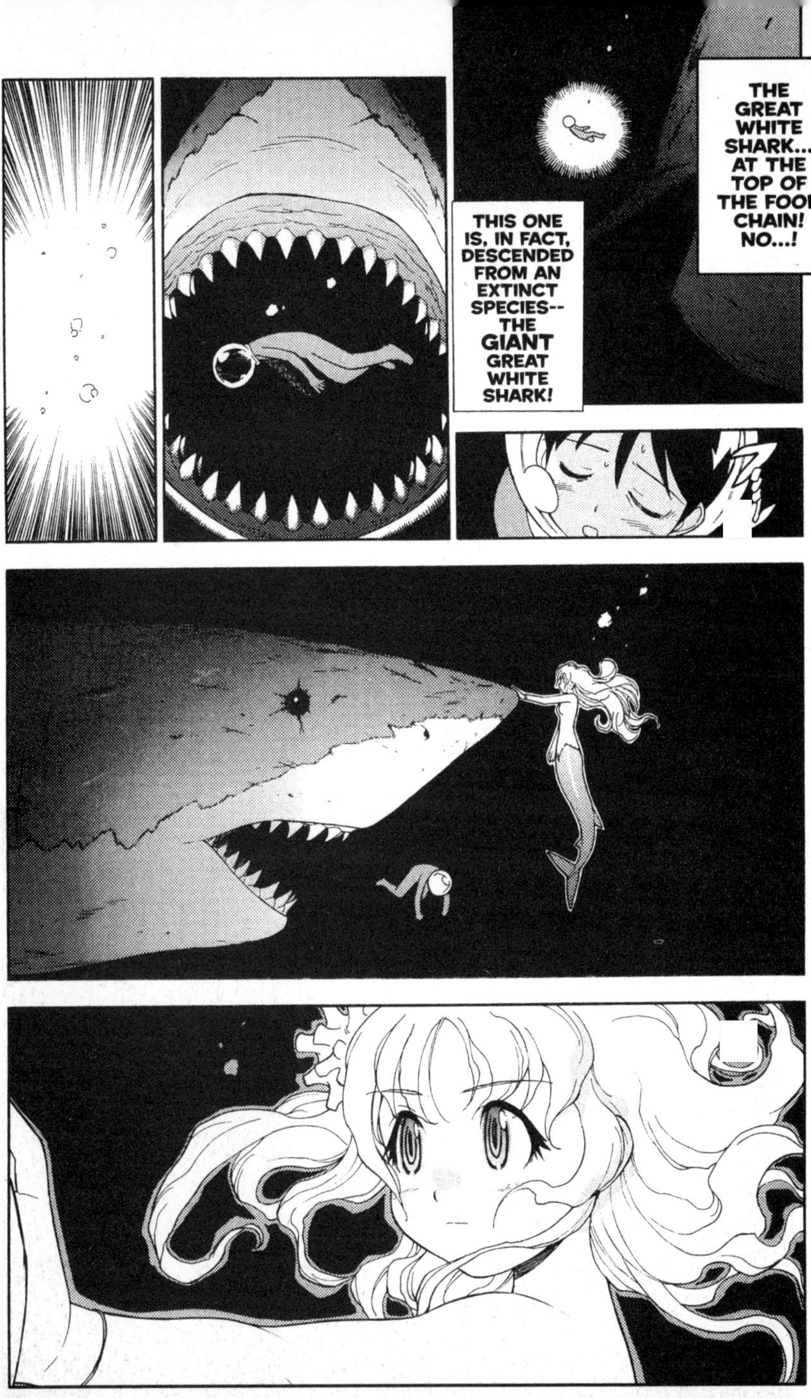
THE GREAT WHITE SHARK... AT THE TOP OF THE FOOD CHAIN! NO...!
THIS ONE IS, IN FACT, DESCENDED FROM AN EXTINCT SPECIES-- THE GIANT GREAT WHITE SHARK!

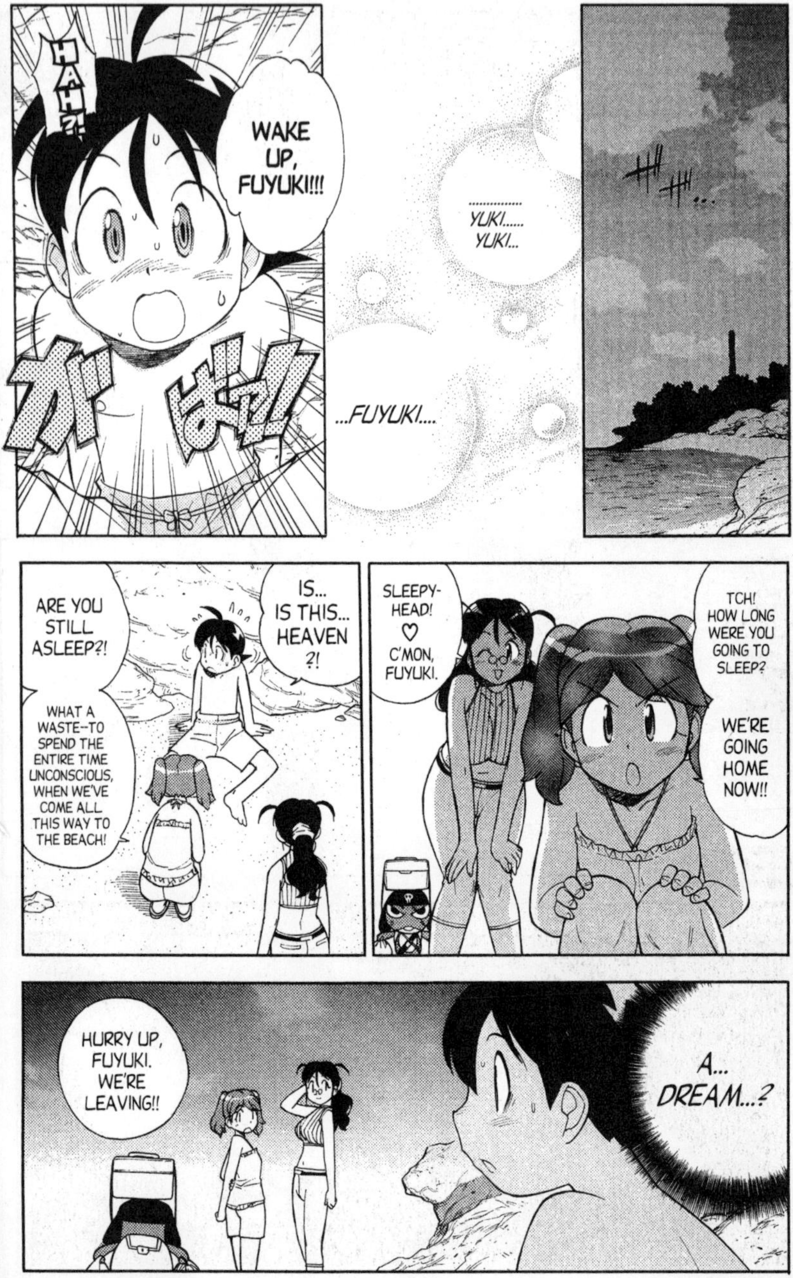

...............YUKI...... YUKI...
...FUYUKI....
WAKE UP, FUYUKI!!!
HAH?!
ガばっ
TCH! HOW LONG WERE YOU GOING TO SLEEP?
WE'RE GOING HOME NOW!!
SLEEPY-HEAD! ♡ C'MON, FUYUKI.
IS... IS THIS... HEAVEN?!
ARE YOU STILL ASLEEP?!
WHAT A WASTE--TO SPEND THE ENTIRE TIME UNCONSCIOUS, WHEN WE'VE COME ALL THIS WAY TO THE BEACH!
A... DREAM...?
HURRY UP, FUYUKI. WE'RE LEAVING!!

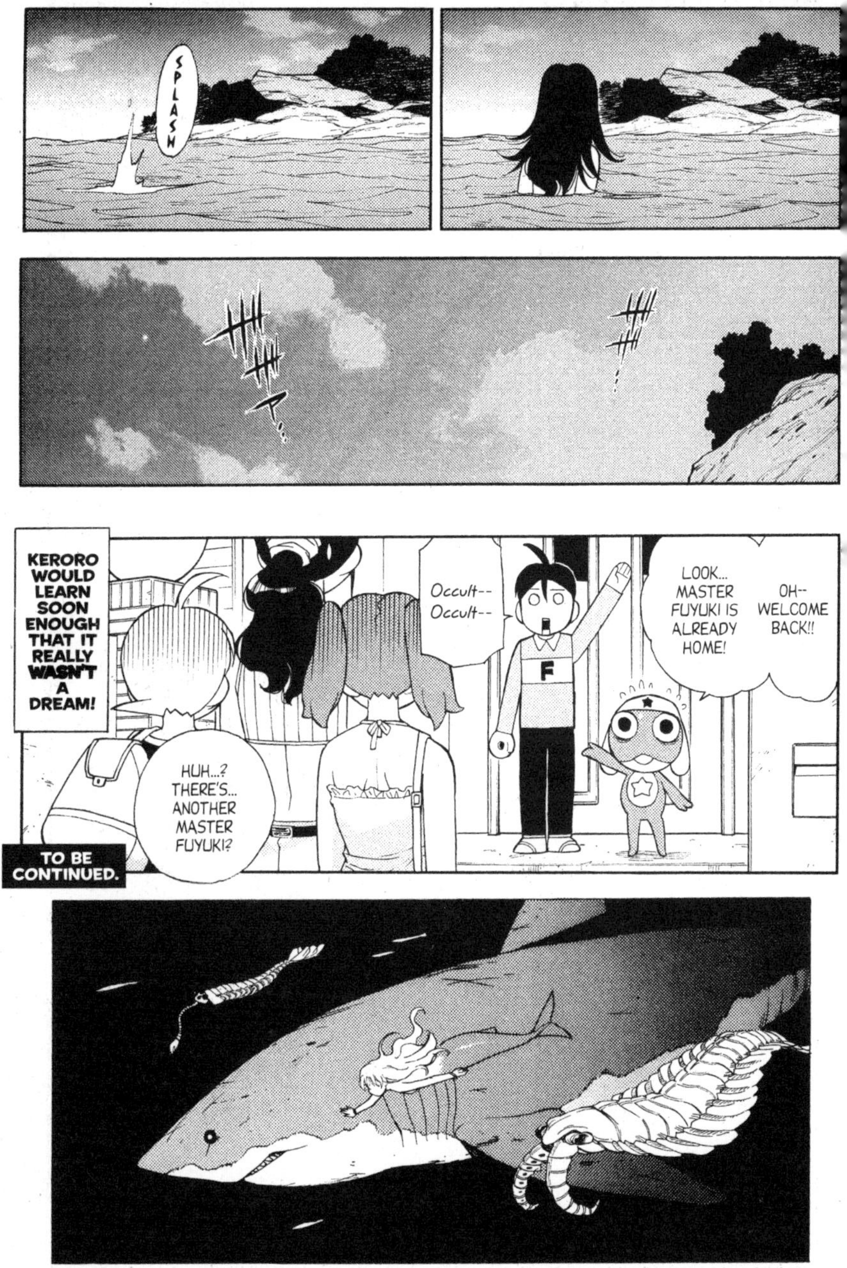
SPLASH
OH-- WELCOME BACK!!
LOOK... MASTER FUYUKI IS ALREADY HOME!
Occult-- Occult--
HUH...? THERE'S... ANOTHER MASTER FUYUKI?
KERORO WOULD LEARN SOON ENOUGH THAT IT REALLY WASN'T A DREAM!
TO BE CONTINUED.

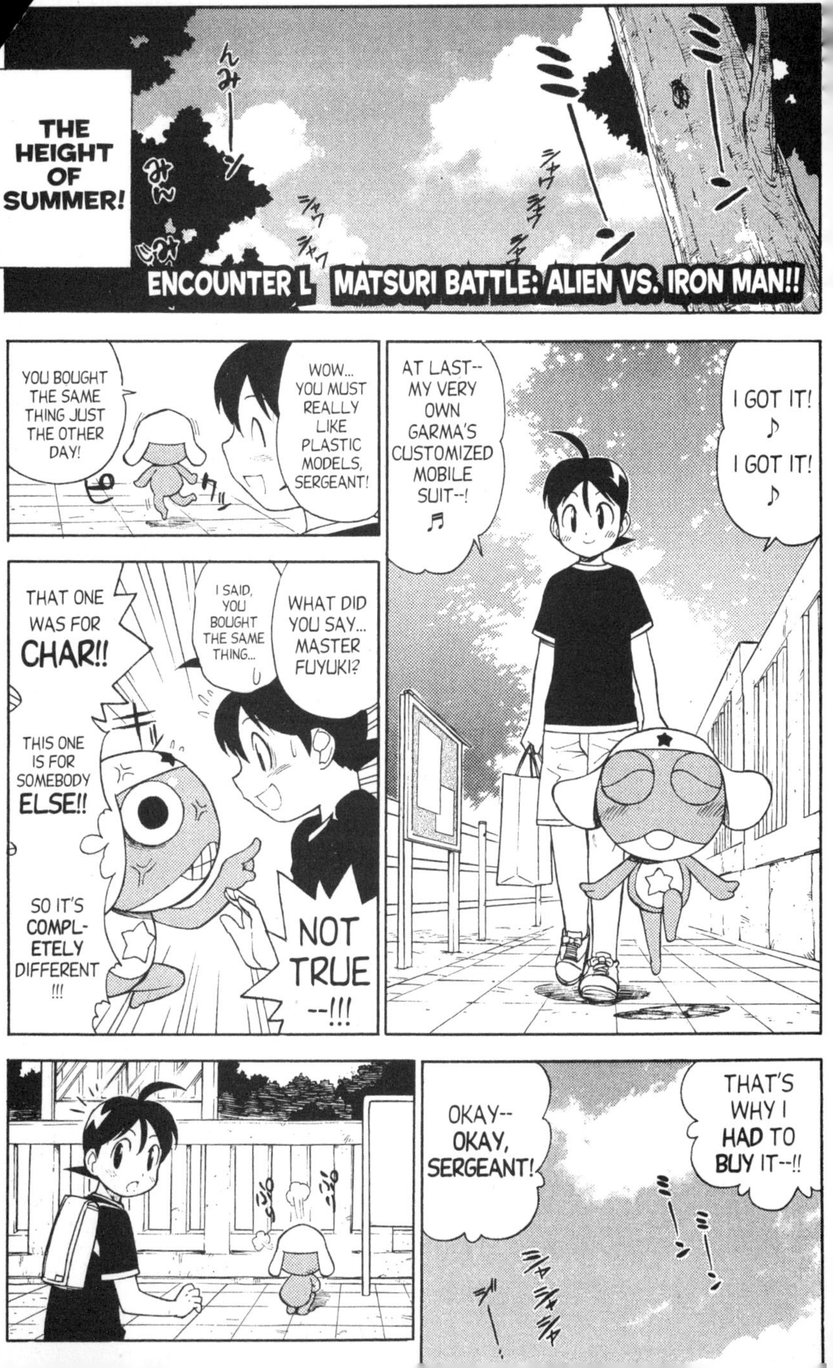
THE HEIGHT OF SUMMER!
ENCOUNTER L MATSURI BATTLE: ALIEN VS. IRON MAN!!
I GOT IT! ♪ I GOT IT! ♪
AT LAST-- MY VERY OWN GARMA'S CUSTOMIZED MOBILE SUIT--! ♬
WOW... YOU MUST REALLY LIKE PLASTIC MODELS, SERGEANT!
YOU BOUGHT THE SAME THING JUST THE OTHER DAY!
WHAT DID YOU SAY... MASTER FUYUKI?
I SAID, YOU BOUGHT THE SAME THING...
THAT ONE WAS FOR CHAR!!
THIS ONE IS FOR SOMEBODY ELSE!!
NOT TRUE--!!!
SO IT'S COMPL-ETELY DIFFERENT!!!
THAT'S WHY I HAD TO BUY IT--!!
OKAY-- OKAY, SERGEANT!

ENCOUNTER L MATSURI BATTLE: ALIEN VS. IRON MAN!!

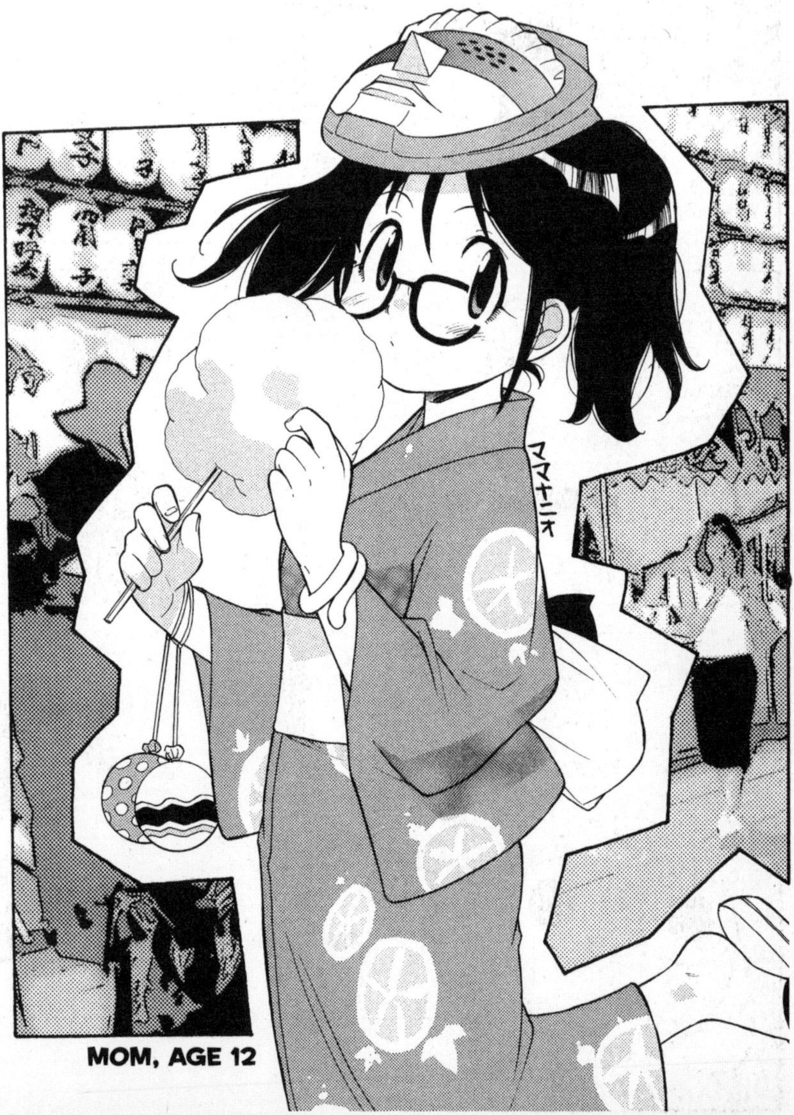

MOM, AGE 12

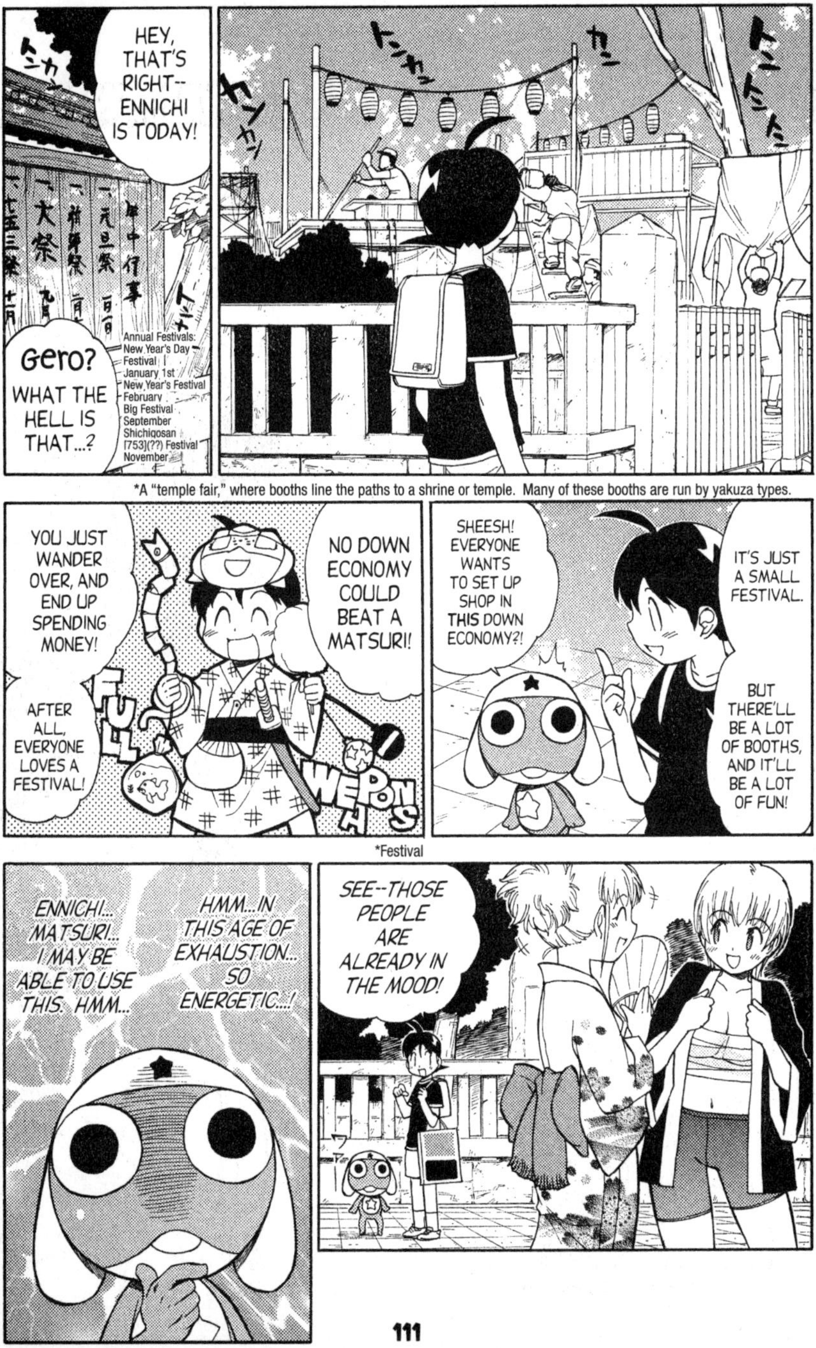
HEY, THAT'S RIGHT-- ENNICHI IS TODAY!
Annual Festivals: New Year's Day Festival January 1st New Year's Festival February Big Festival September Shichigosan [753](??) Festival November
Gero? WHAT THE HELL IS THAT...?
IT'S JUST A SMALL FESTIVAL.
SHEESH! EVERYONE WANTS TO SET UP SHOP IN THIS DOWN ECONOMY?!
BUT THERE'LL BE A LOT OF BOOTHS, AND IT'LL BE A LOT OF FUN!
NO DOWN ECONOMY COULD BEAT A MATSURI!
YOU JUST WANDER OVER, AND END UP SPENDING MONEY!
AFTER ALL, EVERYONE LOVES A FESTIVAL!
FULL
WEAPONS
SEE--THOSE PEOPLE ARE ALREADY IN THE MOOD!
HMM...IN THIS AGE OF EXHAUSTION... SO ENERGETIC...!
ENNICHI... MATSURI... I MAY BE ABLE TO USE THIS. HMM...

*A "temple fair," where booths line the paths to a shrine or temple. Many of these booths are run by yakuza types.

*Festival

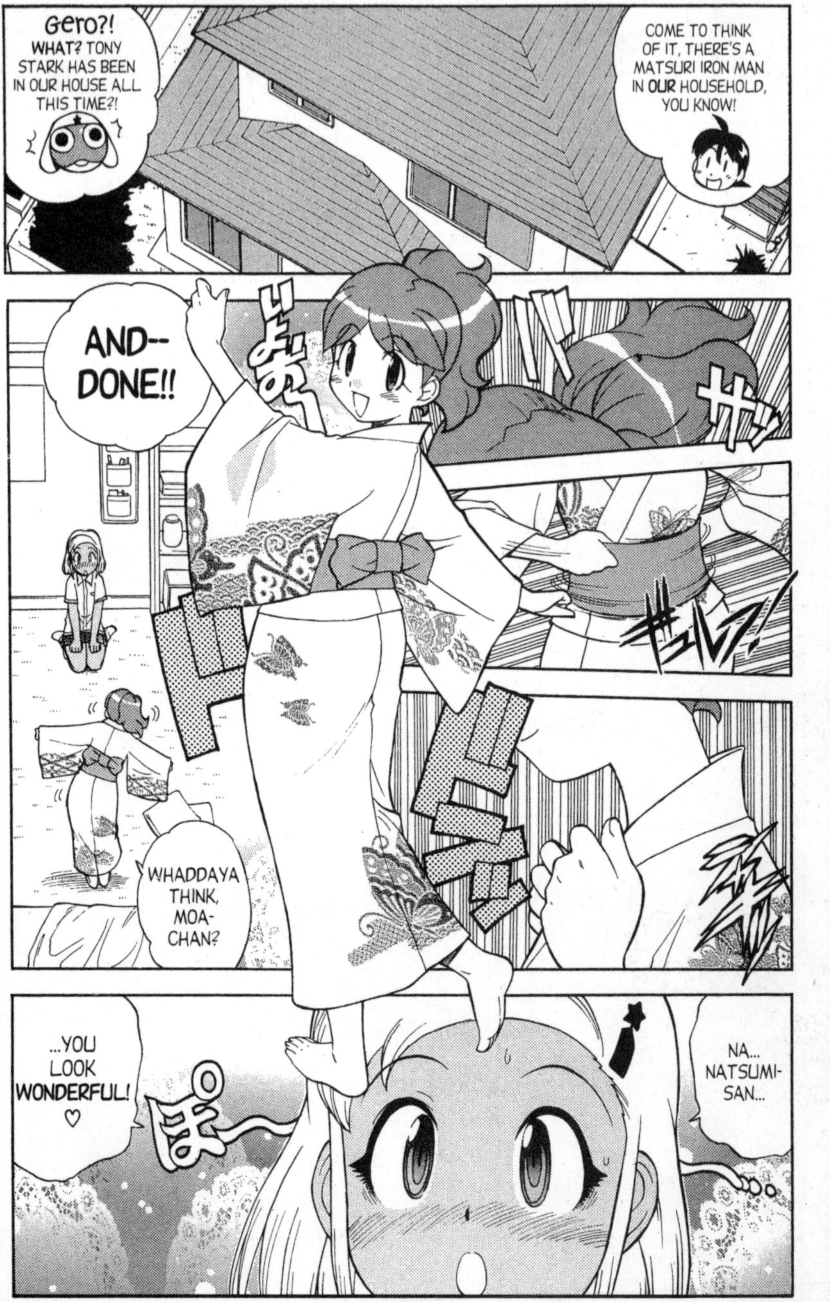
COME TO THINK OF IT, THERE'S A MATSURI IRON MAN IN OUR HOUSEHOLD, YOU KNOW!
Gero?! WHAT? TONY STARK HAS BEEN IN OUR HOUSE ALL THIS TIME?!
AND-- DONE!!
WHADDAYA THINK, MOA-CHAN?
NA... NATSUMI-SAN...
ぽ~
...YOU LOOK WONDERFUL! ♡

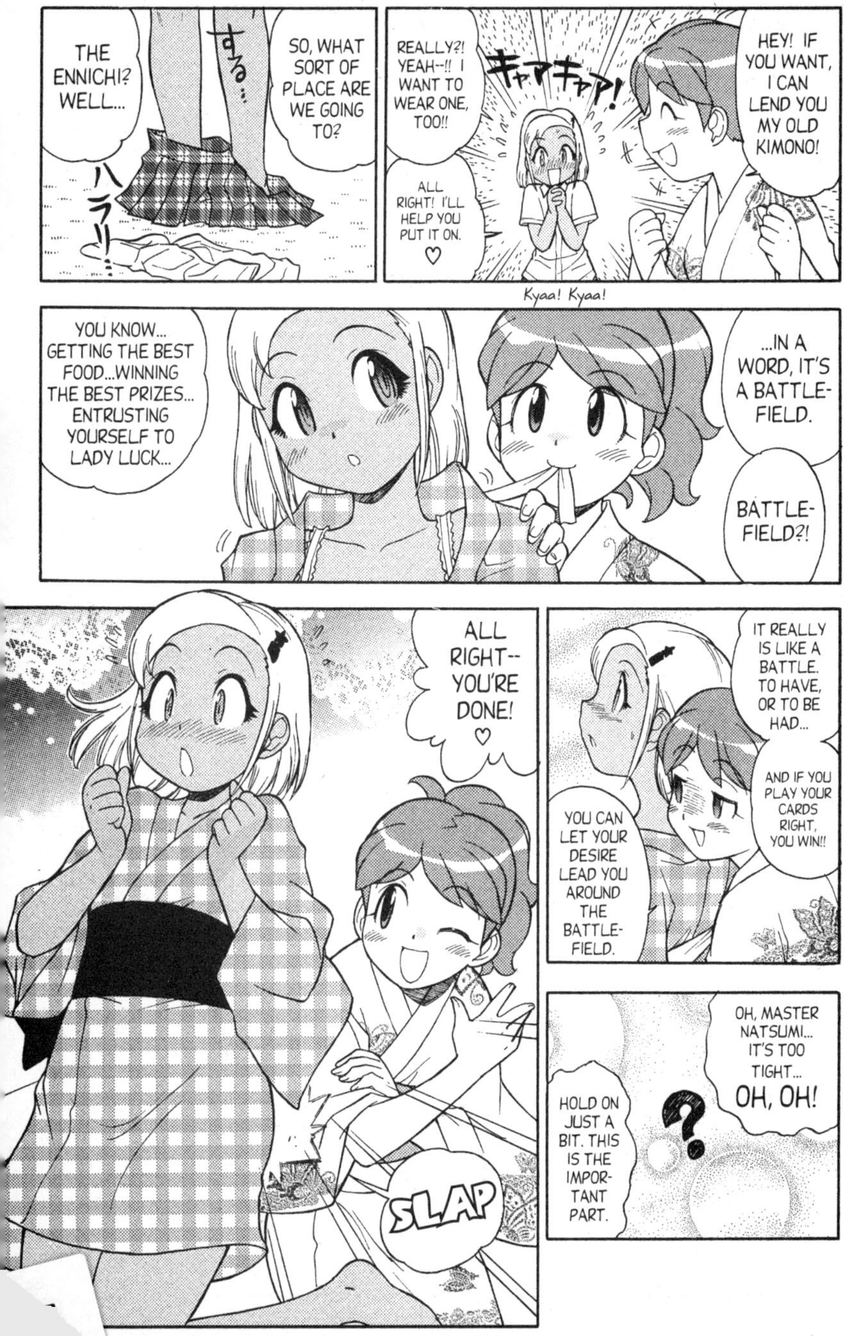
HEY! IF YOU WANT, I CAN LEND YOU MY OLD KIMONO!
REALLY?! YEAH--!! I WANT TO WEAR ONE, TOO!!
キャアキャア!
ALL RIGHT! I'LL HELP YOU PUT IT ON. ♡
Kyaa! Kyaa!
SO, WHAT SORT OF PLACE ARE WE GOING TO?
THE ENNICHI? WELL...
する…
ハラリ…
...IN A WORD, IT'S A BATTLE-FIELD.
BATTLE-FIELD?!
YOU KNOW... GETTING THE BEST FOOD...WINNING THE BEST PRIZES... ENTRUSTING YOURSELF TO LADY LUCK...
IT REALLY IS LIKE A BATTLE. TO HAVE, OR TO BE HAD...
AND IF YOU PLAY YOUR CARDS RIGHT, YOU WIN!!
YOU CAN LET YOUR DESIRE LEAD YOU AROUND THE BATTLE-FIELD.
OH, MASTER NATSUMI... IT'S TOO TIGHT... OH, OH!
?
HOLD ON JUST A BIT. THIS IS THE IMPOR-TANT PART.
ALL RIGHT-- YOU'RE DONE! ♡
SLAP

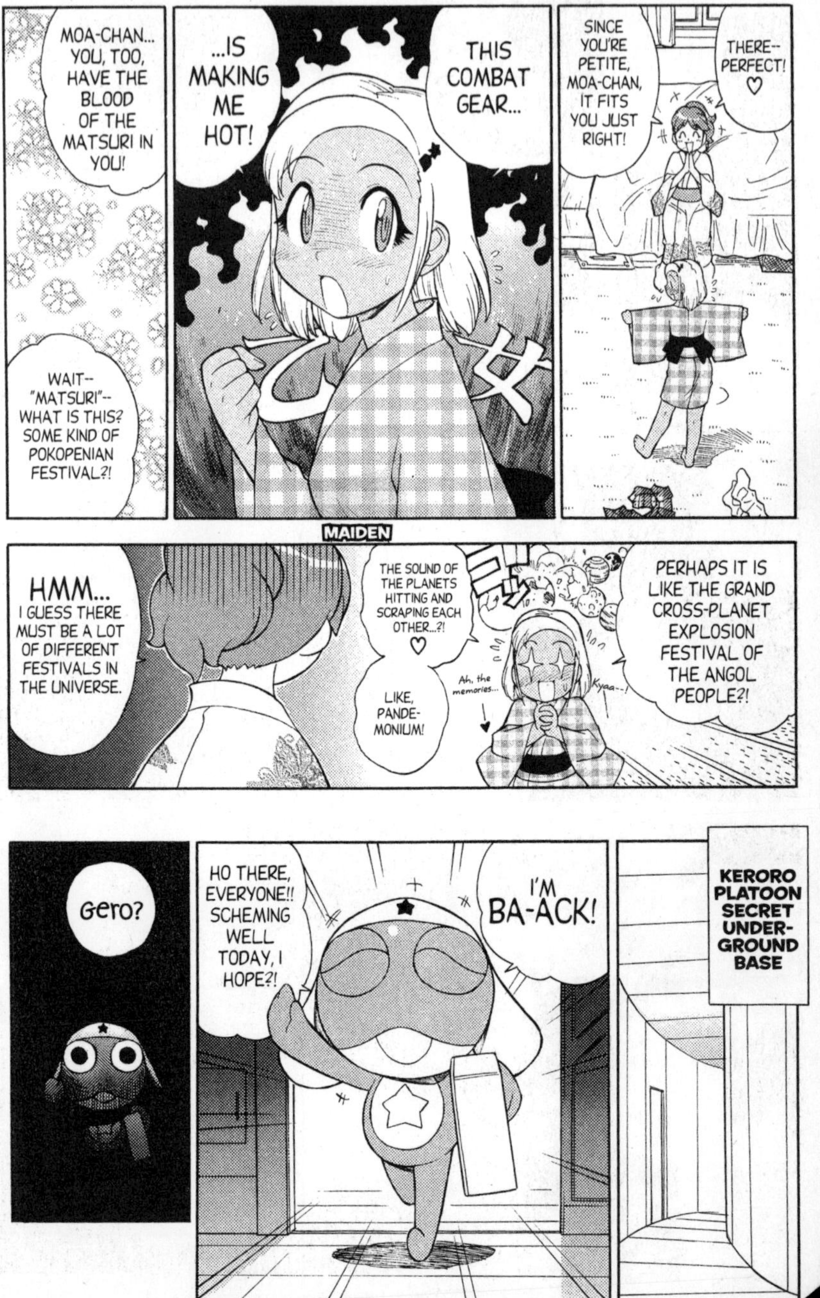
THERE-- PERFECT! ♡
SINCE YOU'RE PETITE, MOA-CHAN, IT FITS YOU JUST RIGHT!
THIS COMBAT GEAR...
...IS MAKING ME HOT!
MOA-CHAN... YOU, TOO, HAVE THE BLOOD OF THE MATSURI IN YOU!
WAIT-- "MATSURI"-- WHAT IS THIS? SOME KIND OF POKOPENIAN FESTIVAL?!
MAIDEN
PERHAPS IT IS LIKE THE GRAND CROSS-PLANET EXPLOSION FESTIVAL OF THE ANGOL PEOPLE?!
Kyaa--!
Ah, the memories...
THE SOUND OF THE PLANETS HITTING AND SCRAPING EACH OTHER...?! ♡
LIKE, PANDE-MONIUM!
HMM... I GUESS THERE MUST BE A LOT OF DIFFERENT FESTIVALS IN THE UNIVERSE.
KERORO PLATOON SECRET UNDER-GROUND BASE
I'M BA-ACK!
HO THERE, EVERYONE!! SCHEMING WELL TODAY, I HOPE?!
Gero?

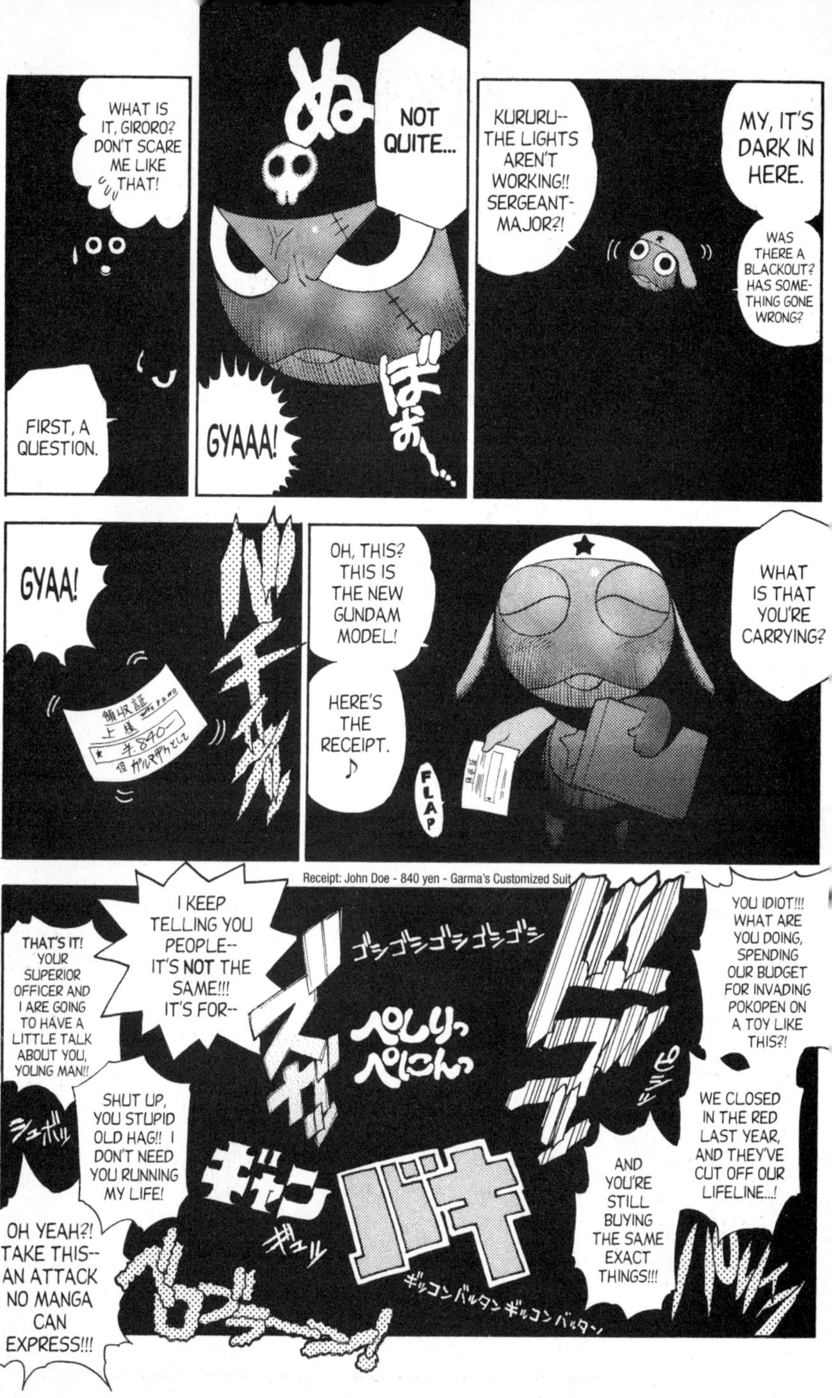
MY, IT'S DARK IN HERE.
WAS THERE A BLACKOUT? HAS SOME-THING GONE WRONG?
KURURU-- THE LIGHTS AREN'T WORKING!! SERGEANT-MAJOR?!
ぬ
NOT QUITE...
GYAAA!
WHAT IS IT, GIRORO? DON'T SCARE ME LIKE THAT!
FIRST, A QUESTION.
WHAT IS THAT YOU'RE CARRYING?
OH, THIS? THIS IS THE NEW GUNDAM MODEL!
HERE'S THE RECEIPT. ♪
FLAP
GYAA!
Receipt: John Doe - 840 yen - Garma's Customized Suit
YOU IDIOT!!! WHAT ARE YOU DOING, SPENDING OUR BUDGET FOR INVADING POKOPEN ON A TOY LIKE THIS?!
WE CLOSED IN THE RED LAST YEAR, AND THEY'VE CUT OFF OUR LIFELINE...!
AND YOU'RE STILL BUYING THE SAME EXACT THINGS!!!
ゴシゴシゴシゴシゴシ
I KEEP TELLING YOU PEOPLE-- IT'S NOT THE SAME!!! IT'S FOR--
THAT'S IT! YOUR SUPERIOR OFFICER AND I ARE GOING TO HAVE A LITTLE TALK ABOUT YOU, YOUNG MAN!!
ぺしりっ ぺにんっ
バキ
ギッコンバッタンギッコンバッタン
SHUT UP, YOU STUPID OLD HAG!! I DON'T NEED YOU RUNNING MY LIFE!
OH YEAH?! TAKE THIS-- AN ATTACK NO MANGA CAN EXPRESS!!!

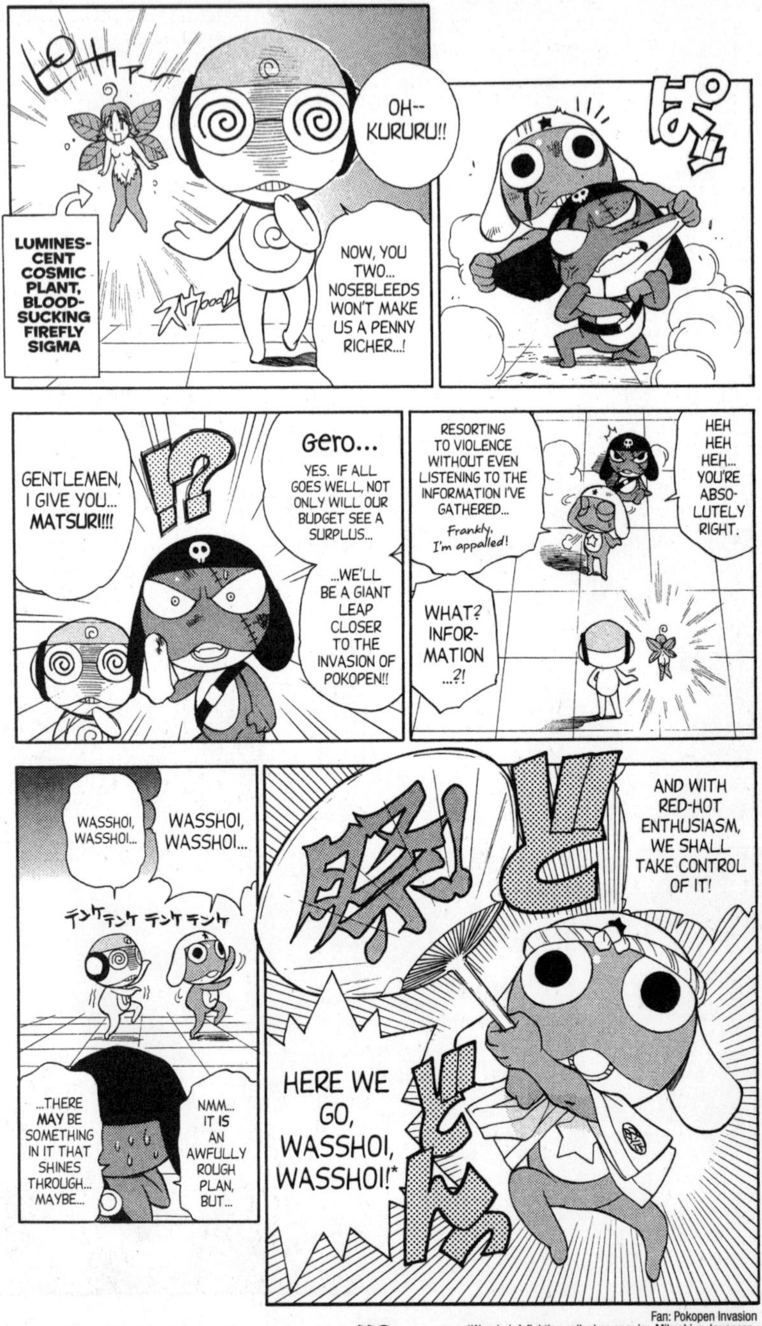
ぱッ
OH-- KURURU!!
NOW, YOU TWO... NOSEBLEEDS WON'T MAKE US A PENNY RICHER...!
ピカァー
LUMINESCENT COSMIC PLANT, BLOOD-SUCKING FIREFLY SIGMA
HEH HEH HEH... YOU'RE ABSOLUTELY RIGHT.
RESORTING TO VIOLENCE WITHOUT EVEN LISTENING TO THE INFORMATION I'VE GATHERED...
Frankly, I'm appalled!
WHAT? INFORMATION ...?!
Gero...
YES. IF ALL GOES WELL, NOT ONLY WILL OUR BUDGET SEE A SURPLUS...
...WE'LL BE A GIANT LEAP CLOSER TO THE INVASION OF POKOPEN!!
!?
GENTLEMEN, I GIVE YOU... MATSURI!!!
AND WITH RED-HOT ENTHUSIASM, WE SHALL TAKE CONTROL OF IT!
祭
HERE WE GO, WASSHOI, WASSHOI!*
WASSHOI, WASSHOI...
WASSHOI, WASSHOI...
テンケテンケ テンケ テンケ
NMM... IT IS AN AWFULLY ROUGH PLAN, BUT...
...THERE MAY BE SOMETHING IN IT THAT SHINES THROUGH... MAYBE...

Fan: Pokopen Invasion

*Wasshoi: A fighting call when carrying Mikoshi, a Japanese-style float carried in parades at Matsuri.

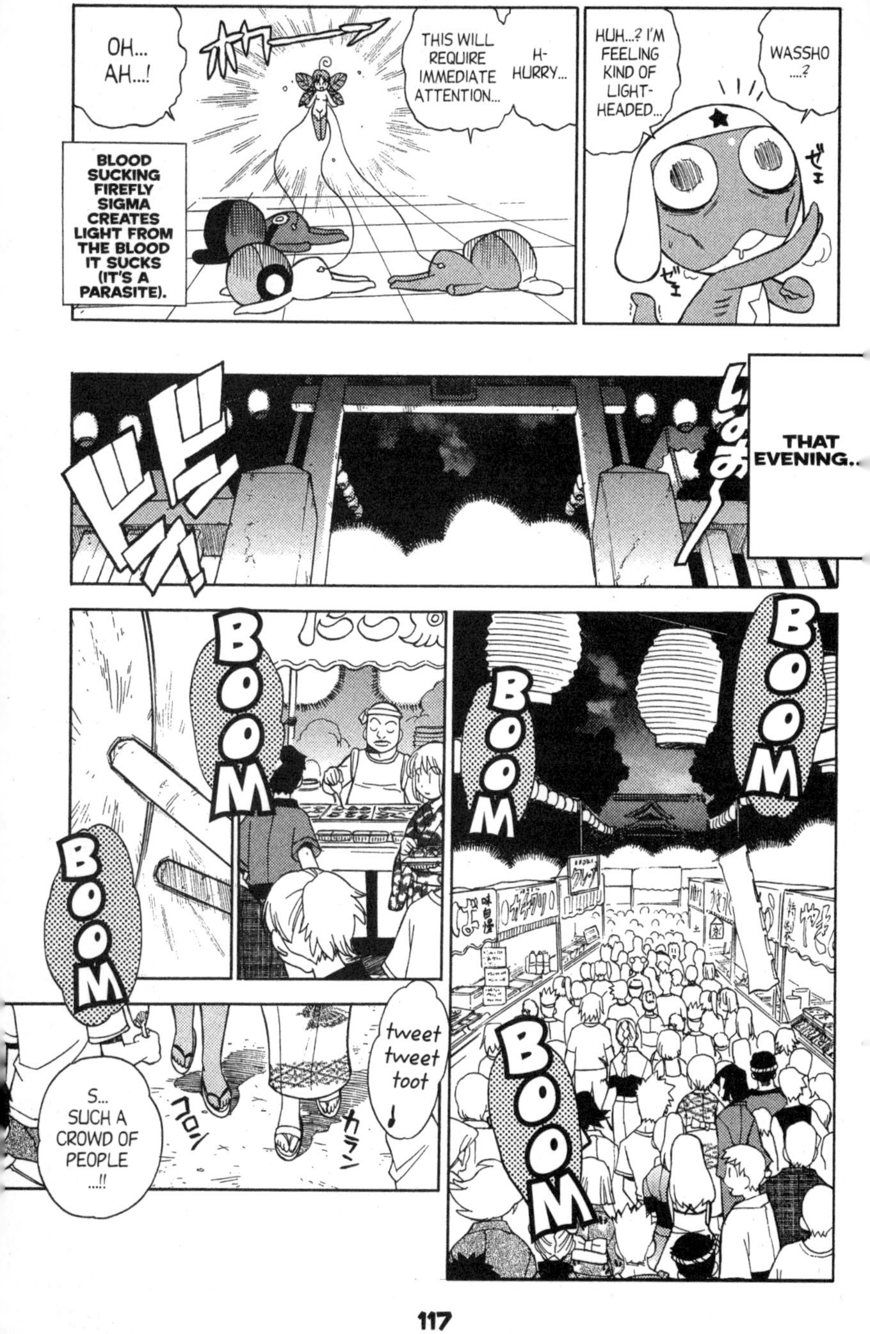
WASSHO ...?
HUH...? I'M FEELING KIND OF LIGHT-HEADED...
H-HURRY...
THIS WILL REQUIRE IMMEDIATE ATTENTION...
OH... AH...!
BLOOD SUCKING FIREFLY SIGMA CREATES LIGHT FROM THE BLOOD IT SUCKS (IT'S A PARASITE).
THAT EVENING...
BOOM
BOOM
BOOM
BOOM
BOOM
tweet tweet toot
S... SUCH A CROWD OF PEOPLE ...!!

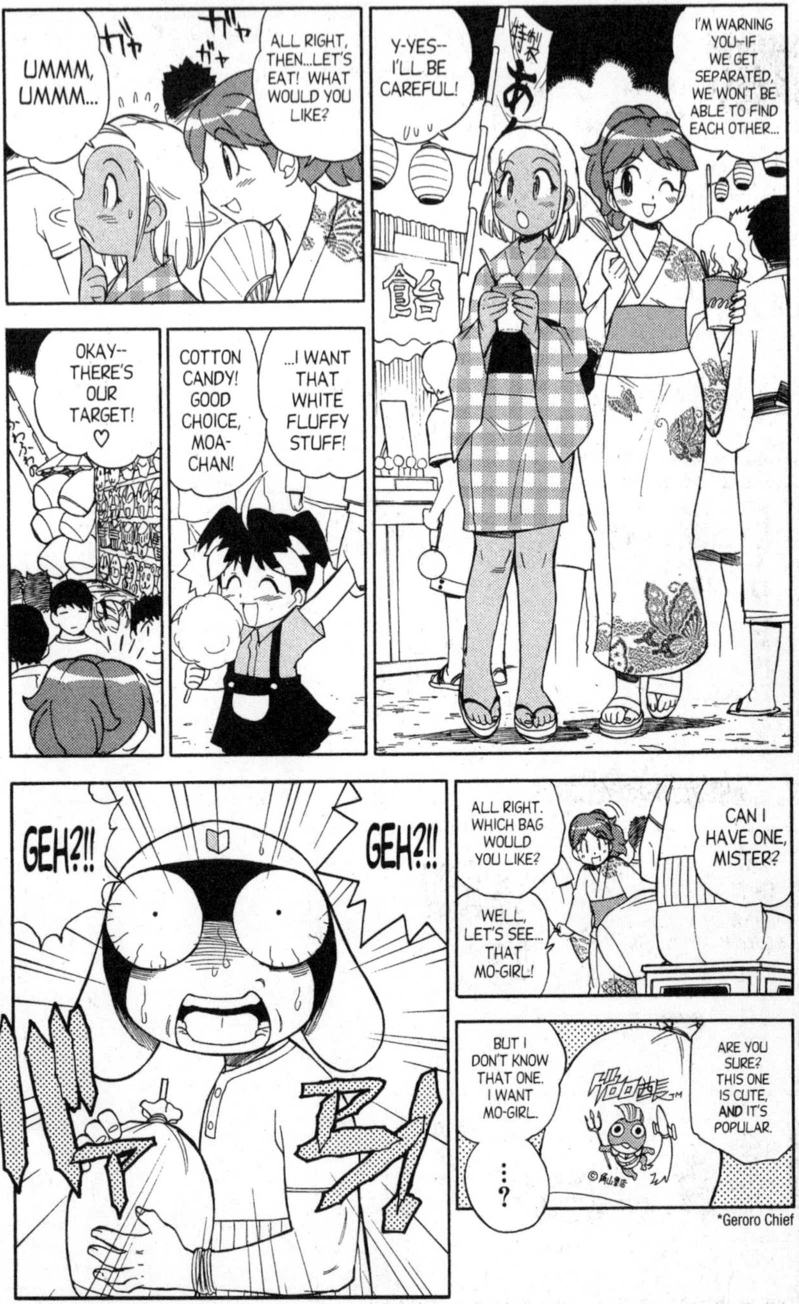
I'M WARNING YOU--IF WE GET SEPARATED, WE WON'T BE ABLE TO FIND EACH OTHER...
Y-YES-- I'LL BE CAREFUL!
ALL RIGHT, THEN...LET'S EAT! WHAT WOULD YOU LIKE?
ガヤ
ガヤ
ガヤ
UMMM, UMMM...
...I WANT THAT WHITE FLUFFY STUFF!
COTTON CANDY! GOOD CHOICE, MOA-CHAN!
OKAY-- THERE'S OUR TARGET! ♡
CAN I HAVE ONE, MISTER?
ALL RIGHT. WHICH BAG WOULD YOU LIKE?
WELL, LET'S SEE... THAT MO-GIRL!
ARE YOU SURE? THIS ONE IS CUTE, AND IT'S POPULAR.
BUT I DON'T KNOW THAT ONE. I WANT MO-GIRL.
...?
GEH?!!
GEH?!!
*Geroro Chief

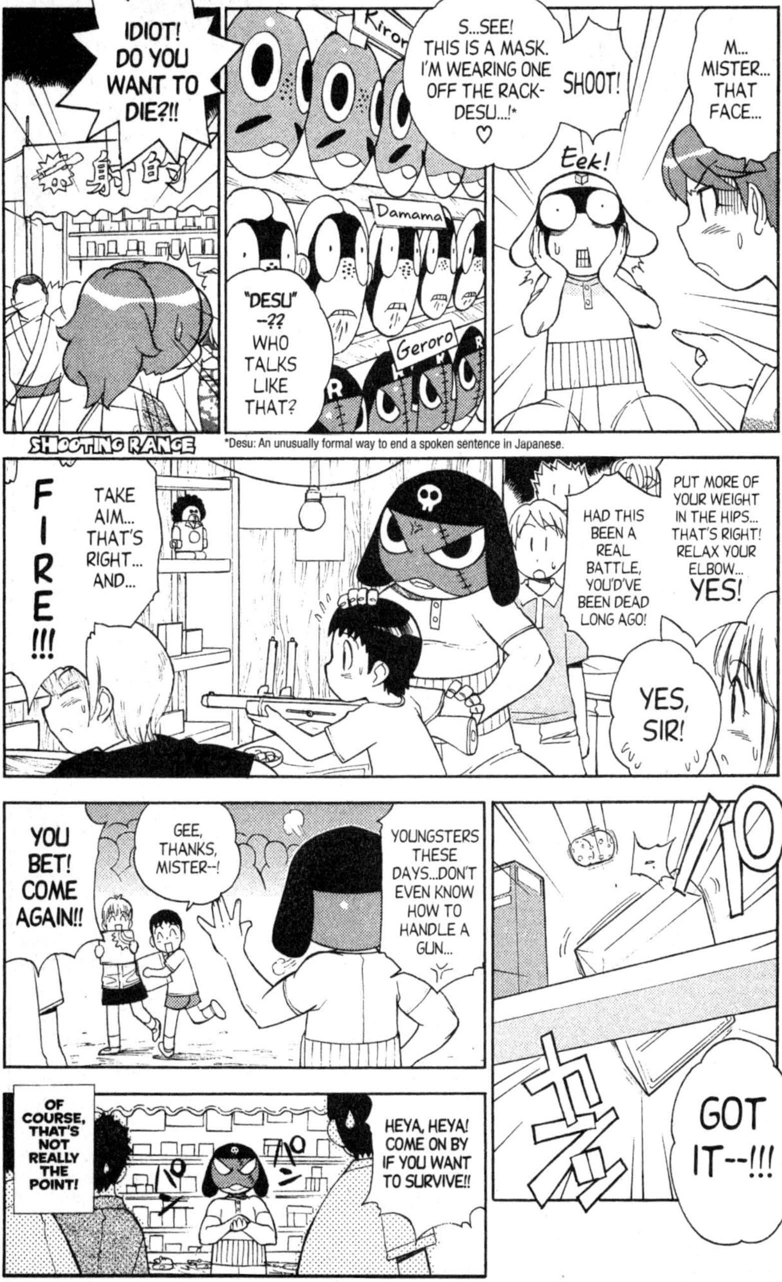
M... MISTER... THAT FACE...
Eek!
SHOOT!
S...SEE! THIS IS A MASK. I'M WEARING ONE OFF THE RACK-DESU...!* ♡
Kiron
Damama
Geroro
"DESU" --?? WHO TALKS LIKE THAT?
IDIOT! DO YOU WANT TO DIE?!!
SHOOTING RANGE
PUT MORE OF YOUR WEIGHT IN THE HIPS... THAT'S RIGHT! RELAX YOUR ELBOW... YES!
HAD THIS BEEN A REAL BATTLE, YOU'D'VE BEEN DEAD LONG AGO!
YES, SIR!
TAKE AIM... THAT'S RIGHT... AND...
FIRE!!!
GOT IT--!!!
YOUNGSTERS THESE DAYS...DON'T EVEN KNOW HOW TO HANDLE A GUN...
GEE, THANKS, MISTER--!
YOU BET! COME AGAIN!!
HEYA, HEYA! COME ON BY IF YOU WANT TO SURVIVE!!
OF COURSE, THAT'S NOT REALLY THE POINT!

*Desu: An unusually formal way to end a spoken sentence in Japanese.

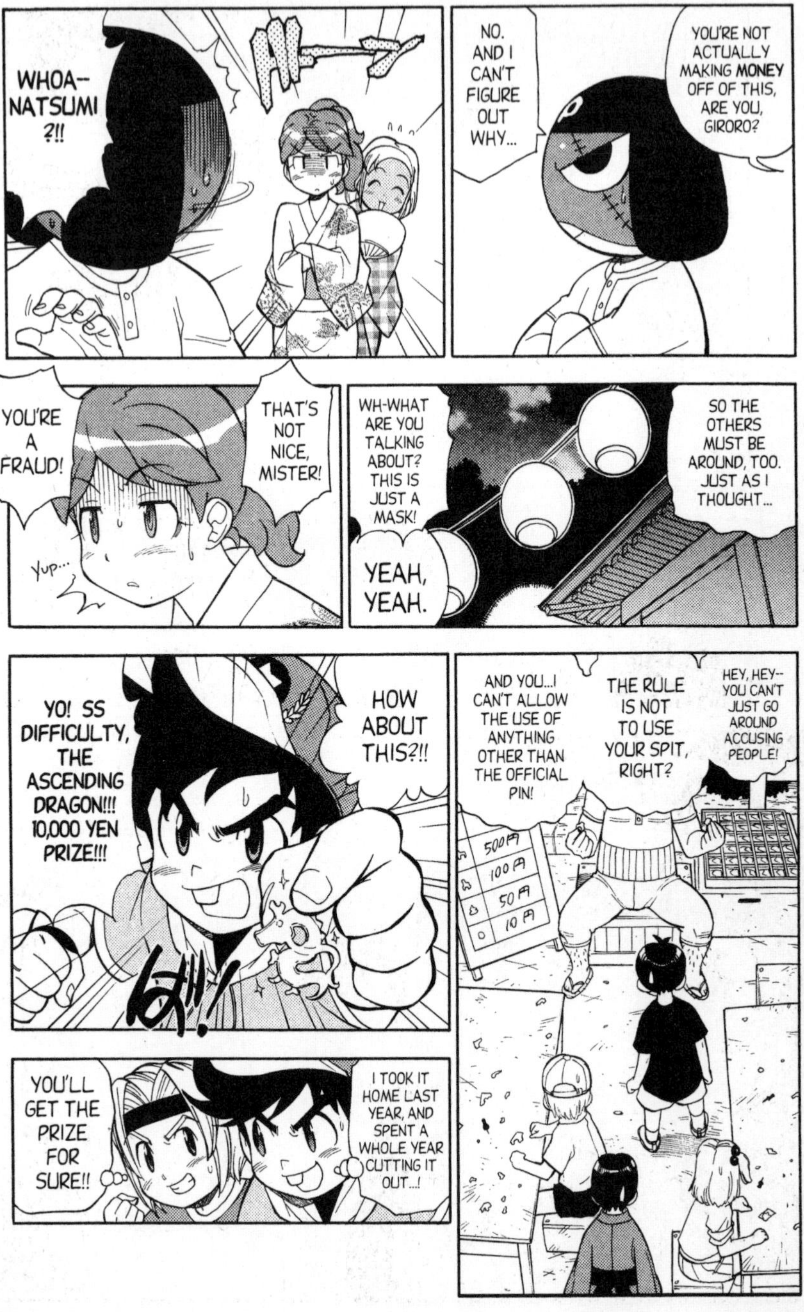
YOU'RE NOT ACTUALLY MAKING MONEY OFF OF THIS, ARE YOU, GIRORO?
NO. AND I CAN'T FIGURE OUT WHY...
WHOA-- NATSUMI?!!
SO THE OTHERS MUST BE AROUND, TOO. JUST AS I THOUGHT...
WH-WHAT ARE YOU TALKING ABOUT? THIS IS JUST A MASK!
YEAH, YEAH.
THAT'S NOT NICE, MISTER!
YOU'RE A FRAUD!
Yup...
HEY, HEY-- YOU CAN'T JUST GO AROUND ACCUSING PEOPLE!
THE RULE IS NOT TO USE YOUR SPIT, RIGHT?
AND YOU...I CAN'T ALLOW THE USE OF ANYTHING OTHER THAN THE OFFICIAL PIN!
500円
100円
50円
10円
HOW ABOUT THIS?!!
YO! SS DIFFICULTY, THE ASCENDING DRAGON!!! 10,000 YEN PRIZE!!!
I TOOK IT HOME LAST YEAR, AND SPENT A WHOLE YEAR CUTTING IT OUT...!
YOU'LL GET THE PRIZE FOR SURE!!

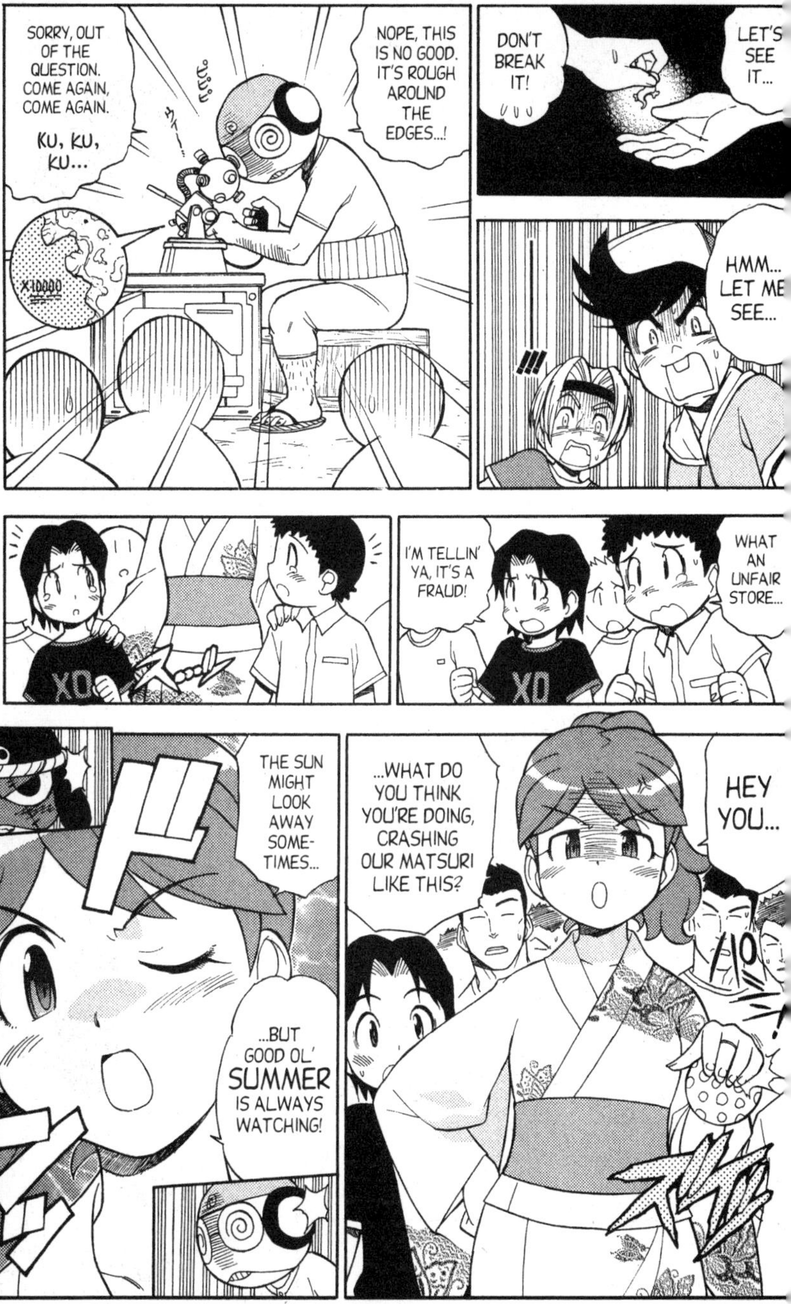
LET'S SEE IT...
DON'T BREAK IT!
HMM... LET ME SEE...
NOPE, THIS IS NO GOOD. IT'S ROUGH AROUND THE EDGES...!
SORRY, OUT OF THE QUESTION. COME AGAIN, COME AGAIN.
KU, KU, KU...
X10000
WHAT AN UNFAIR STORE...
I'M TELLIN' YA, IT'S A FRAUD!
HEY YOU...
...WHAT DO YOU THINK YOU'RE DOING, CRASHING OUR MATSURI LIKE THIS?
THE SUN MIGHT LOOK AWAY SOMETIMES...
...BUT GOOD OL' SUMMER IS ALWAYS WATCHING!

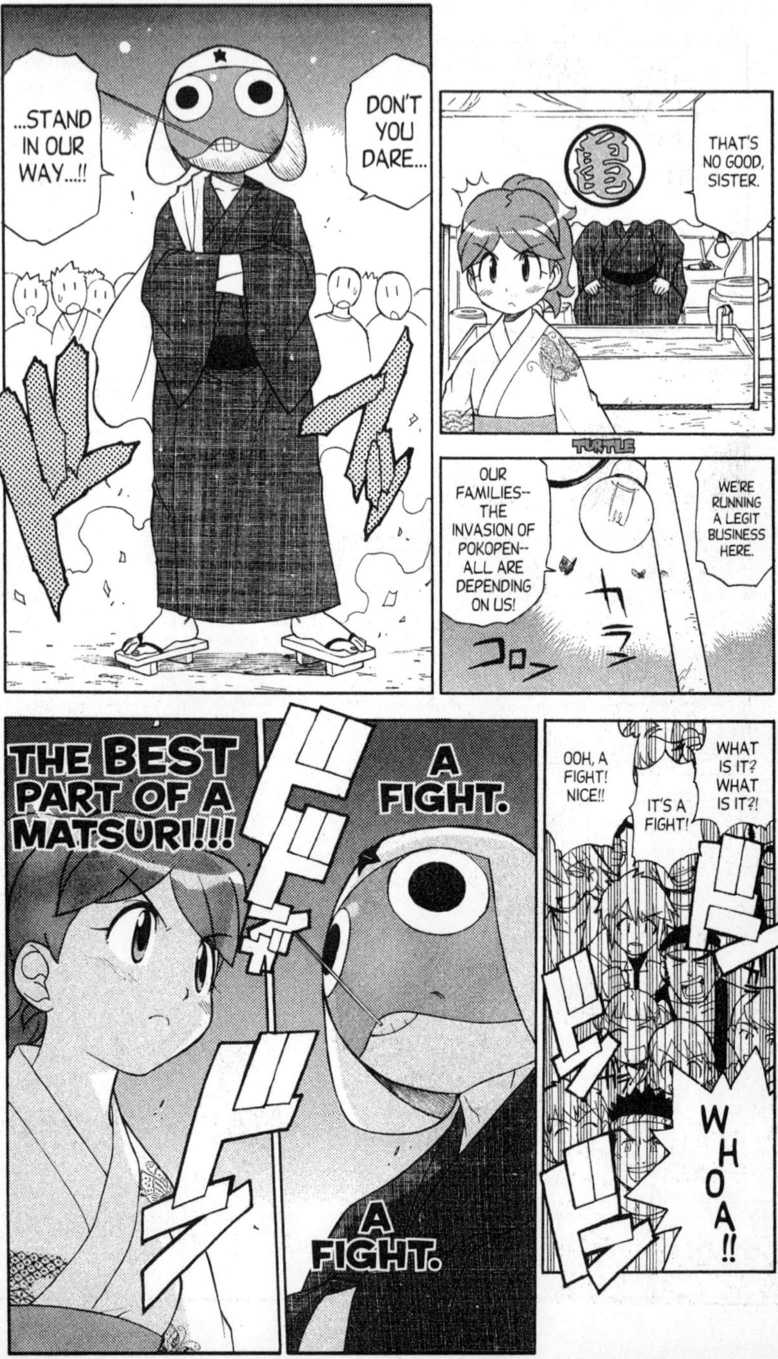
THAT'S NO GOOD, SISTER.
TURTLE
WE'RE RUNNING A LEGIT BUSINESS HERE.
OUR FAMILIES-- THE INVASION OF POKOPEN-- ALL ARE DEPENDING ON US!
カラ
コロッ
DON'T YOU DARE...
...STAND IN OUR WAY...!!
WHAT IS IT? WHAT IS IT?!
IT'S A FIGHT!
OOH, A FIGHT! NICE!!
WHOA!!
A FIGHT.
A FIGHT.
THE BEST PART OF A MATSURI!!!

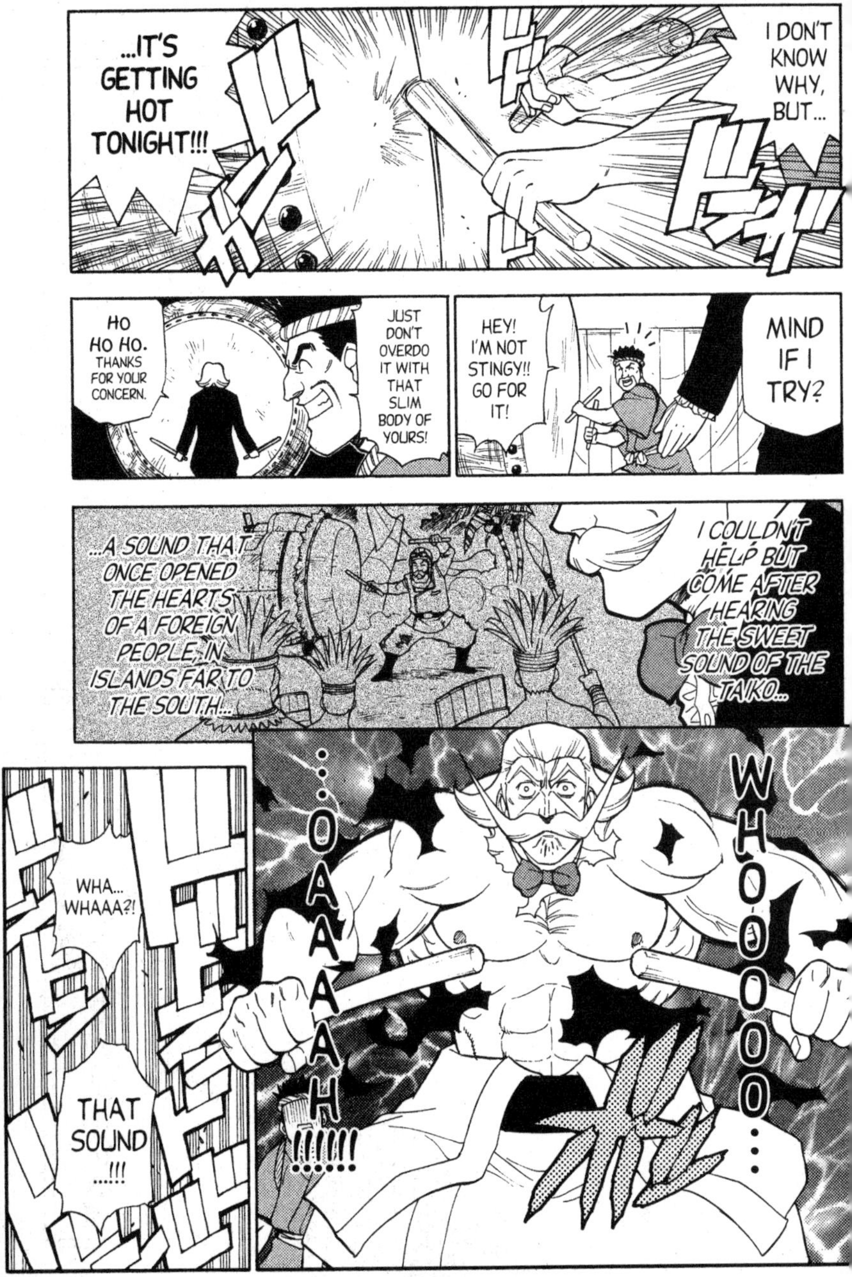

I DON'T KNOW WHY, BUT...
...IT'S GETTING HOT TONIGHT!!!
MIND IF I TRY?
HEY! I'M NOT STINGY!! GO FOR IT!
JUST DON'T OVERDO IT WITH THAT SLIM BODY OF YOURS!
HO HO HO. THANKS FOR YOUR CONCERN.
I COULDN'T HELP BUT COME AFTER HEARING THE SWEET SOUND OF THE TAIKO...
...A SOUND THAT ONCE OPENED THE HEARTS OF A FOREIGN PEOPLE, IN ISLANDS FAR TO THE SOUTH...
WHOOOOOO...
...OAAAAAH!!!!!!
WHA... WHAAA?!
THAT SOUND ...!!!

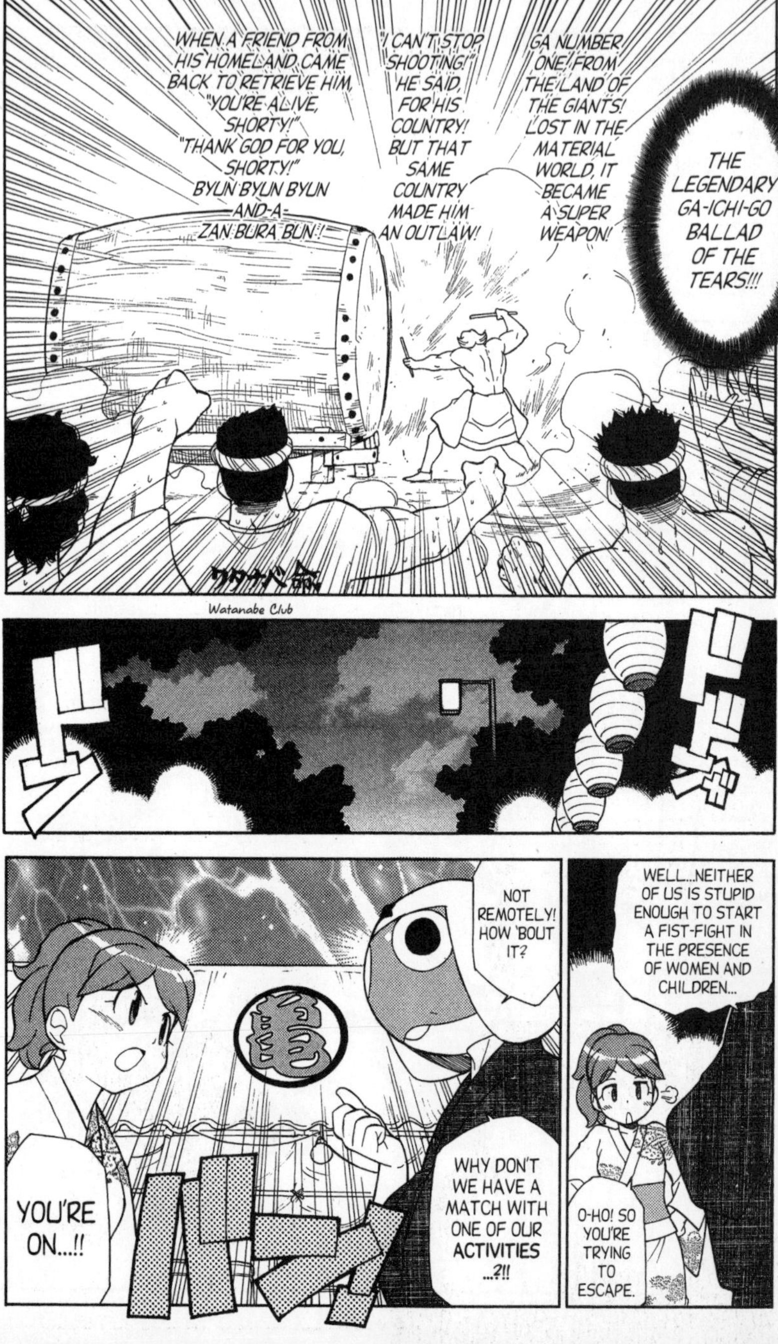
THE LEGENDARY GA-ICHI-GO BALLAD OF THE TEARS!!!
GA NUMBER ONE FROM THE LAND OF THE GIANTS! LOST IN THE MATERIAL WORLD, IT BECAME A SUPER WEAPON!
"I CAN'T STOP SHOOTING!" HE SAID, FOR HIS COUNTRY! BUT THAT SAME COUNTRY MADE HIM AN OUTLAW!
WHEN A FRIEND FROM HIS HOMELAND CAME BACK TO RETRIEVE HIM, "YOU'RE ALIVE, SHORTY!" "THANK GOD FOR YOU, SHORTY!" BYUN BYUN BYUN AND-A- ZAN BURA BUN!
ワタナベ命
Watanabe Club
WELL...NEITHER OF US IS STUPID ENOUGH TO START A FIST-FIGHT IN THE PRESENCE OF WOMEN AND CHILDREN...
O-HO! SO YOU'RE TRYING TO ESCAPE.
NOT REMOTELY! HOW 'BOUT IT?
WHY DON'T WE HAVE A MATCH WITH ONE OF OUR **ACTIVITIES** ...?!!
YOU'RE ON...!!

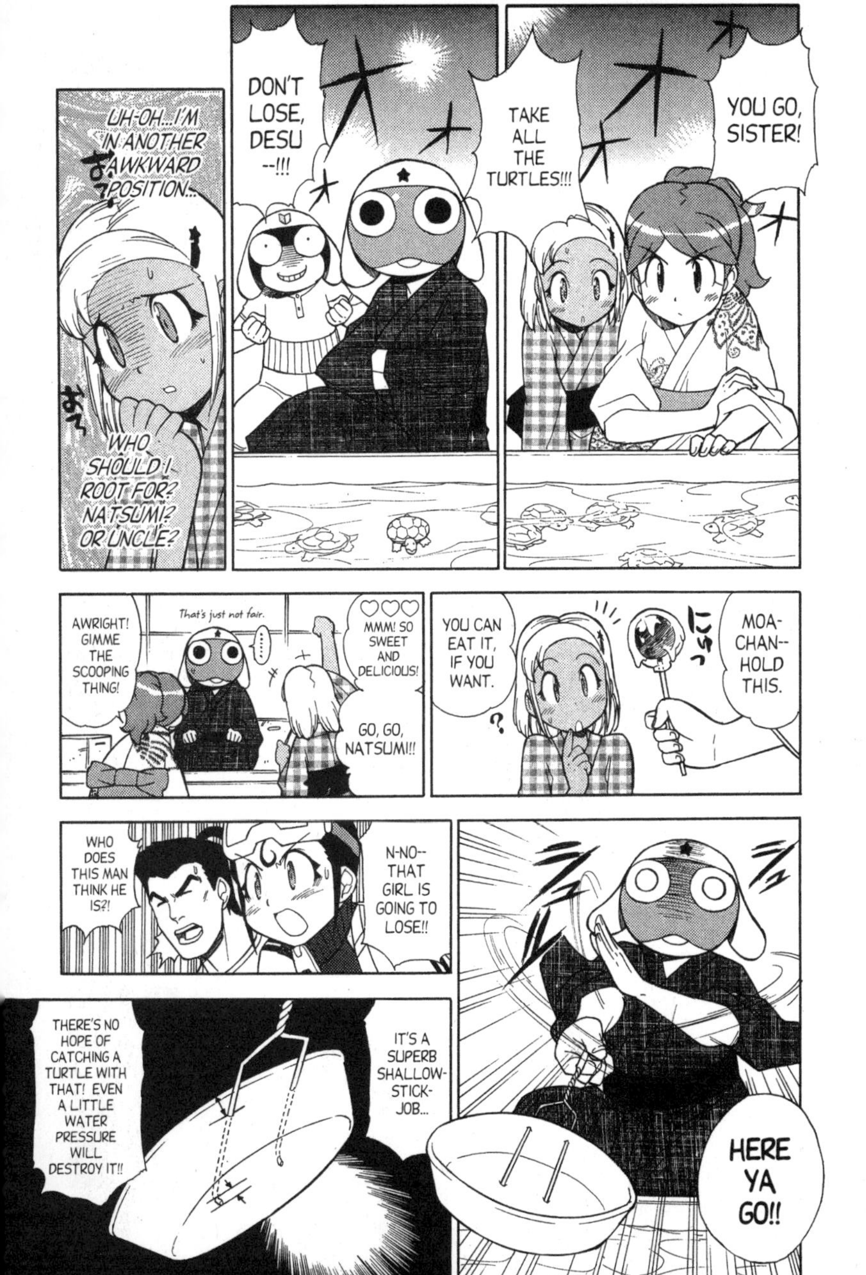
YOU GO, SISTER!
TAKE ALL THE TURTLES!!!
DON'T LOSE, DESU --!!!
UH-OH...I'M IN ANOTHER AWKWARD POSITION...
WHO SHOULD I ROOT FOR? NATSUMI? OR UNCLE?
MOA-CHAN-- HOLD THIS.
YOU CAN EAT IT, IF YOU WANT.
MMM! SO SWEET AND DELICIOUS!
GO, GO, NATSUMI!!
......
That's just not fair.
AWRIGHT! GIMME THE SCOOPING THING!
HERE YA GO!!
N-NO-- THAT GIRL IS GOING TO LOSE!!
WHO DOES THIS MAN THINK HE IS?!
IT'S A SUPERB SHALLOW-STICK-JOB...
THERE'S NO HOPE OF CATCHING A TURTLE WITH THAT! EVEN A LITTLE WATER PRESSURE WILL DESTROY IT!!

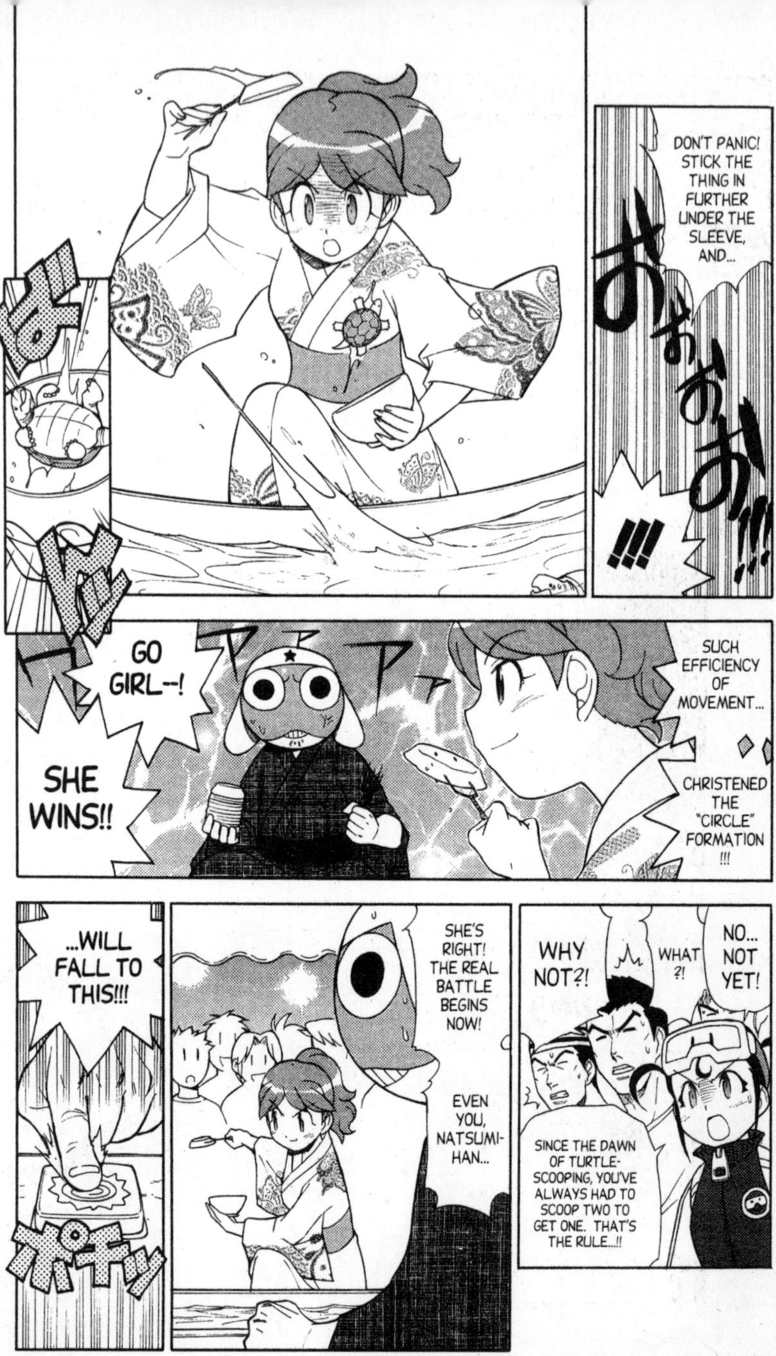

DON'T PANIC! STICK THE THING IN FURTHER UNDER THE SLEEVE, AND...
SUCH EFFICIENCY OF MOVEMENT...
CHRISTENED THE "CIRCLE" FORMATION !!!
GO GIRL--!
SHE WINS!!
NO... NOT YET!
WHAT?!
WHY NOT?!
SINCE THE DAWN OF TURTLE-SCOOPING, YOU'VE ALWAYS HAD TO SCOOP TWO TO GET ONE. THAT'S THE RULE...!!
SHE'S RIGHT! THE REAL BATTLE BEGINS NOW!
EVEN YOU, NATSUMI-HAN...
...WILL FALL TO THIS!!!

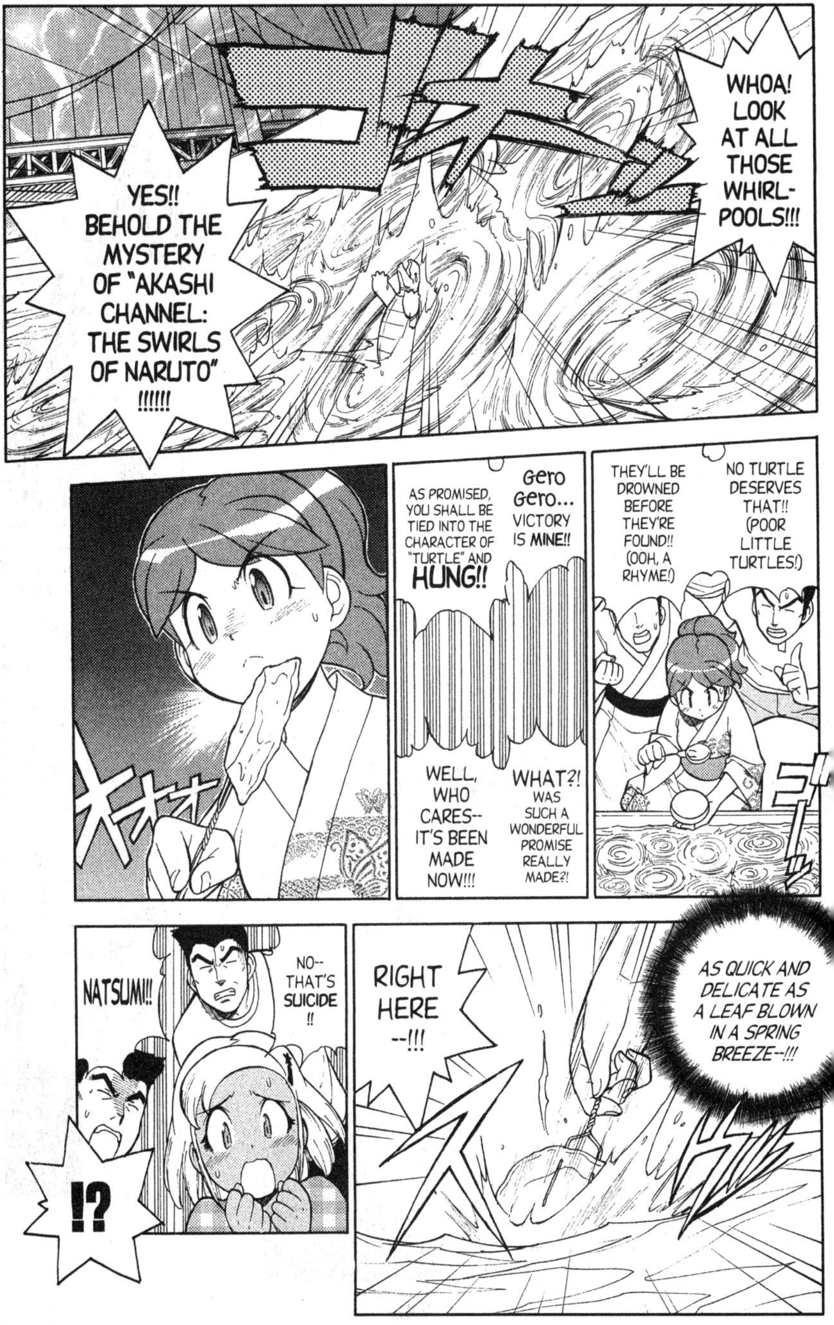
WHOA! LOOK AT ALL THOSE WHIRLPOOLS!!!
YES!! BEHOLD THE MYSTERY OF "AKASHI CHANNEL: THE SWIRLS OF NARUTO" !!!!!!
NO TURTLE DESERVES THAT!! (POOR LITTLE TURTLES!)
THEY'LL BE DROWNED BEFORE THEY'RE FOUND!! (OOH, A RHYME!)
Gero Gero... VICTORY IS MINE!!
AS PROMISED, YOU SHALL BE TIED INTO THE CHARACTER OF "TURTLE" AND HUNG!!
WHAT?! WAS SUCH A WONDERFUL PROMISE REALLY MADE?!
WELL, WHO CARES-- IT'S BEEN MADE NOW!!!
AS QUICK AND DELICATE AS A LEAF BLOWN IN A SPRING BREEZE--!!!
RIGHT HERE --!!!
NO-- THAT'S SUICIDE !!
NATSUMI!!
!?

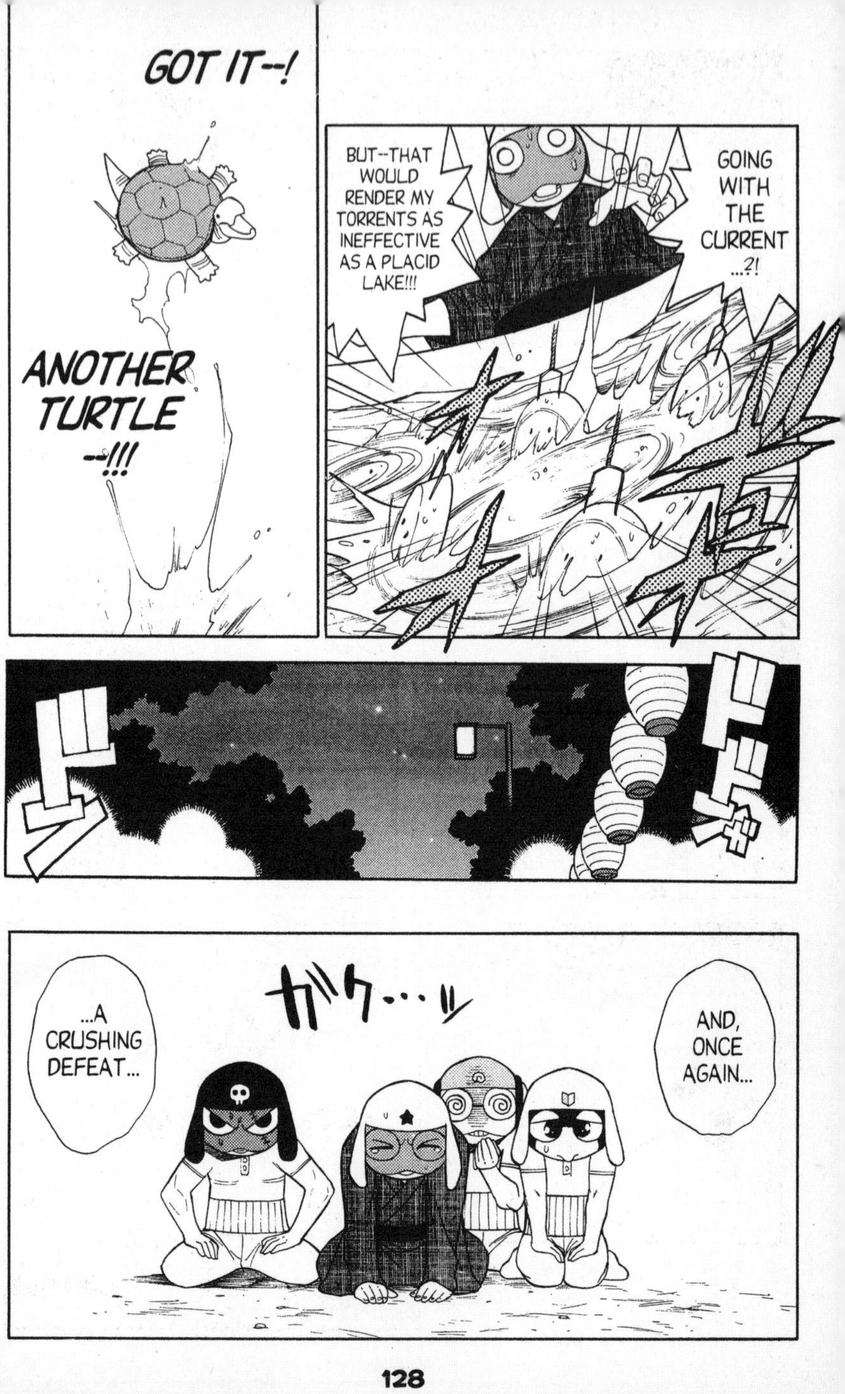
GOING WITH THE CURRENT ...?!
BUT--THAT WOULD RENDER MY TORRENTS AS INEFFECTIVE AS A PLACID LAKE!!!
GOT IT--!
ANOTHER TURTLE--!!!
AND, ONCE AGAIN...
...A CRUSHING DEFEAT...

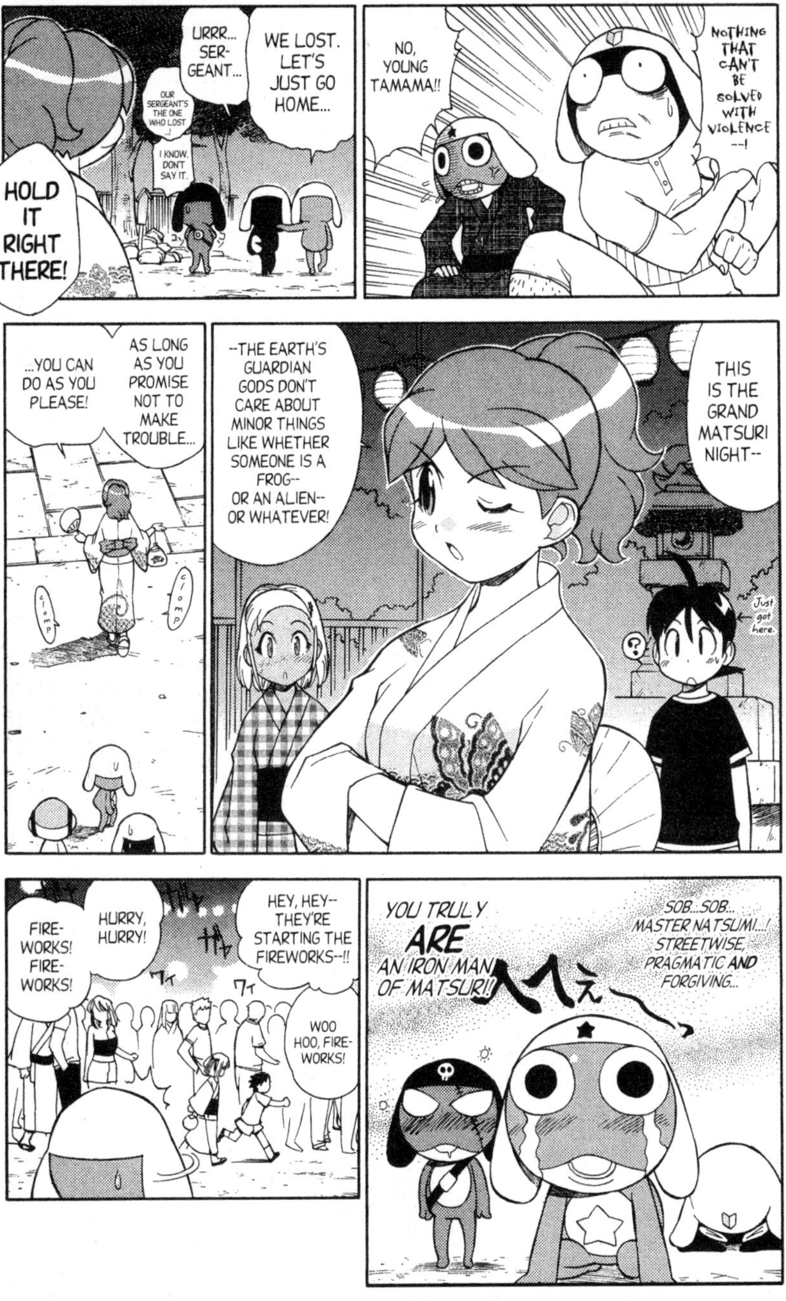

NOTHING THAT CAN'T BE SOLVED WITH VIOLENCE--!
NO, YOUNG TAMAMA!!
WE LOST. LET'S JUST GO HOME...
URRR... SERGEANT...
OUR SERGEANT'S THE ONE WHO LOST...!
I KNOW. DON'T SAY IT.
HOLD IT RIGHT THERE!
THIS IS THE GRAND MATSURI NIGHT--
Just got here.
--THE EARTH'S GUARDIAN GODS DON'T CARE ABOUT MINOR THINGS LIKE WHETHER SOMEONE IS A FROG-- OR AN ALIEN-- OR WHATEVER!
AS LONG AS YOU PROMISE NOT TO MAKE TROUBLE...
...YOU CAN DO AS YOU PLEASE!
clomp
clomp
SOB...SOB... MASTER NATSUMI...! STREETWISE, PRAGMATIC AND FORGIVING...
YOU TRULY ARE AN IRON MAN OF MATSURI!!
へへえ〜
HEY, HEY-- THEY'RE STARTING THE FIREWORKS--!!
WOO HOO, FIREWORKS!
HURRY, HURRY!
FIRE-WORKS! FIRE-WORKS!

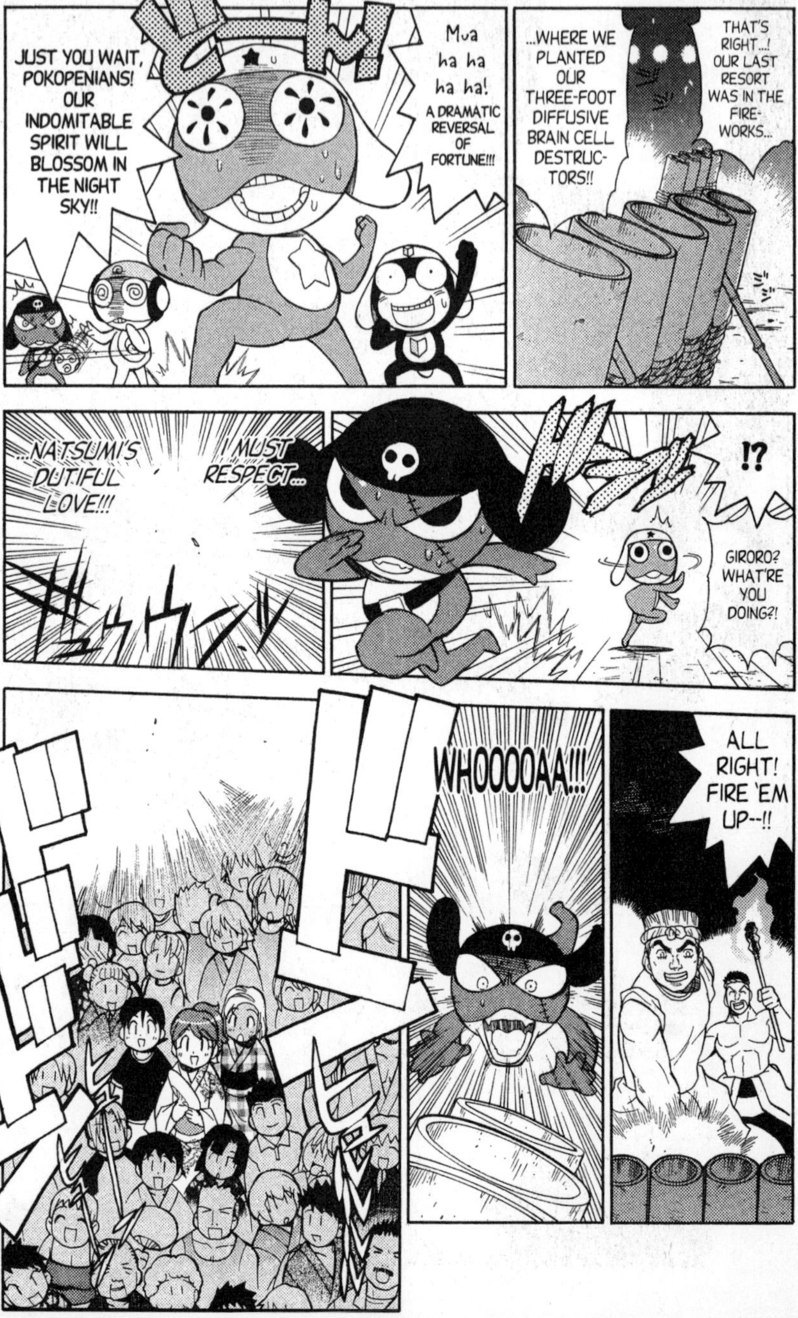
THAT'S RIGHT...! OUR LAST RESORT WAS IN THE FIRE-WORKS...
...WHERE WE PLANTED OUR THREE-FOOT DIFFUSIVE BRAIN CELL DESTRUC-TORS!!
Mua ha ha ha ha!
A DRAMATIC REVERSAL OF FORTUNE!!!
JUST YOU WAIT, POKOPENIANS! OUR INDOMITABLE SPIRIT WILL BLOSSOM IN THE NIGHT SKY!!
!?
GIRORO? WHAT'RE YOU DOING?!
I MUST RESPECT...
...NATSUMI'S DUTIFUL LOVE!!!
ALL RIGHT! FIRE 'EM UP--!!
WHOOOOAA!!!

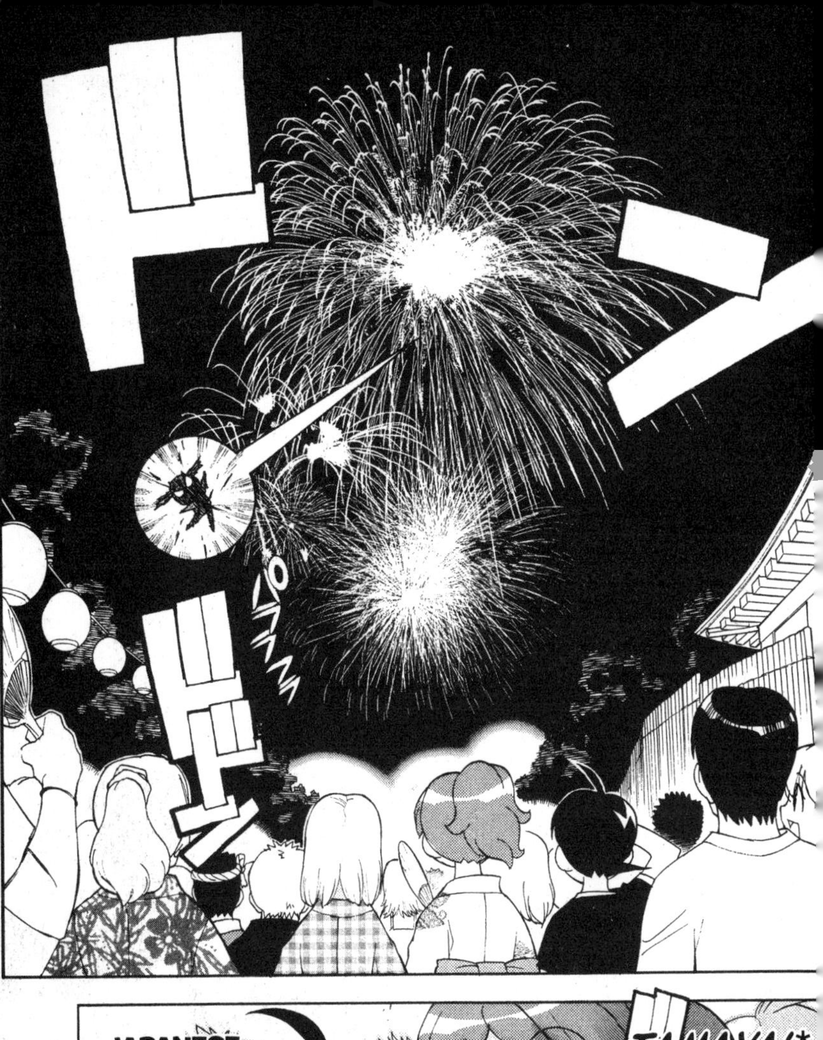

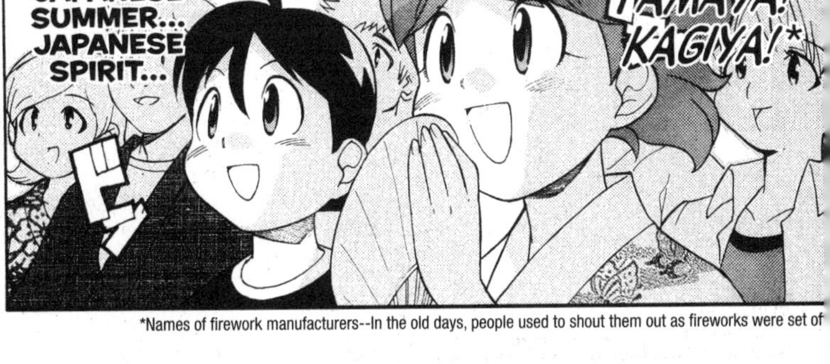
TAMAYA!* KAGIYA!*
JAPANESE SUMMER... JAPANESE SPIRIT...

*Names of firework manufacturers--In the old days, people used to shout them out as fireworks were set of

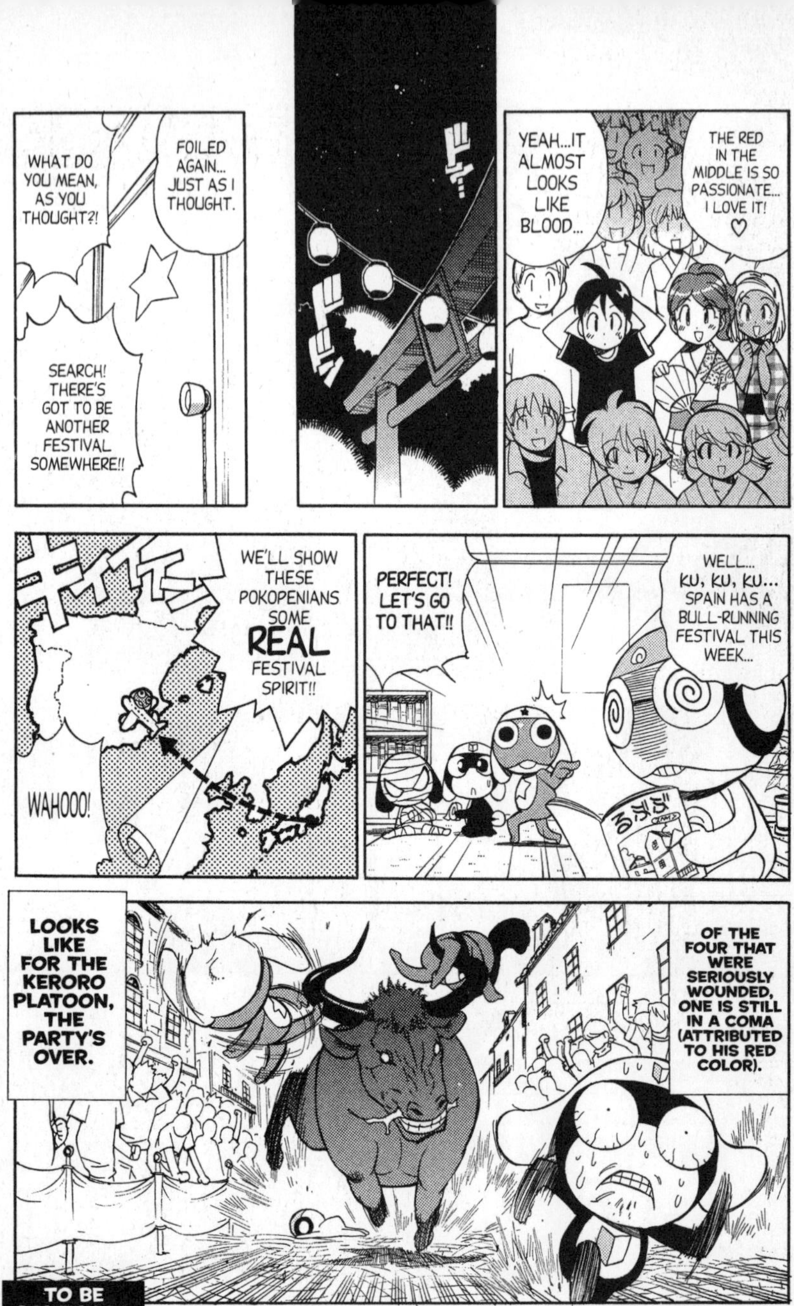

THE RED IN THE MIDDLE IS SO PASSIONATE... I LOVE IT! ♡
YEAH...IT ALMOST LOOKS LIKE BLOOD...
FOILED AGAIN... JUST AS I THOUGHT.
WHAT DO YOU MEAN, AS YOU THOUGHT?!
SEARCH! THERE'S GOT TO BE ANOTHER FESTIVAL SOMEWHERE!!
WELL... KU, KU, KU... SPAIN HAS A BULL-RUNNING FESTIVAL THIS WEEK...
PERFECT! LET'S GO TO THAT!!
WE'LL SHOW THESE POKOPENIANS SOME REAL FESTIVAL SPIRIT!!
WAHOOO!
OF THE FOUR THAT WERE SERIOUSLY WOUNDED, ONE IS STILL IN A COMA (ATTRIBUTED TO HIS RED COLOR).
LOOKS LIKE FOR THE KERORO PLATOON, THE PARTY'S OVER.
TO BE CONTINUED

ENCOUNTER LI

A JERK AND A GENIUS! THE LEGEND OF A SERGEANT-MAJOR

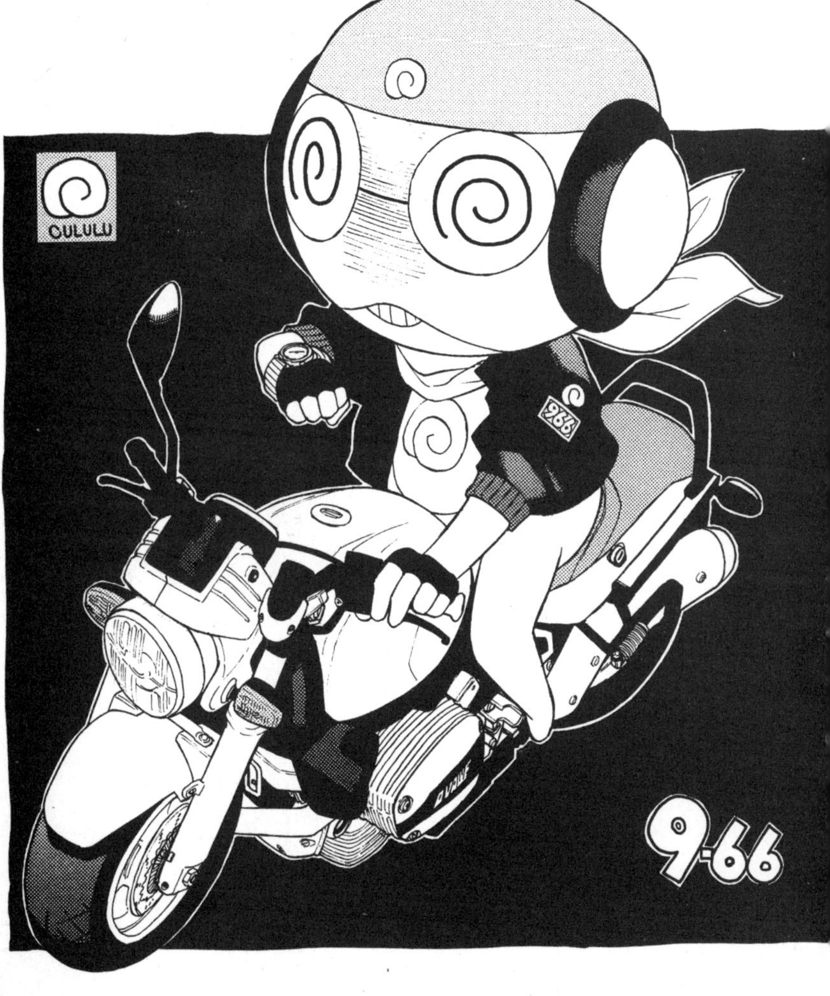
CULULU
9-66

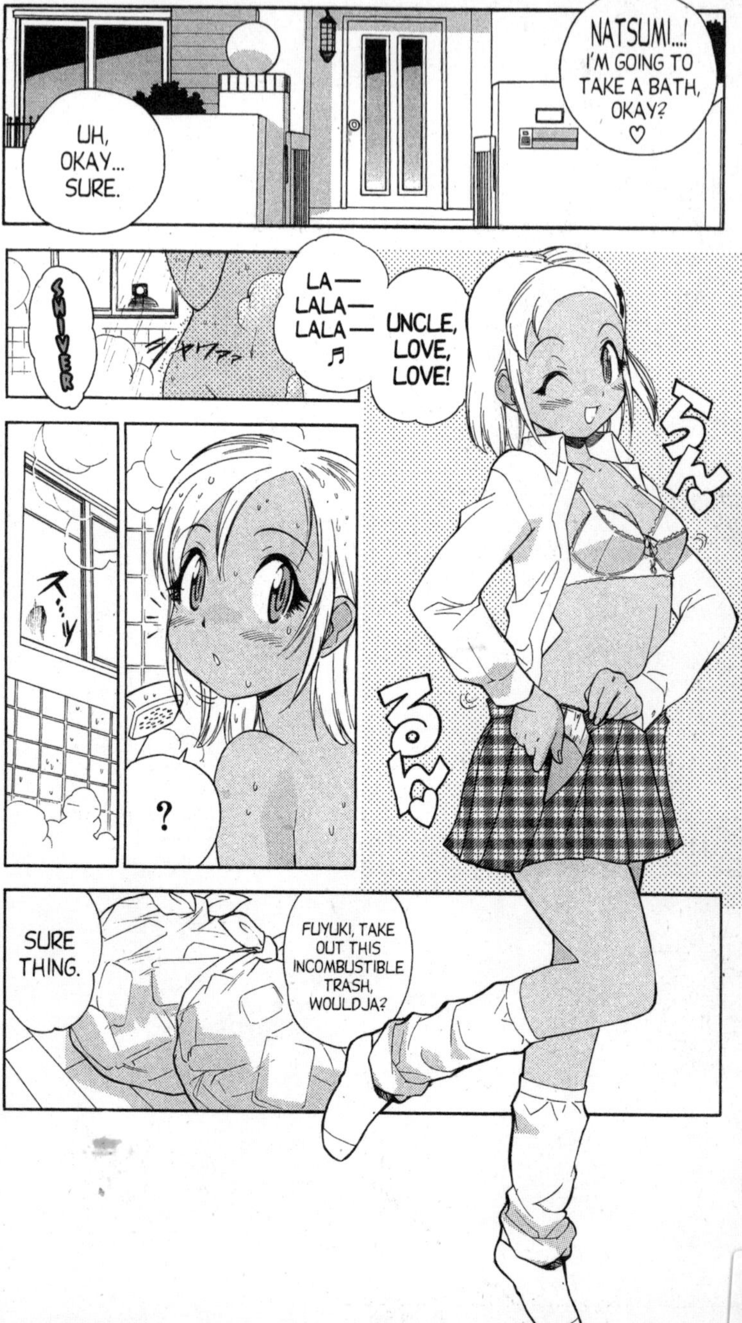
NATSUMI...! I'M GOING TO TAKE A BATH, OKAY? ♡
UH, OKAY... SURE.
UNCLE, LOVE, LOVE!
らん♡
るん♡
LA— LALA— LALA— ♪
SHIVER
シャワァァ
?
ス…ッ
FUYUKI, TAKE OUT THIS INCOMBUSTIBLE TRASH, WOULDJA?
SURE THING.

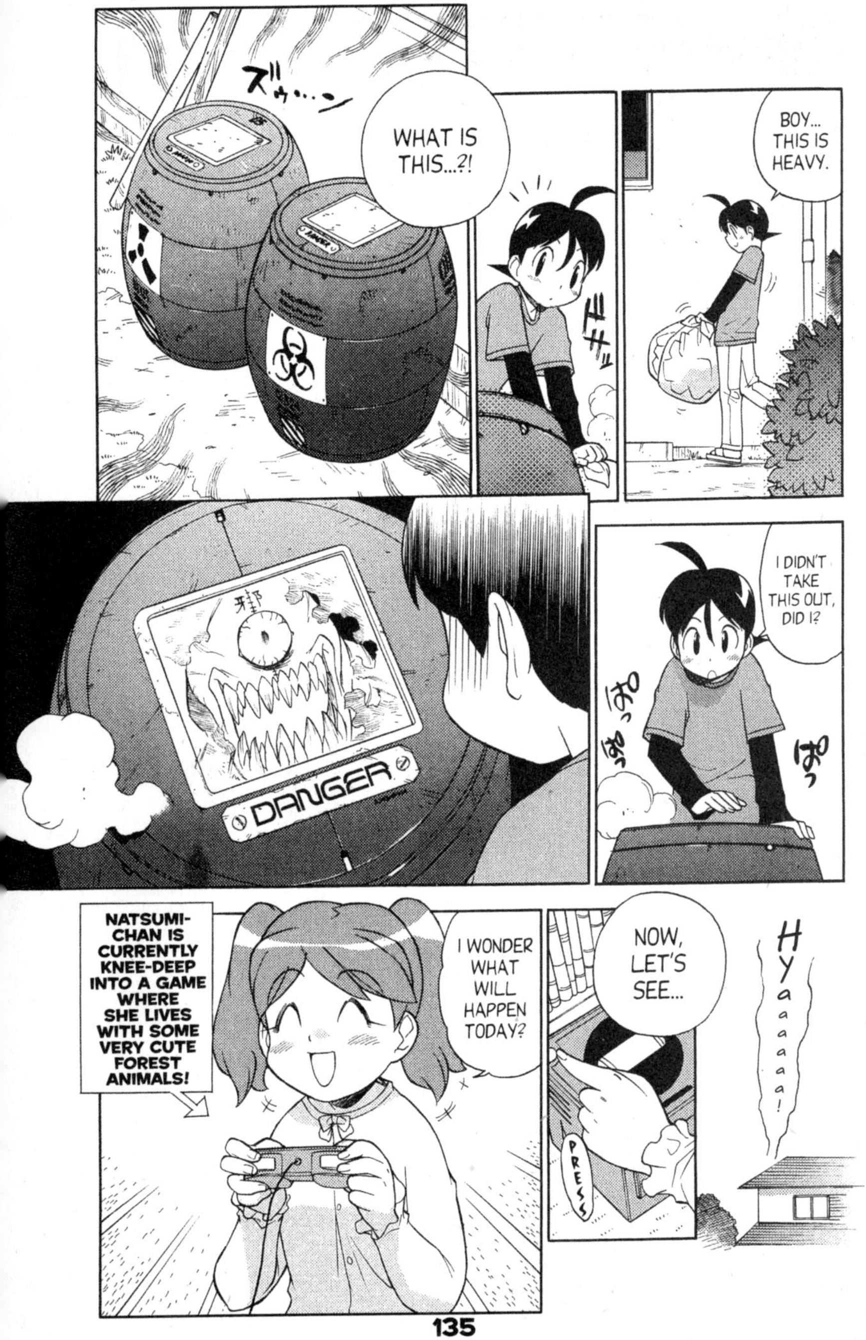
BOY... THIS IS HEAVY.
WHAT IS THIS...?!
I DIDN'T TAKE THIS OUT, DID I?
DANGER
HYaaaaaaa!
NOW, LET'S SEE...
PRESS
I WONDER WHAT WILL HAPPEN TODAY?
NATSUMI-CHAN IS CURRENTLY KNEE-DEEP INTO A GAME WHERE SHE LIVES WITH SOME VERY CUTE FOREST ANIMALS!

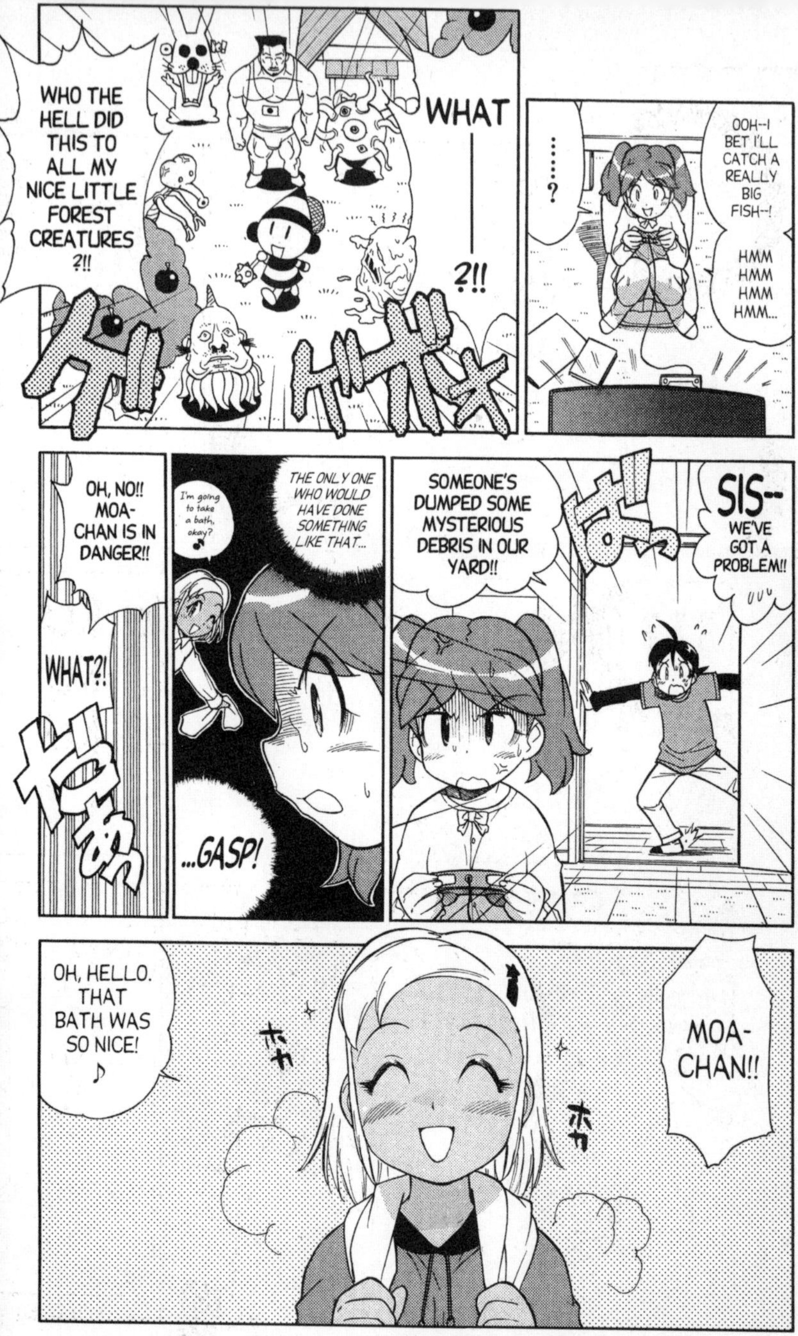

OOH--I BET I'LL CATCH A REALLY BIG FISH--!
HMM HMM HMM HMM...
......?
WHAT ―― ?!!
WHO THE HELL DID THIS TO ALL MY NICE LITTLE FOREST CREATURES ?!!
SIS-- WE'VE GOT A PROBLEM!!
SOMEONE'S DUMPED SOME MYSTERIOUS DEBRIS IN OUR YARD!!
THE ONLY ONE WHO WOULD HAVE DONE SOMETHING LIKE THAT...
I'm going to take a bath, okay? ♪
...GASP!
OH, NO!! MOA-CHAN IS IN DANGER!!
WHAT?!
MOA-CHAN!!
OH, HELLO. THAT BATH WAS SO NICE! ♪

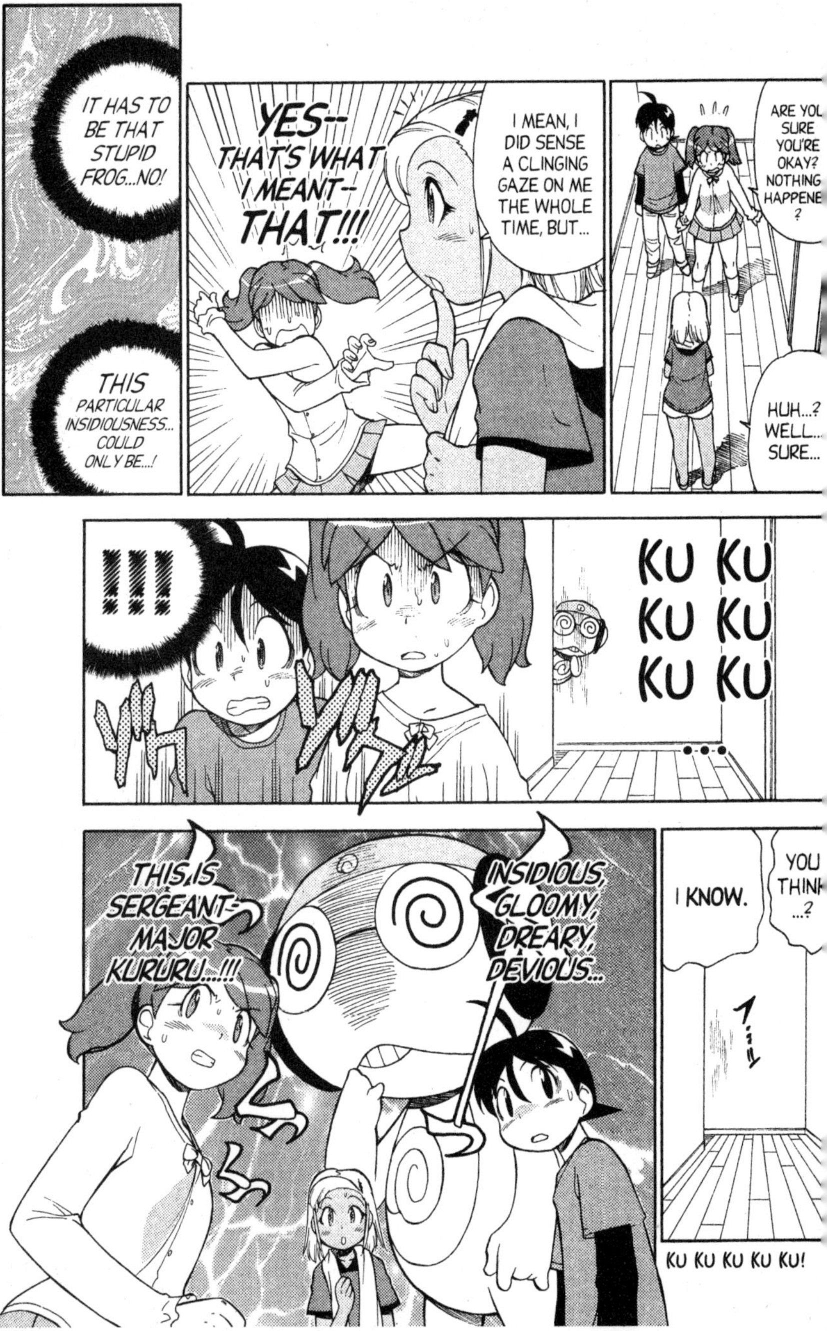
ARE YOU SURE YOU'RE OKAY? NOTHING HAPPENE?
HUH...? WELL... SURE...
I MEAN, I DID SENSE A CLINGING GAZE ON ME THE WHOLE TIME, BUT...
YES-- THAT'S WHAT I MEANT-- THAT!!!
IT HAS TO BE THAT STUPID FROG...NO!
THIS PARTICULAR INSIDIOUSNESS... COULD ONLY BE...!
KU KU KU KU KU KU
...
!!!
YOU THINK...?
I KNOW.
KU KU KU KU KU!
INSIDIOUS, GLOOMY, DREARY, DEVIOUS...
THIS IS SERGEANT-MAJOR KURURU...!!!

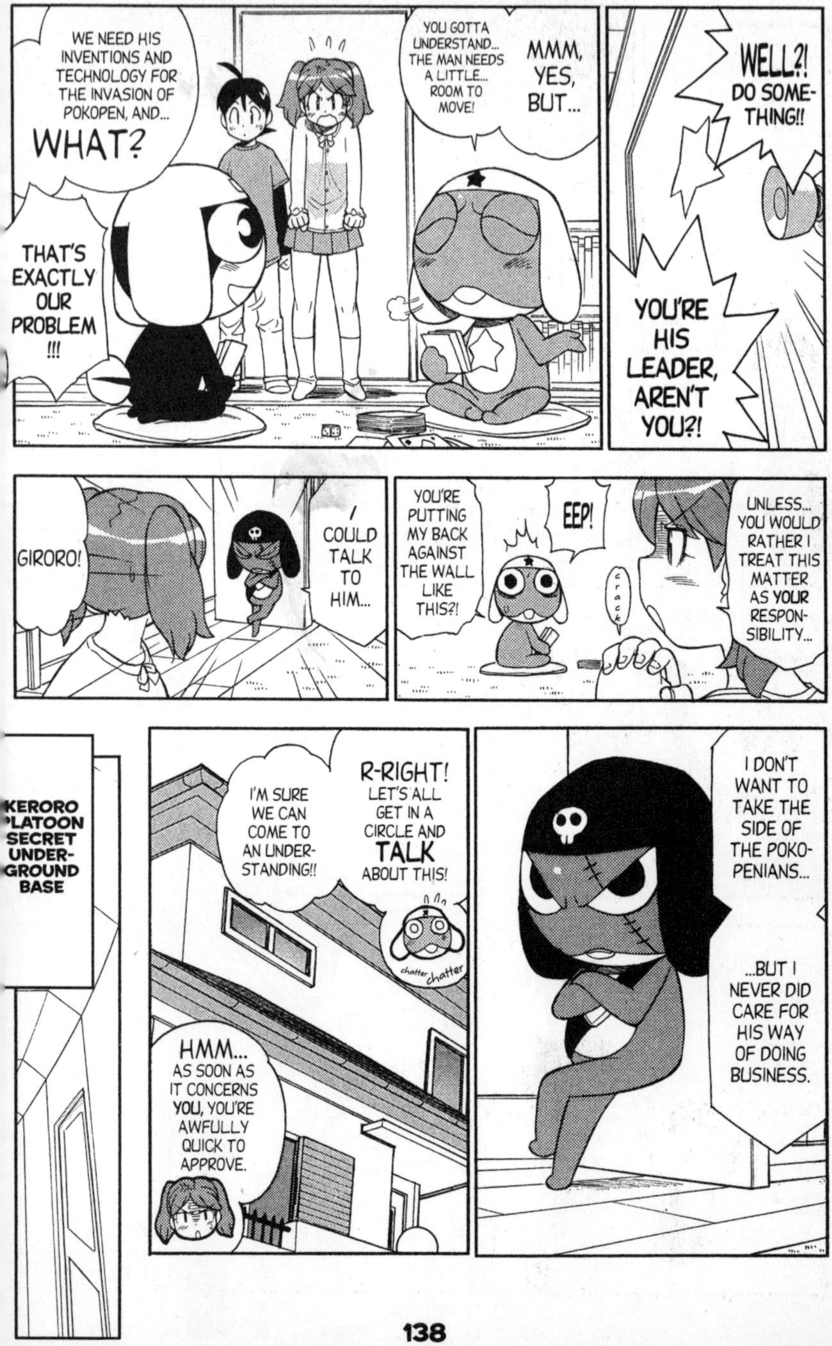
WELL?! DO SOME-THING!!
YOU'RE HIS LEADER, AREN'T YOU?!
MMM, YES, BUT...
YOU GOTTA UNDERSTAND... THE MAN NEEDS A LITTLE... ROOM TO MOVE!
WE NEED HIS INVENTIONS AND TECHNOLOGY FOR THE INVASION OF POKOPEN, AND... WHAT?
THAT'S EXACTLY OUR PROBLEM!!!
UNLESS... YOU WOULD RATHER I TREAT THIS MATTER AS YOUR RESPON-SIBILITY...
crack
EEP!
YOU'RE PUTTING MY BACK AGAINST THE WALL LIKE THIS?!
I COULD TALK TO HIM...
GIRORO!
I DON'T WANT TO TAKE THE SIDE OF THE POKO-PENIANS...
...BUT I NEVER DID CARE FOR HIS WAY OF DOING BUSINESS.
R-RIGHT! LET'S ALL GET IN A CIRCLE AND TALK ABOUT THIS!
I'M SURE WE CAN COME TO AN UNDER-STANDING!!
chatter chatter
HMM... AS SOON AS IT CONCERNS YOU, YOU'RE AWFULLY QUICK TO APPROVE.
KERORO PLATOON SECRET UNDER-GROUND BASE

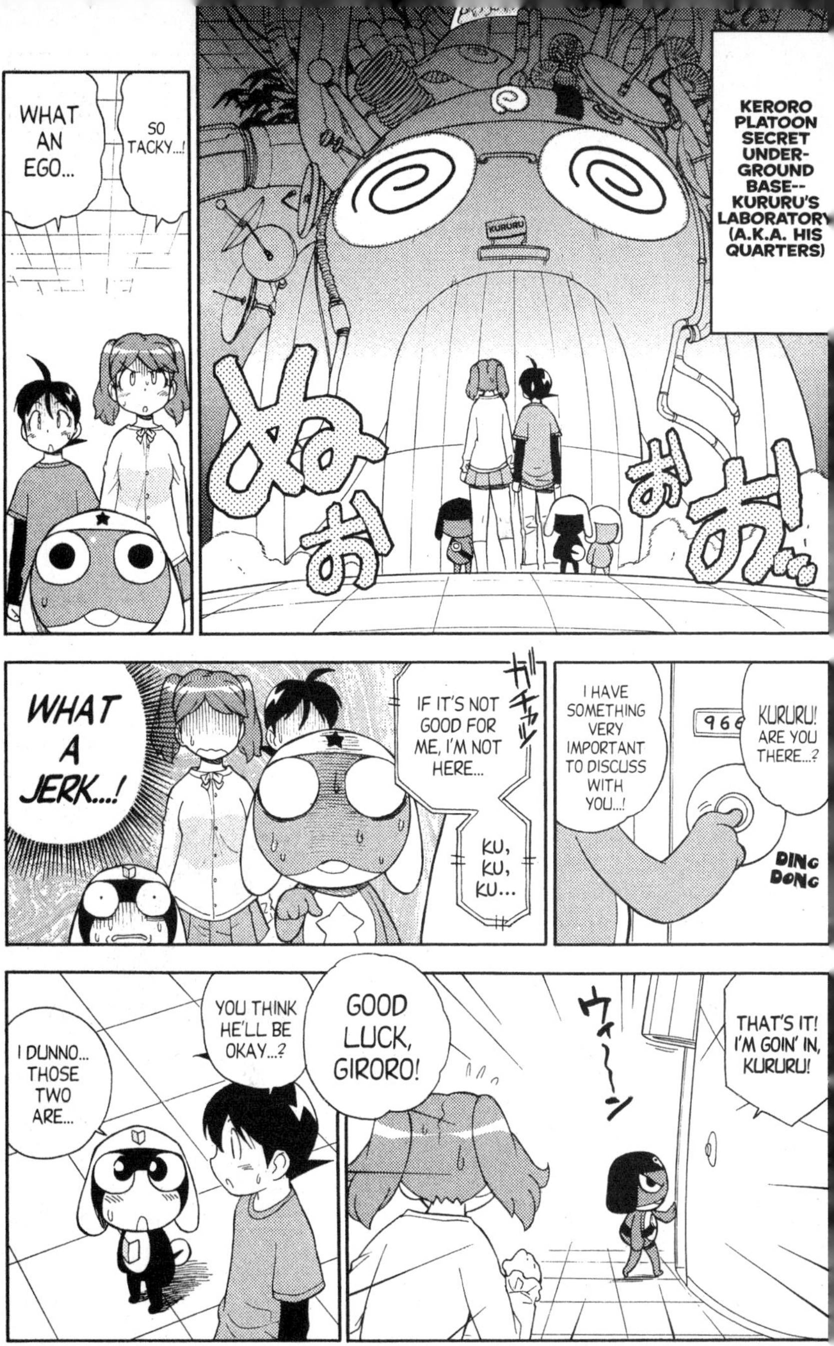
KERORO PLATOON SECRET UNDERGROUND BASE-- KURURU'S LABORATORY (A.K.A. HIS QUARTERS)
KURURU
ぬおおお…
SO TACKY...!
WHAT AN EGO...
KURURU! ARE YOU THERE...?
I HAVE SOMETHING VERY IMPORTANT TO DISCUSS WITH YOU...!
DING DONG
ガチャッ
IF IT'S NOT GOOD FOR ME, I'M NOT HERE...
KU, KU, KU...
WHAT A JERK...!
THAT'S IT! I'M GOIN' IN, KURURU!
ウィ～～ン
GOOD LUCK, GIRORO!
YOU THINK HE'LL BE OKAY...?
I DUNNO... THOSE TWO ARE...

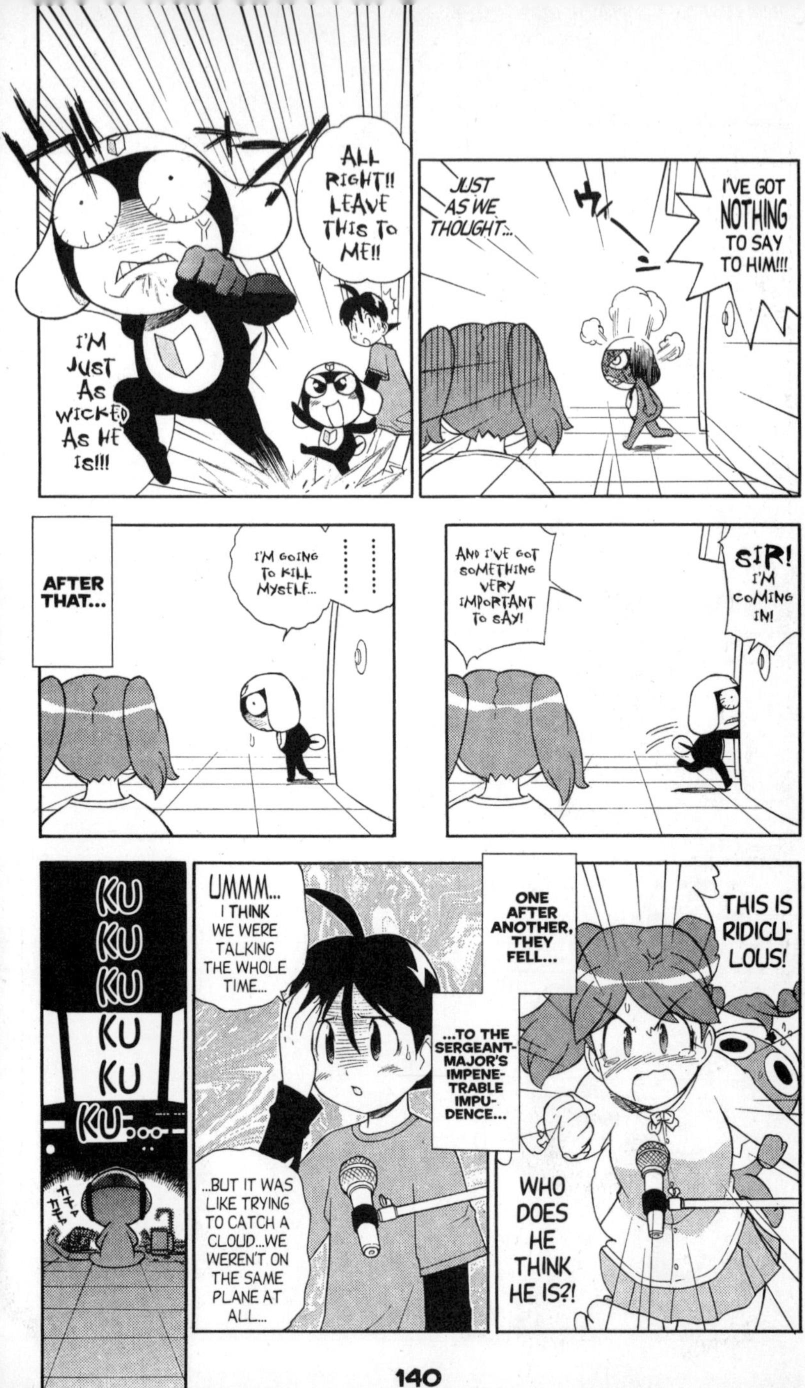
I'VE GOT NOTHING TO SAY TO HIM!!!
JUST AS WE THOUGHT...
ALL RIGHT!! LEAVE THIS TO ME!!
I'M JUST AS WICKED AS HE IS!!!
SIR! I'M COMING IN!
AND I'VE GOT SOMETHING VERY IMPORTANT TO SAY!
......
I'M GOING TO KILL MYSELF...
AFTER THAT...
THIS IS RIDICU-LOUS!
ONE AFTER ANOTHER, THEY FELL...
...TO THE SERGEANT-MAJOR'S IMPENE-TRABLE IMPU-DENCE...
WHO DOES HE THINK HE IS?!
UMMM... I THINK WE WERE TALKING THE WHOLE TIME...
...BUT IT WAS LIKE TRYING TO CATCH A CLOUD...WE WEREN'T ON THE SAME PLANE AT ALL...
KU KU KU KU KU KU...

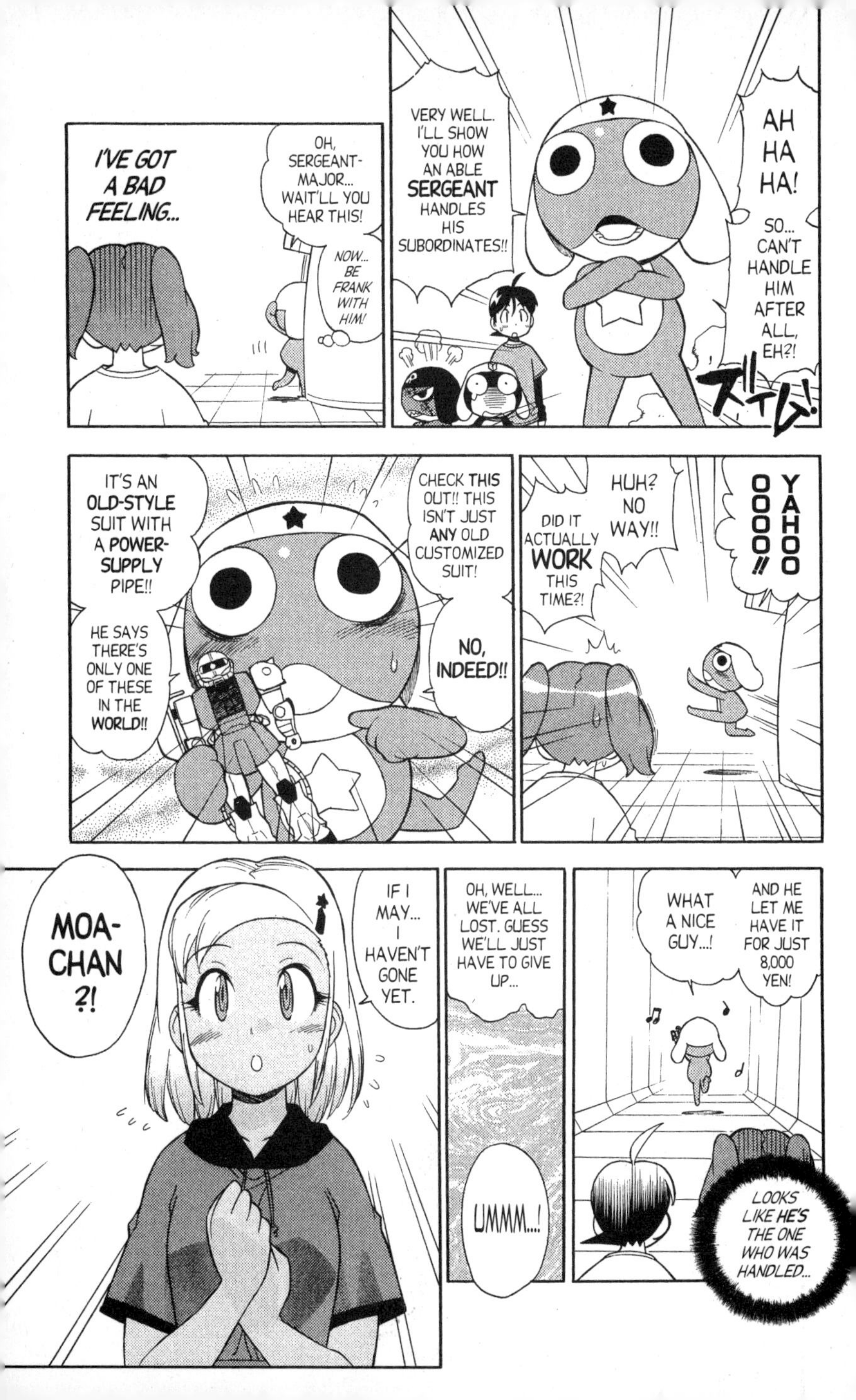
AH HA HA! SO... CAN'T HANDLE HIM AFTER ALL, EH?!
VERY WELL. I'LL SHOW YOU HOW AN ABLE SERGEANT HANDLES HIS SUBORDINATES!!
OH, SERGEANT-MAJOR... WAIT'LL YOU HEAR THIS!
NOW... BE FRANK WITH HIM!
I'VE GOT A BAD FEELING...
YAHOOOOOO!!
HUH? NO WAY!!
DID IT ACTUALLY WORK THIS TIME?!
CHECK THIS OUT!! THIS ISN'T JUST ANY OLD CUSTOMIZED SUIT!
NO, INDEED!!
IT'S AN OLD-STYLE SUIT WITH A POWER-SUPPLY PIPE!!
HE SAYS THERE'S ONLY ONE OF THESE IN THE WORLD!!
AND HE LET ME HAVE IT FOR JUST 8,000 YEN!
WHAT A NICE GUY...!
LOOKS LIKE HE'S THE ONE WHO WAS HANDLED...
OH, WELL... WE'VE ALL LOST. GUESS WE'LL JUST HAVE TO GIVE UP...
UMMM...!
IF I MAY... I HAVEN'T GONE YET.
MOA-CHAN?!

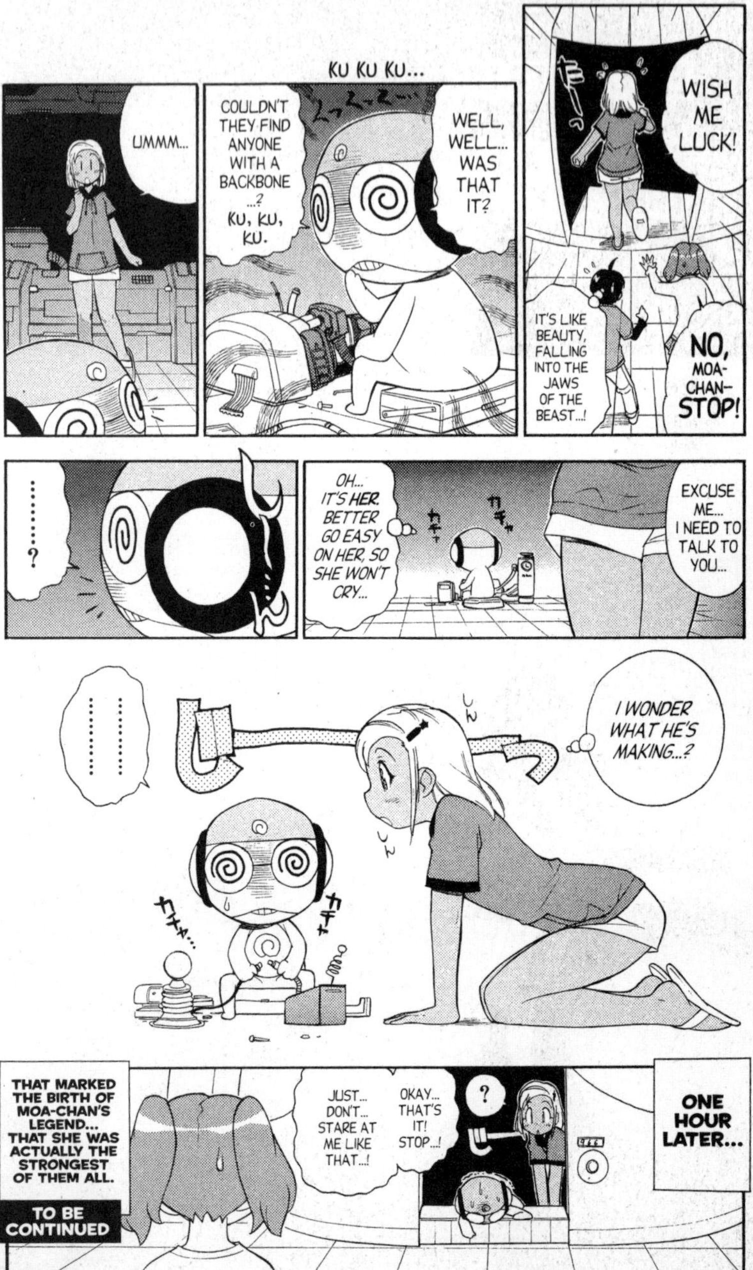
WISH ME LUCK!
NO, MOA-CHAN-STOP!
IT'S LIKE BEAUTY, FALLING INTO THE JAWS OF THE BEAST...!
KU KU KU...
WELL, WELL... WAS THAT IT?
COULDN'T THEY FIND ANYONE WITH A BACKBONE...? KU, KU, KU.
UMMM...
EXCUSE ME... I NEED TO TALK TO YOU...
OH... IT'S HER. BETTER GO EASY ON HER, SO SHE WON'T CRY...
.......?
I WONDER WHAT HE'S MAKING...?
....
ONE HOUR LATER...
?
OKAY... THAT'S IT! STOP...!
JUST... DON'T... STARE AT ME LIKE THAT...!
THAT MARKED THE BIRTH OF MOA-CHAN'S LEGEND... THAT SHE WAS ACTUALLY THE STRONGEST OF THEM ALL.
TO BE CONTINUED

ENCOUNTER LII

FEELINGS ALL THE WAY! THE LEGEND OF A CORPORAL

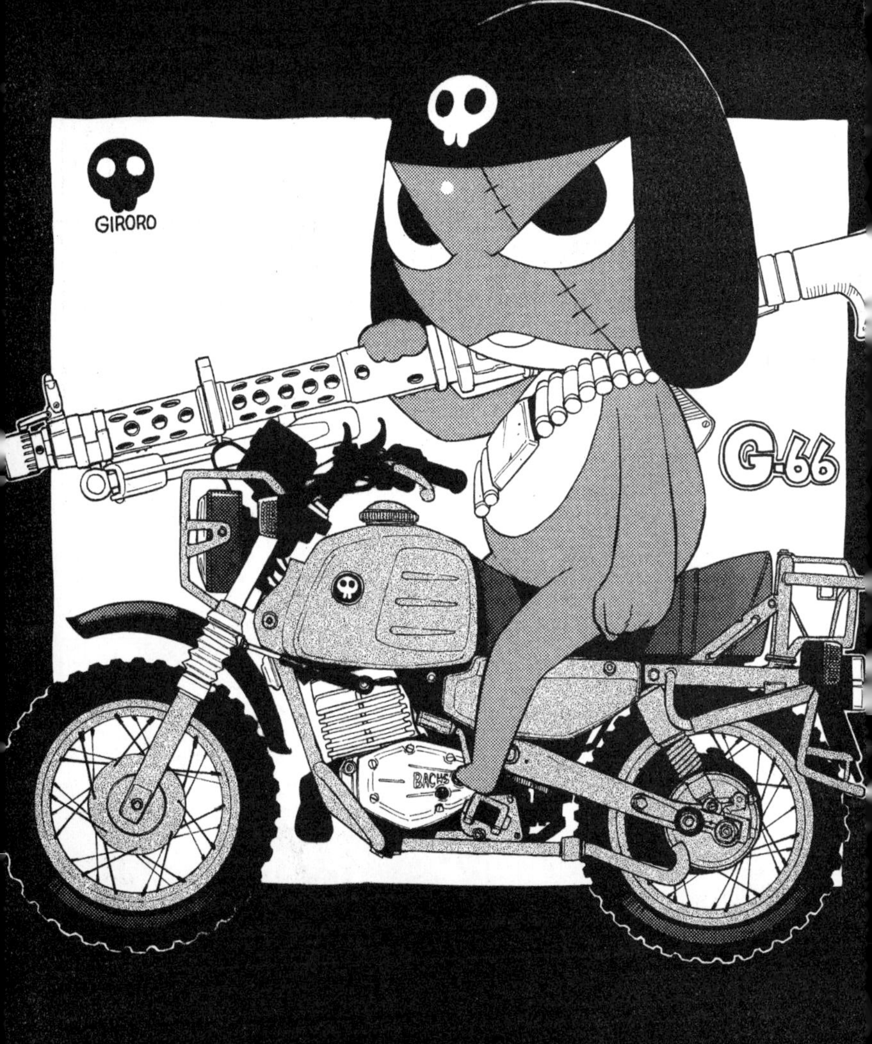
GIRORO
G.66

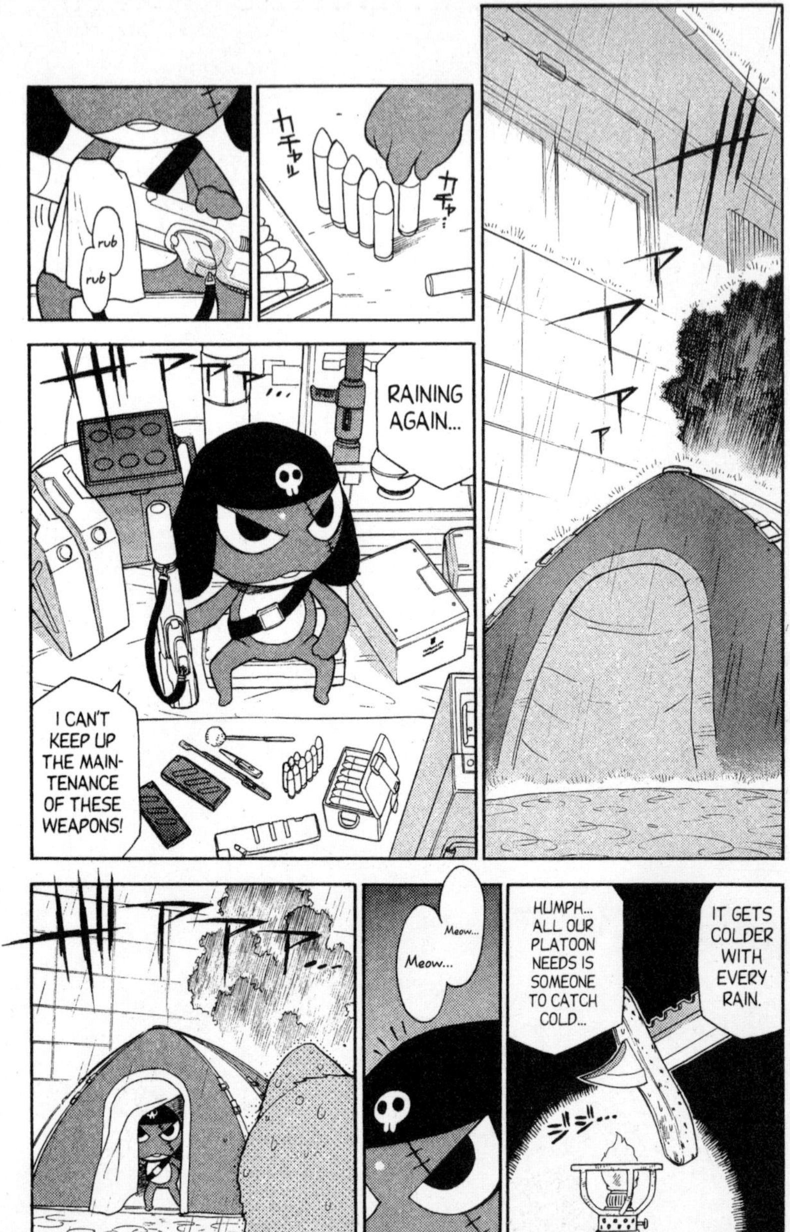
カチャッ
カチャ…
rub
rub
RAINING AGAIN...
I CAN'T KEEP UP THE MAIN-TENANCE OF THESE WEAPONS!
IT GETS COLDER WITH EVERY RAIN.
HUMPH... ALL OUR PLATOON NEEDS IS SOMEONE TO CATCH COLD...
ジジ…
Meow...
Meow...

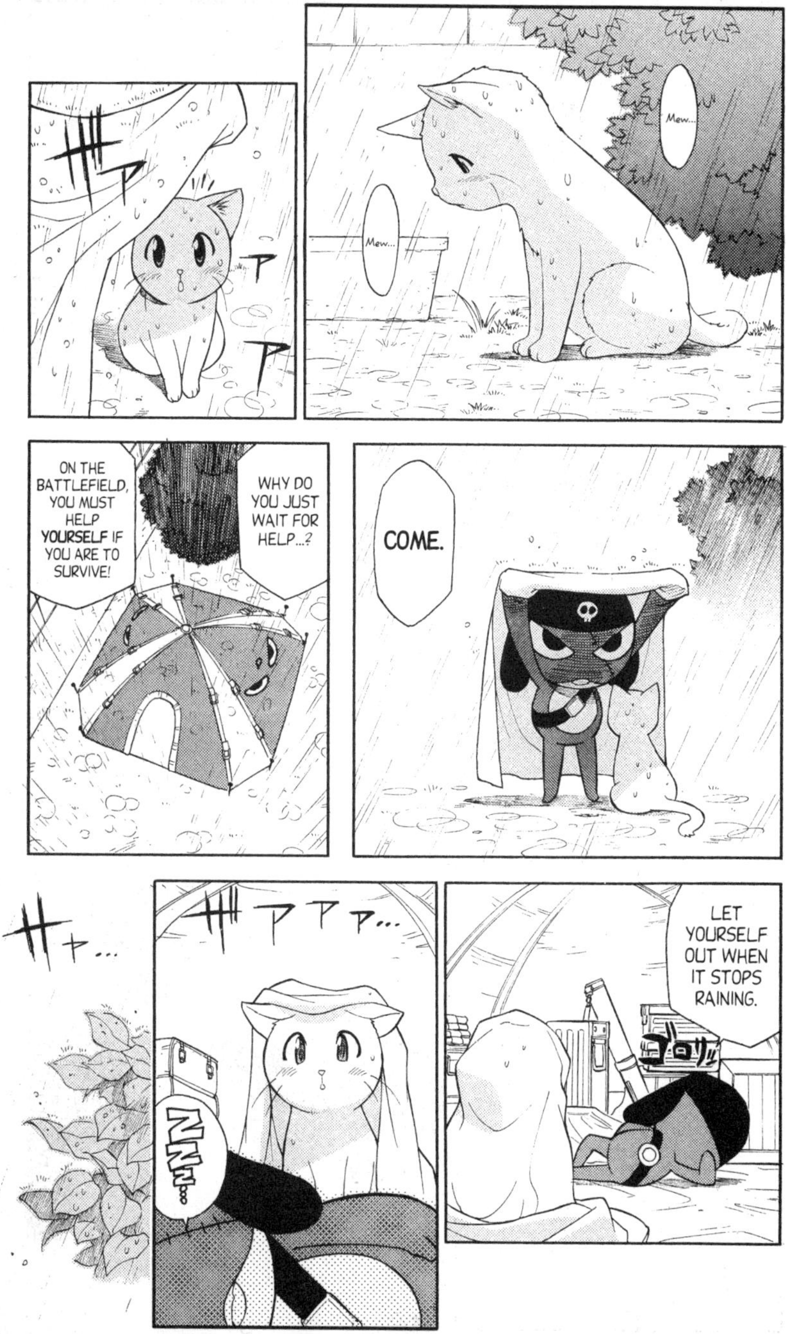
Mew...
Mew...
COME.
WHY DO YOU JUST WAIT FOR HELP...?
ON THE BATTLEFIELD, YOU MUST HELP **YOURSELF** IF YOU ARE TO SURVIVE!
LET YOURSELF OUT WHEN IT STOPS RAINING.
ZNN...

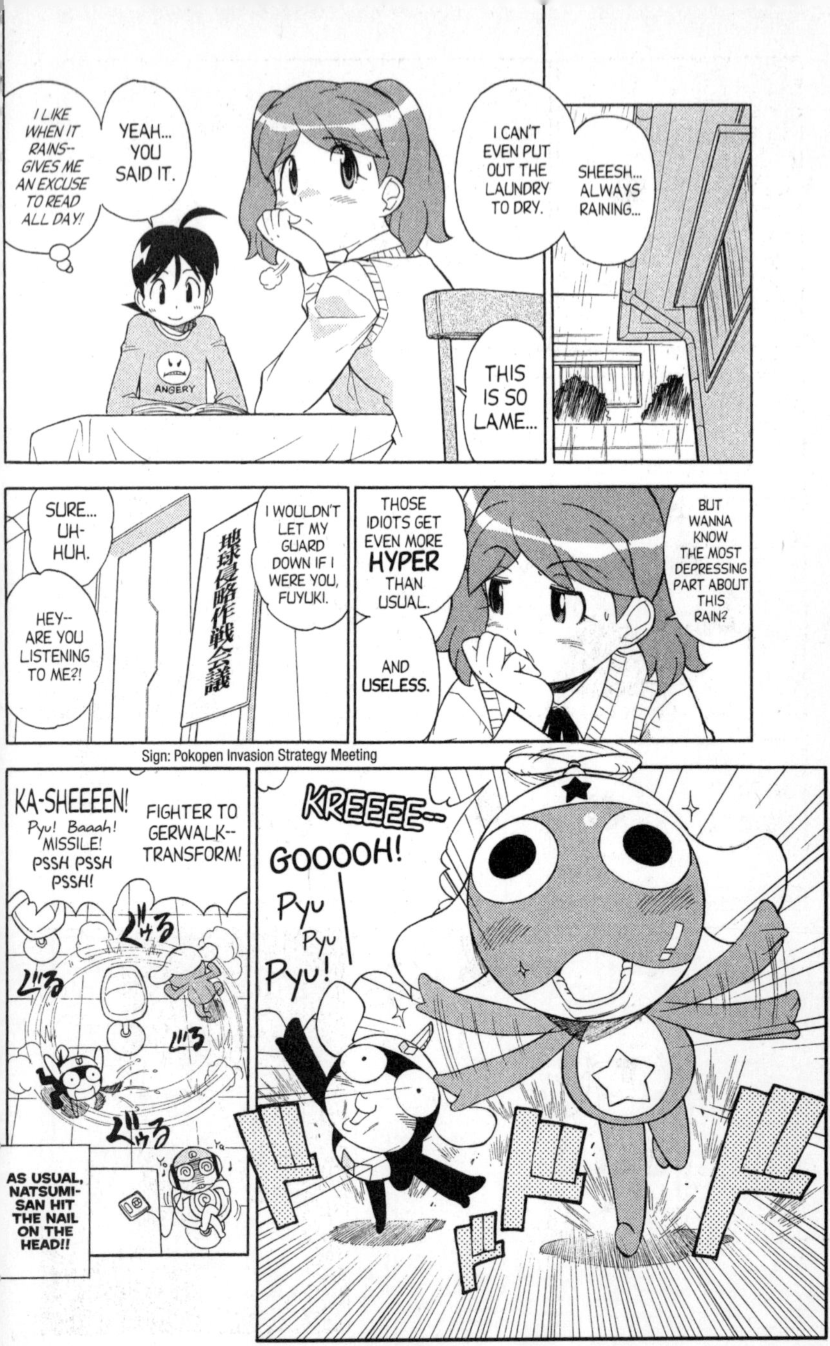
SHEESH... ALWAYS RAINING...
I CAN'T EVEN PUT OUT THE LAUNDRY TO DRY.
THIS IS SO LAME...
YEAH... YOU SAID IT.
I LIKE WHEN IT RAINS-- GIVES ME AN EXCUSE TO READ ALL DAY!
ANGERY
BUT WANNA KNOW THE MOST DEPRESSING PART ABOUT THIS RAIN?
THOSE IDIOTS GET EVEN MORE HYPER THAN USUAL.
AND USELESS.
I WOULDN'T LET MY GUARD DOWN IF I WERE YOU, FUYUKI.
地球侵略作戦会議
SURE... UH-HUH.
HEY-- ARE YOU LISTENING TO ME?!
Sign: Pokopen Invasion Strategy Meeting
KREEEE-- GOOOOH!
Pyu Pyu Pyu!
ドドドド
FIGHTER TO GERWALK-- TRANSFORM!
KA-SHEEEEN! Pyu! Baaah! MISSILE! PSSH PSSH PSSH!
ぐる ぐる ぐる ぐる
Yo Ya
AS USUAL, NATSUMI-SAN HIT THE NAIL ON THE HEAD!!

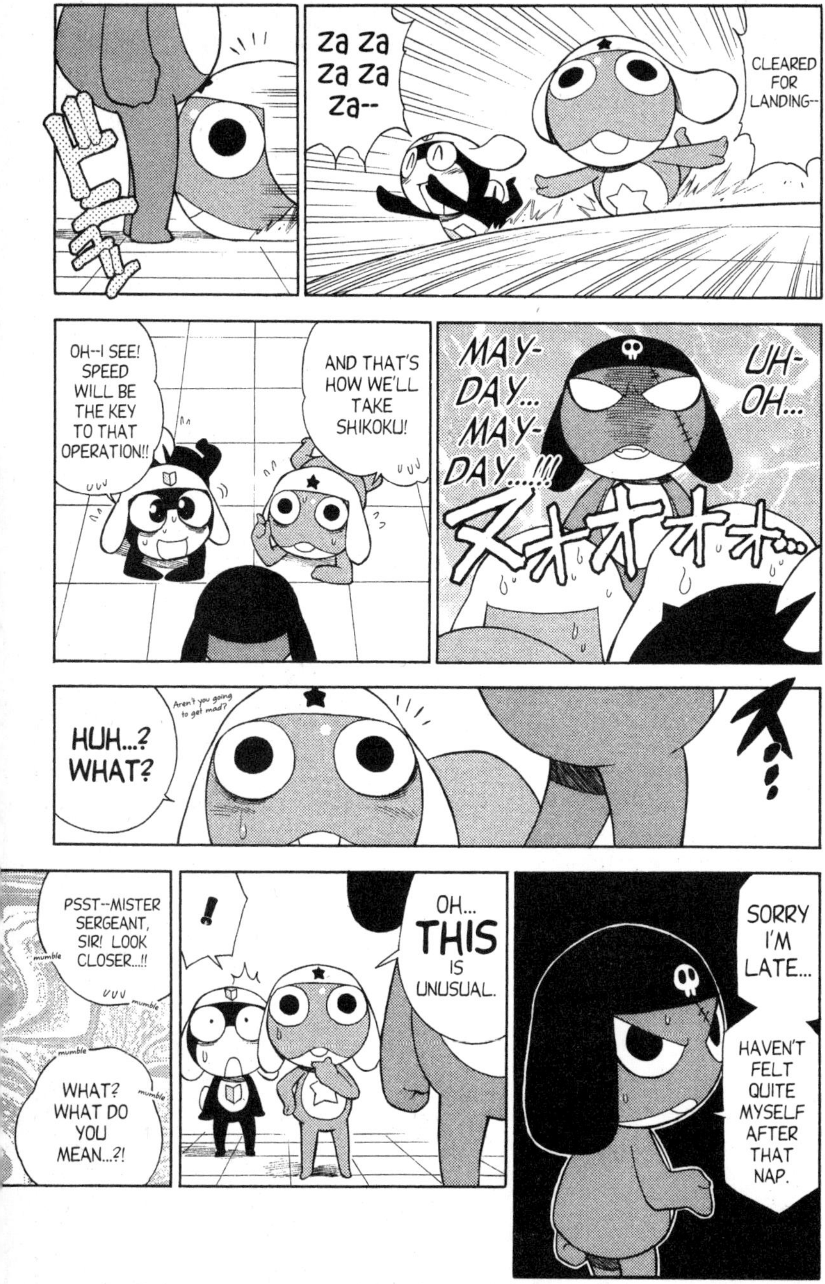
CLEARED FOR LANDING--
Za Za Za Za Za--
UH-OH...
MAY-DAY... MAY-DAY...!!!
AND THAT'S HOW WE'LL TAKE SHIKOKU!
OH--I SEE! SPEED WILL BE THE KEY TO THAT OPERATION!!
Aren't you going to get mad?
HUH...? WHAT?
SORRY I'M LATE...
HAVEN'T FELT QUITE MYSELF AFTER THAT NAP.
OH... THIS IS UNUSUAL.
!
PSST--MISTER SERGEANT, SIR! LOOK CLOSER...!!
mumble
mumble
mumble
WHAT? WHAT DO YOU MEAN...?!
mumble

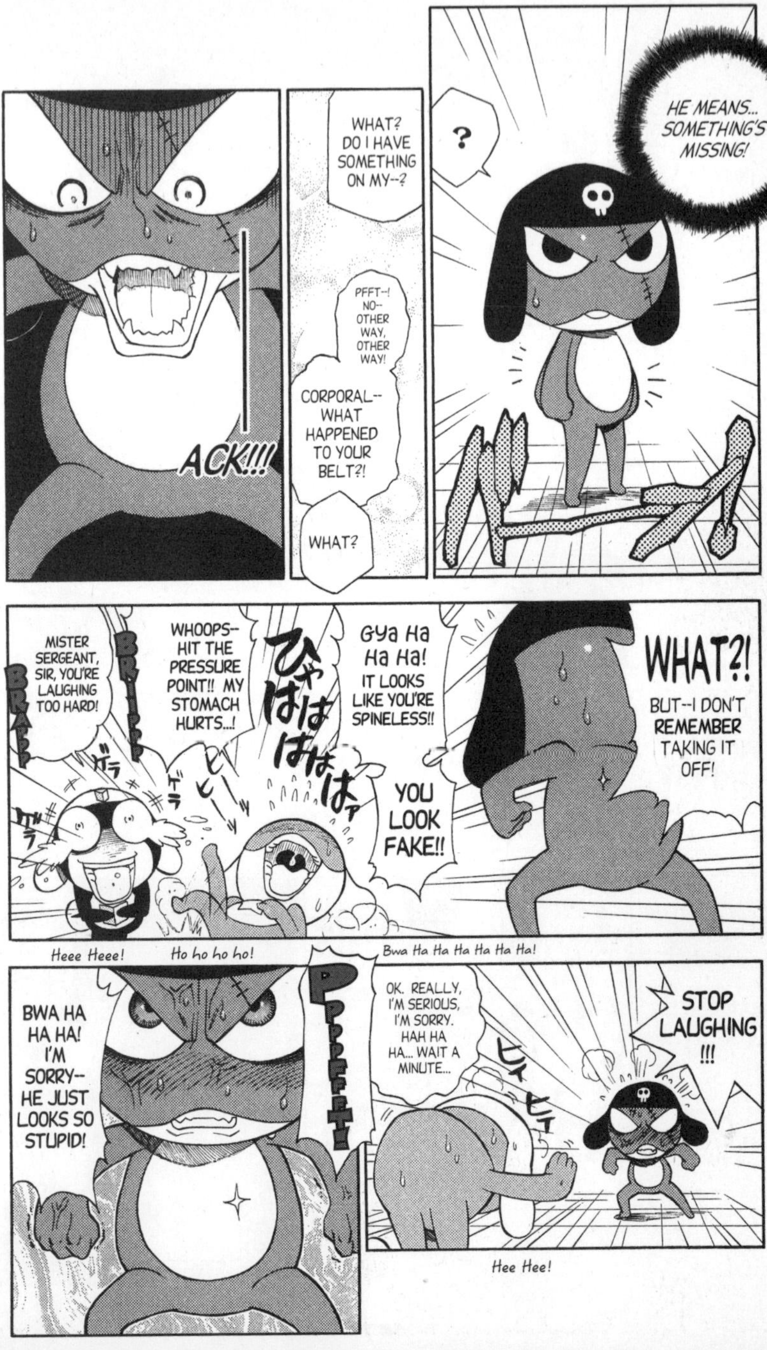
HE MEANS... SOMETHING'S MISSING!
?
WHAT? DO I HAVE SOMETHING ON MY--?
PFFT--! NO-- OTHER WAY, OTHER WAY!
CORPORAL-- WHAT HAPPENED TO YOUR BELT?!
WHAT?
ACK!!!
WHAT?!
BUT--I DON'T REMEMBER TAKING IT OFF!
GYA HA HA HA! IT LOOKS LIKE YOU'RE SPINELESS!!
YOU LOOK FAKE!!
ひゃははははァ
WHOOPS-- HIT THE PRESSURE POINT!! MY STOMACH HURTS...!
MISTER SERGEANT, SIR, YOU'RE LAUGHING TOO HARD!
BRAPP
BRIPPP
Bwa Ha Ha Ha Ha Ha Ha!
Ho ho ho ho!
Heee Heee!
STOP LAUGHING!!!
OK. REALLY, I'M SERIOUS, I'M SORRY. HAH HA HA... WAIT A MINUTE...
Hee Hee!
PPPPFFFT!
BWA HA HA HA! I'M SORRY-- HE JUST LOOKS SO STUPID!

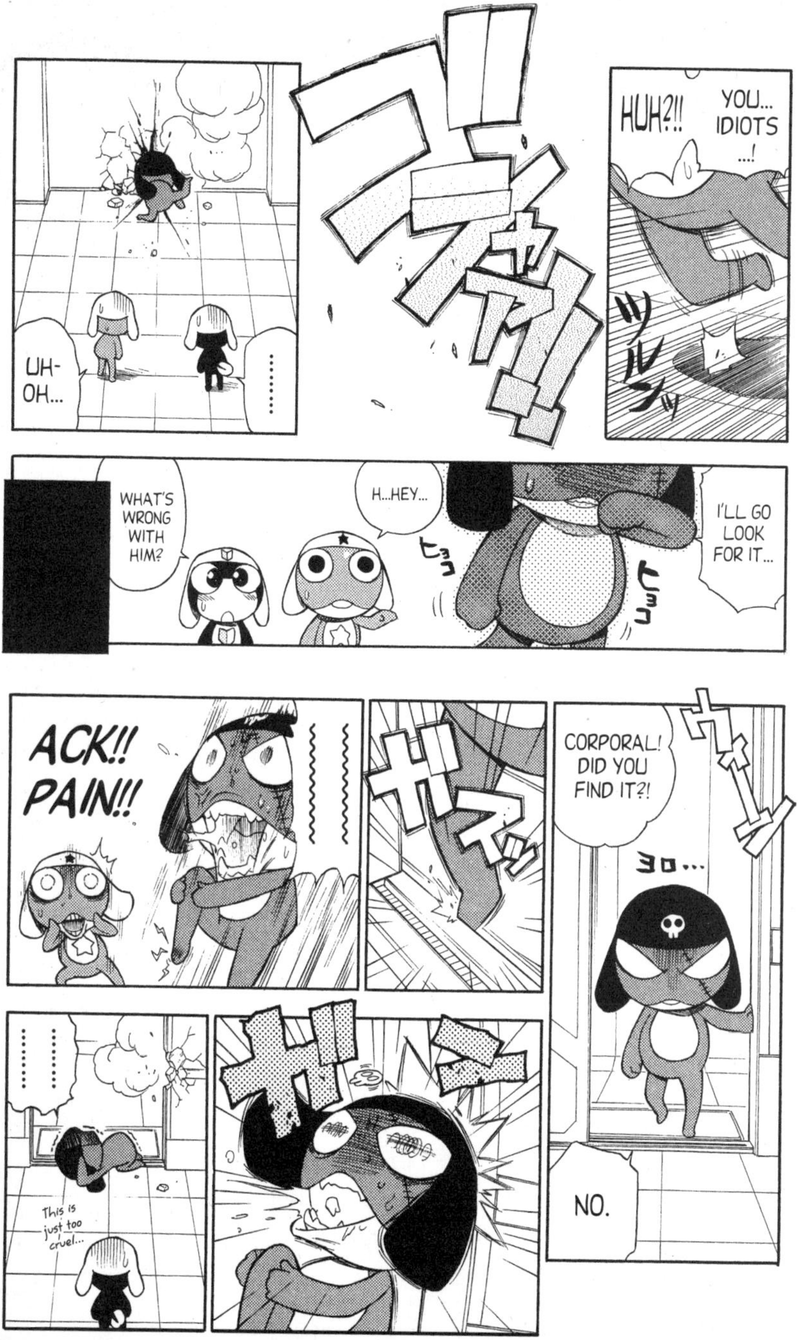
YOU... IDIOTS ...!
HUH?!!
UH-OH...
....
I'LL GO LOOK FOR IT...
H...HEY...
WHAT'S WRONG WITH HIM?
CORPORAL! DID YOU FIND IT?!
ヨロ...
NO.
ACK!! PAIN!!
......
......
This is just too cruel...

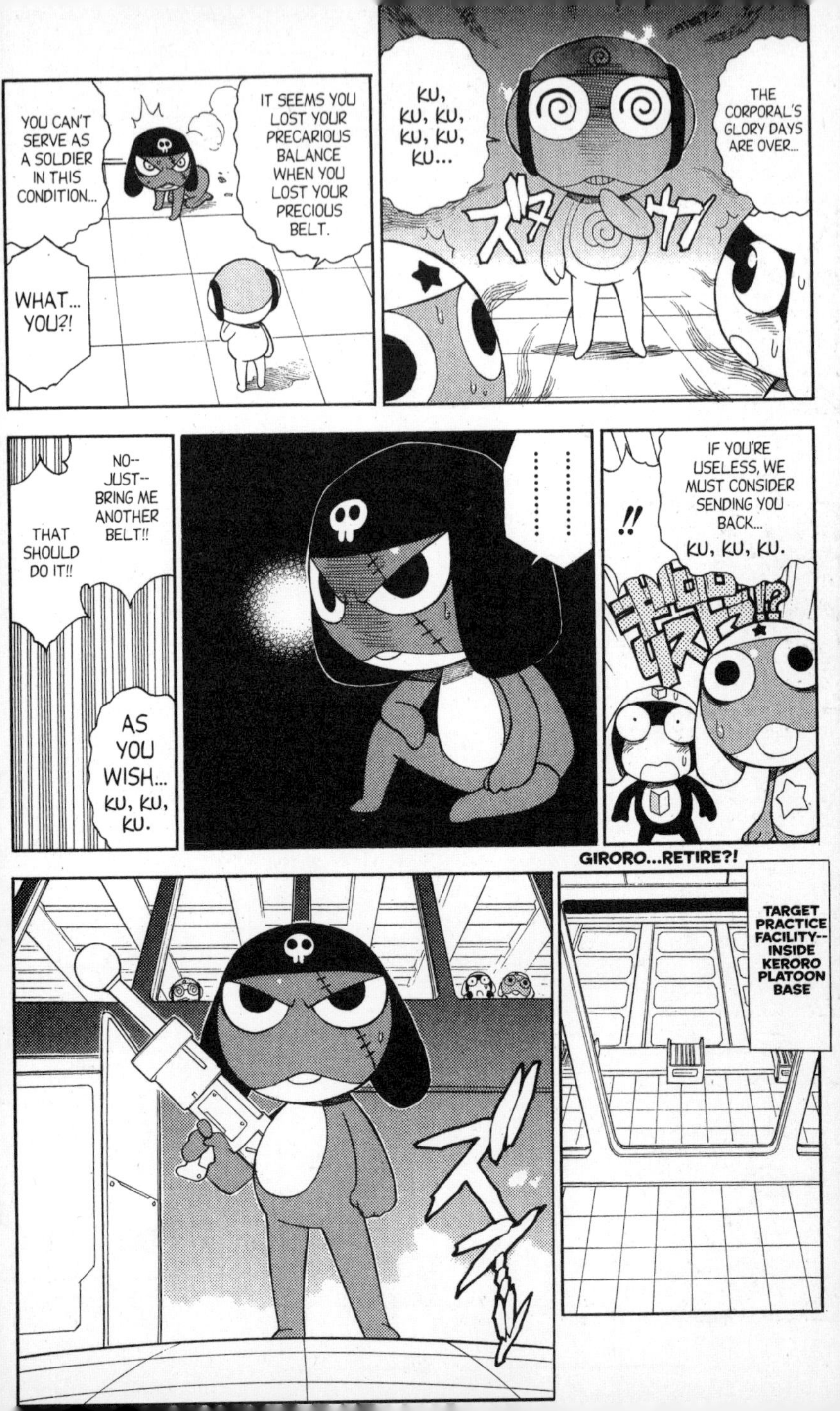
THE CORPORAL'S GLORY DAYS ARE OVER...
KU, KU, KU, KU, KU, KU...
IT SEEMS YOU LOST YOUR PRECARIOUS BALANCE WHEN YOU LOST YOUR PRECIOUS BELT.
YOU CAN'T SERVE AS A SOLDIER IN THIS CONDITION...
WHAT... YOU?!
IF YOU'RE USELESS, WE MUST CONSIDER SENDING YOU BACK... KU, KU, KU.
!!
......
NO-- JUST-- BRING ME ANOTHER BELT!!
THAT SHOULD DO IT!!
AS YOU WISH... KU, KU, KU.
GIRORO...RETIRE?!
TARGET PRACTICE FACILITY-- INSIDE KERORO PLATOON BASE

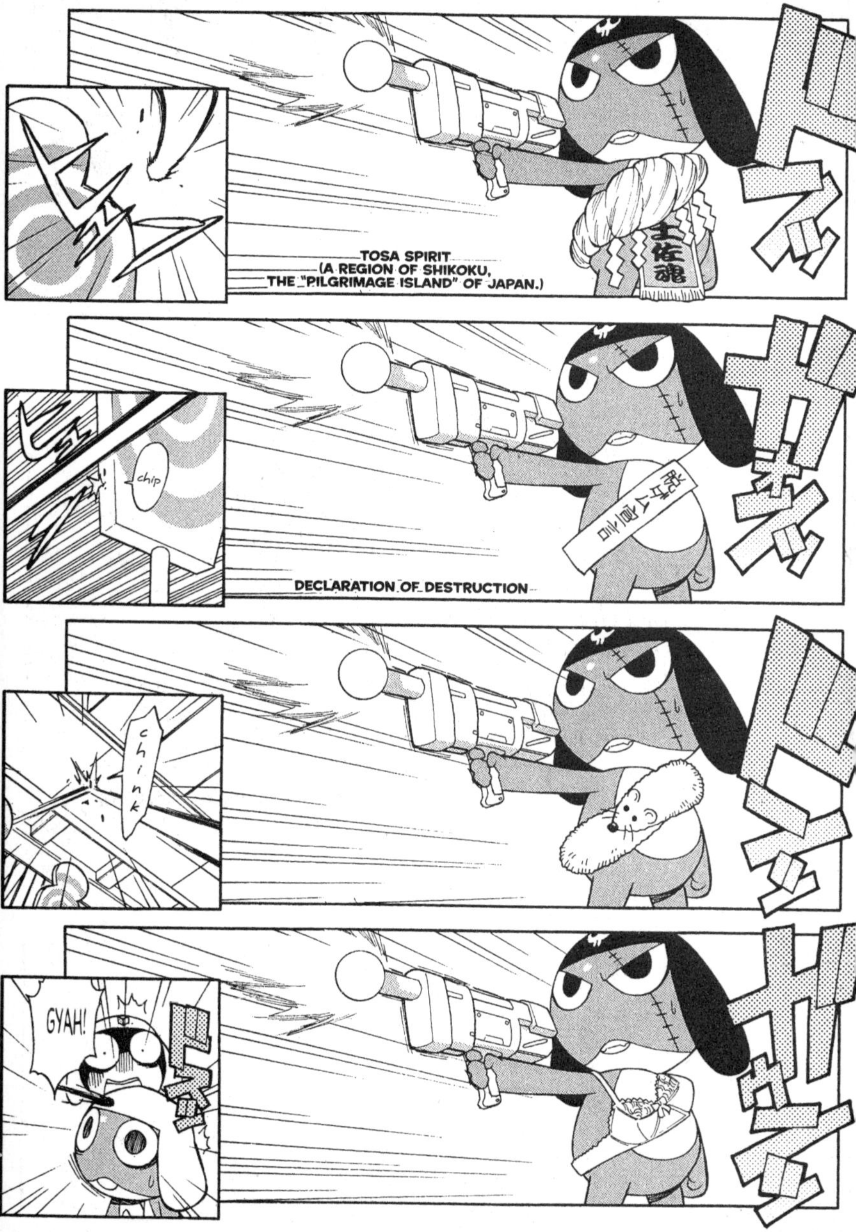
土佐魂
TOSA SPIRIT
(A REGION OF SHIKOKU,
THE "PILGRIMAGE ISLAND" OF JAPAN.)
DECLARATION OF DESTRUCTION
chip
chink
GYAH!

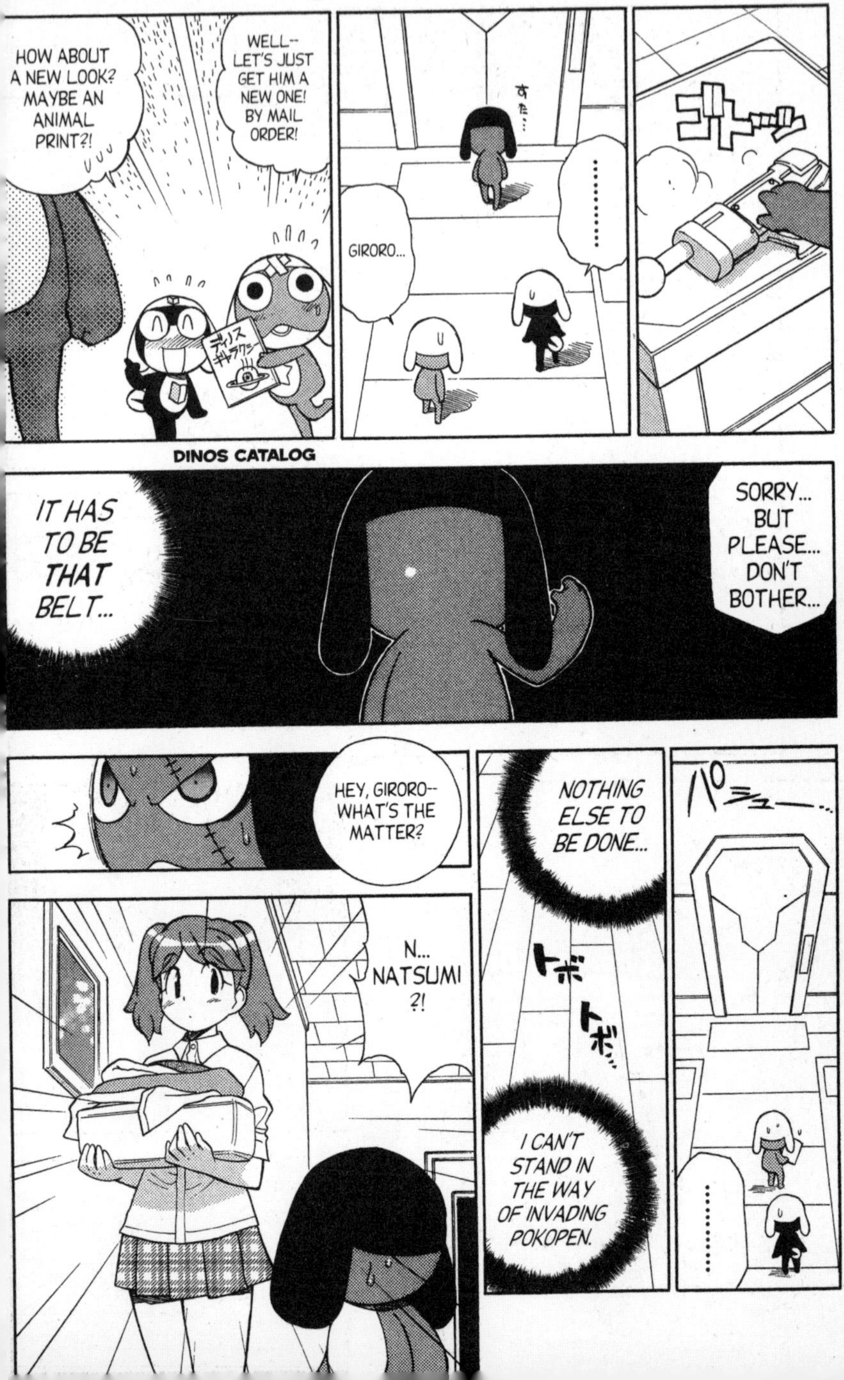
すた...
....
GIRORO...
WELL-- LET'S JUST GET HIM A NEW ONE! BY MAIL ORDER!
HOW ABOUT A NEW LOOK? MAYBE AN ANIMAL PRINT?!
ディノス ギャラクシー
DINOS CATALOG
SORRY... BUT PLEASE... DON'T BOTHER...
IT HAS TO BE THAT BELT...
パシュー...
....
NOTHING ELSE TO BE DONE...
トボ トボ...
I CAN'T STAND IN THE WAY OF INVADING POKOPEN.
HEY, GIRORO-- WHAT'S THE MATTER?
N... NATSUMI?!

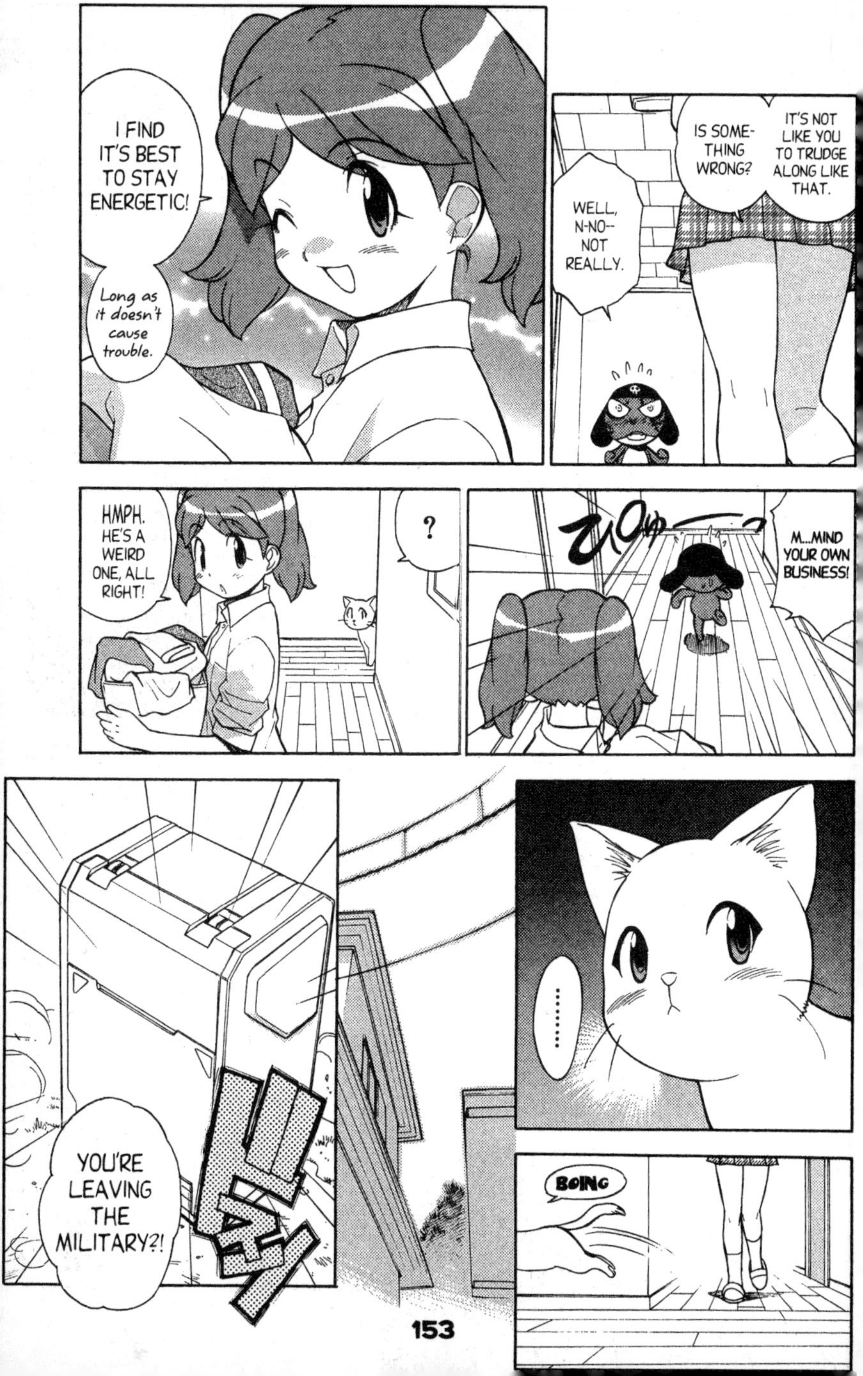
IT'S NOT LIKE YOU TO TRUDGE ALONG LIKE THAT.
IS SOME-THING WRONG?
WELL, N-NO-- NOT REALLY.
I FIND IT'S BEST TO STAY ENERGETIC!
Long as it doesn't cause trouble.
M...MIND YOUR OWN BUSINESS!
?
HMPH. HE'S A WEIRD ONE, ALL RIGHT!
....
BOING
YOU'RE LEAVING THE MILITARY?!

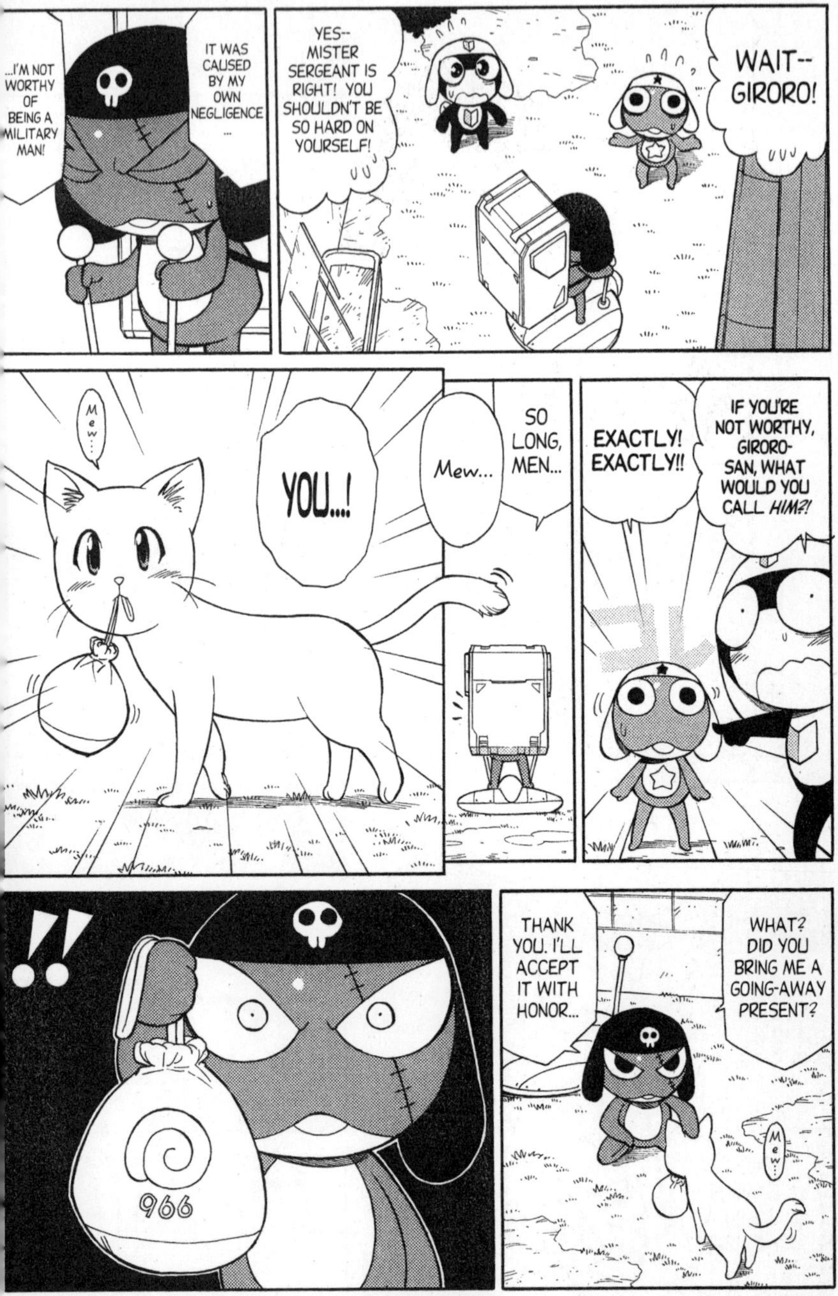
WAIT-- GIRORO!
YES-- MISTER SERGEANT IS RIGHT! YOU SHOULDN'T BE SO HARD ON YOURSELF!
IT WAS CAUSED BY MY OWN NEGLIGENCE...
...I'M NOT WORTHY OF BEING A MILITARY MAN!
IF YOU'RE NOT WORTHY, GIRORO-SAN, WHAT WOULD YOU CALL *HIM?!*
EXACTLY! EXACTLY!!
SO LONG, MEN...
Mew...
YOU...!
Mew...
WHAT? DID YOU BRING ME A GOING-AWAY PRESENT?
THANK YOU. I'LL ACCEPT IT WITH HONOR...
Mew...
!!
966

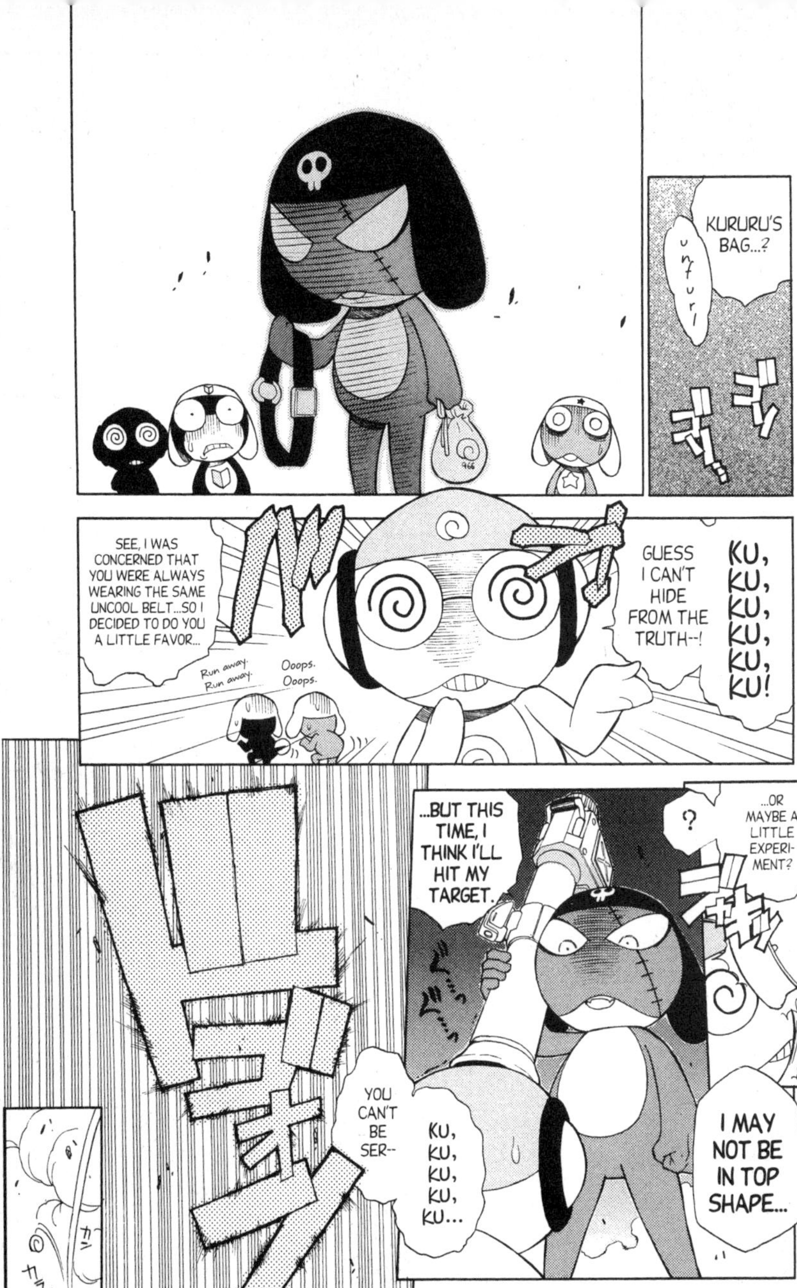
KURURU'S BAG...?
unfuri
GUESS I CAN'T HIDE FROM THE TRUTH--!
KU, KU, KU, KU, KU, KU!
SEE, I WAS CONCERNED THAT YOU WERE ALWAYS WEARING THE SAME UNCOOL BELT...SO I DECIDED TO DO YOU A LITTLE FAVOR...
Ooops. Ooops.
Run away. Run away.
...OR MAYBE A LITTLE EXPERIMENT?
?
...BUT THIS TIME, I THINK I'LL HIT MY TARGET.
I MAY NOT BE IN TOP SHAPE...
KU, KU, KU, KU, KU...
YOU CAN'T BE SER--

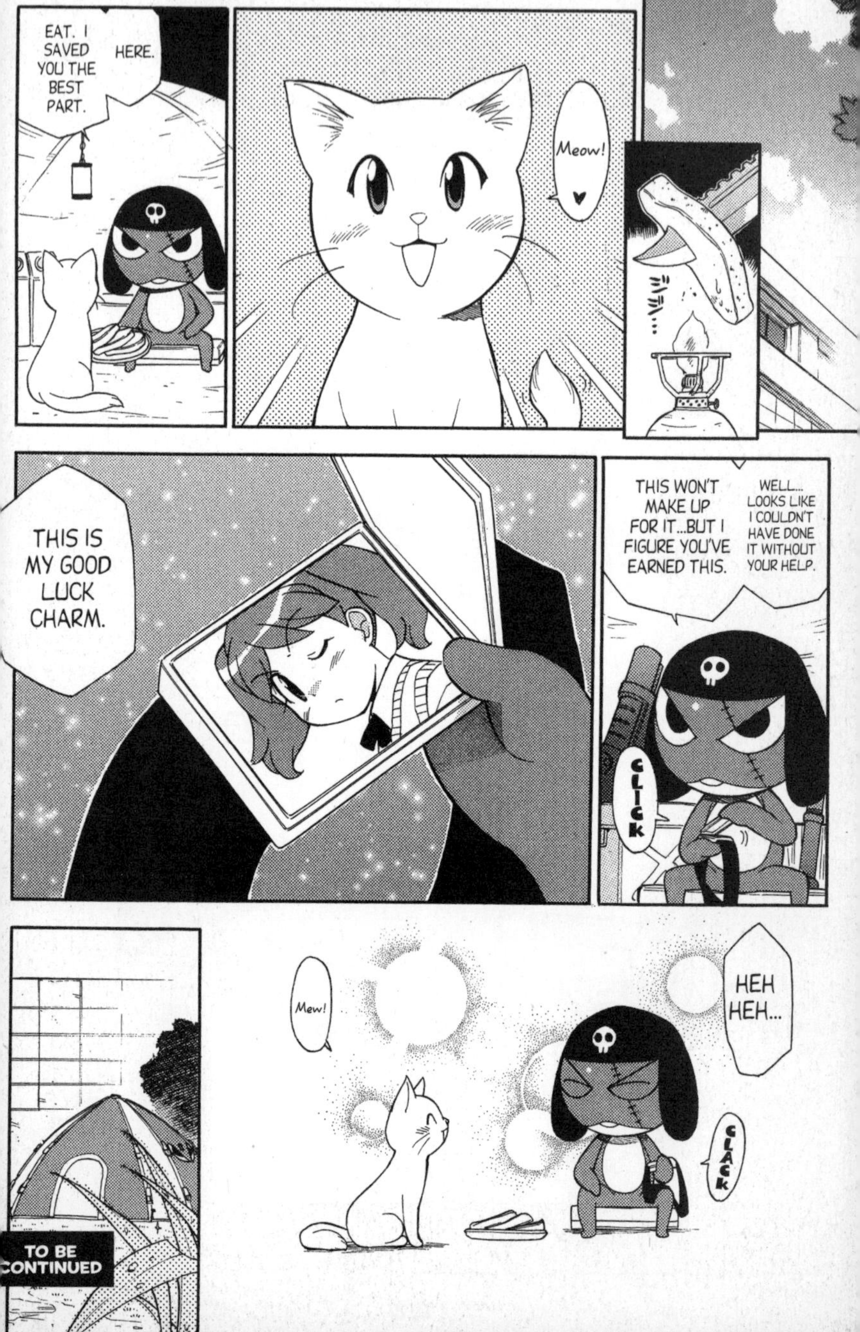
ジジジ…
Meow! ♥
HERE.
EAT. I SAVED YOU THE BEST PART.
WELL... LOOKS LIKE I COULDN'T HAVE DONE IT WITHOUT YOUR HELP.
THIS WON'T MAKE UP FOR IT...BUT I FIGURE YOU'VE EARNED THIS.
CLICK
THIS IS MY GOOD LUCK CHARM.
HEH HEH...
CLACK
Mew!
TO BE CONTINUED

ENCOUNTER LIII
THE WORLD'S SMALLEST INVASION: PART I

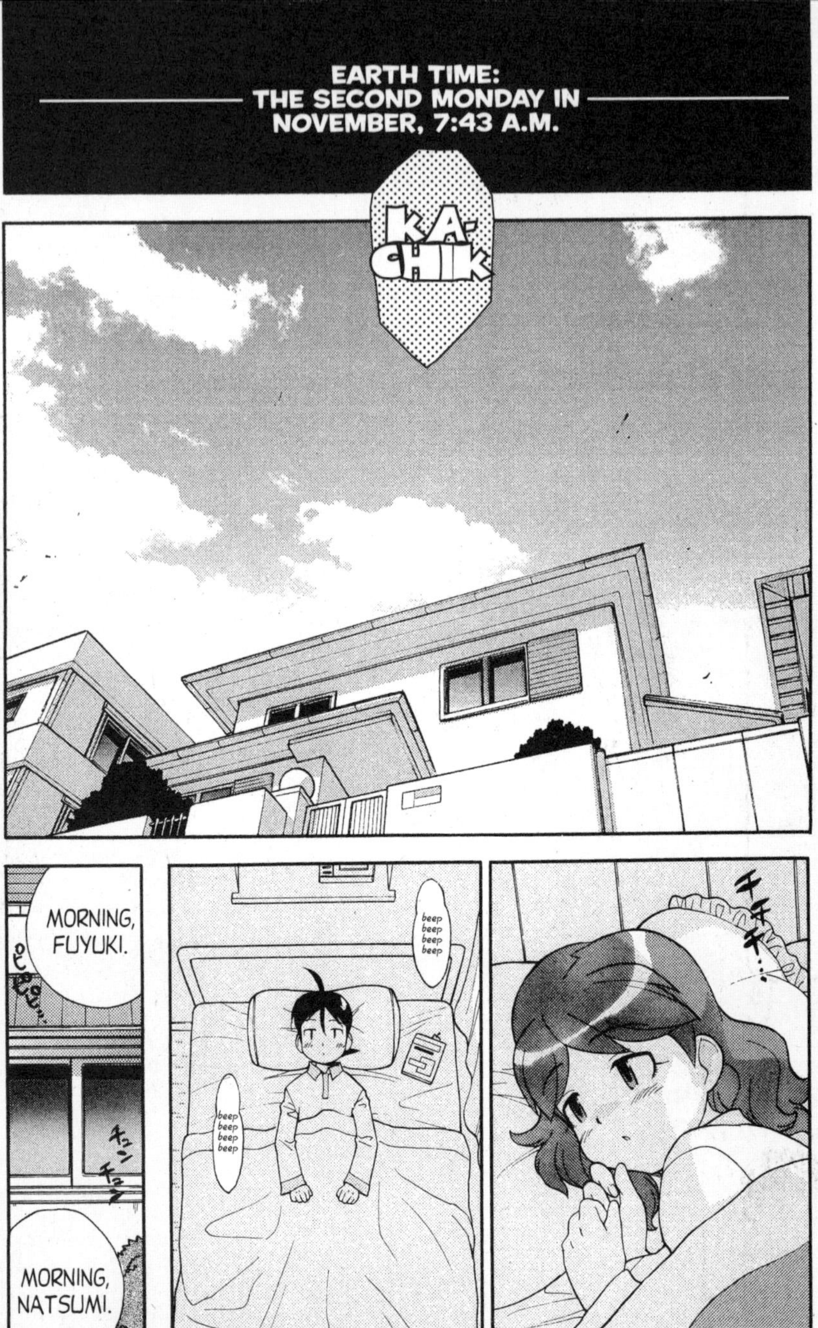
EARTH TIME:
THE SECOND MONDAY IN NOVEMBER, 7:43 A.M.
KA-CHIK
チチチ...
beep beep beep beep
beep beep beep beep
MORNING, FUYUKI.
チュン チュン
MORNING, NATSUMI.

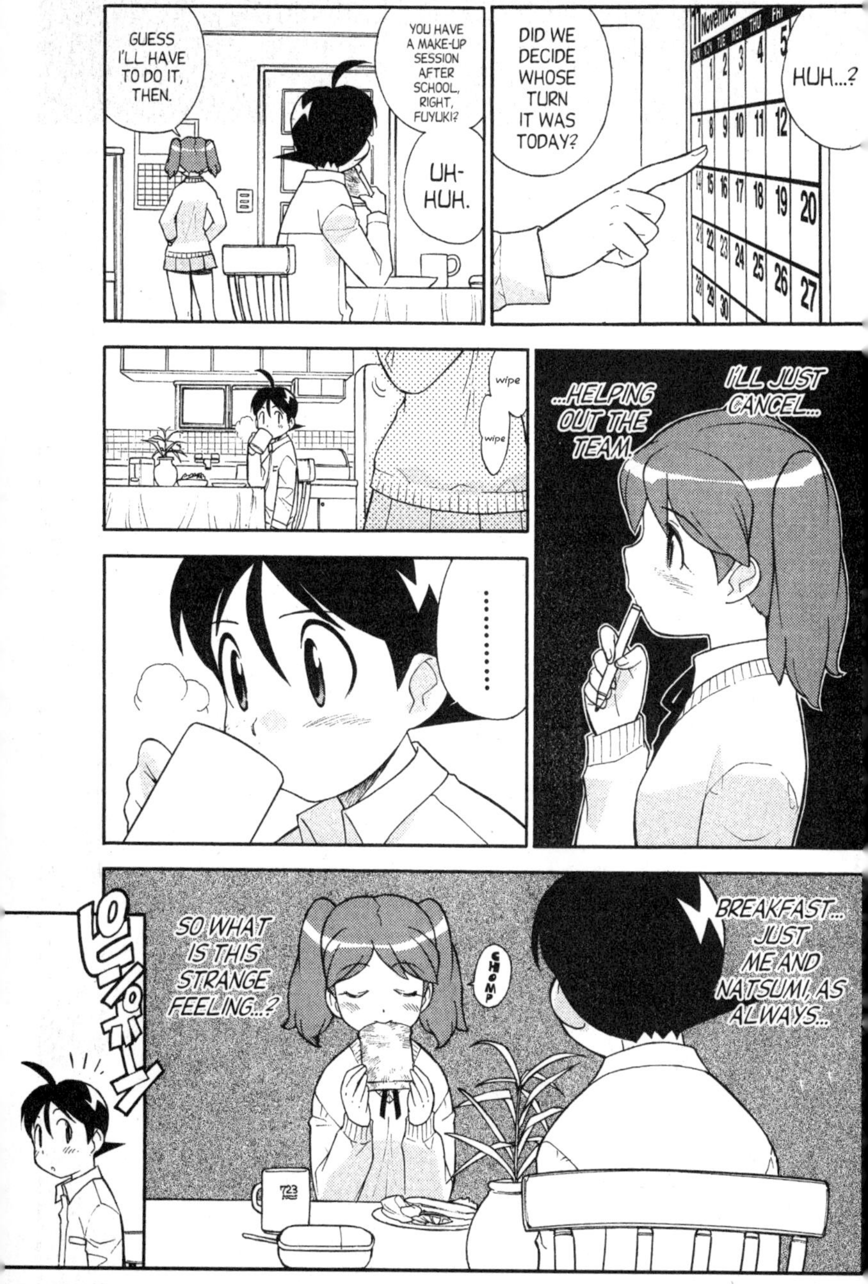
DID WE DECIDE WHOSE TURN IT WAS TODAY?
HUH...?
YOU HAVE A MAKE-UP SESSION AFTER SCHOOL, RIGHT, FUYUKI?
UH-HUH.
GUESS I'LL HAVE TO DO IT, THEN.
I'LL JUST CANCEL...
...HELPING OUT THE TEAM.
wipe
wipe
......
BREAKFAST... JUST ME AND NATSUMI, AS ALWAYS...
CHOMP
SO WHAT IS THIS STRANGE FEELING...?

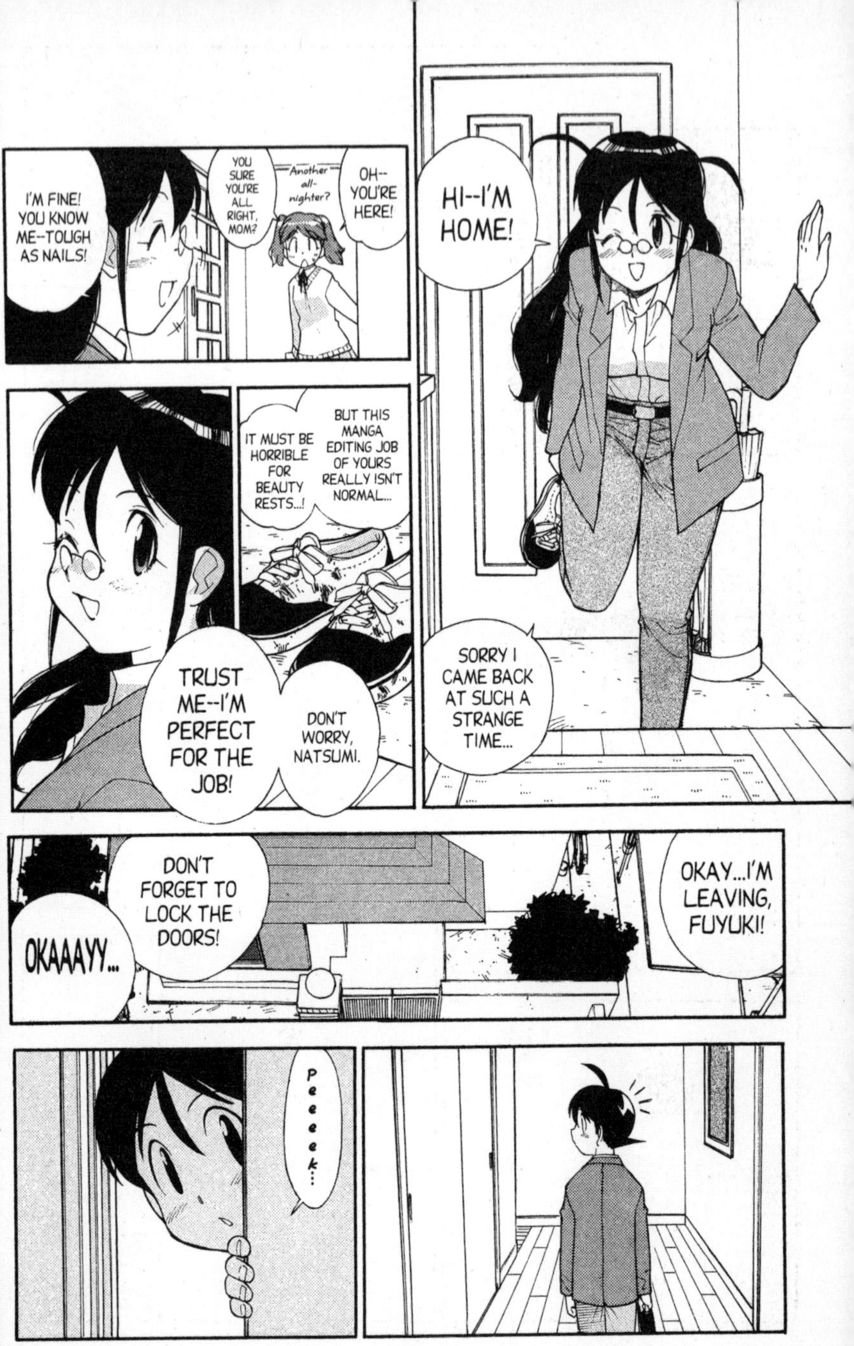
HI--I'M HOME!
SORRY I CAME BACK AT SUCH A STRANGE TIME...
OH-- YOU'RE HERE!
Another all-nighter?
YOU SURE YOU'RE ALL RIGHT, MOM?
I'M FINE! YOU KNOW ME--TOUGH AS NAILS!
BUT THIS MANGA EDITING JOB OF YOURS REALLY ISN'T NORMAL...
IT MUST BE HORRIBLE FOR BEAUTY RESTS...!
DON'T WORRY, NATSUMI.
TRUST ME--I'M PERFECT FOR THE JOB!
OKAY...I'M LEAVING, FUYUKI!
DON'T FORGET TO LOCK THE DOORS!
OKAAAYY...
Peeeeek...

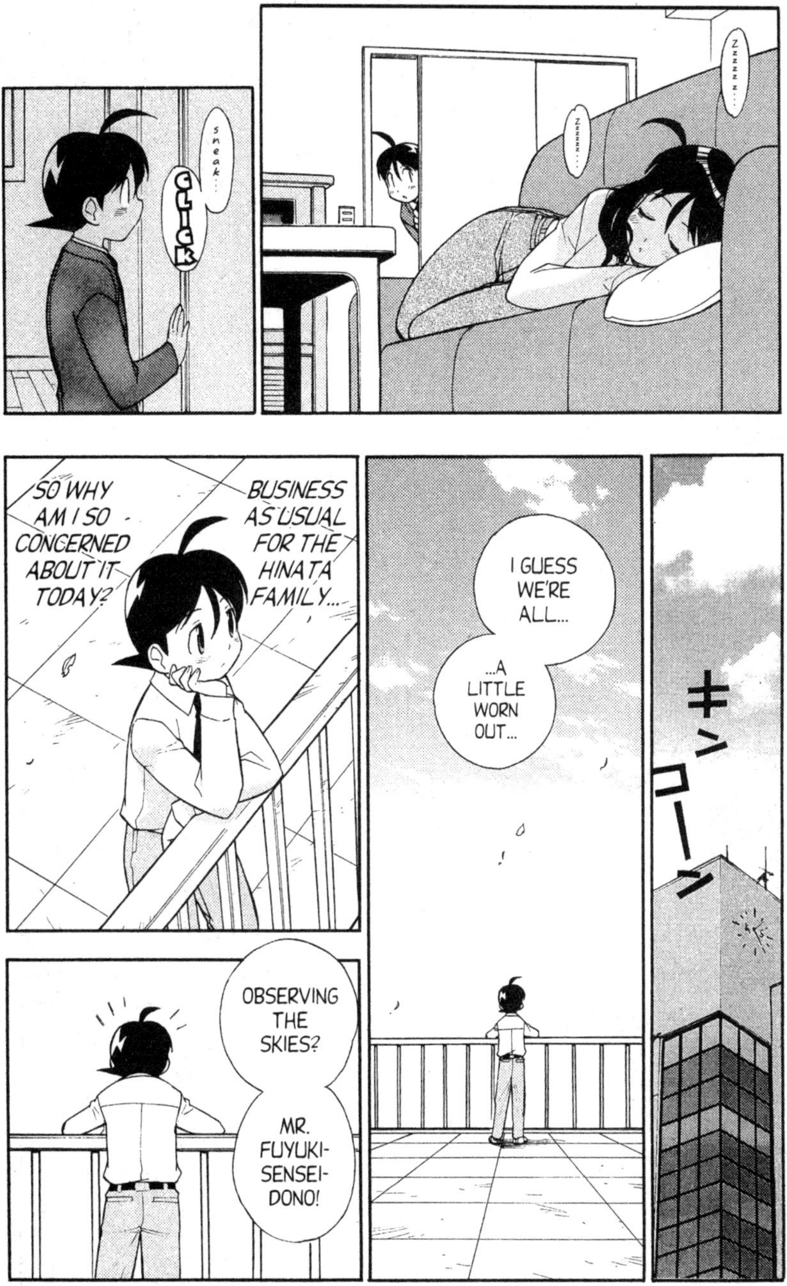
Zzzzz z...
Zzzzzz...
sneak...
CLICK
キンコーン
I GUESS WE'RE ALL...
...A LITTLE WORN OUT...
BUSINESS AS USUAL FOR THE HINATA FAMILY...
SO WHY AM I SO CONCERNED ABOUT IT TODAY?
OBSERVING THE SKIES?
MR. FUYUKI-SENSEI-DONO!

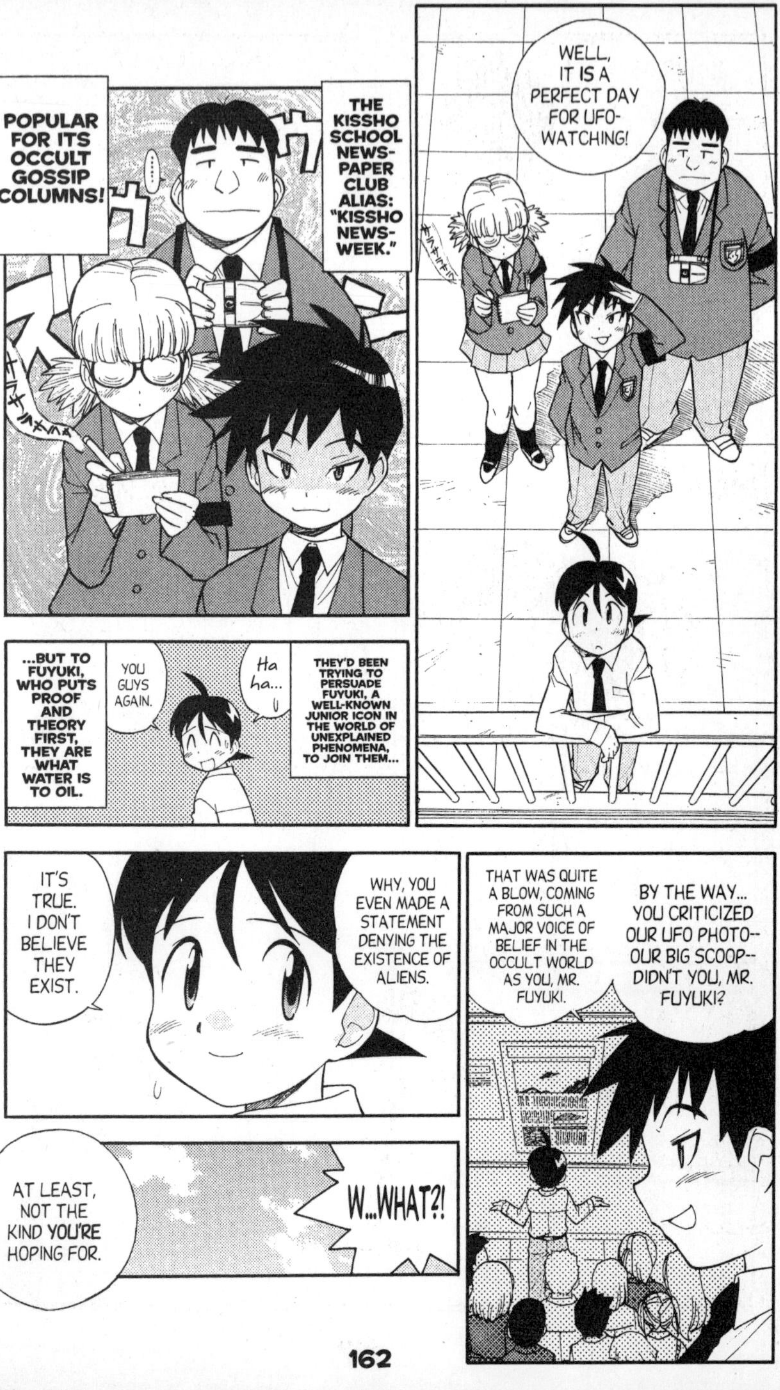

WELL, IT IS A PERFECT DAY FOR UFO-WATCHING!
THE KISSHO SCHOOL NEWSPAPER CLUB ALIAS: "KISSHO NEWSWEEK."
POPULAR FOR ITS OCCULT GOSSIP COLUMNS!
......
THEY'D BEEN TRYING TO PERSUADE FUYUKI, A WELL-KNOWN JUNIOR ICON IN THE WORLD OF UNEXPLAINED PHENOMENA, TO JOIN THEM...
Ha ha...
YOU GUYS AGAIN.
...BUT TO FUYUKI, WHO PUTS PROOF AND THEORY FIRST, THEY ARE WHAT WATER IS TO OIL.
BY THE WAY... YOU CRITICIZED OUR UFO PHOTO-- OUR BIG SCOOP-- DIDN'T YOU, MR. FUYUKI?
THAT WAS QUITE A BLOW, COMING FROM SUCH A MAJOR VOICE OF BELIEF IN THE OCCULT WORLD AS YOU, MR. FUYUKI.
WHY, YOU EVEN MADE A STATEMENT DENYING THE EXISTENCE OF ALIENS.
IT'S TRUE. I DON'T BELIEVE THEY EXIST.
W...WHAT?!
AT LEAST, NOT THE KIND YOU'RE HOPING FOR.

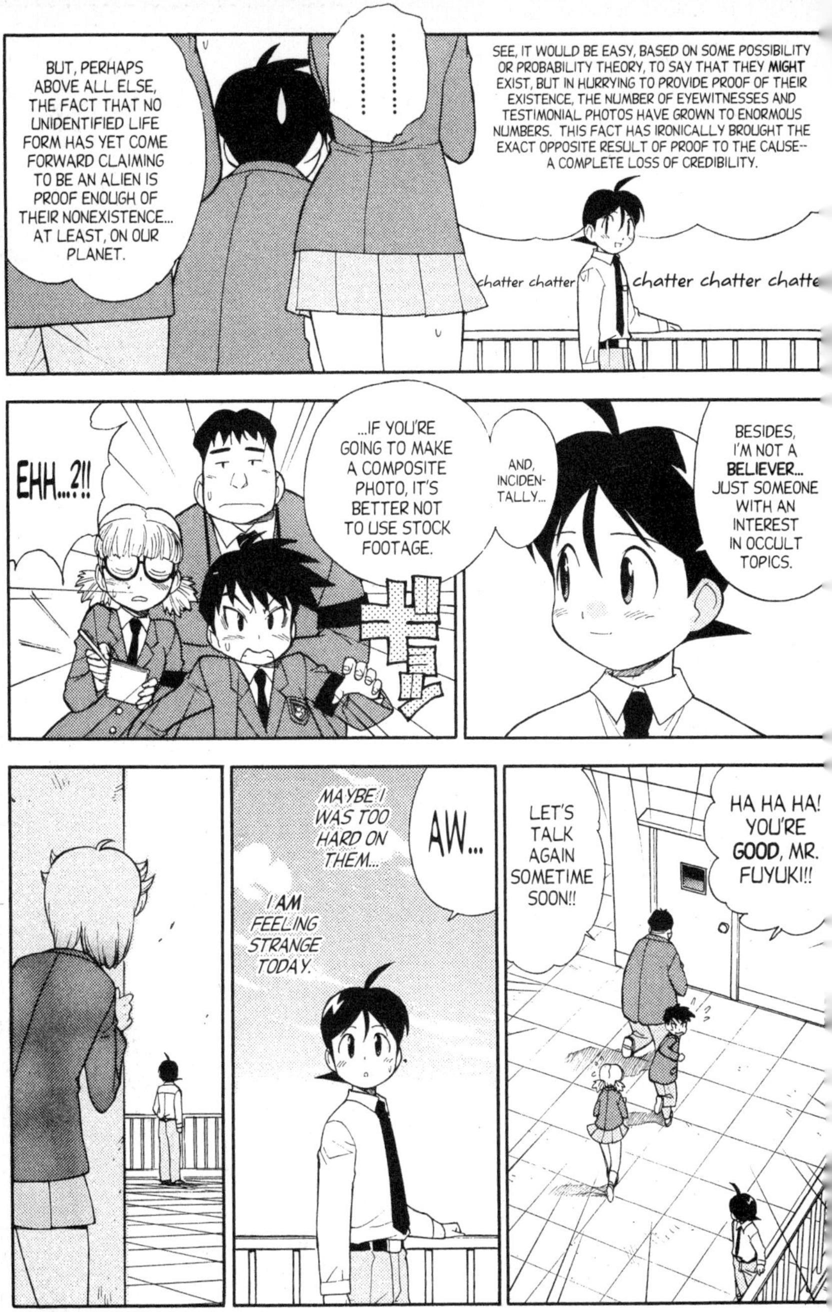
SEE, IT WOULD BE EASY, BASED ON SOME POSSIBILITY OR PROBABILITY THEORY, TO SAY THAT THEY **MIGHT** EXIST, BUT IN HURRYING TO PROVIDE PROOF OF THEIR EXISTENCE, THE NUMBER OF EYEWITNESSES AND TESTIMONIAL PHOTOS HAVE GROWN TO ENORMOUS NUMBERS. THIS FACT HAS IRONICALLY BROUGHT THE EXACT OPPOSITE RESULT OF PROOF TO THE CAUSE-- A COMPLETE LOSS OF CREDIBILITY.
chatter chatter chatte
chatter chatter
......
BUT, PERHAPS ABOVE ALL ELSE, THE FACT THAT NO UNIDENTIFIED LIFE FORM HAS YET COME FORWARD CLAIMING TO BE AN ALIEN IS PROOF ENOUGH OF THEIR NONEXISTENCE... AT LEAST, ON OUR PLANET.
BESIDES, I'M NOT A **BELIEVER**... JUST SOMEONE WITH AN INTEREST IN OCCULT TOPICS.
AND, INCIDEN-TALLY...
...IF YOU'RE GOING TO MAKE A COMPOSITE PHOTO, IT'S BETTER NOT TO USE STOCK FOOTAGE.
EHH...?!!
HA HA HA! YOU'RE **GOOD**, MR. FUYUKI!!
LET'S TALK AGAIN SOMETIME SOON!!
AW...
MAYBE I WAS TOO HARD ON THEM...
*I **AM** FEELING STRANGE TODAY.*

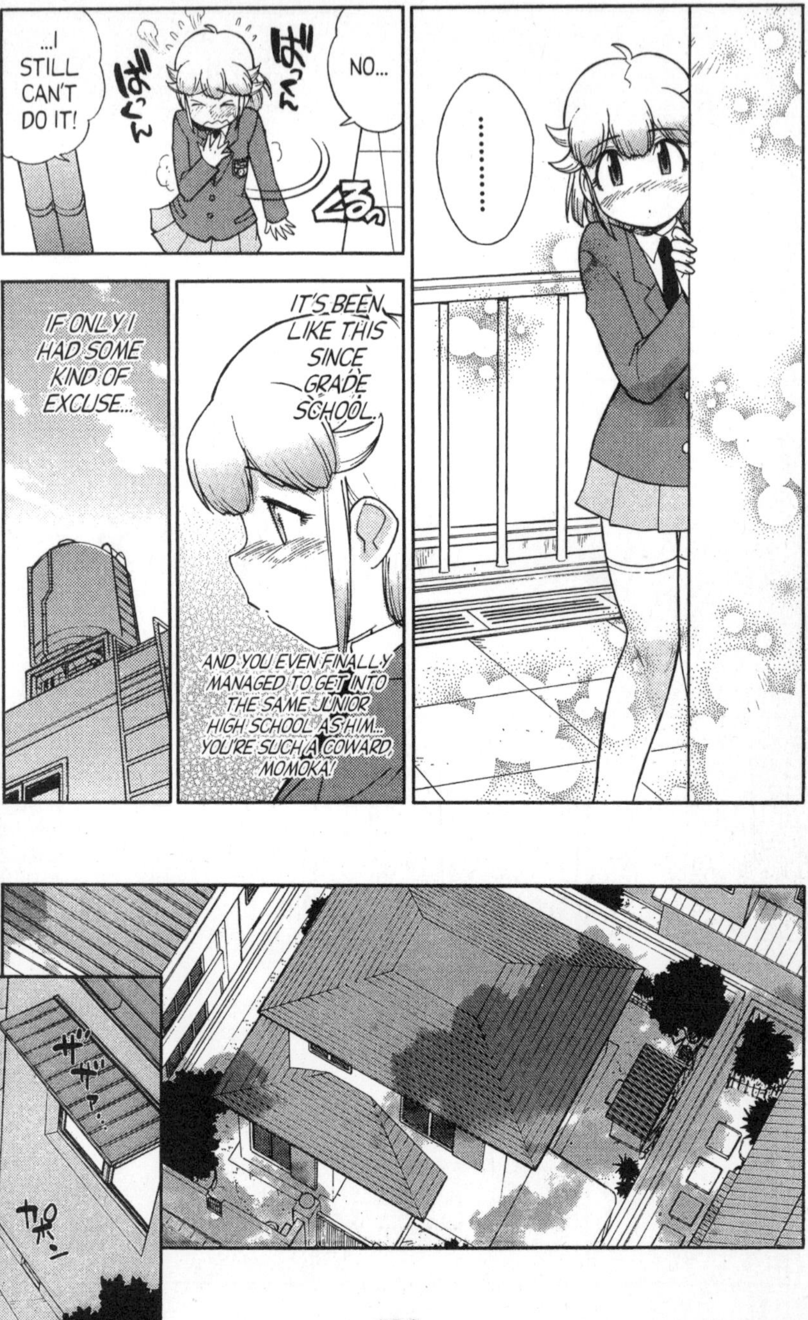
……………
NO...
...I STILL CAN'T DO IT!
IT'S BEEN LIKE THIS SINCE GRADE SCHOOL.
AND YOU EVEN FINALLY MANAGED TO GET INTO THE SAME JUNIOR HIGH SCHOOL AS HIM... YOU'RE SUCH A COWARD, MOMOKA!
IF ONLY I HAD SOME KIND OF EXCUSE...
ザザァ…

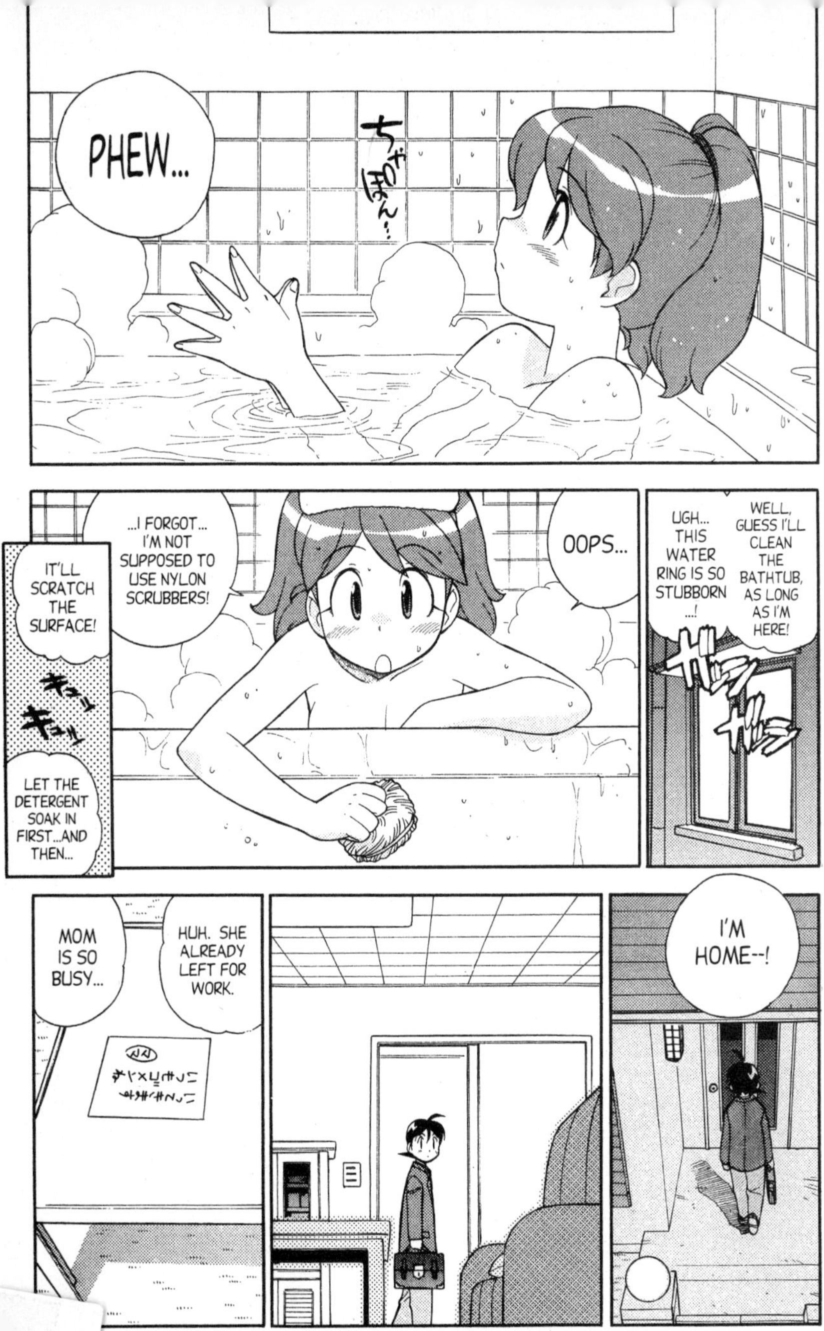
PHEW...
ちゃぽん...
WELL, GUESS I'LL CLEAN THE BATHTUB, AS LONG AS I'M HERE!
UGH... THIS WATER RING IS SO STUBBORN ...!
OOPS...
...I FORGOT... I'M NOT SUPPOSED TO USE NYLON SCRUBBERS!
IT'LL SCRATCH THE SURFACE!
キュッ キュッ
LET THE DETERGENT SOAK IN FIRST...AND THEN...
I'M HOME--!
HUH. SHE ALREADY LEFT FOR WORK.
MOM IS SO BUSY...

Well, back to the salt mines! Sorry I'm never home. —Mom

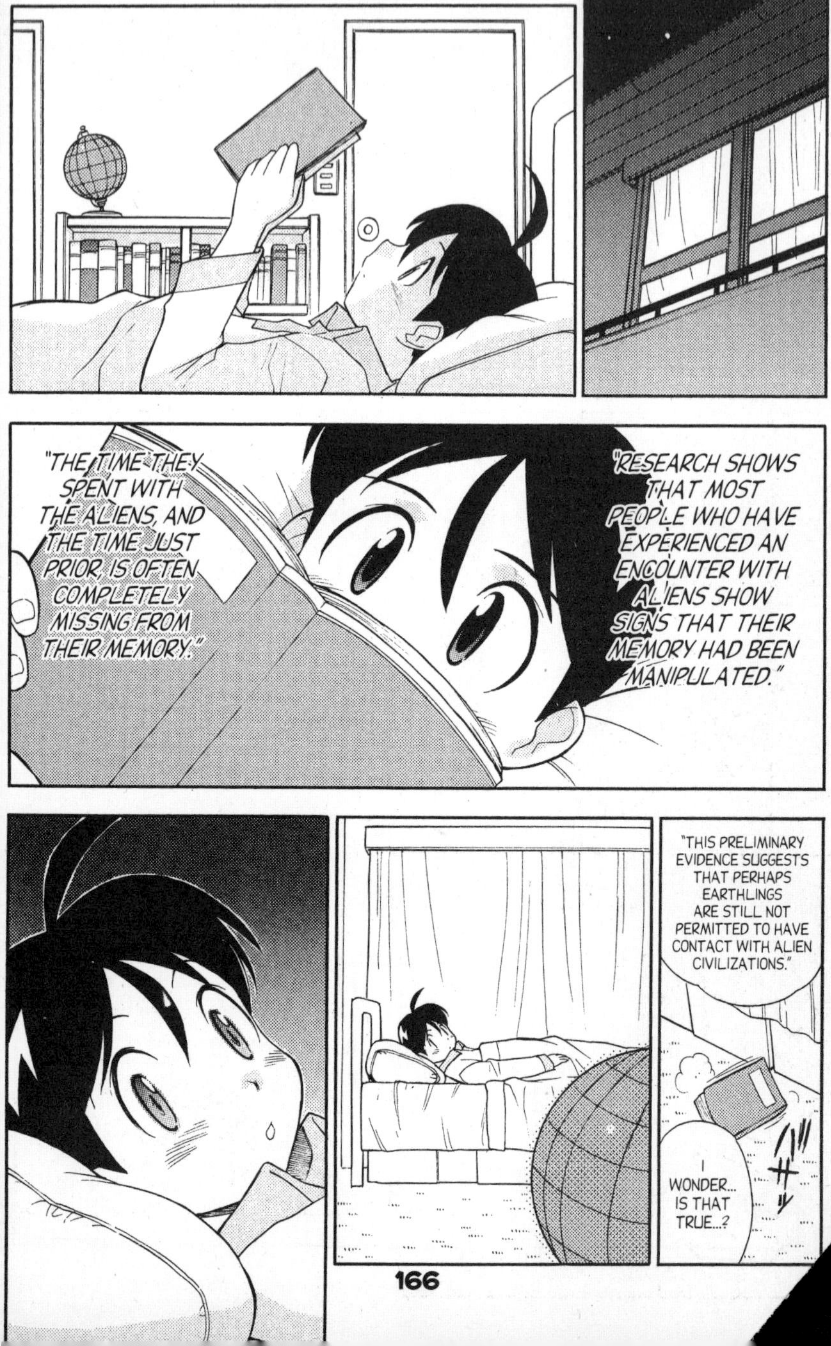
"RESEARCH SHOWS THAT MOST PEOPLE WHO HAVE EXPERIENCED AN ENCOUNTER WITH ALIENS SHOW SIGNS THAT THEIR MEMORY HAD BEEN MANIPULATED."
"THE TIME THEY SPENT WITH THE ALIENS, AND THE TIME JUST PRIOR, IS OFTEN COMPLETELY MISSING FROM THEIR MEMORY."
"THIS PRELIMINARY EVIDENCE SUGGESTS THAT PERHAPS EARTHLINGS ARE STILL NOT PERMITTED TO HAVE CONTACT WITH ALIEN CIVILIZATIONS."
I WONDER... IS THAT TRUE...?

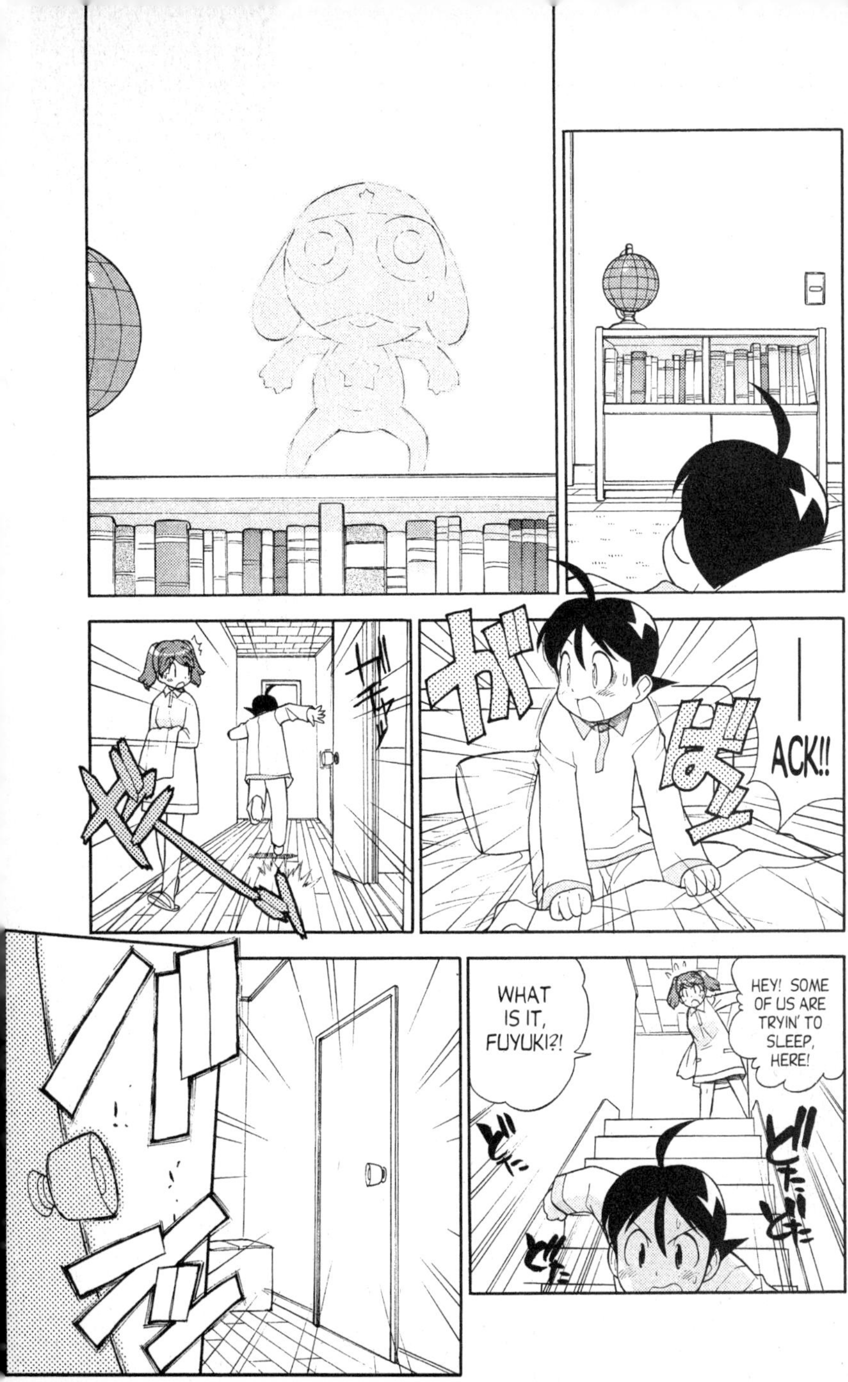
ACK!!
HEY! SOME OF US ARE TRYIN' TO SLEEP, HERE!
WHAT IS IT, FUYUKI?!

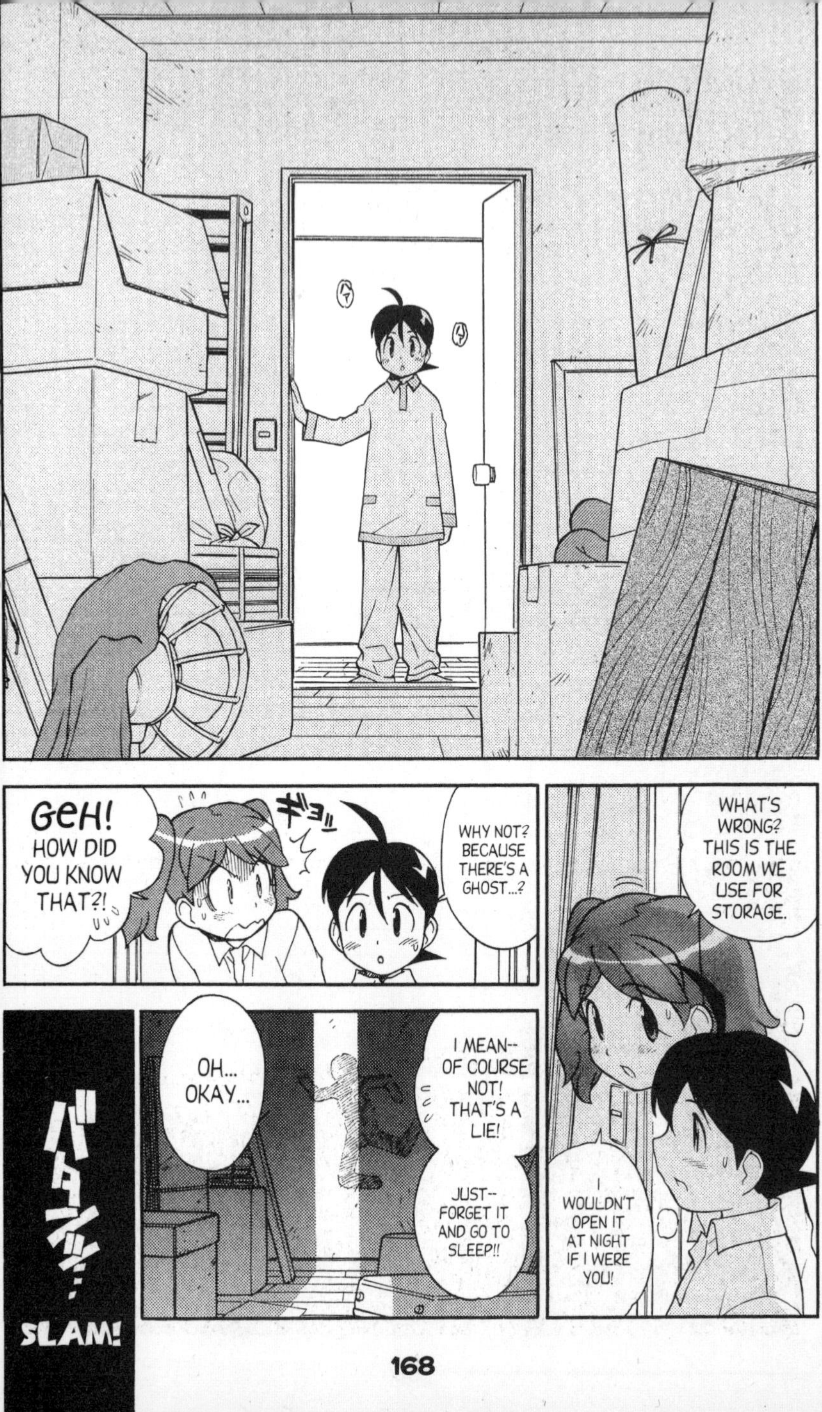
WHAT'S WRONG? THIS IS THE ROOM WE USE FOR STORAGE.
I WOULDN'T OPEN IT AT NIGHT IF I WERE YOU!
WHY NOT? BECAUSE THERE'S A GHOST...?
GEH! HOW DID YOU KNOW THAT?!
I MEAN-- OF COURSE NOT! THAT'S A LIE!
JUST-- FORGET IT AND GO TO SLEEP!!
OH... OKAY...
バタンッ
SLAM!

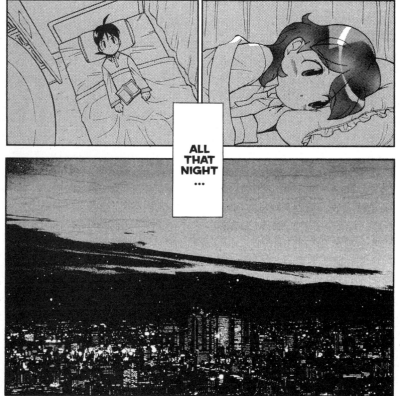

Sob...sob...

ALL
THAT
NIGHT
...

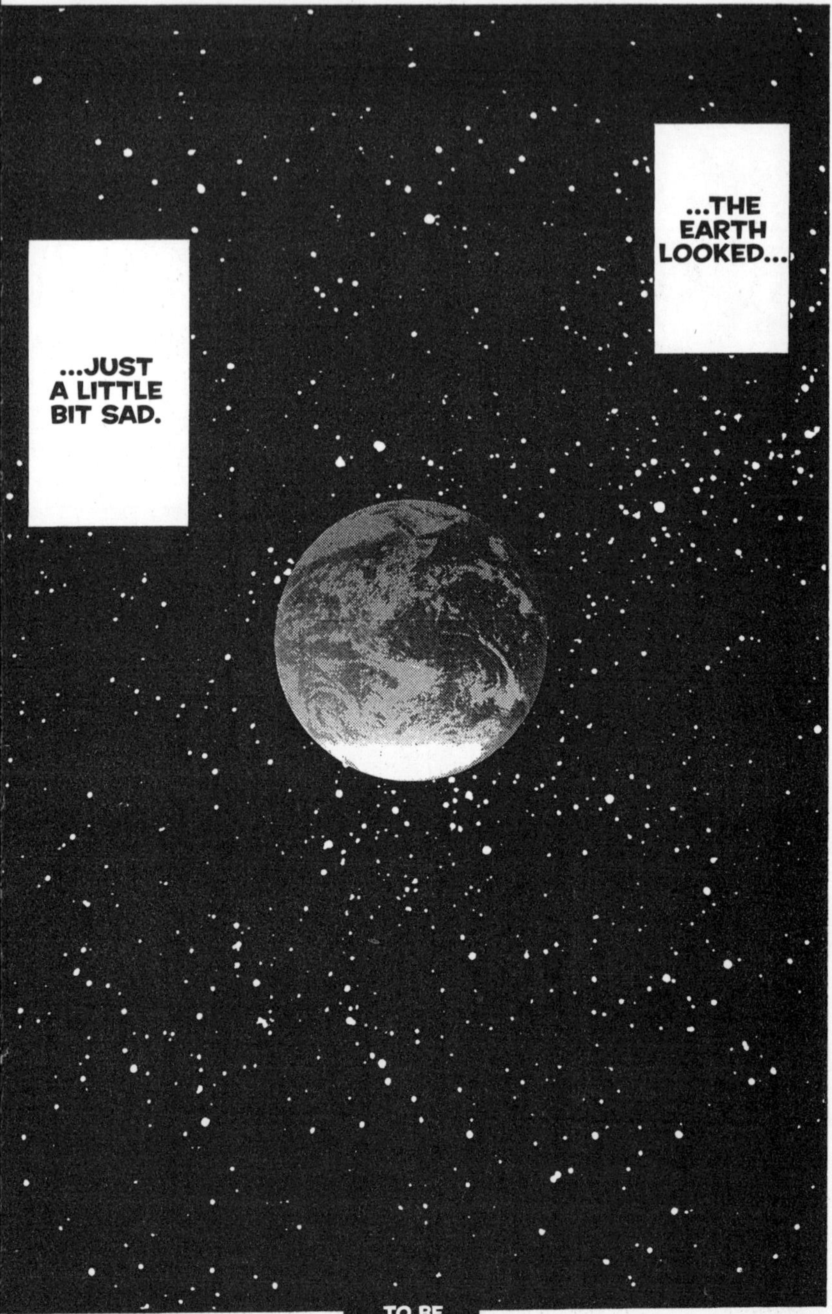
...THE EARTH LOOKED...
...JUST A LITTLE BIT SAD.

TO BE CONTINUED

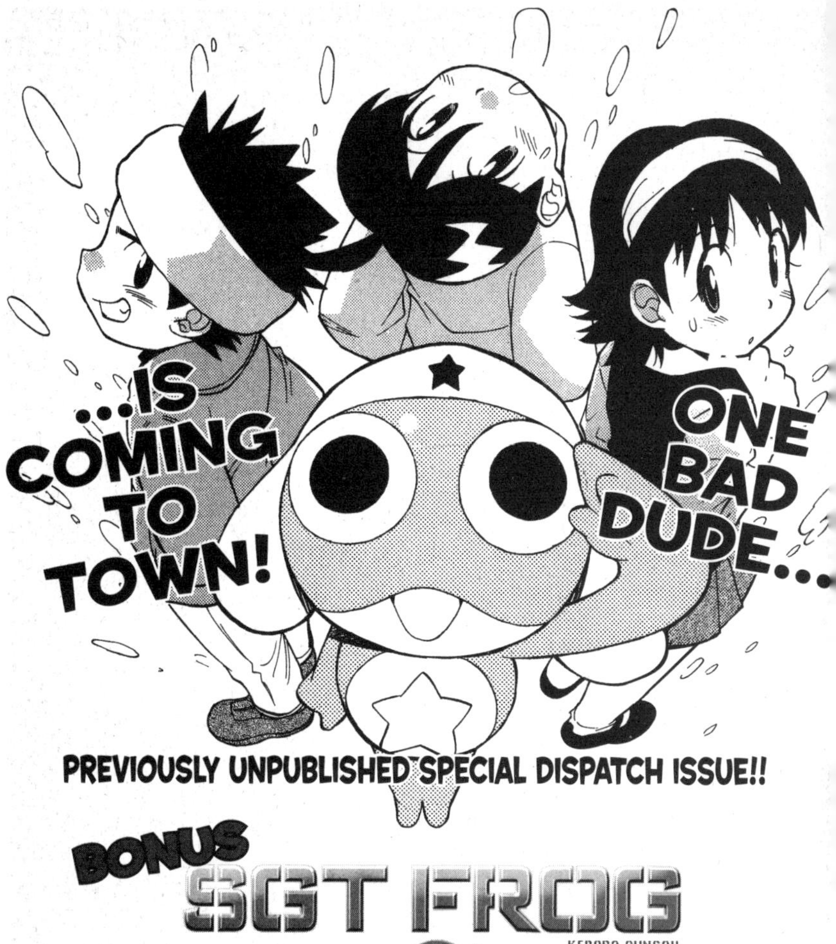
ONE BAD DUDE...
...IS COMING TO TOWN!

PREVIOUSLY UNPUBLISHED SPECIAL DISPATCH ISSUE!!

BONUS SGT FROG

KERORO GUNSOU

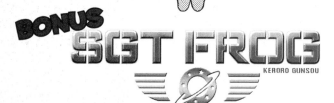

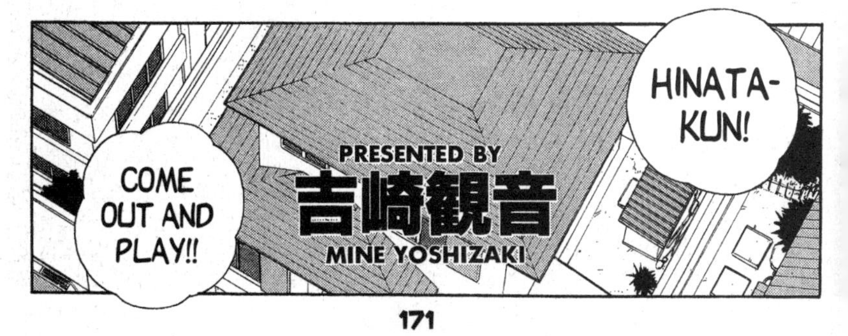
HINATA-KUN!
PRESENTED BY
吉崎観音
MINE YOSHIZAKI
COME OUT AND PLAY!!

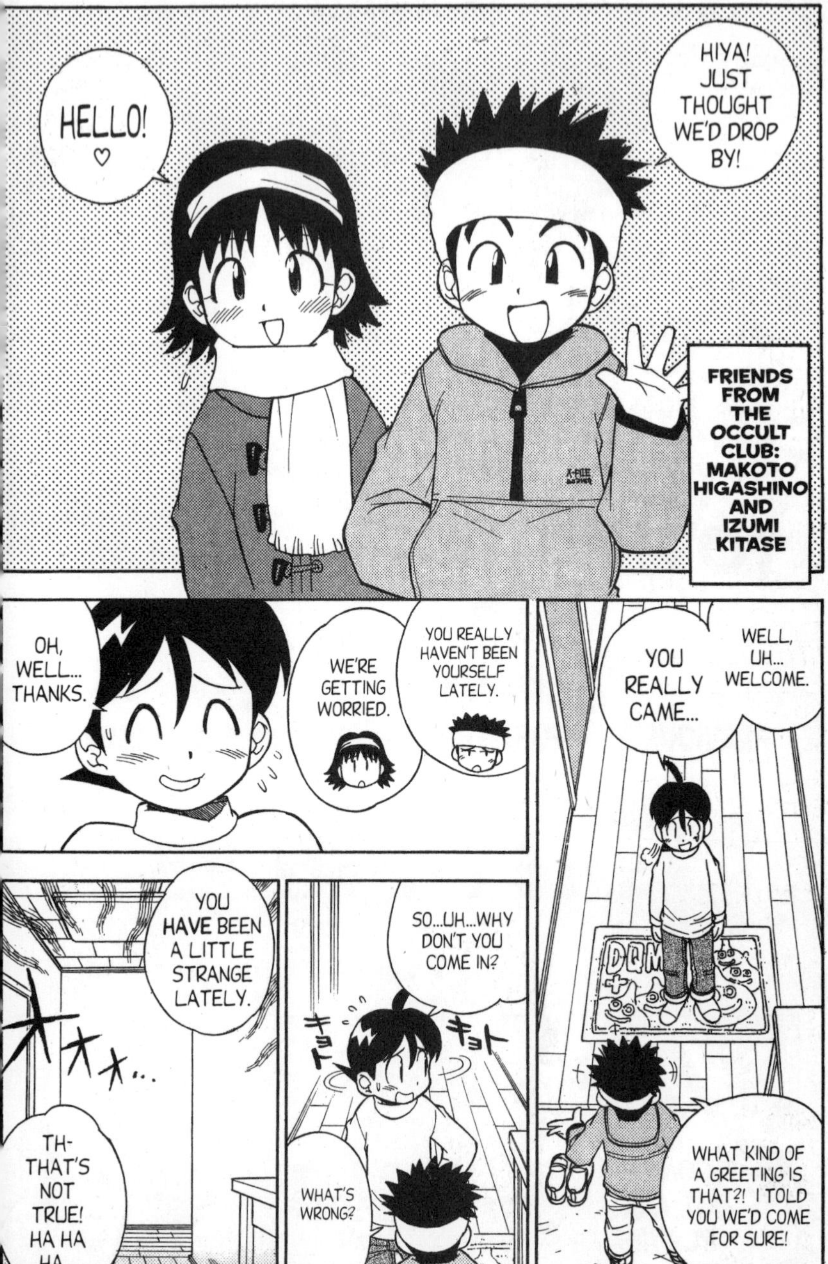
HIYA! JUST THOUGHT WE'D DROP BY!
FRIENDS FROM THE OCCULT CLUB: MAKOTO HIGASHINO AND IZUMI KITASE
HELLO! ♡
WELL, UH... WELCOME.
YOU REALLY CAME...
DQM
WHAT KIND OF A GREETING IS THAT?! I TOLD YOU WE'D COME FOR SURE!
YOU REALLY HAVEN'T BEEN YOURSELF LATELY.
WE'RE GETTING WORRIED.
OH, WELL... THANKS.
SO...UH...WHY DON'T YOU COME IN?
キョト
キョト
WHAT'S WRONG?
YOU HAVE BEEN A LITTLE STRANGE LATELY.
オォォ...
TH- THAT'S NOT TRUE! HA HA HA...

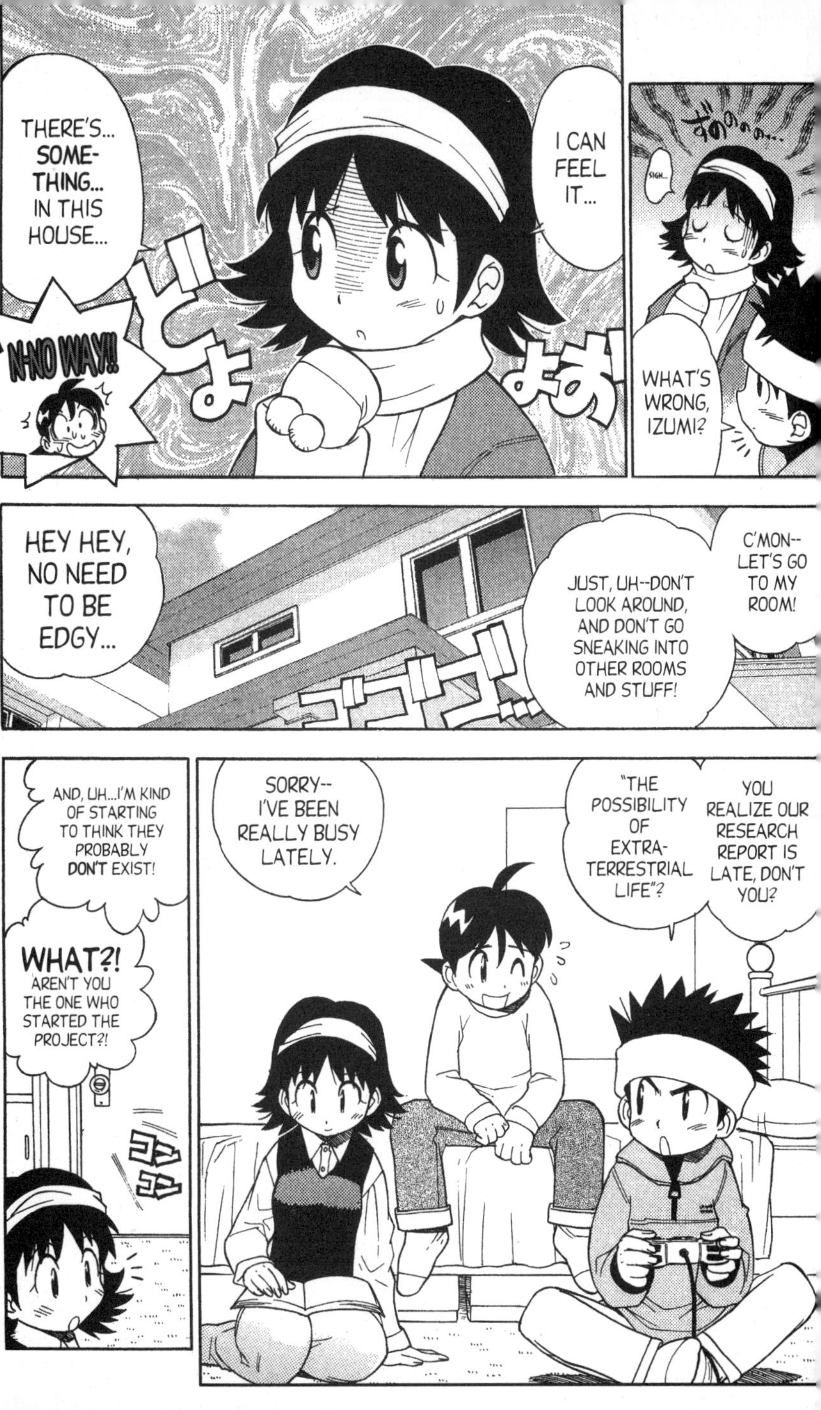
SIGH...
WHAT'S WRONG, IZUMI?
I CAN FEEL IT...
THERE'S... SOME-THING... IN THIS HOUSE...
N-NO WAY!!
C'MON-- LET'S GO TO MY ROOM!
JUST, UH--DON'T LOOK AROUND, AND DON'T GO SNEAKING INTO OTHER ROOMS AND STUFF!
HEY HEY, NO NEED TO BE EDGY...
YOU REALIZE OUR RESEARCH REPORT IS LATE, DON'T YOU?
"THE POSSIBILITY OF EXTRA-TERRESTRIAL LIFE"?
SORRY-- I'VE BEEN REALLY BUSY LATELY.
AND, UH...I'M KIND OF STARTING TO THINK THEY PROBABLY DON'T EXIST!
WHAT?! AREN'T YOU THE ONE WHO STARTED THE PROJECT?!

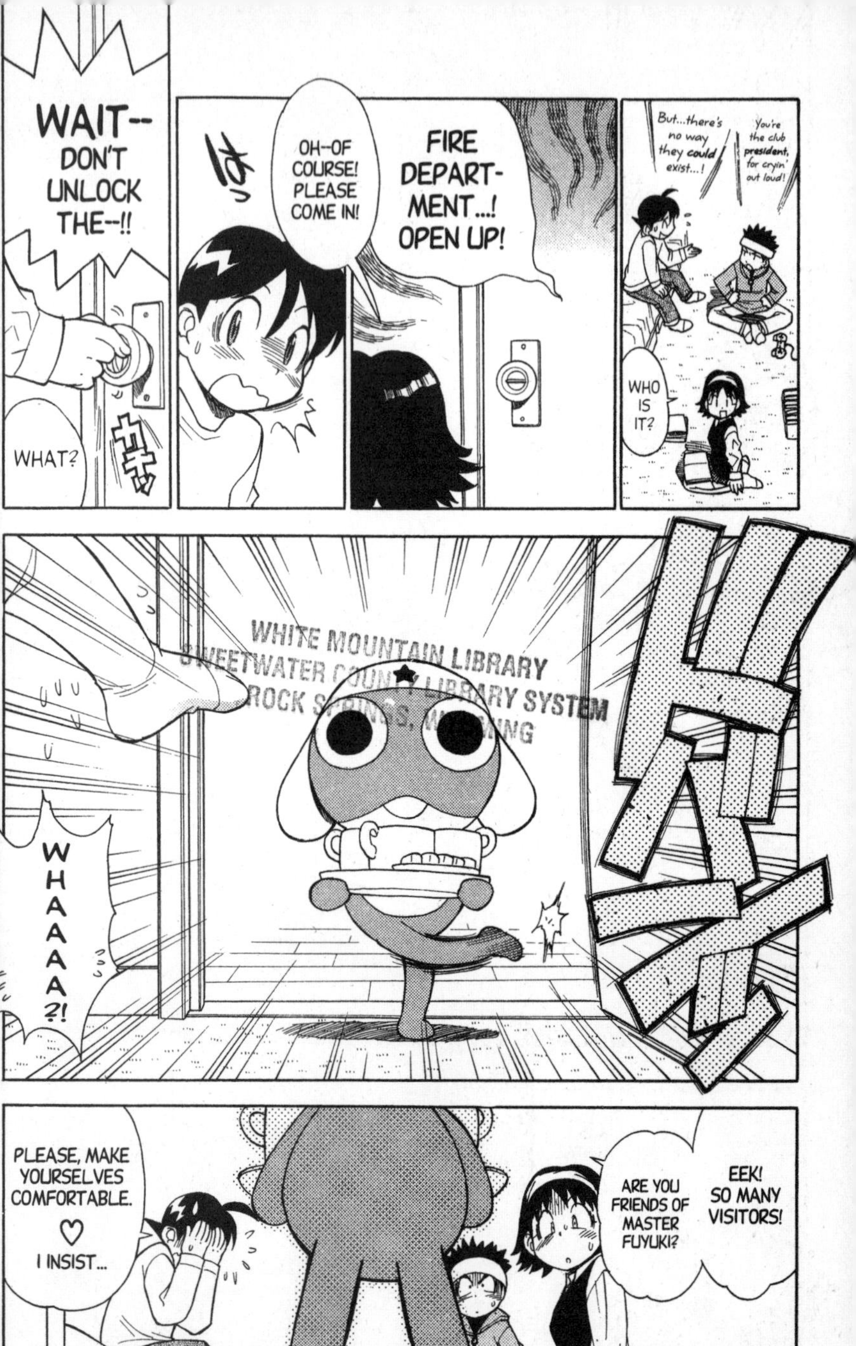
You're the club president, for cryin' out loud!
But...there's no way they could exist...!
WHO IS IT?
FIRE DEPARTMENT...! OPEN UP!
OH--OF COURSE! PLEASE COME IN!
はっ
WAIT-- DON'T UNLOCK THE--!!
WHAT?
WHAAAAA?!
EEK! SO MANY VISITORS!
ARE YOU FRIENDS OF MASTER FUYUKI?
PLEASE, MAKE YOURSELVES COMFORTABLE. ♡ I INSIST...

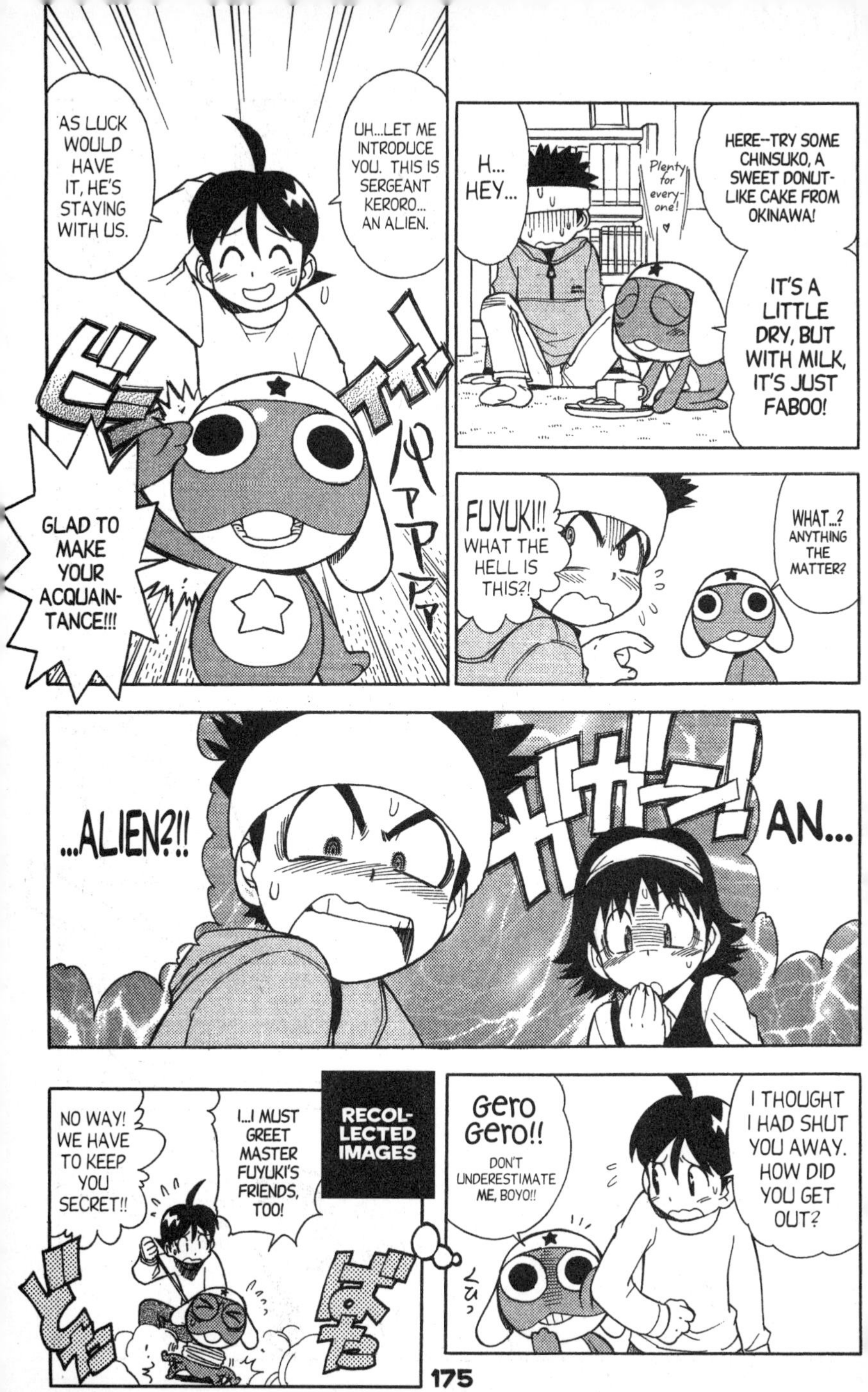
HERE--TRY SOME CHINSUKO, A SWEET DONUT-LIKE CAKE FROM OKINAWA!
Plenty for every-one!
IT'S A LITTLE DRY, BUT WITH MILK, IT'S JUST FABOO!
H... HEY...
WHAT...? ANYTHING THE MATTER?
FUYUKI!! WHAT THE HELL IS THIS?!
UH...LET ME INTRODUCE YOU. THIS IS SERGEANT KERORO... AN ALIEN.
AS LUCK WOULD HAVE IT, HE'S STAYING WITH US.
GLAD TO MAKE YOUR ACQUAINTANCE!!!
AN...
...ALIEN?!!
I THOUGHT I HAD SHUT YOU AWAY. HOW DID YOU GET OUT?
Gero Gero!!
DON'T UNDERESTIMATE ME, BOYO!!
RECOL-LECTED IMAGES
I...I MUST GREET MASTER FUYUKI'S FRIENDS, TOO!
NO WAY! WE HAVE TO KEEP YOU SECRET!!

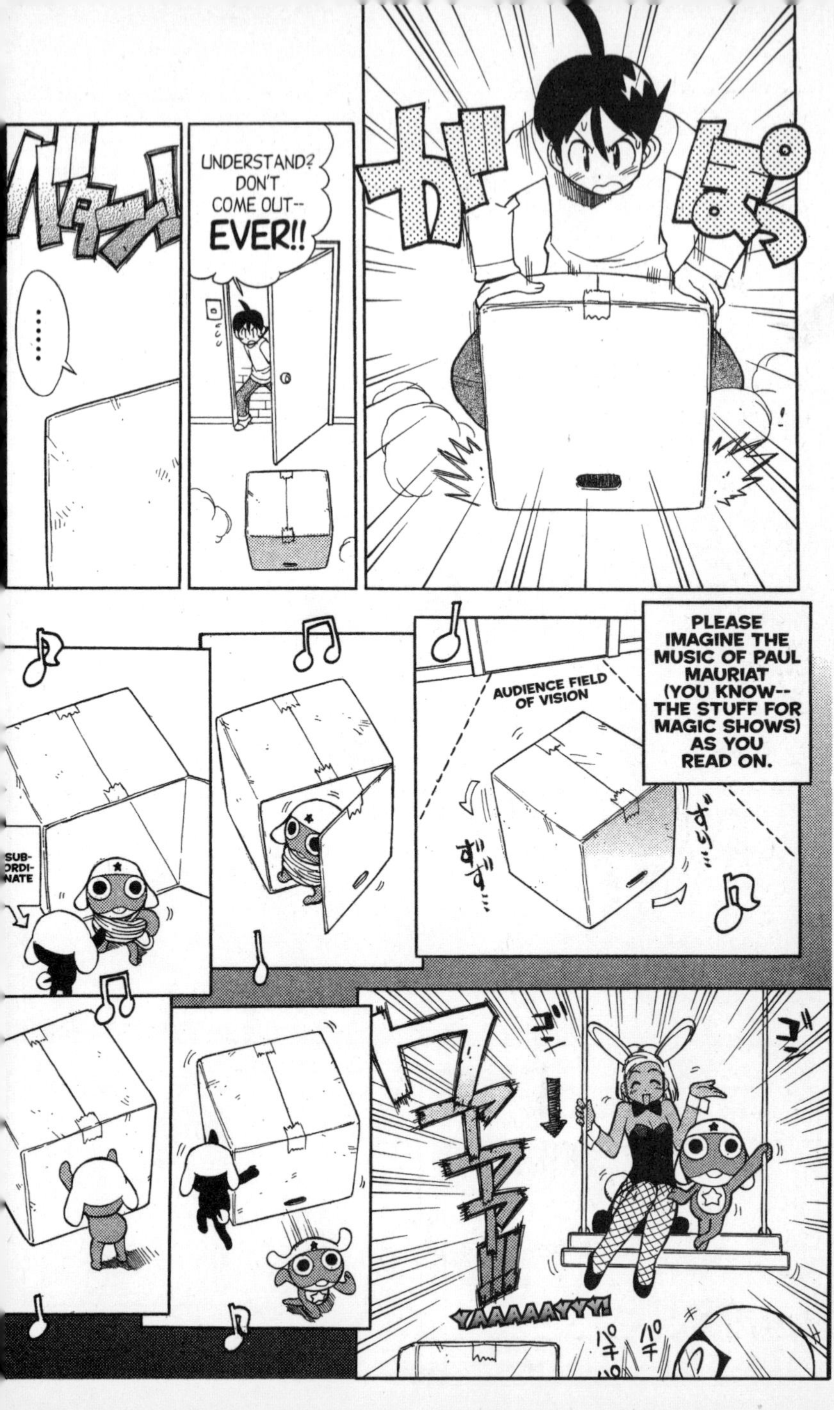
UNDERSTAND? DON'T COME OUT-- EVER!!
......
PLEASE IMAGINE THE MUSIC OF PAUL MAURIAT (YOU KNOW-- THE STUFF FOR MAGIC SHOWS) AS YOU READ ON.
AUDIENCE FIELD OF VISION
SUB-ORDI-NATE
YAAAAAYYY!

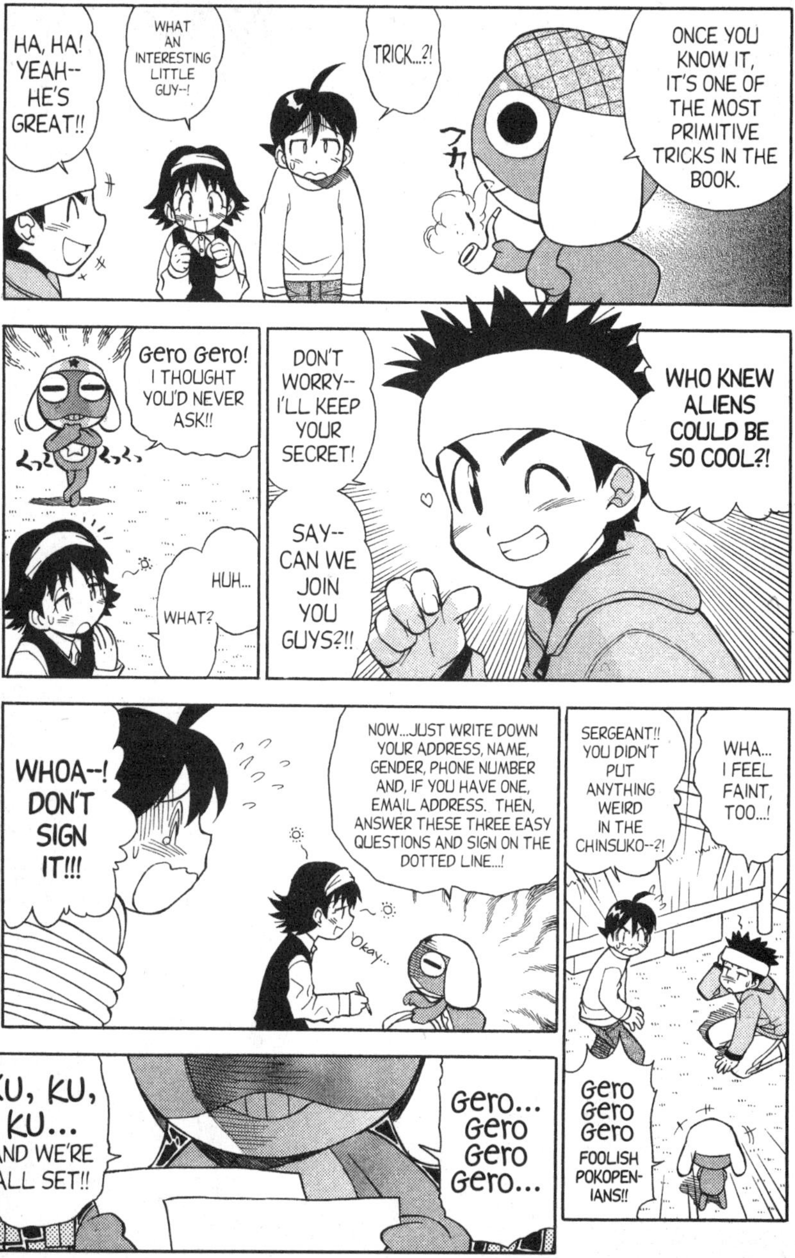
ONCE YOU KNOW IT, IT'S ONE OF THE MOST PRIMITIVE TRICKS IN THE BOOK.
TRICK...?!
WHAT AN INTERESTING LITTLE GUY--!
HA, HA! YEAH-- HE'S GREAT!!
WHO KNEW ALIENS COULD BE SO COOL?!
DON'T WORRY-- I'LL KEEP YOUR SECRET!
SAY-- CAN WE JOIN YOU GUYS?!!
Gero Gero! I THOUGHT YOU'D NEVER ASK!!
HUH... WHAT?
WHA... I FEEL FAINT, TOO...!
SERGEANT!! YOU DIDN'T PUT ANYTHING WEIRD IN THE CHINSUKO--?!
Gero Gero Gero FOOLISH POKOPEN-IANS!!
NOW...JUST WRITE DOWN YOUR ADDRESS, NAME, GENDER, PHONE NUMBER AND, IF YOU HAVE ONE, EMAIL ADDRESS. THEN, ANSWER THESE THREE EASY QUESTIONS AND SIGN ON THE DOTTED LINE...!
Okay...
WHOA--! DON'T SIGN IT!!!
Gero... Gero Gero Gero...
KU, KU, KU... AND WE'RE ALL SET!!

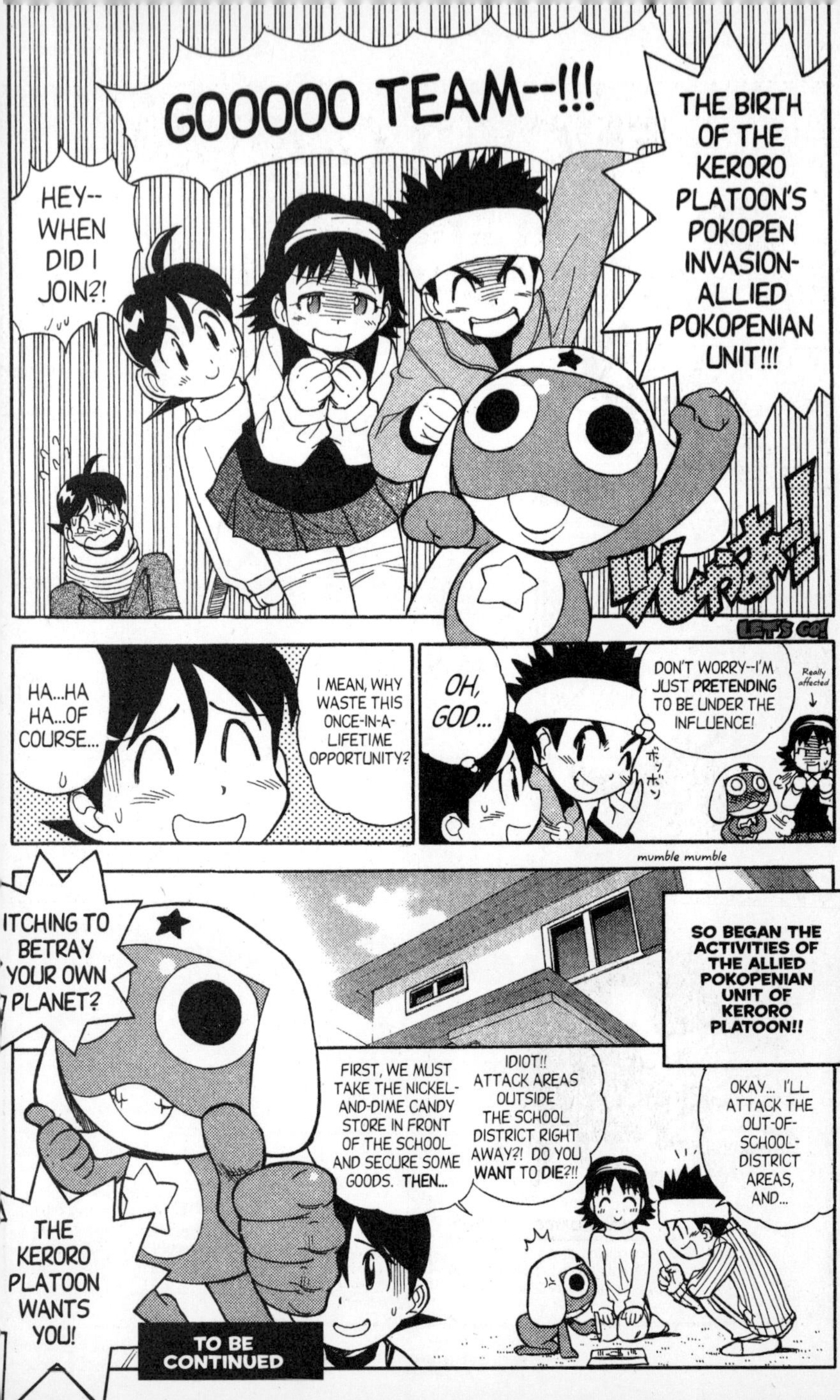
GOOOOO TEAM--!!!
THE BIRTH OF THE KERORO PLATOON'S POKOPEN INVASION-ALLIED POKOPENIAN UNIT!!!
LET'S GO!
HEY--WHEN DID I JOIN?!
Really affected
DON'T WORRY--I'M JUST PRETENDING TO BE UNDER THE INFLUENCE!
OH, GOD...
mumble mumble
I MEAN, WHY WASTE THIS ONCE-IN-A-LIFETIME OPPORTUNITY?
HA...HA HA...OF COURSE...
SO BEGAN THE ACTIVITIES OF THE ALLIED POKOPENIAN UNIT OF KERORO PLATOON!!
OKAY... I'LL ATTACK THE OUT-OF-SCHOOL-DISTRICT AREAS, AND...
IDIOT!! ATTACK AREAS OUTSIDE THE SCHOOL DISTRICT RIGHT AWAY?! DO YOU WANT TO DIE?!!
FIRST, WE MUST TAKE THE NICKEL-AND-DIME CANDY STORE IN FRONT OF THE SCHOOL AND SECURE SOME GOODS. THEN...
ITCHING TO BETRAY YOUR OWN PLANET?
THE KERORO PLATOON WANTS YOU!
TO BE CONTINUED

ENCYCLOPEDIA KERONIA

(A.K.A. A GUIDE TO VARIOUS DUBIOUS TOOLS)

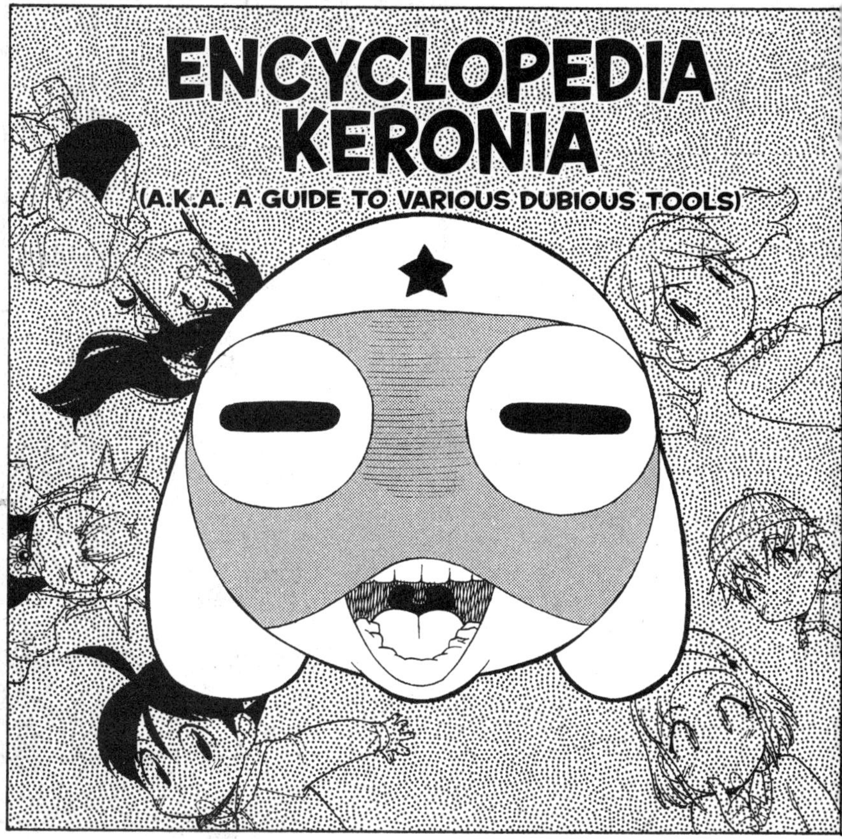

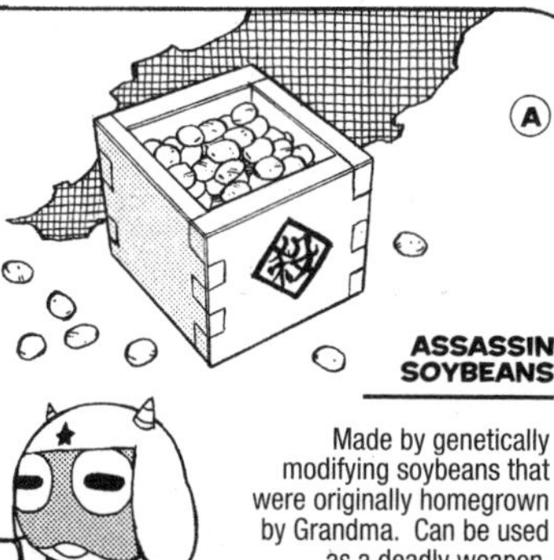
A

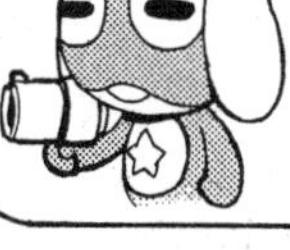

ASSASSIN SOYBEANS

Made by genetically modifying soybeans that were originally homegrown by Grandma. Can be used as a deadly weapon.

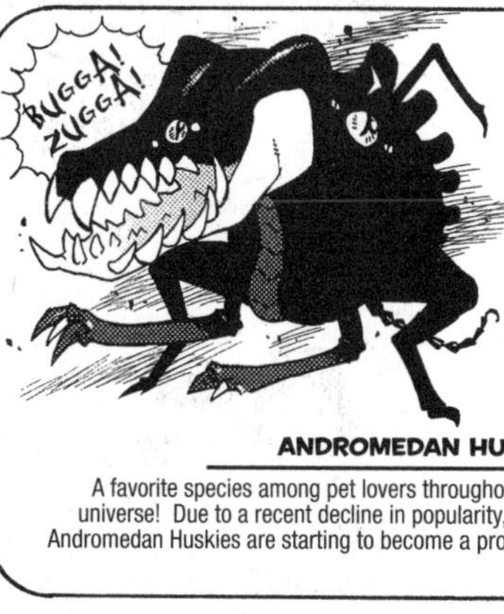
BUGGA! ZUGGA!

ANDROMEDAN HUSKY

A favorite species among pet lovers throughout the universe! Due to a recent decline in popularity, stray Andromedan Huskies are starting to become a problem.

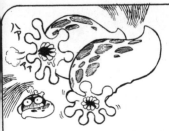

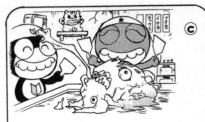

COSMIC OKONOMIYAKI

A delicacy favored in the Kaisai area of the Cosmos. Its popularity is attributed to the thrill of "eat or be eaten."

ハア
アア

COSMIC LEECH

A leech that lives in the swamps of Planet Keron. Its warm breath is highly unpleasant. Mostly captured for use in torture.

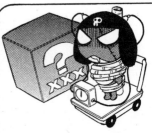

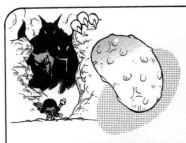

COSMIC KEROPES LIVER

Reported to cure any disease--ironically, many lives are required for its procurement.

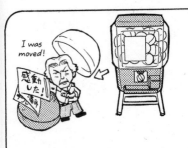

FRIGHT COUNTER AND FRIGHT PENALTY BOX

Originally developed to measure the scariness of horror stories. Its precision is contantly being improved upon, using organisms that are sensitive to fright.

COSMIC NYORO

A quasi-plant that lives near the waters of Planet Keron. Perfect for use as rope, they tie up nice and tight.

I was moved!
感動した!

FOURTH DIMENSION GACHA

Changes the person who turns the knob into a figurine inside of a capsule. By pressing on the figurine's nose, you can interchange your body with his/hers.

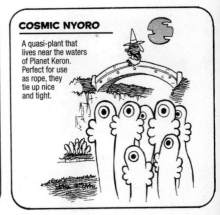

G
Dar-ling!

GOBLIN GIRL SPECIAL TRANSFORMATION BEAM

Transforms Pokopenian girls into "That Electric Goblin Girl" types. [Alluding to Lum from the manga Urusei Yatsura.]

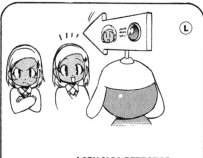

L

LADY MOA DETECTOR

Can detect Lady Moa. I want one, too!

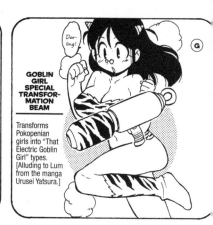

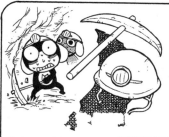

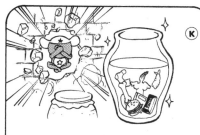

K

KERO JUMP SUI

The ultimate in soup technology, made from a variety of ingredients. Named for the delicious taste that makes Sgt. Keroro jump over walls to get it, even when he is in the midst of model building.

LOCATION SET

These famous-name products (sold at better J-Marts everywhere!) are of reputable quality. With patience and dilligence, they can be used to dig a tunnel.

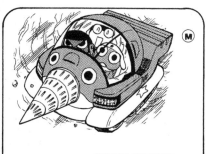

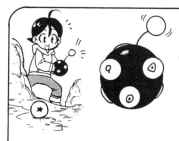

KERO BALL

A mobile communication device provided to Keron Force officers. Its most important features are always malfunctioning, whereas convenience features are constantly being added.

M

MAGMA SWIMMER

A vehicle that purportedly can dig freely in any direction underground. It has yet to be made clear whether the drill actually works.

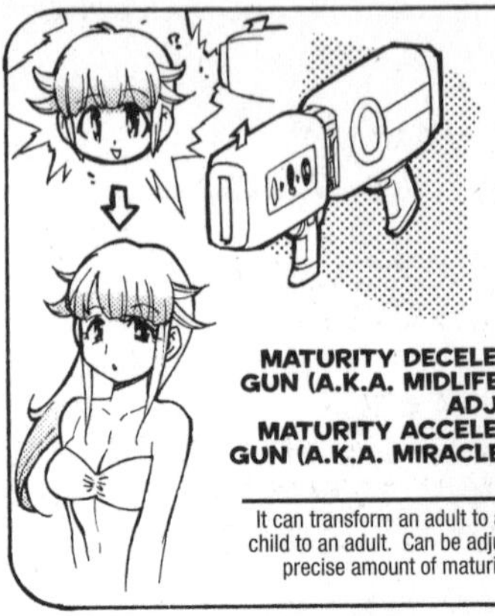

MATURITY DECELERATION GUN (A.K.A. MIDLIFE CRISIS ADJUSTOR)
MATURITY ACCELERATION GUN (A.K.A. MIRACLE-GROW GUN)

It can transform an adult to a child, or a child to an adult. Can be adjusted to the precise amount of maturity required.

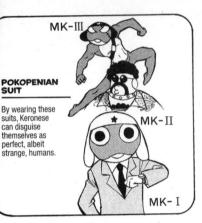

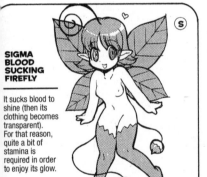

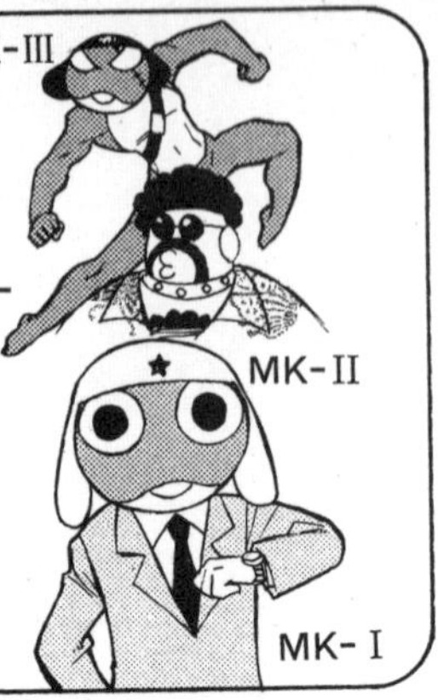
MK-III
MK-II
MK-I

POKOPENIAN SUIT

By wearing these suits, Keronese can disguise themselves as perfect, albeit strange, humans.

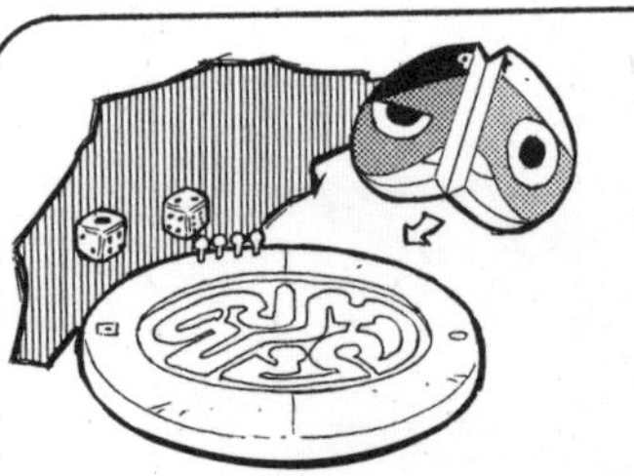

POKOPEN INVASION LIFE-OR-DEATH PARCHEESI DX

A high-performance, life-sized version of Parcheesi. Turns the details of each square you land on into reality. The sergeant's invasion suffered unusual setbacks during the development of this game.

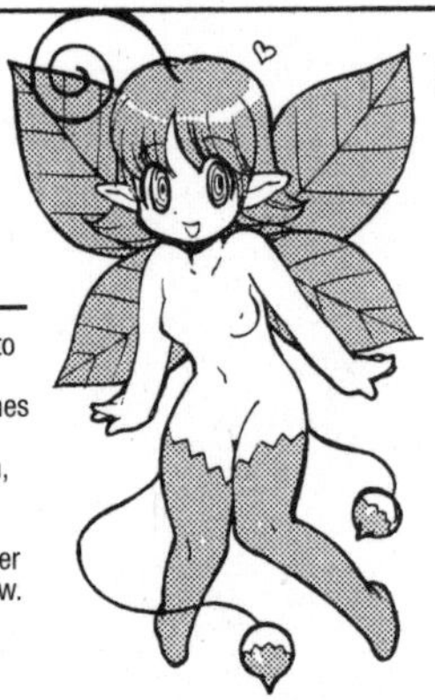

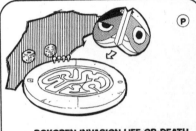

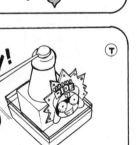

SIGMA BLOOD SUCKING FIREFLY

It sucks blood to shine (then its clothing becomes transparent). For that reason, quite a bit of stamina is required in order to enjoy its glow.

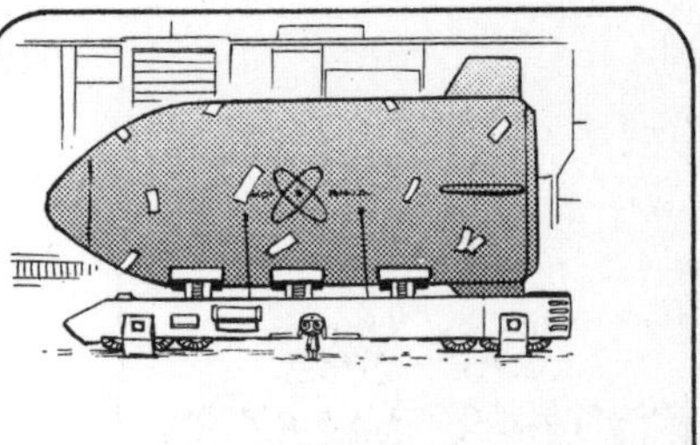

POKOPENIAN ONE-SWEEP MISSILE

A weapon with the power to burn the entire surface of the Earth three times over. However, destruction is considered uncool in most of the Cosmos, so the chances of its use are slim.

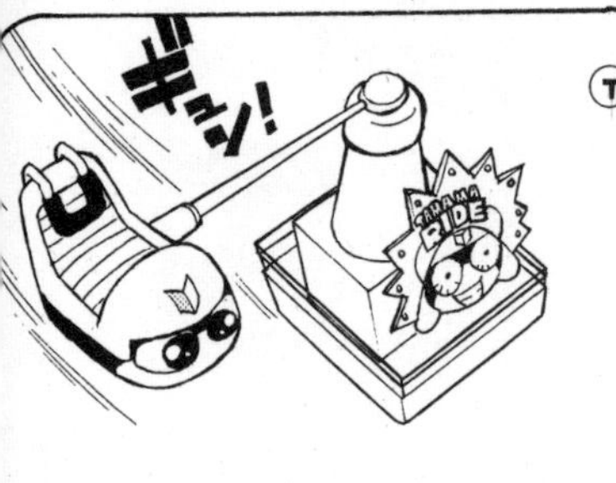
TAMAMA RIDE

TAMAMA RIDE

An attraction boasting the thrilling sensation of 500G's to the body! Derived from a ride that has killed many at amusement parks on Planet Keron.

CREATOR
MINE YOSHIZAKI

BACKGROUNDS
OYSTER

FINISH
GOMOKU AKATSUKI
ROBIN TOKYO
TONMI NARIHARA

TO BE CONTINUED IN VOLUME 7

COMIC POLICEWOMAN
POYON-CHAN

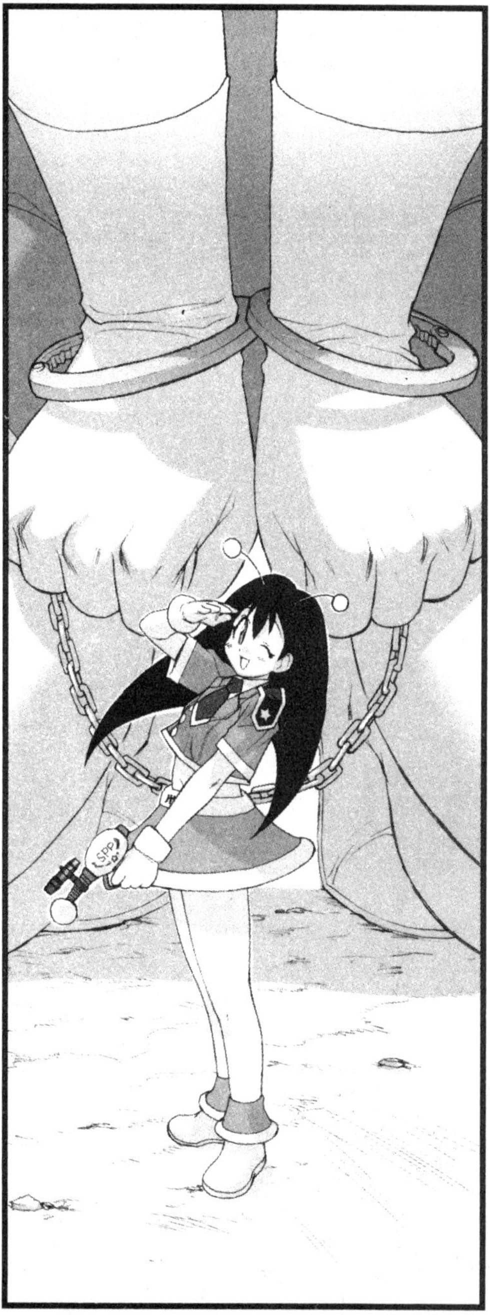

TOKYOPOP PRESS

LOS ANGELES • TOKYO • LONDON • HAMBURG

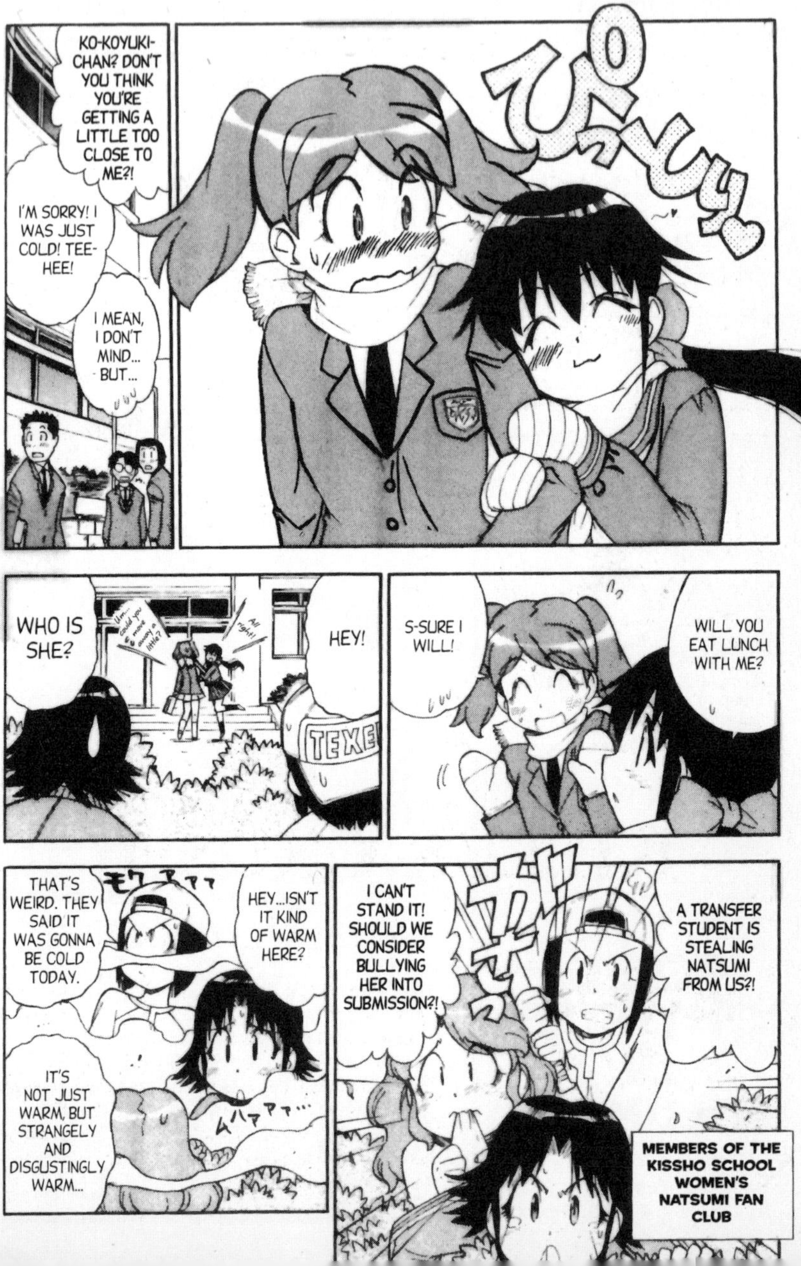
ぴっとり
KO-KOYUKI-CHAN? DON'T YOU THINK YOU'RE GETTING A LITTLE TOO CLOSE TO ME?!
I'M SORRY! I WAS JUST COLD! TEE-HEE!
I MEAN, I DON'T MIND... BUT...
WILL YOU EAT LUNCH WITH ME?
S-SURE I WILL!
HEY!
All right!
Um... could you move away a little?
TEXE
WHO IS SHE?
A TRANSFER STUDENT IS STEALING NATSUMI FROM US?!
I CAN'T STAND IT! SHOULD WE CONSIDER BULLYING HER INTO SUBMISSION?!
MEMBERS OF THE KISSHO SCHOOL WOMEN'S NATSUMI FAN CLUB
HEY...ISN'T IT KIND OF WARM HERE?
THAT'S WEIRD. THEY SAID IT WAS GONNA BE COLD TODAY.
IT'S NOT JUST WARM, BUT STRANGELY AND DISGUSTINGLY WARM...

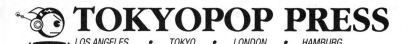

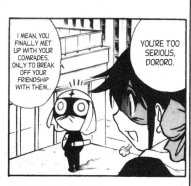

TOKYOPOP PRESS

LOS ANGELES • TOKYO • LONDON • HAMBURG

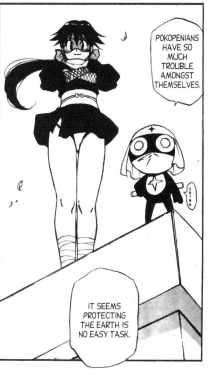

POKOPENIANS HAVE SO MUCH TROUBLE AMONGST THEMSELVES.
SHING
IT SEEMS PROTECTING THE EARTH IS NO EASY TASK.
YOU'RE TOO SERIOUS, DORORO.
I MEAN, YOU FINALLY MET UP WITH YOUR COMRADES, ONLY TO BREAK OFF YOUR FRIENDSHIP WITH THEM...
NO...IT WAS THE RIGHT THING TO DO.
AFTER ALL, I AM NOW ON THE SIDE OF EARTH.
SO ALL HER INVADERS--INCLUDING KERORO--ARE NOW MY ENEMIES!

KILLER CRUSH!

NEXT IN VOLUME 7 OF

SGT FROG

KERORO GUNSO

IN STORES THE MONTH OF MARCH!

Nefarious, nosy neighbor!

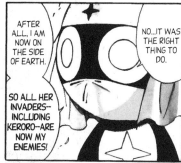

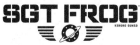

Koyuki, a new student, instantly falls in love with a startled Natsumi. And when Koyuki's obsession compels her to move next door, the secret of the Hinata family might be exposed! Are Koyuki's amorous advances pure of heart...or does she have insidious intent? Koyuki is full of secrets, especially regarding the otherworldly company she keeps! Yes, she's an ally with a little blue alien named Dororo--the Keroro Platoon's long-lost fifth member!

She crash-landed on earth...

now she has a thing or two to get off her chest.

DearS
ディアーズ

The hit series that inspired the anime and video game!

EXPERIENCE THE MANGA

www.TOKYOPOP.com/dears

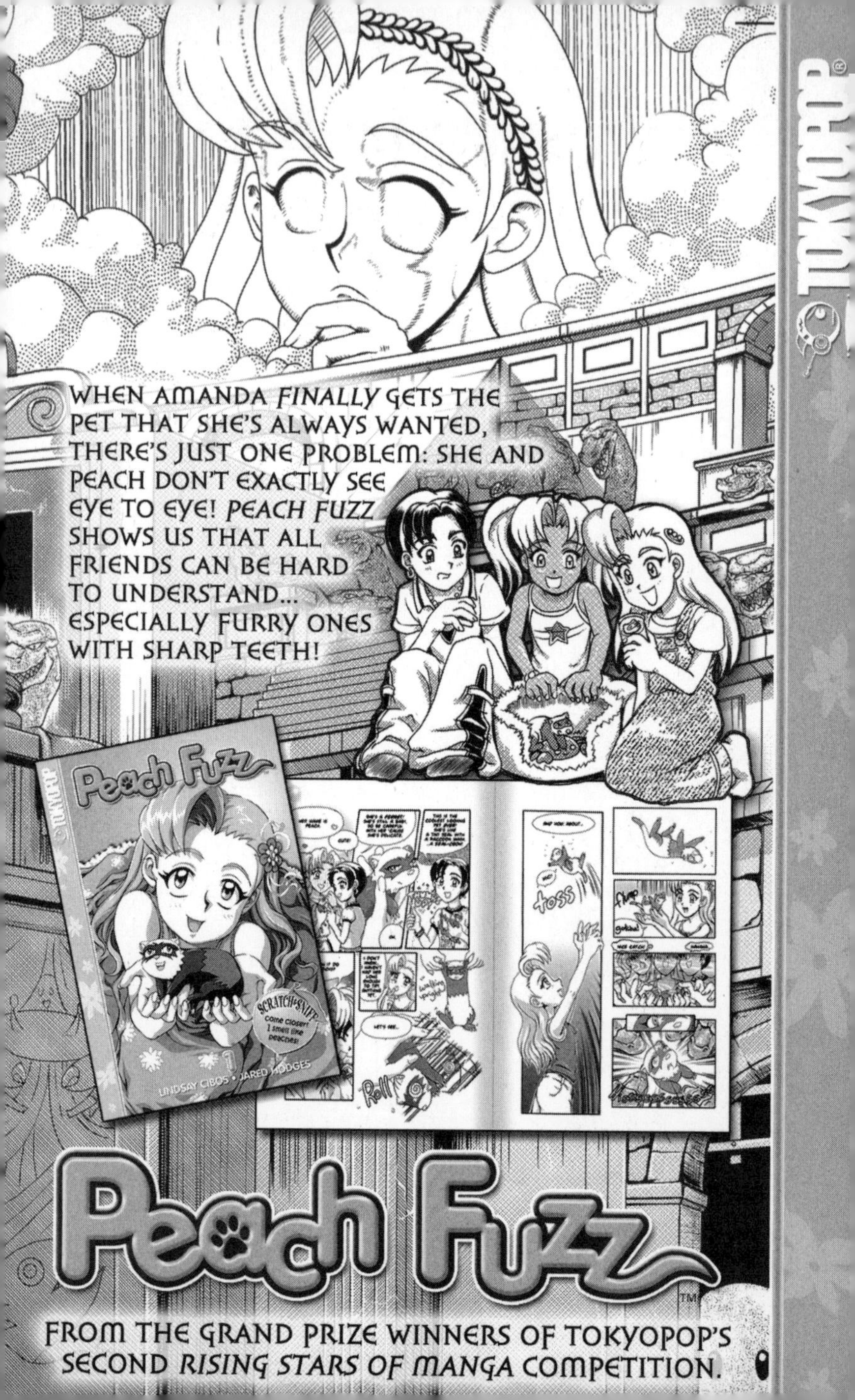
TOKYOPOP®
WHEN AMANDA *FINALLY* GETS THE PET THAT SHE'S ALWAYS WANTED, THERE'S JUST ONE PROBLEM: SHE AND PEACH DON'T EXACTLY SEE EYE TO EYE! *PEACH FUZZ* SHOWS US THAT ALL FRIENDS CAN BE HARD TO UNDERSTAND... ESPECIALLY FURRY ONES WITH SHARP TEETH!
Peach Fuzz
TOKYOPOP
SCRATCH & SNIFF
Come closer! I smell like peaches!
#1
LINDSAY CIBOS • JARED HODGES
toss
Roll
Peach Fuzz™
FROM THE GRAND PRIZE WINNERS OF TOKYOPOP'S SECOND *RISING STARS OF MANGA* COMPETITION.

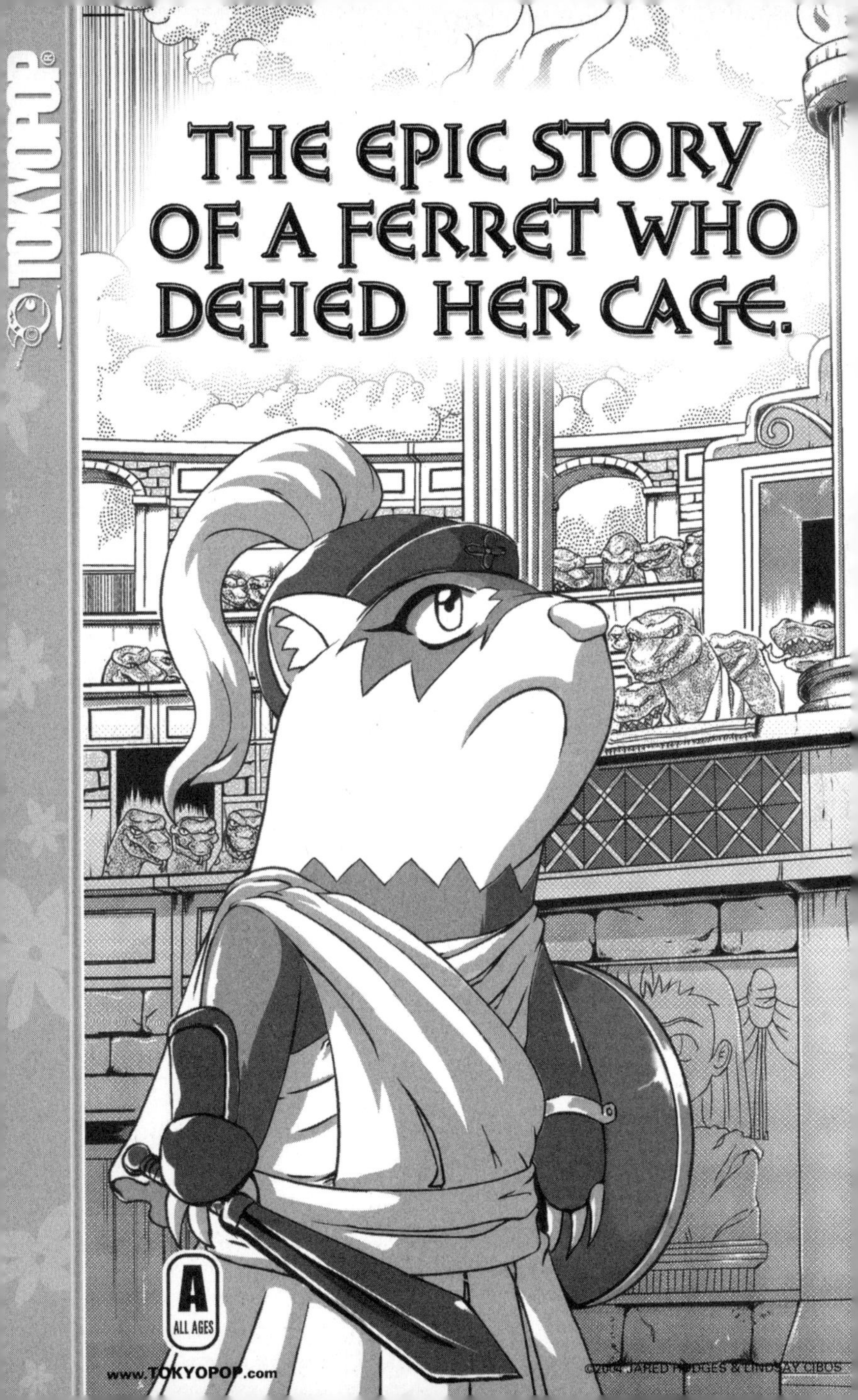
TOKYOPOP
THE EPIC STORY OF A FERRET WHO DEFIED HER CAGE.
A ALL AGES
www.TOKYOPOP.com
©2004 JARED HODGES & LINDSAY CIBOS

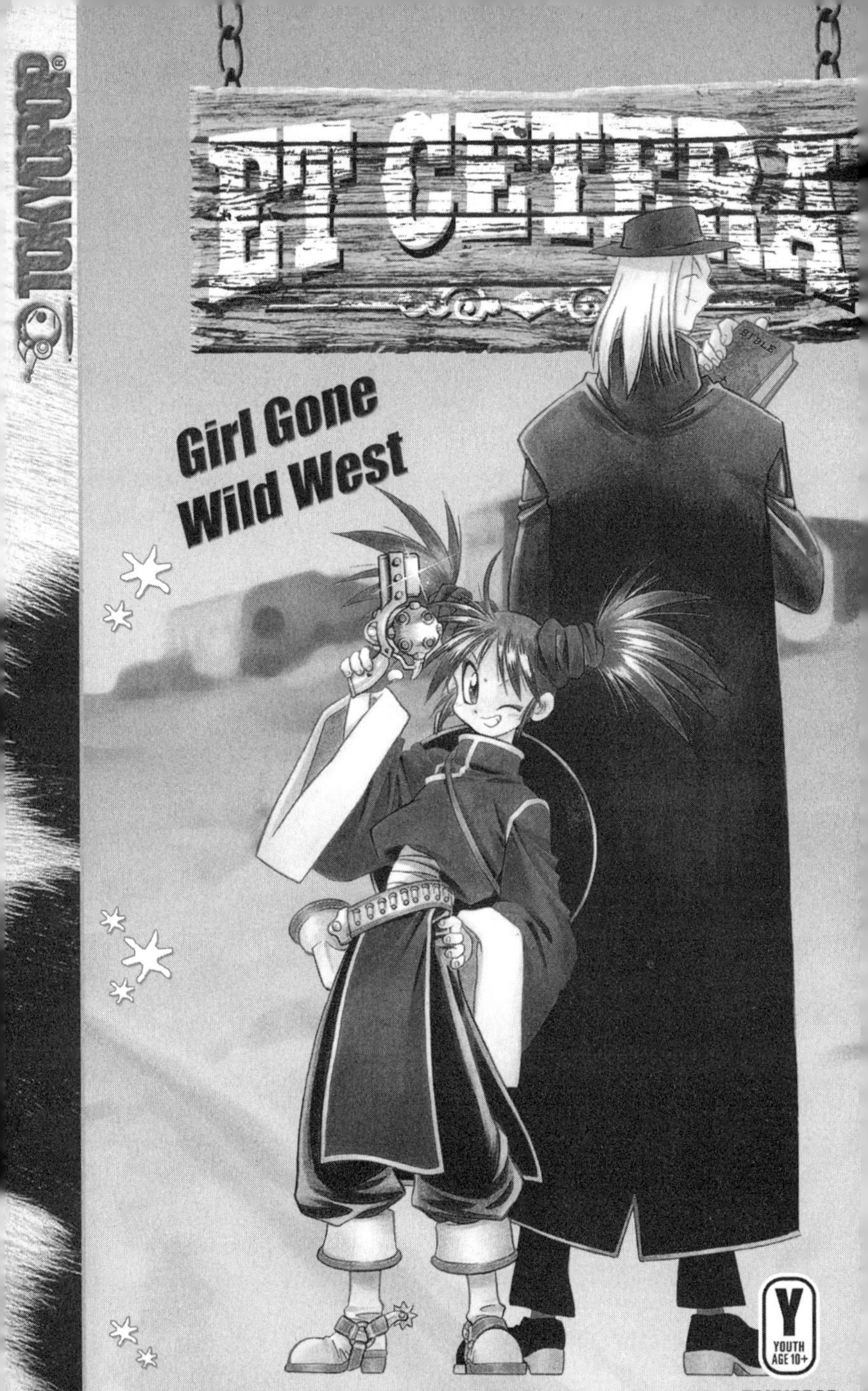

TOKYOPOP
Girl Gone
Wild West
BIBLE
Y
YOUTH
AGE 10+

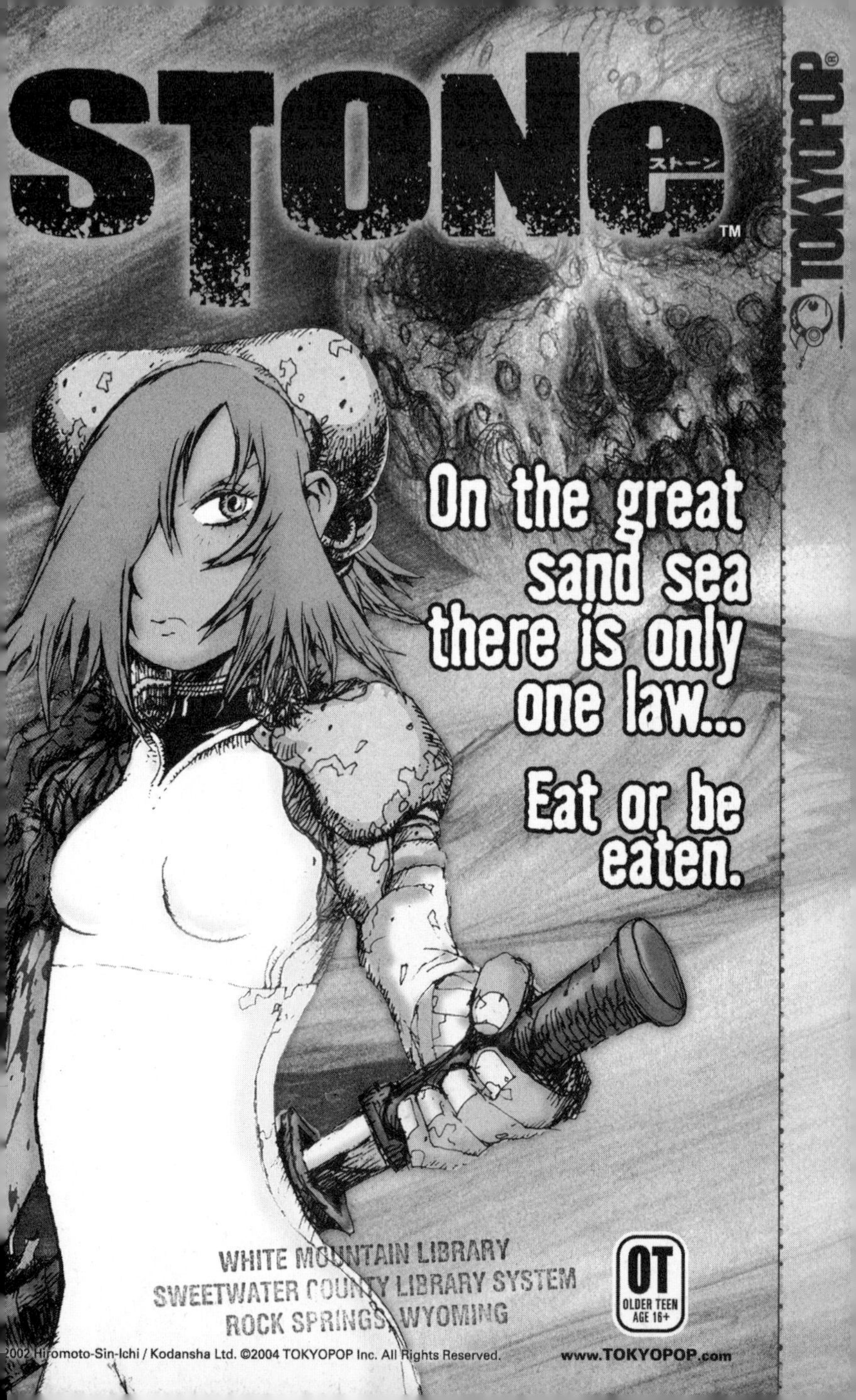
STONe
ストーン
TM
TOKYOPOP®
On the great sand sea there is only one law...
Eat or be eaten.
OT
OLDER TEEN AGE 16+
2002 Hiromoto-Sin-Ichi / Kodansha Ltd. ©2004 TOKYOPOP Inc. All Rights Reserved.
www.TOKYOPOP.com

Heaven help you...
Faerie tales *do* come true!

FAERIE'S LANDING™

ALSO AVAILABLE FROM TOKYOPOP

You want it? We got it!
A full range of TOKYOPOP
products are available now at:
www.TOKYOPOP.com/shop

09.21.04T

MANGA

.HACK//LEGEND OF THE TWILIGHT
@LARGE
ABENOBASHI: MAGICAL SHOPPING ARCADE
A.I. LOVE YOU
AI YORI AOSHI
ALICHINO
ANGELIC LAYER
ARM OF KANNON
BABY BIRTH
BATTLE ROYALE
BATTLE VIXENS
BOYS BE...
BRAIN POWERED
BRIGADOON
B'TX
CANDIDATE FOR GODDESS, THE
CARDCAPTOR SAKURA
CARDCAPTOR SAKURA - MASTER OF THE CLOW
CHOBITS
CHRONICLES OF THE CURSED SWORD
CLAMP SCHOOL DETECTIVES
CLOVER
COMIC PARTY
CONFIDENTIAL CONFESSIONS
CORRECTOR YUI
COWBOY BEBOP
COWBOY BEBOP: SHOOTING STAR
CRAZY LOVE STORY
CRESCENT MOON
CROSS
CULDCEPT
CYBORG 009
D•N•ANGEL
DEARS
DEMON DIARY
DEMON ORORON, THE
DEUS VITAE
DIABOLO
DIGIMON
DIGIMON TAMERS
DIGIMON ZERO TWO
DOLL
DRAGON HUNTER
DRAGON KNIGHTS
DRAGON VOICE
DREAM SAGA
DUKLYON: CLAMP SCHOOL DEFENDERS
EERIE QUEERIE!
ERICA SAKURAZAWA: COLLECTED WORKS
ET CETERA
ETERNITY
EVIL'S RETURN
FAERIES' LANDING
FAKE
FLCL
FLOWER OF THE DEEP SLEEP
FORBIDDEN DANCE
FRUITS BASKET

G GUNDAM
GATEKEEPERS
GETBACKERS
GIRL GOT GAME
GRAVITATION
GTO
GUNDAM SEED ASTRAY
GUNDAM WING
GUNDAM WING: BATTLEFIELD OF PACIFISTS
GUNDAM WING: ENDLESS WALTZ
GUNDAM WING: THE LAST OUTPOST (G-UNIT)
HANDS OFF!
HAPPY MANIA
HARLEM BEAT
HYPER RUNE
I.N.V.U.
IMMORTAL RAIN
INITIAL D
INSTANT TEEN: JUST ADD NUTS
ISLAND
JING: KING OF BANDITS
JING: KING OF BANDITS - TWILIGHT TALES
JULINE
KARE KANO
KILL ME, KISS ME
KINDAICHI CASE FILES, THE
KING OF HELL
KODOCHA: SANA'S STAGE
LAMENT OF THE LAMB
LEGAL DRUG
LEGEND OF CHUN HYANG, THE
LES BIJOUX
LOVE HINA
LOVE OR MONEY
LUPIN III
LUPIN III: WORLD'S MOST WANTED
MAGIC KNIGHT RAYEARTH I
MAGIC KNIGHT RAYEARTH II
MAHOROMATIC: AUTOMATIC MAIDEN
MAN OF MANY FACES
MARMALADE BOY
MARS
MARS: HORSE WITH NO NAME
MINK
MIRACLE GIRLS
MIYUKI-CHAN IN WONDERLAND
MODEL
MOURYOU KIDEN: LEGEND OF THE NYMPH
NECK AND NECK
ONE
ONE I LOVE, THE
PARADISE KISS
PARASYTE
PASSION FRUIT
PEACH FUZZ
PEACH GIRL
PEACH GIRL: CHANGE OF HEART
PET SHOP OF HORRORS
PITA-TEN
PLANET LADDER

09.2

STOP!

This is the back of the book.
You wouldn't want to spoil a great ending!

This book is printed "manga-style," in the authentic Japanese right-to-left format. Since none of the artwork has been flipped or altered, readers get to experience the story just as the creator intended. You've been asking for it, so TOKYOPOP® delivered: authentic, hot-off-the-press, and far more fun!

DIRECTIONS

If this is your first time reading manga-style, here's a quick guide to help you understand how it works.

It's easy... just start in the top right panel and follow the numbers. Have fun, and look for more 100% authentic manga from TOKYOPOP®!